Getting into the Text

Getting into the Text

New Testament Essays in Honor of David Alan Black

Edited by DANIEL L. AKIN
and THOMAS W. HUDGINS

☙PICKWICK *Publications* • Eugene, Oregon

GETTING INTO THE TEXT
New Testament Essays in Honor of David Alan Black

Copyright © 2017 Wipf and Stock Publishers. All rights reserved. Except for brief quotations in critical publications or reviews, no part of this book may be reproduced in any manner without prior written permission from the publisher. Write: Permissions, Wipf and Stock Publishers, 199 W. 8th Ave., Suite 3, Eugene, OR 97401.

Pickwick Publications
An Imprint of Wipf and Stock Publishers
199 W. 8th Ave., Suite 3
Eugene, OR 97401

www.wipfandstock.com

PAPERBACK ISBN: 978-1-4982-3759-8
HARDCOVER ISBN: 978-1-4982-3761-1
EBOOK ISBN: 978-1-4982-3760-4

Cataloging-in-Publication data:

Names: Akin, Daniel L., editor. | Hudgins, Thomas W., editor.

Title: Getting into the text : New Testament essays in honor of David Alan Black / edited by Daniel L. Akin and Thomas W. Hudgins.

Description: Eugene, OR : Pickwick Publications, 2017 | Includes bibliographical references.

Identifiers: ISBN 978-1-4982-3759-8 (paperback) | ISBN 978-1-4982-3761-1 (hardcover) | ISBN 978-1-4982-3760-4 (ebook)

Subjects: LCSH: Bible. New Testament. | Black, David Alan, 1952–.

Classification: LCC BS2395 G37 2017 (print) | LCC BS2395 (ebook)

Manufactured in the U.S.A.   02/24/17

In Memory of

Becky Lynn Black

Contents

Permissions | ix
Contributors | xi
Foreword | xiii
—Daniel L. Akin
Introduction | xv
—Thomas W. Hudgins

List of Works Published by David Alan Black | 1

1. So What Have We Learned in the Last Thirty Years of Greek Linguistic Study? | 9
   —Stanley E. Porter

2. Prepositions and Exegesis: What's in a Word? | 39
   —Constantine R. Campbell

3. Reclaiming Γάρ: Correcting the Conjunctive Errors of New Testament Lexicography | 55
   —Michael Rudolph

4. Majority Text or Not: Which Criteria Should Be Adopted When Assessing Textual Variation in the Greek New Testament? | 77
   —J. K. Elliott

5. A Short Textual Commentary on the Lucan Travel Narrative (Luke 9:51—19:46) | 90
   —Tommy Wasserman

6. "It's All About Variants"—Unless "No Longer Written" | 116
   —Maurice Robinson

7. L'origine de la parole de Jésus sur la réunion du masculin et du féminin | 154
   —Christian-B. Amphoux

8   The Definition and Translation of ἀλήθεια in the Gospel According to John: The Case of John 1:14, 17 | 169
    —Jesús Peláez and GASCO

9   The Meaning of πίστις in the Framework of the *Diccionario griego-español del Nuevo Testamento* | 179
    —Israel Muñoz Gallarte

10 The Infancy Narratives and the Synoptic Problem: Reassessing the Evidence and Arguments | 191
    —Alexander E. Stewart

11 The Origin of Jesus' Speeches in the Fourth Gospel | 211
    —Antonio Piñero

12 Wisdom and the Sojourning Saints or Christ and the Wandering Sinners? The Wilderness Wandering Motif in Hebrews as a Reaction to Wisdom of Solomon | 227
    —Paul A. Himes

13 Contextualizando y actualizando la traducción al español de la gramática griega de David Alan Black | 250
    —Stephen H. Levinsohn

Permissions

Scripture quotations taken from the New American Standard Bible® (NASB), Copyright © 1960, 1962, 1963, 1968, 1971, 1972, 1973, 1975, 1977, 1995 by The Lockman Foundation Used by permission. www.Lockman.org.

Scripture quotations are from the ESV® Bible (The Holy Bible, English Standard Version®), copyright © 2001 by Crossway, a publishing ministry of Good News Publishers. Used by permission. All rights reserved.

Scriptures taken from the Holy Bible, New International Version®, NIV®. Copyright © 1973, 1978, 1984, 2011 by Biblica, Inc.™ Used by permission of Zondervan. All rights reserved worldwide. www.zondervan.com The "NIV" and "New International Version" are trademarks registered in the United States Patent and Trademark Office by Biblica, Inc.™

New Revised Standard Version Bible, copyright 1989, Division of Christian Education of the National Council of the Churches of Christ in the United States of America. Used by permission. All rights reserved.

Scripture taken from LA BIBLIA DE LAS AMERICAS®, Copyright © 1986, 1995, 1997 by The Lockman Foundation. Used by permission.

La Santa Biblia, Nueva Versión Internacional® NVI® Copyright © 1999 by Biblica, Inc.® Used by permission. All rights reserved worldwide.

El texto Bíblico ha sido tomado de la versión Reina-Valera © 1960 Sociedades Bíblicas en América Latina © renovado 1988 Sociedades Bíblicas Unidas. Utilizado con permiso.

Scriptures marked as "RVR1995" are taken from the Reina-Valera 1995 version Reina-Valera 95® © Sociedades Bíblicas Unidas, 1995. Used by permission.

Biblia Hebraica Stuttgartensia, edited by Karl Elliger and Wilhelm Rudolph, Fifth Revised Edition, edited by Adrian Schenker, © 1977 and 1997 Deutsche Bibelgesellschaft, Stuttgart. Used by permission.

Nestle-Aland, Novum Testamentum Graece, 28th Revised Edition, edited by Barbara and Kurt Aland, Johannes Karavidopoulos, Carlo M. Martini, and Bruce M. Metzger in cooperation with the Institute for New Testament Textual Research, Münster/Westphalia, © 2012 Deutsche Bibelgesellschaft, Stuttgart. Used by permission.

Septuaginta, edited by Alfred Rahlfs, Second Revised Edition, edited by Robert Hanhart, © 2006 Deutsche Bibelgesellschaft, Stuttgart. Used by permission.

Contributors

Daniel L. Akin President, Ed Young, Sr. Chair of Expository Preaching, and Professor of Preaching and Theology, Southeastern Baptist Theological Seminary in Wake Forest, NC

Christian-B. Amphoux chercheur CNRS (1974-2008), membre associé, Centre Paul-Albert Février, Aix-Marseille Université in Marseille, France

Constantine R. Campbell Professor of New Testament, Trinity Evangelical Divinity School in Deerfield, IL

J. K. Elliott Emeritus Professor of New Testament Textual Criticism, The University of Leeds in Leeds, England

Paul A. Himes Professor of Bible and Ancient Languages, Baptist College of Ministry in Menomonee Falls, WI

Thomas W. Hudgins Assistant Professor of Biblical and Theological Studies, Capital Seminary and Graduate School in Washington, D.C.

Stephen H. Levinsohn Senior Linguistics Consultant, SIL International

Israel Muñoz Gallarte Profesor de Filología Griega, Universidad de Córdoba in Cordoba, Spain

Jesús Peláez Catedrático de Filología Griega y Editor de *Filología Neotestamentaria*, Universidad de Córdoba in Cordoba, Spain

Antonio Piñero Catedrático Emérito de Filología Griega, Universidad Complutense de Madrid in Madrid, Spain

Stanley E. Porter President and Dean, Professor of New Testament, and Roy A. Hope Chair in Christian Worldview, McMaster Divinity College in Hamilton, ON, Canada

Maurice Robinson Research Professor of New Testament (ret.), Southeastern Baptist Theological Seminary in Wake Forest, NC

Michael Rudolph PhD Graduate, Southeastern Baptist Theological Seminary in Wake Forest, NC

Alexander E. Stewart Academic Dean and Associate Professor of New Testament Language and Literature, Tyndale Theological Seminary in Badhoevedorp, Netherlands

Tommy Wasserman Professor of Biblical Studies, Ansgar Teologiske Høgskole, Kristiansand, Norway

Foreword

Daniel L. Akin
Southeastern Baptist Theological Seminary

One of the most memorable moments on the campus of Southeastern Baptist Theological Seminary that I can remember was hosting Dr. M. O. Owens Jr. on April 26, 2012. The purpose was twofold. First, we wanted to honor the former pastor of Parkwood Baptist Church in Gastonia, NC for his lifetime of faithful service in pastoral ministry. Dr. Owens is one of the best examples our students have of what it looks like to live a life that counts, and he is undoubtedly one of the closest friends and strongest supporters of the seminary. Second, we wanted to honor David Alan Black (Professor of New Testament and Greek) for his many years of faithful service. It was an opportune time for the faculty, staff, and students of Southeastern to recognize Black's many accomplishments and express our gratitude for his many contributions towards what makes Southeastern such a special place. I had the privilege of naming Black as the inaugural recipient of the Dr. M. O. Owens Jr. Chair of New Testament Studies.

This Festschrift is another opportunity to honor him, but this time for a much larger community, consisting of his friends, colleagues, and former students from around the world. I am extremely thankful for each of them for their contributions. Preparing a book to honor a scholar who has engaged almost every corner of the field of New Testament studies is a difficult endeavor. We could have limited the focus, but, in our opinion, it would have only acknowledged a limited portion of Black's scholarly contributions and it would have unnecessarily limited the Festschrift contributors. By not doing so, the contributors were free to choose the subject of their contributions, and as a result, free to write their own congratulations to our honoree.

Each of them has provided a high quality study on a subject that Black has engaged during his lifetime of research and teaching. And it is our hope that in reading them he will sense our deepest appreciation for all that he has offered to field of New Testament studies.

He has challenged numerous students on the campus on Southeastern to grow in the grace and knowledge of Jesus Christ, and he has inspired even more throughout the world to study the New Testament with a humble heart and with the greatest precision, which it deserves. I often tell people that Southeastern is a Great-Commission seminary and every classroom a Great-Commission classroom. That only happens when you have a faculty that is committed to the Great Commission. And David Alan Black is an example par excellence, having the sort of devotion that I hope to see in my own life and that of every graduate of Southeastern. His contributions to the field of New Testament studies are many, but they pale in comparison to the investment he has made (and continues to make) in people and seeing them come to know and love the one who gave his life for us on the cross.

Introduction

Thomas W. Hudgins
Capital Seminary and Graduate School

This collection of essays is offered to David Alan Black in recognition of his many contributions to the field of New Testament studies over the last forty years. He has served at Southeastern Baptist Theological Seminary since 1998 as Professor of New Testament and Greek. And in April 2012 he was named the Dr. M. O. Owens Jr. Chair of New Testament Studies. Before coming to Southeastern, Black served full-time at Biola University and Grace Theological Seminary, as well as an adjunct for Talbot School of Theology, Grace Bible Institute, Simon Greenleaf University, Golden Gate Baptist Theological Seminary, Chong Shin Theological Seminary, Fuller Theological Seminary, and American Theological Seminary. Since coming to Southeastern, Black has traveled extensively and taught across the United States and abroad as a visiting professor, including at the Complutense University in Madrid and the Universities of Oxford and Leeds in England. He is a member of the prestigious *Studiorum Novi Testamenti Societas* and a founding editor of the renowned journal *Filología Neotestamentaria*.

He completed his undergraduate studies at Biola University in 1975 and went on for his MDiv in New Testament at Talbot School of Theology, graduating in 1980. He began teaching Greek at Biola while he was a student at Talbot. The year 2016 marked his fortieth year of teaching Greek, a remarkable accomplishment to say the least. His masters thesis at Talbot was titled "The Address of the Ephesian Epistle," leading to the publication of "The Peculiarities of Ephesians and the Ephesian Address" in *Grace Theological Journal* the following year. In 1980, he and his wife Becky moved to Switzerland to study at the University of Basel under the direction of Bo

Reicke. His dissertation was titled "The Pauline Weakness Motif," and he graduated magna cum laude in 1983. A number of publications involving his research on Paul and weakness were published during this time. The first was "The Weak in Thessalonica: A Study in Pauline Lexicography" (1982), followed by "Weakness Language in Galatians" (1983), "A Note on 'the Weak' in 1 Corinthians 9,22" (1983), and *"Paulus Infirmus*: The Pauline Concept of Weakness" (1984). His comprehensive lexical-theological study was published in the American University Studies series in 1984 with the title *Paul, Apostle of Weakness: Astheneia and Its Cognates in the Pauline Literature*. It was recently republished (with updated discussions and bibliography) by Wipf & Stock in 2012.

Those studies at Biola, Talbot, and Basel (as well as two summer courses at Jerusalem University College in Israel) were the foundation of what has become a successful and renowned academic career. He has offered numerous contributions to the field of New Testament studies, ranging from textual criticism to discourse analyses of New Testament texts. His introduction to textual criticism, *New Testament Textual Criticism: A Concise Guide*, is one of the easiest to understand on the subject. Not only does he explain *why* textual criticism matters for students of the New Testament, he shows readers *how* to think through select textual issues (e.g., John 3:13) by considering both the internal and external evidence. This book has also been translated into Chinese.

His books on Greek grammar have been used all over the world to learn the original language of the New Testament and study it with precision:

1. *Learn to Read New Testament Greek*, his beginning Greek grammar, is in its third edition and was recently translated into Spanish (*Aprenda a leer el griego del Nuevo Testamento*) and Chinese. There are a number of reasons why I feel this is the best introductory New Testament Greek grammar, among which are its affordability, its simplified (and linguistically informed) discussions of grammatical concepts, its pairing of verb tenses in the indicative mood (present and future, aorist and imperfect, and perfect and pluperfect). A supplemental workbook for this grammar was put out by the publisher in 2009 (the same year as the third edition), edited by David A. Croteau et al. It should be mentioned, however, that Black's grammar contains translation exercises at the end of almost every chapter with an answer key located at the end of the book in an appendix, making it a suitable resource for self-study and classroom use. A professional recording (24 DVDs) of Black's beginning Greek course, taught at the Evangelical Theological College in Addis Ababa, Ethiopia, also became available in 2009.

2. His intermediate Greek grammar, *It's Still Greek to Me: An Easy to Understand Guide to Intermediate Greek*, is very different than most intermediate grammars. Like all of Black's books, he keeps the subject matter as simple as possible—never cumbersome or overloaded—and he even injects some humor to make the experience more enjoyable (and memorable). Even though learning Greek makes students gnash their teeth at times, Black's grammar keeps the focus on the essentials, even offering discussions on English grammar and terminology (Greek professors often assume that students know English just because they speak it!), while challenging students to engage more than individual words in their Greek New Testament.

3. *Using New Testament Greek in Ministry: A Practical Guide for Students and Pastors*, which is translated into Korean, Russian, and Chinese, is an update to A. T. Robertson's *The Minister and His Greek New Testament*. A course on Greek is not the most difficult part in learning Greek—actually *using* Greek is! Black has challenged his students to view their studies as a stewardship, and a good steward seeks maximum return for what has been entrusted to him. Greek should be no different. The last chapter and epilogue of *Learn to Read New Testament Greek* introduce students to using Greek. In *Using New Testament Greek in Ministry*, though, Black focuses on how to use Greek and frames the discussion around a ten-step exegetical method.

4. In *Linguistics for Students of New Testament Greek*, first published in 1988 and now in its second edition (1995), Black bridged together the fields of Greek studies and linguistics, focusing on the language as a whole like never before. One of the book's most valuable contributions is Black's discourse analysis of Paul's letter to the Philippians found in the last chapter. Before the mid-twentieth century, Greek studies were bound to traditional grammars and lexicons, and exegesis focused almost entirely on the meaning of words. In the 1960's modern linguistics was a blossoming field, and some scholars began to recognize not only that it *could* have an impact on the study of the New Testament, but that it *should*. For many students of the New Testament, Black's book was the introduction they needed to move beyond the study of words and to study the actual language instead.

In addition to these works, Black has published a number of resources on the background and theology of the New Testament. He was asked by Broadman & Holman to revise, ever so slightly (e.g., updated bibliographies and enlarged discussions on certain topics [e.g., textual criticism]), Thomas

D. Lea's (1938–1999) *The New Testament: Its Background and Message*. His books *Why Four Gospels? The Historical Origins of the Gospels* and *The Authorship of Hebrews: The Case for Paul* are quite unique. In them he argues for positions that are unquestionably rare in the present day. Almost no one in the present day argues for Matthean priority, and even fewer in favor of Paul as the author of Hebrews. He invites every student of the New Testament to consider the evidence afresh—including the Church Fathers—and make an informed decision about these issues. He has published numerous articles in various journals and multi-author books/series on a wide number of topics—text-critical studies on Matt 5:22a and Mark 6:20, rhetorical studies (e.g., John 17), discourse analyses on Heb 1:1–4 and Paul's letter to the Philippians, the Synoptic problem, and the translation of certain New Testament passages.

Black has been involved with organizing three major New Testament conferences on the campus of Southeastern Baptist Theological Seminary. In April 2000, some of the world's finest and most renowned New Testament scholars visited Wake Forest for a conference titled "Symposium on New Testament Studies: A Time for Reappraisal." Three topics were discussed: the Synoptic problem, the authorship of Hebrews, and New Testament textual criticism in general. The contributions from that symposium on the Synoptic problem were published in 2001, edited by Black and his colleague David Beck, with the title *Rethinking the Synoptic Problem*. The contributors were Craig L. Blomberg, Darrell L. Bock, Scot McKnight, William R. Farmer, and Grant R. Osborne. One year later the second "rethinking" book was published: *Rethinking New Testmaent Textual Criticism*. It features the contributions of Eldon Jay Epp, Michael W. Holmes, J. K. Elliott, Maurice A. Robinson, and Moisés Silva. In April 2007, Southeastern hosted another conference, focusing specifically on one particular textual issue—the ending of Mark (16:9–20). The presentations of Daniel B. Wallace, Darrell Bock, Maurice Robinson, J. K. Elliott, and Black were published under the title *Perspectives on the Ending of Mark: 4 Views*, edited by our honoree. Southeastern hosted a third conference, focusing on the *Pericope Adulterae* (John 7:53–8:11), in April 2014, featuring presentations by John David Punch, Tommy Wasserman, Jennifer Knust, Chris Keith, and Maurice Robinson. Those presentations, along with a foreword by Gary M. Burge, were published in a book titled *The Pericope of the Adulteress in Contemporary Research*, edited by Black and Jacob N. Cerone, in the Library of New Testament Studies series.

He has also edited/co-edited six other books, including two *Festshcriften*—one honoring J. Harold Greenlee (1918–2015), an eminent New Testament scholar and author of the widely praised *Introduction to New*

Testament Textual Criticism, and the other for Paige Patterson, a renowned Baptist leader and former president of Southeastern Baptist Theological Seminary (who invited Black to join the faculty in 1988). David S. Dockery and Black edited *New Testament Criticism and Interpretation* (1991) and *Interpreting the New Testament: Essays on Methods and Issues* (2001). In 1992, he, along with Katharine Barnwell and Stephen Levinsohn, edited a book titled *Linguistics and New Testament Interpretation: Essays on Discourse Analysis*, which discusses methodology (chs. 1–5) and offers examples of how discourse analysis contributes to the study of the New Testament (chs. 6–14). He also served as the New Testament editor of the International Standard Version (ISV) and provided the base translation from which the committee worked. More recently, he was among the twenty-one scholars that made up the Holman Christian Standard Bible translation and review team, whose work led to the publication of the Christian Standard Bible in 2017.

He was married to Becky Lynn Black for thirty-seven years. They met in the cafeteria line at Biola University in 1973 and married three years later. To them were born two children, Nathan Alan Black and Matthew David Black. Dave and Becky served together in training and mentoring numerous students over the years, partnering local churches in the states with churches abroad, and leading trips across the globe to serve others and share the significance of what Jesus did on the cross. Becky (who my wife and I [and many others] affectionately called "MamaB") was a truly amazing woman. Before she entered the presence of the Lord, Becky dictated her life's story, appropriately titled *My Life Story*, and it was published in 2014. And while the story is Becky's, the book offers a beautiful picture of the Black's marriage and how they wanted to live for something bigger than themselves and their relationship. Readers can get another picture of this in Black's booklet *Will You Join the Cause of Global Missions?* For anyone who wants to know more about Black's academic career and how God took him from surfing to church in Hawaii to studying in Basel and all the way to Southeastern, his book *It's All Greek to Me: Confessions of an Unlikely Academic* will no doubt be of great interest. By the way, he still surfs! And these days he is running a 5k race (literally) almost every single weekend. He also maintains two websites: (1) Dave Black Online (www.daveblackonline.com), which features a blog that he updates daily (unless he is traveling), and (2) Dave Black's New Testament Greek Portal (www.newtestamentgreekportal.blogspot.com), a hub for all things related to learning Koine Greek and using it in ministry.

David Alan Black has inspired countless students to get into the text of the New Testament and to be serious about presenting themselves as approved workers in their study of God's Word. He has challenged his students to live for something bigger than the status quo—to live for the only thing that matters (Phil 1:27–30). He has challenged his students to think for themselves, to study hard, and to make informed decisions as they study the New Testament. He encourages them to proclaim the amazing love of what Jesus has done on the cross not just with their words, but through serving others with simple acts of love and kindness. And even though he would deny it, Dave is a world-class scholar, whose contributions to the field of New Testament studies have long been recognized and appreciated by his friends, colleagues, and students. And to him is now offered this small token of our gratitude, a sort of applause for his faithful career and ministry, and our wishes for continued success in the years ahead.

List of Works Published by David Alan Black

BOOKS WRITTEN

———. *Paul, Apostle of Weakness: Astheneia and Its Cognates in the Pauline Literature.* American University Studies 7/3. New York: Lang, 1984.
———. *Linguistics for Students of New Testament Greek: A Survey of Basic Concepts and Applications.* Grand Rapids: Baker, 1988.
———. *Learn to Read New Testament Greek.* Nashville: Broadman & Holman, 1993.
———. *Using New Testament Greek in Ministry: A Practical Guide for Students and Pastors.* Grand Rapids: Baker, 1993.
———. *Learn to Read New Testament Greek.* Exp. ed. Nashville: Broadman & Holman, 1994.
———. *New Testament Textual Criticism: A Concise Guide.* Grand Rapids: Baker, 1994.
———. *Linguistics for Students of New Testament Greek: A Survey of Basic Concepts and Applications.* 2nd ed. Grand Rapids: Baker, 1995.
———. *It's Still Greek to Me: An Easy to Understand Guide to Intermediate Greek.* Grand Rapids: Baker, 1998.
———. *The Myth of Adolescence: Raising Responsible Children in an Irresponsible Society.* Yorba Linda, CA: Davidson, 1999.
———. *Why Four Gospels? The Historical Origins of the Gospels.* Grand Rapids: Kregel, 2001.
———, and Thomas D. Lea. *The New Testament: Its Background and Message.* Nashville: Broadman & Holman, 2003.
———. *Why I Stopped Listening to Rush: Confessions of a Recovering Neocon.* Baltimore: Publish America, 2004.
———. *Learn to Read New Testament Greek.* 3rd ed. Nashville: Broadman & Holman, 2009.
———. *The Jesus Paradigm.* Gonzalez, FL: Energion, 2009.
———. *Christian Archy.* Edited by David Alan Black and Allan R. Bevere. Areopagus: Critical Christian Issues 1. Gonzalez, FL: Energion, 2009.
———. *Why Four Gospels? The Historical Origins of the Gospels.* 2nd rev. ed. Gonzalez, FL: Energion, 2010.
———. *Will You Join the Cause of Global Missions?* Gonzalez, FL: Energion, 2012.
———. *Paul, Apostle of Weakness: Astheneia and Its Cognates in the Pauline Literature.* Rev. ed. Eugene, OR: Wipf & Stock, 2012.

2 Getting into the Text

———. *The Authorship of Hebrews: The Case for Paul*. Gonzalez, FL: Energion, 2013.
———. *It's All Greek to Me: Confessions of an Unlikely Academic*. Gonzalez, FL: Energion, 2014.
———. *Seven Marks of a New Testament Church: A Guide for Christians of All Ages*. Gonzalez, FL: Energion, 2014.
———. *Running My Race: Reflections on Life, Loss, Aging, and 40 Years of Christian Ministry*. Gonzalez, FL: Energion, 2016.

BOOKS EDITED

———, and David Dockery, eds. *New Testament Criticism and Interpretation*. Grand Rapids: Zondervan, 1991.
———, ed. *Linguistics and New Testament Interpretation: Essays on Discourse Analysis*. Nashville: Broadman, 1992.
———, ed. *Scribes and Scripture: New Testament Essays in Honor of J. Harold Greenlee*. Winona Lake, IN: Eisenbrauns, 1992.
———, (New Testament ed.). *The Holy Bible: International Standard Version New Testament*. Yorba Linda, CA: Davidson, 1999.
———, et al., eds. *Here I Stand: Essays in Honor of Paige Patterson*. Yorba Linda, CA: Davidson, 2000.
———, and David Dockery, eds. *Interpreting the New Testament: Essays on Methods and Issues*. Nashville: Broadman & Holman, 2001.
———, and David Beck, eds. *Rethinking the Synoptic Problem*. Grand Rapids: Baker, 2001.
———, ed. *Rethinking New Testament Textual Criticism*. Grand Rapids: Baker, 2002.
———, ed. *Perspectives on the Ending of Mark*. Nashville: B&H, 2008.
———, and JacobnCerone, eds. *The Pericope of the Adulteress in Contemporary Research*. The Library of New Testament Studies. New York: Bloomsbury, 2016.

SERIES EDITOR

Cornwall, Robert D. *Ultimate Allegiance: The Subversive Nature of the Lord's Prayer*. Edited by David Alan Black and Allan R. Bevere. Areopagus: Critical Christian Issues Series 2. Gonzalez, FL: Energion, 2010.
Bevere, Allan R. *The Politics of Witness: The Character of the Church in the World*. Edited by David Alan Black and Allan R. Bevere. Areopagus: Critical Christian Issues Series 3. Gonzalez, FL: Energion, 2011.
Parunak, H. Van Dyke. *Except for Fornication: The Teaching of the Lord Jesus on Divorce and Remarriage*. Edited by David Alan Black and Allan R. Bevere. Areopagus: Critical Christian Issues Series 4. Gonzalez, FL: Energion, 2011.
Baxter, Benjamin J. *"In the Original Text It Says": Word Study Fallacies and How to Avoid Them*. Edited by David Alan Black and Allan R. Bevere. Areopagus: Critical Christian Issues Series 5. Gonzalez, FL: Energion, 2012.
Greenham, Ant. *The Questioning God: An Inquiry for Muslims, Jews and Christians*. Edited by David Alan Black and Allan R. Bevere. Areopagus: Critical Christian Issues Series 6. Gonzalez, FL: Energion, 2012.

Croteau, David A. *Tithing after the Cross: A Refutation of the Top Arguments for Tithing and New Paradigm for Giving*. Edited by David Alan Black and Allan R. Bevere. Areopagus: Critical Christian Issues Series 7. Gonzalez, FL: Energion, 2013.

Freet, Christopher J. *A New Look at Hospitality as a Guide to Missions*. Edited by David Alan Black and Allan R. Bevere. Areopagus: Critical Christian Issues Series 8. Gonzalez, FL: Energion, 2014.

CHAPTERS IN BOOKS

———. "Blood in the New Testament." In *Mercer Dictionary of the Bible*, edited by Watson E. Mills et al., 118–19. Macon, GA: Mercer, 1990.

———. "Food Offered to Idols." In *Mercer Dictionary of the Bible*, edited by Watson E. Mills et al., 305. Macon, GA: Mercer, 1990.

———. "Luke." In *Mercer Dictionary of the Bible*, edited by Watson E. Mills et al., 529. Macon, GA: Mercer, 1990.

———. "Trinity." In *Mercer Dictionary of the Bible*, edited by Watson E. Mills et al., 934–35. Macon, GA: Mercer, 1990.

———. "El grupo de Juan: Helenismo y Gnosis." In *Orígenes del cristianismo: Antecedentes y primeros pasos*, edited by Antonio Piñero, 303–23. Translated by Antonio Piñero. Córdoba: Ediciones El Almendro, 1991.

———. "The Study of New Testament Greek in the Light of Ancient and Modern Linguistics." In *New Testament Criticism and Interpretation*, edited by David Alan Black and David S. Dockery, 379–406. Grand Rapids: Zondervan, 1991.

——— (contributor). *Complete Bible Dictionary*. Springfield, MO: Gospel Publishing House, 1992–93.

———. "Discourse Analysis, Synoptic Criticism, and the Problem of Markan Grammar: Some Methodological Considerations." In *Linguistics and New Testament Interpretation: Essays on Discourse Analysis*, edited by David Alan Black et al., 90–98. Nashville: Broadman, 1992.

———. "Dreams." In *Dictionary of Jesus and the Gospels*, edited by Joel B. Green et al., 199–200. Downers Grove, IL: InterVarsity, 1992.

———. "On Translating New Testament Poetry." In *Scribes and Scripture: New Testament Essays in Honor of J. Harold Greenlee*, edited by David Alan Black, 117–27. Winona Lake, IN: Eisenbrauns, 1992.

———. "The Unity and Variety of the Bible." In *Holman Bible Handbook*, edited by David S. Dockery et al., 23–27. Nashville: Holman, 1992.

———. "Weakness." In *Dictionary of Paul and His Letters*, edited by Gerald F. Hawthorne, et al., 966–67. Downers Grove, IL: InterVarsity, 1993.

———. "New Testament Textual Criticism." In *Foundations for Biblical Interpretation*, edited by David S. Dockery et al., 396–413. Nashville: Broadman & Holman, 1994.

———. "The Study of New Testament Greek in the Light of Ancient and Modern Linguistics." In *Interpreting the New Testament: Essays on Methods and Issues*, edited by David Alan Black and David S. Dockery, 230–52. Nashville: Broadman and Holman, 2001.

———. "Mark 16:9–20 as Markan Supplement." In *Perspectives on the Ending of Mark*, edited by David Alan Black, 103–23. Nashville: B&H, 2008.

———. "Exegesis for the Text-Driven Sermon." In *Text-Driven Preaching*, edited by Daniel L. Akin et al., 135–62. Nashville: B&H, 2010.

———, and Thomas W. Hudgins. "Jesus on Anger (Matt 5,22a): A History of Recent Scholarship." In *Greeks, Jews, and Christians: Historical, Religious, and Philological Studies in Honor of Jesús Peláez del Rosal*, edited by L. Roig Lanzillotta and I. Muñoz Gallarte, 91–104. Estudios de Filología Neotestamentaria 10. Córdoba: El Almendro, 2013.

———. "Greek Grammar." In *Encyclopedia of the Bible and Its Reception*, vol. 10, edited by Dale C. Allison Jr. et al., 908–910. Berlin: De Gruyter, 2015.

———. "Notes on the Translation of Hebrews 6,1." In *Nova et Vetera: Philological Studies in Honor of Professor Antonio Piñero*, edited by Israel M. Gallarte and Jesús Peláez, 455–66. Estudios de Filología Neotestamentaria 11. Córdoba: El Almendro, 2016.

BOOKS TRANSLATED INTO FOREIGN LANGUAGES

———. *Shin Yak Seok Euy Ip Moon*. [Korean ed. of *Using New Testament Greek in Ministry*.] Translated by Kyoung-Jin Kim. Seoul: Solomon, 1997.

———. *Por Que 4 Evangelhos?* Sao Paulo: Vida, 2004.

———. Russian edition of *Using New Testament Greek in Ministry*. Moscow: Smirna, 2004.

———. Chinese translation of *New Testament Textual Criticism*. Taiwan: China Evangelical Seminary Press, 2009.

———. *Aprenda a leer el griego del Nuevo Testamento*. [Spanish Translation of *Learn to Read New Testament Greek*.] Translated by Thomas W. Hudgins, Lesly J. Hudgins, and Fiorella J. Polo. Gonzalez, FL: Energion Publications, 2015.

———. Chinese Translation of *Learn to Read New Testament Greek*. Shanghai: Shanghai Translation Publishing, Forthcoming.

———. Chinese translation of *Using New Testament Greek in Ministry*. Gonzalez, FL: Energion Publications, Forthcoming.

———. Chinese Translation of *Seven Marks of a New Testament Church*. Gonzalez, FL: Energion Publications, Forthcoming.

———. Spanish Translation of *Seven Marks of a New Testament Church*. Gonzalez, FL: Energion Publications, Forthcoming.

PAMPHLETS

———. "Linguistics, Biblical Semantics, and Bible Translation: An Annotated Bibliography of Periodical Literature from 1961." Biola Bibliographies. La Mirada: Biola University, Rose Memorial Library, 1984.

———. "Articles on Hebrews, Annotated." Issue 1 of Biola Bibliographies: Talbot Bibliography. La Mirada: Biola University, Rose Memorial Library, 1984.

JOURNAL ARTICLES

———. "The Peculiarities of Ephesians and the Ephesian Address." *Grace Theological Journal* 2/1 (Spring 1981) 59–73.
———. "The Weak in Thessalonica: A Study in Pauline Lexicography." *Journal of the Evangelical Theological Society* 25/3 (September 1982) 307–21.
———. "Weakness Language in Galatians." *Grace Theological Journal* 4/1 (Spring 1983) 15–36.
———. "A Note on 'the Weak' in 1 Corinthians 9,22." *Biblica* 64/2 (1983) 240–42.
———. "*Paulus Infirmus*: The Pauline Concept of Weakness." *Grace Theological Journal* 5/1 (Spring 1984) 77–93.
———. "The Evangelical and Redaction Criticism in the Synoptic Gospels." *Talbot Review* 1 (1985) 6–13.
———. "The Text of John 3:13." *Grace Theological Journal* 6/1 (Spring 1985) 49–66.
———. "Paul and Christian Unity: A Formal Analysis of Philippians 2:1–4." *Journal of the Evangelical Theological Society* 28/3 (September 1985) 299–308.
———. "The Problem of the Literary Structure of Hebrews: An Evaluation and a Proposal." *Grace Theological Journal* 7/2 (Fall 1986) 163–77.
———. "Hebrews 1:1–4: A Study in Discourse Analysis." *Westminster Theological Journal* 49/1 (Spring 1987) 175–94.
———. "The Translation of Matthew 5:2." *Bible Translator* 38/2 (April 1987) 241–43.
———. "A Note on the Structure of Hebrews 12,1–2." *Biblica* 68/4 (1987) 543–51.
———. "Jesus on Anger: The Text of Matthew 5:22a Revisited." *Novum Testamentum* 30/1 (January 1988) 1–8.
———. "The Text of Mark 6.20." *New Testament Studies* 34 (1988) 141–45.
———. "The Authorship of Philippians 2:6–11: Some Literary-Critical Observations." *Criswell Theological Review* 2 (Spring 1988) 269–89.
———. "New Testament Semitisms." *Bible Translator* 39/2 (April 1988) 215–23.
———. "On the Style and Significance of John 17." *Criswell Theological Review* 3 (Fall 1988) 141–59.
———. "Some Dissenting Notes on R. Stein's The Synoptic Problem and Markan 'Errors.'" *Filología Neotestamentaria* 1/1 (May 1988) 95–101.
———. "Lasting Lessons from Philemon." *Grace Magazine* 4 (1988) 24–25.
———. "The Pauline Love Command: Structure, Style, and Ethics in Romans 12:9–21." *Filología Neotestamentaria* 2/1 (May 1989) 3–22.
———. "Conjectural Emendations in the Gospel of Matthew." *Novum Testamentum* 31/1 (January 1989) 1–15.
———. "Remarks on the Translation of Matthew 7:14." *Filología Neotestamentaria* 2/4 (November 1989) 193–95.
———. "Literary Artistry in the Epistle to the Hebrews." *Filología Neotestamentaria* 7/13 (May 1994) 43–52.
———. "Section Headings in Philippians." *Notes on Translation* 8 (1994) 27–33.
———. "The Discourse Structure of Philippians: A Study in Textlinguistics." *Novum Testamentum* 37/1 (January 1995) 16–49.
———. "Greek for Bible Readers" (former bimonthly column). *Bible Review* (Washington, D.C.: Biblical Archaeological Society).
———. "How Much Lettuce Is There in the New Testament? (and Other Musings of a Bible Translator)." *Notes on Translation* 12 (1998) 16–26.

———. "The Literary Structure of 1 and 2 Thessalonians." *Southern Baptist Journal of Theology* 3/3 (Fall 1999) 46–57.

———. "On the Pauline Authorship of Hebrews (Part 1): Overlooked Affinities between Hebrews and Paul." *Faith and Mission* 16/2 (Spring 1999) 32–51.

———. "On the Pauline Authorship of Hebrews (Part 2): The External Evidence Reconsidered." *Faith and Mission* 16/3 (Summer 1999) 78–86.

———. "The Historical Origins of the Gospels." *Faith and Mission* 18/1 (Fall 2000) 21–42.

BOOK REVIEWS

———. Review of *Gesundheit um jeden Preis?*, by S. Pfeifer. *Journal of Psychology and Theology* 11 (1983) 68–69.

———. Review of *Der heilige Geist in der Theologie von Heribert Mühlen*, by J. Banawiratma. *Journal of Psychology and Theology* 11 (1983) 72.

———. Review of *Justification: The Doctrine of Karl Barth and a Catholic Reflection*, by H. Kung. *Journal of Psychology and Theology* 11 (1983) 73–74.

———. Review of *Immanente Transzendenz*, by P. Ullrich. *Journal of Psychology and Theology* 11 (1983) 75.

———. Review of *Matthew: A Commentary on His Literary and Theological Art*, by R. Gundry. *Journal of Psychology and Theology* 11 (1983) 57.

———. Review of *Christliches Sterben als Gabe und Aufgabe*, by W. Klein. *Journal of Psychology and Theology* 12 (1984) 157.

———. Review of *Das Leben Meistern*, by W. Wanner. *Journal of Psychology and Theology* 12 (1984) 160.

———. Review of *Religionspädagogische Psychologie des Kleinkind-, Schul- und Jugendalters*, by B. Grom. *Journal of Psychology and Theology* 12 (1984) 154.

———. Review of *Ermutigung zur Nachfolge*, by I. Hoffmann. *Journal of Psychology and Theology* 12 (1984) 155.

———. Review of *Theorie und Experiment in der Psychologie*, by K. Holzkamp. *Journal of Psychology* 12 (1984) 332.

———. Review of *Die religionspädagogische Vertretbarkeit der biblischen Vaterfigur*, by R. Guist. *Journal of Psychology and Theology* 12 (1984) 331–32.

———. Review of *The Power of the Powerless*, by J. Moltmann. *Journal of the Evangelical Theological Society* 27 (1984) 340–42.

———. Review of *James Barr and the Beginnings of Biblical Semantics*, by R. Erickson. *Journal of the Evangelical Theological Society* 27 (1984) 500–501.

———. Review of *Die Sinnfrage in Psychotherapie und Theologie*, by U. Böschemeyer. *Journal of the Evangelical Theological Society* 27 (1984) 153.

———. Review of *Style and Discourse*, by E. Nida et al. *Journal of the Evangelical Theological Society* 27 (1984) 346–47.

———. Review of *Crisis and Catharsis: The Power of the Apocalypse*, by A. Collins. *Perspectives in Religious Studies* 12 (1985) 163–64.

———. Review of *The Message of Philippians*, by A. Motyer. *Grace Theological Journal* 6 (1985) 135–37.

———. Review of *Galatians*, by C. Cousar. *Talbot Review* 1 (1985) 6–7.

———. Review of *A Concise Guide to the Catholic Church*, by F. Foy. *Journal of Psychology and Theology* 13 (1985) 222–23.
———. Review of *The Pastoral Epistles*, by H. Kent. *Talbot Review* 1 (1985) 14–15.
———. Review of *Authority: The Critical Issue for Southern Baptists*, by J. Draper. *Journal of Psychology and Theology* 13 (1985) 72–73.
———. Review of *Nineteenth Century Evangelical Theology*, by F. Humphreys (ed.). *Journal of Psychology and Theology* 13 (1985) 76–77.
———. Review of *The Letter to the Colossians*, by E. Schweizer. *Talbot Review* 1 (1985) 13–14.
———. Review of *Style and Discourse*, by E. Nida et al. *Grace Theological Journal* 7 (1986) 133–34.
———. Review of *Layman's Library of Christian Doctrine*, by J. Newport. *Journal of Psychology and Theology* 14 (1986) 82.
———. Review of *The Pauline Circle*, by F. F. Bruce. *Grace Theological Journal* 7 (1986) 247–48.
———. Review of *The Pastoral Epistles*, by G. Clark. *Grace Theological Journal* 7 (1986) 248–50.
———. Review of *The Apostolic Church*, by E. F. Harrison. *Grace Theological Journal* 7 (1986) 263–64.
———. Review of *New Testament Exposition*, by W. Liefeld. *Journal of the Evangelical Theological Society* 29 (1986) 358–60.
———. Review of *First Corinthians*, by R. Hughes. *Grace Theological Journal* 8 (1987) 148–50.
———. Review of *Hebrews: A Call to Commitment*, by W. Lane. *Grace Theological Journal* 8 (1987) 150–52.
———. Review of *How Karl Barth Changed My Mind*, by D. McKim et al. *Criswell Theological Review* 2 (1987) 183–84.
———. Review of *Mach mehr aus Dir*, by W. Wanner. *Journal of Psychology and Theology* 15 (1987) 259.
———. Review of *Theological German: A Reader*, by H. Ziefle. *Criswell Theological Review* (1987) 181–83.
———. Review of *Suffering and the Spirit*, by S. Hafemann. *Journal of Biblical Literature* 107 (1988) 553–55.
———. Review of *The Text of the New Testament*, by K. Aland and B. Aland. *Criswell Theological Review* 2 (1988) 432–34.
———. Review of *The Gospel According to Matthew*, by D. Patte. *Criswell Theological Review* 3 (1988) 432–34.
———. Review of *Style and Discourse*, by E. Nida et al. In *Filología Neotestamentaria* 1 (1988) 112–13.
———. Review of *Sociolinguistics and Communication*, by J. Louw (ed.). In *Filología Neotestamentaria* 1 (1988) 111–12.
———. Review of *A New Testament Greek Morpheme Lexicon*, by J. H. Greenlee. *Filología Neotestamentaria* 1 (1988) 113–14.
———. Review of *A South African Perspective on the New Testament*, by J. H. Petzer and P. J. Harten (eds.). *Filología Neotestamentaria* 1 (1988) 117.
———. Review of *Greek-English Lexicon of the New Testament Based on Semantic Domains*, by J. P. Louw and E. A. Nida (eds.). *Filología Neotestamentaria* 1 (1988) 217–18.

———. Review of *Paul's Letter to the Romans*, by J. P. Heil. *Filología Neotestamentaria* 1 (1988) 220.

———. Review of *Reading Corinthians*, by C. H. Talbert. *Filología Neotestamentaria* 1 (1988) 220–21.

———. Review of *Interpreting the Synoptic Gospels*, by S. McKnight. *Filología Neotestamentaria* 1 (1988) 221.

———. Review of *Matthew as Story*, by J. D. Kingsbury. *Filología Neotestamentaria* 1 (1988) 221.

———. Review of *La proclama del Reino*, by F. Camacho. *Filología Neotestamentaria* 2 (1989) 99–100.

———. Review of *Difficult Passages in the Epistles*, by R. Stein. *Filología Neotestamentaria* 2 (1989) 212.

———. Review of *The Epistle to the Romans*, by L. Morris. *Filología Neotestamentaria* 2 (1989) 212.

———. Review of *The Epistle to the Hebrews*, by H. W. Attridge. *Filología Neotestamentaria* 3 (1990) 76–77.

———. Review of *De Jerusalén a Antioquía*, by J. Rius-Camps. *Filología Neotestamentaria* 3 (1990) 169–70.

———. Review of *El origen divino del poder*, by A. Urban. *Filología Neotestamentaria* 4 (1991) 222–23.

———. Review of *So wird Gott in dir geboren*, by H. Walach. *Journal of Psychology and Theology* 19/3 (1991) 309.

———. Review of *The Gifts of God and the Authentication of a Christian*, by Paul Gardner. *Critical Review of Books in Religion* 9 (1996) 204–7.

———. Review of *Textual Optimism: A Critique of the United Bible Societies' Greek New Testament*, by K. Clarke. *Filología Neotestamentaria* 10 (1997) 157–58.

———. Review of *Paul's Letter to the Philippians in the Light of the Disunity in the Church*, by D. Peterlin. *Filología Neotestamentaria* 10 (1997) 162–64.

———. Review of *Christ and the Bible*, by John Wenham. *Journal of the Evangelical Theological Society* 40 (1997) 313–14.

———. Review of *A Critical and Exegetical Commentary on Ephesians*, by Ernest Best. *Faith and Mission* 16 (1999) 87–88.

———. Review of *The Paul Quest*, by Ben Witherington. *Faith and Mission* 16 (1999) 112–14.

———. Review of *Griechischer Lehrgang zum Neuen Testament*, by R. Schoch. *Novum testamentum* 43/4 (2001) 393–95.

———. Review of *Analytical Lexicon of the Greek New Testament*, by T. Friberg. *Novum testamentum* 44/2 (2002) 192–95.

———. Review of *Das Studium des Neuen Testaments Bd 2*, by H.-W. Neudorfer. *Novum testamentum* 44/2 (2002) 189–92.

———. Review of *Syntax Lists for Students of New Testament Greek*, by nH. Young. *Novum testamentum* 47/3 (2005) 296–97.

Bowden, Andrew M., and David Alan Black. Review of *Introducing the New Testament*, by D. A. Carson and D. J. Moo. *Criswell Theological Review* 8/2 (2011) 93–95.

1

So What Have We Learned in the Last Thirty Years of Greek Linguistic Study?

STANLEY E. PORTER
McMaster Divinity College

INTRODUCTION

I HAVE KNOWN DAVID Alan Black for the entire length of my academic career. In fact, I knew *of* him, even if I did not know him directly, before I began my academic career. Then, once I had finished my PhD and began teaching at an institution where David himself had taught, I sought his advice regarding publishing my recently completed thesis (as it is called in the UK system). He gave me excellent advice based upon his own experience with what became the publisher of my thesis, and I have never regretted it. In fact, I published another book with the same publisher, and they have kept my first book in print to this day. That early conversation was a (relatively) long time ago. However, it was soon after that time that David published his *Linguistics for Students of New Testament Greek*.[1] This book occupies an interesting and quite possibly even unique place in New Testament studies. For those in New Testament studies, the field of linguis-

---

1. Black, *Linguistics for Students* (1988). A second edition of this book appeared in 1995, but I am not concerned with that book here, for reasons made clear above.

tics had been brought to our serious attention (at least for those who were not aware of the field of linguistics) by James Barr's *The Semantics of Biblical Language*, which drew upon general and basic principles of linguistics in the Saussurian mode.[2] However, for all of its great worth (and its still immediate importance), Barr's *Semantics* focused upon a few major issues, especially related to how biblical scholars abuse and misunderstand words, with serious theological and other consequences. What was needed in the field of biblical studies was an accessible introduction to the field of modern linguistics for those unfamiliar with its basic concepts and ways of thinking about things. It took over twenty-five years from the first appearance of Barr's work until such a work was provided. David provided such an introduction in 1988, with a second edition in 1995. There is only one other book in English that I can think of that attempts something similar.[3] The subtitle of David's book provides a useful orientation to what he was attempting: *A Survey of Basic Concepts and Applications*, even if the nature of the subject matter in more than a few instances requires (especially for the previously uninitiated) more understanding than is implied in the words "survey" and "basic." Nevertheless, this was a noble attempt to draw upon the wide range of linguistic thought then available to provide a necessary introduction for those in New Testament studies who wanted to know more about a variety of topics that they had perhaps heard of (although many had not), that they arguably needed to know (and still do, even if they don't), and which had not been adequately treated in the standard works used in Greek language study, many of which had been written many years earlier.

Linguistics for Students of New Testament Greek is organized as one might expect such a book to be that reflects the way that much linguistics of the time was done (and as much of it is still done today). In that sense, this book is very similar to many other introductions to general linguistics.[4] Black starts with a broad discussion of what linguistics is all about, including what exactly a linguist is and how linguistics differs from such things as traditional grammar. He then treats the standard categories found in many

---

2. Barr, *Semantics*. Cf. de Saussure, *General Linguistics*. This is not the place to discuss the history and development of the field of linguistics. For a brief history, see Robins, *Linguistics*, and on structuralism in particular, see Lepschy, *Structural Linguistics*.

3. That work is Cotterell and Turner, *Linguistics and Biblical Interpretation*. Along somewhat similar lines, see also Silva, *God, Language, and Scripture*.

4. There are numerous introductions to linguistics available for comparison, and their basic topics are often quite similar. This was certainly true in 1988. As an example, see O'Grady and Archibald, *Contemporary Linguistic Analysis*, with the following chapters: Language: A Preview, Phonetics, Phonology, Morphology, Syntax, Semantics, Historical Linguistics, Classification of Languages, and then a number of chapters on social and psychological issues in language, not treated by Black.

general linguistics introductions, including phonology, morphology, syntax, semantics, and historical and comparative linguistics. In this essay, I wish to use the same categories as Black used in his book to briefly comment upon what has happened in each of these fields since his original book was published in 1988. I use his book as a platform for exploring the developments in linguistic study of the New Testament over the last thirty years, not as an opportunity to quibble over Black's treatment of the subject, but as a means of exploring what we have learned in the last thirty or so years.[5] I am furthermore not concerned to treat all or even a major portion of the studies produced since his book was published, but to survey what I see as important developments over this span of time. Others will no doubt have different perspectives on these developments.

WHAT IS LINGUISTICS?

In the first chapter, Black asks a number of questions and proposes answers to them that encourage the study and use of linguistics. From the beginning, he points out that linguistics is no different from any other academic discipline in having its own complexity including technical vocabulary and that, rather than being in a state of perilous change, it has arrived at many conclusions worth understanding.[6] When written in 1988, one might not have understood the importance of such a comment, as the field of linguistics was reasonably new to New Testament studies—especially if this was the first book one might have read on the topic. In his recent treatment of advances in Greek study, Constantine Campbell, claiming that New Testament studies have not been linguistically strong (I would perhaps state instead that they have not been particularly widespread), raises the same possible objections to linguistics.[7] He in fact quotes Black on this very set of issues. There is, however, a difference in Campbell's approach to the subject of the complexity and fluidity of linguistics from that of Black. Whereas Black states that linguistics is no more intimidating than any other intellectual discipline, Campbell seems to concede that linguistics being a changing and developing field with differing schools of thought does indeed present legitimate difficulties for the study of the Greek New Testament—even

---

5. This essay is to be distinguished from the attempt by Campbell (*Advances in the Study of Greek*) to treat what he calls "advances" in New Testament linguistic study, by focusing upon the categories that Black uses, whether there have been advances or not. There is inevitably some overlap.

6. Black, *Linguistics for Students*, 1–2.

7. Campbell, *Advances*, 52–53.

though he is also quick to point out that one pays a high price for ignoring linguistics.

The shift in perspective, even if it is subtle, is not encouraging. There may well be more schools of linguistic thought now than there were thirty years ago (as there probably are in New Testament studies), but that does not seem to be the main point. There seems to have been a shift in attitude from Black to Campbell that makes linguistics, at least in Campbell's eyes, more intimidating and potentially more confusing for the student of the New Testament who wishes to embrace a linguistic orientation to ancient Greek. This has not, to be sure, hindered a number of scholars from wading into the treacherous waters of linguistic study, but the fact that Campbell's statement raises the same issue, even to the point of quoting Black on it, indicates that there has been less progress in the adoption of linguistics over the last thirty years than hoped. Numerous reasons come to mind as to why this might be thought to be so—such as students being less well academically prepared, their being less well linguistically prepared, their having less exposure to other languages and matters of language, their teachers being the same, their all being less willing to invest the time to overcome their deficiencies especially in a field that is seen to be ancillary, etc.—but the fact that the sentiment persists does not bode well for linguistics and New Testament studies. The evidence for such a claim is all too readily to hand. The fact that this persists as a problem is clearly evident in the lack of attention to linguistics in recent commentaries, including in commentaries that purport to focus upon linguistic matters.[8]

One of the further insights of Black's book is the identification of differences between linguistics and traditional grammar, where he identifies three major features of linguistics: being scientific, descriptive, and focused upon spoken language.[9] These are solid insights, even if they require nuance. In an article published in 1989, I noted that modern linguistics is not to be confused with traditional grammar, and identified seven differences between them. These include: (1) the priority of spoken over written language in linguistics, (2) the unrepresentative nature of literary remains often used as the basis of traditional grammatical studies, (3) the regularized forms of language found in traditional grammars, (4) the dominance of language descriptions in terms of languages of study, (5) the imposition of logic on language, (6) the imposition of other interests, such as theology,

---

8. See Porter, "Linguistic Competence," 33–56; cf. also Porter, "Commentaries," 365–404, in the same volume, where it is seen that several earlier commentaries are more linguistically aware than later ones.

9. Black, *Linguistics for Students*, 12–14.

history, philosophy, rhetoric or literature, upon language, and (7) the tendency towards atomistic analysis in traditional grammar.[10]

What is surprising is how traditional grammar has continued to have such an important influence upon the study of New Testament Greek, even if there has been noteworthy work in linguistics. This is seen in a variety of ways in which traditional grammar still dominates our discipline. These include the publishing of traditional grammars since Black wrote in 1988, numerous Greek grammatical studies written from the standpoint of traditional grammar, and the continued use of traditional grammar in the vast majority of commentaries (as already noted above). Even though Daniel Wallace claims to be informed by linguistics, his book *Greek Grammar Beyond the Basics* is probably better described as an attempt to salvage traditional grammar through select (just a few) principles formulated to sound linguistic.[11] Several of his principles regarding his approach have linguistic potential, such as his reference to "semantic situation," "unaffected vs. affected meaning," and "synchronic priority,"[12] but even these raise questions. For example, why does Wallace feel compelled to use the labels he does when there are suitable terms from the broader field of linguistics? I fear that it is because he means something different by them. For example, his notion of semantics is extensive and inclusive, to the point that he cannot use the typical semantics vs. pragmatics distinction. He recognizes the tension, but it appears that he wishes to categorize and discuss pragmatics but arrive at semantic conclusions. However, on a number of other issues, he appears very unlinguistic, such as what seems to be confusion over the notion of structure in language. His notion of "structural priority" seems to be confined to individual structures,[13] rather than the structure of language (or even of a given language), a notion that seems absent from his approach. Most disconcerting is his statement regarding "the cryptic nature

---

10. Porter, "Studying Ancient Languages," 165–66.

11. Wallace, *Greek Grammar*, esp. 1–11. His definition of syntax is also to be questioned (e.g., p. xv). The one linguistic theory that Wallace seems to acknowledge he clearly disagrees with is Chomsky's transformational grammar, based upon the work of Ian Robinson (*New Grammarians' Funeral*), whose work is interesting but cannot be said to speak for the field of linguistics in its reaction to Chomsky (e.g., Robinson's statement that linguistic fashions come and go, with the implication that Chomsky's will soon go!). Wallace seems to draw upon the work of P. H. Matthews (*Syntax*), but I am not convinced that he has always understood Matthews (e.g., p. xv notes 14 and 15), and more than that, what syntax is. A similar approach is taken in Wallace, *Granville Sharp's Canon*. Cf. Porter, *Idioms*.

12. Wallace, *Greek Grammar*, 2–5.

13. Ibid., 5–7.

of language."[14] The matter is not nearly as cryptic as he contends, except that he has unnecessarily restricted himself to a minimal notion of context, wants to deal predominantly with what he variously calls "morpho-syntactic uses/element(s)/categories/features/structure(s)/construction,"[15] and arrive at semantics through forms (what he apparently labels a type of word grammar).[16] In relation to the three criteria of Black that distinguish linguistics from traditional grammar, Wallace rejects the notion of being scientific, clearly calls into question descriptivism by advocating a form of prescriptivism (as well as mistaking the notion of what it means to be ungrammatical), and does not address the issue of spoken vs. written language apart possibly from recognizing the need for sufficient data. In relation to the further seven criteria, he does not address problems related to the priority of spoken language, he only tacitly acknowledges problems regarding the corpus, he apparently makes a plea for regularization (and this is exemplified in his work), his actual descriptions are often in terms of English (e.g., the use of English-based sentence diagramming, description of the genitive in relation to English "of"),[17] he seems to adopt a logical view of language (hence his discussion of "ontological" meaning in relation to other types of meaning),[18] the importance of theology is seen in his overall discussion, and there is a definite tendency to atomization (and categorization—note the 33 uses of the genitive).[19] Hence he summarizes his approach as a type of (unstable) hybrid that continues to endorse traditional grammar.[20] This is all to say that those wanting a linguistic approach to Greek will not find it here.

The use of traditional grammatical works in so much further exegetical work, including many if not most commentaries, as I have documented elsewhere (note above), shows that there has been minimal progress in many if not most areas of linguistic thinking in New Testament studies. Black was at the forefront of identifying some of the major issues, so much so that Campbell makes many of the same observations nearly thirty years

---

14. Ibid., 7–9.

15. These various terms are found (inter alia?) in Wallace, *Greek Grammar*, x, xii, xiii, xiv, xvi, 5, 6, 10, 11.

16. Ibid., xvi. His treatment does not have the other characteristics of a word grammar, such as dependency syntax (see below).

17. Ibid., 73–74, 86, 88, 118.

18. Ibid., 2n8.

19. Ibid., 72. Wallace notes at the beginning that he has developed categorizes "some of which have never been in print before" (xii). This is believable but often regrettable that some of them made it into print.

20. Ibid., 7n32; cf. 5n20.

later. This is not a particularly auspicious beginning to an examination of what we have learned from Greek linguistic study of the last thirty years.

PHONOLOGY

Phonology is concerned with the sounds of language. Black lays out both a conspectus of articulatory phonetics and the Greek phonological system. I do not think that I know of another such treatment of both phonetics and phonology of the Greek sound system since Black's book. Although his phonological theory is not entirely clear to me, it appears that he uses some type of generative phonological theory.[21] Since his writing, however, there has been significant discussion of matters related to the sounds of Greek. In fact, this has perhaps been one of the most vocal areas of discussion in New Testament Greek linguistics, even if there has not been as much genuine progress in understanding the language. The major issue has been concerning whether the traditional Erasmian pronunciation should be retained or whether some form of pronunciation that approximates to a reconstruction of the Greek used during the Greco-Roman period or even modern pronunciation should be utilized. Chrys Caragounis has been one of the most outspoken advocates for what he calls Historic Greek Pronunciation, that is, a form of pronunciation based upon his reconstruction of what the sound system of Greek may have been like during the time of the turn of the millennia.[22] He has been followed by a number of others, including Randall Buth, among others (although not all of them agree on the pronunciation).[23] There are also those who advocate the use of a system of pronunciation similar to that of modern Greek, such as John Lee and Constantine Campbell, among others.[24] The result is, for the most part, very similar to that of those who advocate the Historic Greek Pronunciation, although there are still some noteworthy differences. For many, this is a new discussion. Black himself, however, anticipated this issue, although without all of the vitriol and posturing that has often accompanied the recent discussion.[25]

---

21. See Black, *Linguistics for Students*, 42. On generative phonology, see Chomsky and Halle, *Sound Pattern of English*. Cf. Anderson, *Phonology*, for discussion of various theories.

22. Caragounis, "Error of Erasmus," 151–85; with further material in Caragounis, *Development of Greek*, esp. 339–564.

23. Buth, *Living Koiné Greek*.

24. Campbell, *Advances*, 192–208, with a guide to pronunciation of Koine based on modern pronunciation by John A. L. Lee on 201–3.

25. Black, *Linguistics for Students*, 38–40.

One feature that emerges in most of the positions is that any attempt to define the sound-system of ancient Greek, including that of the first century, requires compromise and accommodation.[26] This compromise and accommodation includes the recognition that some of the evidence cited is stronger and clearer than other evidence, especially if we consider the mixed attestation found in the papyri. We must also recognize that there would have been dialectal and idiolectal variations according to a range of factors, so we are talking in any case about an idealized pronunciation.[27] Regional varieties are usually not taken into account, as much of the evidence discussed comes from Egypt, but other places in the Roman world may well have pronounced their Greek with other variations. So it is not quite as easy as simply saying that one might adopt Erasmian or historic Greek or modern pronunciation, and that one of these is necessarily a more accurate reflection of what an ancient Greek speaker of the first century would have sounded like. None of the discussions that I have seen, it should be noted, are grounded in an explicit phonological theory.

Some of the reasons for continued use of the Erasmian pronunciation—which itself varies depending upon whether the modern user is from North America, Europe, or elsewhere (see above on accommodation and compromise, found here as well)—are the general (though not invariable) differentiation of individual letters and letter combinations by a distinct sound and the resulting consistency. Since we are primarily dealing with the ancient language (regardless of one's thought on its modern form), this arguably makes communication with other scholars and the teaching of the language easier to facilitate, especially its reading. The vowel system of Greek is the place most affected by the differentiation between the Erasmian and other types of pronunciation, due to the process of itacism that occurred in Greek. The result is the tendency toward use of the high front vowel sound /i/ for many vowels and vowel combinations. There was also a process of monophthongization, in which diphthongs became monothongs, some of them also with the high front vowel sound. The result of such vowel shifts was widespread vowel interchange in spelling, witnessed by numerous documentary (and other) papyri from the period.[28] These vowel (and consonant) interchanges provide the evidence for the reconstructed sound system of the turn of the millennia, although the evidence requires that the interpreter make sometimes variable judgments on the resulting sound pat-

---

26. See, e.g., Lee, in Campbell, *Advances*, 201, where he refers to there being what he calls "anachronism" in adopting modern pronunciation.

27. I owe some of these insights here and below to my colleague David I. Yoon.

28. The best source of this information for the papyri is found in Gignac, *Greek Papyri*, who had already published by the time Black wrote.

terns. There were also several consonants that were affected, including some aspirates (e.g., φ, θ, χ). The Historic Greek and modern pronunciations are arguably closer to a more consistent reconstruction of the sounds used by the ancients of this time period and for that reason alone may well be convincing for those who wish to believe that they are sounding more like the ancients than those using the Erasmian pronunciation. It has been suggested that further arguments for the Hellenistic Greek or modern pronunciation are that it sounds more like a real language (whatever that means), this pronunciation connects one more fully with Greek culture and history, it potentially saves one from embarrassment when speaking with modern Greeks (I didn't know that the modern Greeks were such an uncharitable people), and it allows one to "speak" with relatives and local merchants more successfully.[29] The last such reasons are not to be taken too seriously.

Since Black himself recognized many if not most of the major differences already in 1988, without resulting in a strident battle over pronunciation, even if there are more advocates for types of historic or modern pronunciation than there were earlier, we may have developed in the depth of our knowledge, but there is little knew that we know now that was not known before. There is much more said, to be sure, but not much development.

MORPHOLOGY

Morphology is concerned with the minimal unit of meaning in a language, and, as in Black's book, is often treated in relation to such topics as lexical roots and their affixes. He offers a fairly detailed set of lists of the various derivational and inflectional morphemes.[30] The only other major work on New Testament Greek morphology published since Black that I am aware of is by William Mounce.[31] This volume is odd, to say the least. He works with the theory that the morphology of the language is determined by the phonology.[32] Mounce includes a brief treatment of what he calls phonology, but which essentially consists of vowel and consonantal change as reflected in graphology, rather than with the sound system of Greek. His treatment of morphology does not include any description of morphological theory,

---

29. Campbell, *Advances*, 206.
30. Black, *Linguistics for Students*, 53–95, the longest chapter in the book.
31. Mounce, *Morphology*.
32. Ibid., 1. Those familiar with the morphology-phonology interface will recognize that many, if not most, theories of morphology take the opposite approach.

but consists primarily of charts of formations, broken down into individual morphemes.

The tradition in Greek language study is to treat morphology in terms of what Gregory Stump calls lexical-incremental morphology.[33] Morphology is analyzable according to two major axes. Lexical morphology, as opposed to inferential morphology, essentially takes the view that each morpheme is equivalent to a lexical entry and is equivalent to a designated set of morphosyntactic properties. Stump uses the example of the English affix –s, which he says indicates the properties "3sg subject agreement," "present tense," and "indicative mood"[34]—even though he is referring to modern English, the similarities for discussion of ancient Greek cannot be missed. Incremental morphology, as opposed to realizational morphology, is what he calls "information-increasing" or might also be called agglutinating; "that is, words acquire morphosyntactic properties only as a concomitant of acquiring the inflectional exponents of those properties."[35] This means that a verb in English that adds the –s ending in doing so gains the indicated properties as above: "3sg subject agreement," "present tense," and "indicative mood." This is similarly reflected in Mounce's statement that when he discusses verbs and their formation, he moves from left to right in the discussion, as the various affixes are added and their morphosyntactic properties are acquired as well.[36] In lexical-incremental morphology, the lexical properties are added by increment, rather than these properties either being inferred or rule-based.

This theory of morphology, the lexical-incremental, seems to reflect the general state of discussion of New Testament Greek morphology. However, the lexical-incremental theory is perhaps not the best approach to Greek morphology. The problems are seen in the fact that the result is, just as Mounce evidences, numerous and varied charts that compile the morphological information (properties) so as to result in the agglutinated meanings of the various word-forms. Each separate morpheme adds to these properties. A better approach might be an inferential-realizational morphological model, or what Stump calls Paradigm Function Morphology. An inferential theory claims that there are "systematic formal relations between a lexeme's root and the fully inflected word forms constituting its paradigm," and that

33. Stump, *Inflectional Morphology*, 1–3.

34. Ibid., 1.

35. Ibid., 2. As an inflectional language, ancient Greek has some properties of agglutinating languages—especially in traditional morphological theory.

36. Mounce, *Morphology*, 63.

these relations are not simply lexically based but rule based.[37] These rules are morphological rules that pertain to the respective paradigms. As an example, for the English word *likes*, there is a rule that associates the use of the suffix –*s* with certain properties, such as "3sg subject agreement," "present tense," and "indicative mood." A realizational theory works from the standpoint that the morphosyntactic properties that are associated with a particular word, that is, its function within a particular paradigm, "licenses" or allows the "indication of those properties' inflectional exponents."[38] Thus, when the verb *like* is associated with the properties of "3sg subject agreement," "present tense," and "indicative mood," the affixation of the –*s* suffix is allowed.

The advantages of this inferential-realizational or paradigmatic morphological model are several. The first is that it avoids the systematic confusion over the meaning of a morpheme or morphemes. In the lexical models, we might have the morpheme –*s* as indicated above. However, if we treat this morpheme lexically, we have confusion over whether it realizes "3sg subject agreement," "present tense," and "indicative mood," or whether it realizes "plural," as it would in its use with *book* and *books*. Is this one morpheme with several meanings or is this several different morphemes? There are numerous instances of such possible confusion in ancient Greek. Instead, we should treat the primary and secondary endings of the Greek aorist indicative as morphologically identical, but with different phonological or graphological realizations. They may vary in how they are realized phonologically or graphologically, but they function in the same way (have the same properties) within their respective places within the aorist paradigm. The lexical theories have difficulty in differentiating these morphemes apart from taking a paradigmatic functional approach. The second advantage is that the inferential-realizational model recognizes what Stump calls "extended exponence."[39] By this he means that the morphosyntactic properties may be realized by a number of morphological markers, rather than a single marker. There has been continuing confusion in discussion of Greek regarding the aorist and imperfect augment. This inflectional prefix is usually isolated and temporal significance given to it, rather than treating the prefix as part of the extended exponence of the aorist or imperfect indicative verbal paradigm morphology. There is much more that can and should be said about Greek morphology, especially from the paradigm functional model.

37. Stump, *Inflectional Morphology*, 1.
38. Ibid., 2.
39. Ibid., 4.

Black chose to place his discussion of verbal aspect within the section on morphology. We see now that this was probably a mistake, as verbal aspect is a semantic category rather than a morphological one, even though it is morphologically realized. However, more to the point here is that Black equates the lexical stem with what he calls "inherent aspect," so that he also ends up equating verbal aspect with *Aktionsart*.[40] The discussion of verbal aspect in New Testament Greek is probably the single biggest area in which there have been major developments in the study of the Greek of the New Testament over the last thirty years and in which we have learned the most as a result. Since Black wrote in 1988, there have been a number of major monographs published—several of them published very soon after—and a number of other works, too numerous to mention here, that have continued to develop and extend the discussion.[41] There are still many unresolved issues, but in light of my discussion above, it becomes clear that at least some of them may have been caused by considering the morphology of verbs from the lexical-incremental rather than the inferential-realizational position.[42] This could have helped to avoid some of the problems that are often introduced regarding the semantics of verbal aspect on the basis of lexical and incremental frameworks, rather than utilizing inferential and realizational, that is, paradigmatic, ones.

Despite this possible confusion, there are a number of generally held principles that have emerged in the study of Greek verbal aspect that illustrate what we have learned in the ensuing discussion. These generalizations include the realization that ancient Greek is what is now often called an aspect prominent language.[43] Within the categories of tense, mood, and aspect, aspect is the most important semantic category for discussing the Greek verbal system (in relation to tense), not some of the time but virtually all of the time, and the semantic category that is focally realized by the Greek

---

40. Black, *Linguistics for Students*, 80, 84.

41. The major works include: Porter, *Verbal Aspect*; Fanning, *Verbal Aspect*; McKay, *Syntax* (whose work was previously published in journal articles on New Testament Greek); Olsen, *Lexical and Grammatical Aspect*; Decker, *Temporal Deixis*; and Campbell, *Verbal Aspect, the Indicative Mood, and Narrative*, and Campbell, *Verbal Aspect and Non-Indicative Verbs*. Some of the extensions include Foley, *Biblical Translation*; Lee, *Paul's Gospel*; Mathewson, *Verbal Aspect in the Book of Revelation*; Cirafesi, *Verbal Aspect*; and Huffman, *Verbal Aspect Theory*. There are of course many other studies, especially in journals and other literature. A summary of some of the issues is found in Porter, *Linguistic Analysis*, 198–203, and elsewhere.

42. This seems to be one among many problems in Ellis et al., "Greek Verbal System," 33–62, along with possibly other studies that rely too heavily upon morphology for their categorizations.

43. E.g., Ellis et al., "Greek Verbal System," 33.

verbal edifice. Even most of those scholars who believe that Greek verbs grammaticalize tense in the indicative mood recognize that verbal aspect is grammaticalized within the indicative and non-indicative mood forms.[44] We have further learned that there are at least two verbal aspects in Greek—the perfective and the imperfective—even if there is still disagreement over how to define the aspect of the perfect tense-form and over what to do with the future form. We have learned further the importance of differentiating verbal aspect from *Aktionsart*, no matter how it is that one defines the various components. Verbal aspect is a paradigmatically driven semantic category, and not to be equated with *Aktionsart* (which is variously defined, although most do not attach the meaning of *Aktionsart* simply to the lexical stem of a Greek verb).[45] Most who discuss the relationship between aspect and *Aktionsart* make a division between them, although recent research has shown that the notion of *Aktionsart* seems to remain inherently imprecise and eludes formulation at any particular rank within the language.[46]

Even if many of the major issues have been resolved within study of verbal aspect—recognition of its importance for understanding the Greek verbal system, the basic definitions of the perfective and imperfective verbal aspects, and that the aspects are not to be considered tenses (apart from the indicative for some interpreters)—there still remain a number of issues to be considered regarding the function of the aspects within various discourse contexts.

SYNTAX

When Black published his introduction, traditional grammar still overwhelmingly dominated the discussion of syntax of New Testament Greek. As a result, he introduces a mix of discussions of various views of syntax. These include a treatment of immediate constituent analysis (IC), phrase structure grammar using kernels, and transformational generative grammar. He also mentions some current interest in stratificational grammar.[47]

---

44. There is a difference of opinion between Porter, McKay, Decker and Campbell, and those who follow them in taking a non-temporal view of the Greek indicative, and Fanning and others who take a temporal view. Nevertheless, most if not all take an aspectual (and non-temporal) view of the non-indicative verbal system.

45. Some of these various theories are discussed in Porter, *Linguistic Analysis*, 202–3.

46. See Pang, *Revisiting Aspect and Aktionsart*. Black's view is closest to that of Fanning, *Verbal Aspect*, 50.

47. Black, *Linguistics for Students*, 96–119.

It is perhaps a testimony to the developments within mainstream study of New Testament Greek and what has been learned along the way that very little work is being done in any of these areas.[48] Immediate constituent analysis was characteristic of American structuralism of the 1920s to 1950s, and then became fully integrated into phrase structure analysis as part of the Chomskyan linguistic movement.[49] Immediate constituent analysis, even as part of phrase structure analysis, has been central to much linguistic theory, and has been used within the study of New Testament Greek as well, especially by those influenced by Chomskyan thought.[50] However, as has been pointed out, there are some possible reasons for the domination of immediate constituent or phrase structure analysis that merit review. The first is that it seems to reflect the domination of English, a configurational language, as the first language of its originators, whereas the outworkings may not have been the same if the originators had used a non-configurational language. This reason immediately raises questions concerning the use of immediate constituent or phrase structure analysis for ancient Greek, which has the characteristics of a non-configurational language. The second reason is the strong domination of formalism at the expense originally of mentalism but also of semantics. Models of language that place semantics over syntax are probably not as well suited to constituent theory. The third reason is the urge toward scientism in modern linguistics, as seen in the work of such linguists as Leonard Bloomfield, Zellig Harris, and Noam Chomsky, which resulted in formal grammars confined to units at the sentence/clause or below. Those linguistic approaches that wish to move to ranks above the clause/sentence may need to rely upon other means of analysis. The fourth reason is the emphasis upon syntax of much modern linguistics, at the expense of semantics, with the original notion being that immediate constituents and later phrase structures could be analyzed apart from meaning. The question of whether this is even possible is an important one, and meaning-based linguistic models have already answered it in the negative. There are in fact a number of grammatical models that have included ele-

---

48. Stratificational grammar, developed by Lamb (*Outline of Stratificational Grammar*), was never widely used within study of New Testament Greek, so far as I know, although it early on was one of the major cognitive-functional grammars. One attempt that combines it with Relevance Theory is Fantin, *Greek Imperative Mood*. Other work in cognitive-oriented linguistics, a topic not treated by Black due to its more recent development, may be found in Howe, *Because You Bear This Name*; Park, *Mark's Memory Resources*; Stovell, *Mappping Metaphorical Discourse*; Howe and Green, *Cognitive Linguistic Explorations*. A related but distinctive approach is taken in Wierzbicka, *What Did Jesus Mean?*

49. This paragraph is dependent upon Mel'čuk, *Dependency Syntax*, 3–6, 12–17.

50. E.g., Palmer, *Constituent Structure*.

ments of an alternative to constituent or phrasal analysis, that is, they have evidence of various dependency relations.[51] Instead, dependency syntax, rather than combining elements into units and then into higher levels of units, shows the relationships among the elements themselves. Dependency syntax categorizes according to function rather than according to syntactic class. The result of such phrase structure is forced groupings of words, not found in dependency syntax that instead tries to maintain a focus upon the individual words. Rather than being strictly linear, dependency syntax is able to handle non-configurational languages with its non-linear ordering. Finally, dependency syntax is able to offer functional rather than formal labels to the dependency relations.

This description possibly explains why so little productive work has continued in New Testament studies based upon the Chomskyan model, and why various functional models are being utilized instead to analyze the non-configurational characteristics of ancient Greek. Some of these include various adaptations of Systemic Functional Linguistics and cognitive-functional linguistics.[52] The variety of approaches continues to grow, but they have in common a number of features. One of these features is their recognition of the non-configurational and hence non-linear nature of Greek, and hence the lack of necessity of a linear ordering. Those who maintain traditional grammars, often linked to traditional English sentence diagramming, continue to see the problems of such an approach. A second feature is the emphasis upon function over form. This is not to say that there is not a relationship between form and function, but that formalization alone and its analysis cannot be separated from function and must be taken into account. One of the ways to do this is to recognize various types of meaningful or dependency relations among the elements involved. A third feature is the ability to appreciate the individualism of a language (a moder-

---

51. Some of these include lexical-functional grammar, which differentiates between constituent structure and functional structure (to use the differentiation in Kroeger, *Analyzing Syntax*, 12, 14); case grammar, in which there are semantic case dependencies (in New Testament studies, see Wong, *Semantic Case-Relations*; cf. also on construction grammar: Danove, *Linguistics and Exegesis*; Danove, *Verbs of Transference*; and Danove, *Verbs of Communication*; relational grammar in which syntax reflects grammatical relations; and word grammar, an explicit dependency relationship grammar. See Mel'čuk, *Dependency Syntax*, 7. In a fuller treatment, Danove's work would merit attention, but to date he seems to be the only one who is pursuing case grammar in a rigorous way. Others of the above models also have promise for New Testament Greek studies.

52. The OpenText.org model has characteristics of both constituent and dependency syntax. See O'Donnell et al., "OpenText.org," 109–21; cf. O'Donnell, *Corpus Linguistics*. For other studies of syntax, in particular word order, see as examples Porter, "Word Order and Clause Structure," 177–206; Levinsohn, *Discourse Features*; Kwong, *Word Order*; Pitts, "Greek Word Order," 311–46; Porter, *Linguistic Analysis*, 347–62.

ate form of the Sapir-Whorf hypothesis) even if this is within a broader linguistic typology. Language typology can be a useful heuristic tool for categorization of some of the features of given languages, but it cannot be determinative for any given language.[53] There is an important role still to be played by descriptivism, even if the conclusions are used to make observations about other languages. The tendency has been to universalize on the basis of phrase structure rules, rather than examine individual languages and describe them on the basis of what Mel'čuk calls their "inventories of surface-syntactic relations."[54]

SEMANTICS

The chapter on semantics in Black's *Linguistics* takes James Barr's work on *The Semantics of Biblical Language* as its starting point for the development of what he calls "biblical lexicography," including the work of such scholars as Anthony Thiselton, J. P. Louw, Moisés Silva, D. A. Carson, Arthur Gibson, and G. B. Caird.[55] As a result, Black discusses several of the major fallacies of biblical lexicography. Black's work just missed the appearance of Louw and Nida's important *Greek-English Lexicon of the New Testament Based on Semantic Domains*.[56] However, Black's treatment of lexicography is consistent with their approach to polysemy in language. There are two other areas that he treats in this chapter that are worth noting. One is rhetorical language and the other is discourse analysis.[57] Black does not raise the question of how semantics relates to pragmatics.

Even though the 1970s and 1980s were something of a highpoint in New Testament Greek lexicographical analysis, there have been major developments in each of the areas that Black discusses, some perhaps much greater than he had anticipated. The first concerns the area of lexical semantics. Most biblical scholars, including those cited above, assume the notion of polysemy, that is, that a word may well represent more than one lexeme. This follows the work of Silva in his *Biblical Words and Their Meaning*, which tends to follow the kind of lexical semantics proposed by John

---

53. Problems with typologies are recognized by Croft, *Verbs*, 128–9.

54. Mel'čuk, *Dependency Syntax*, 16. Some other studies in syntax worth noting include Black, *Sentence Conjunctions*; and Sim, *Marking Thought and Talk*.

55. Black, *Linguistics for Students*, 120–21, referring in the chapter to works such as Thiselton, "Semantics and New Testament Interpretation," 75–104; Louw, *Semantics*; Silva, *Biblical Words*; Carson, *Exegetical Fallacies*; Gibson, *Biblical Semantic Logic*; and Caird, *Language and Imagery*.

56. Louw and Nida, *Greek-English Lexicon*.

57. Black, *Linguistics for Students*, 132–36, 138–41.

Lyons, in which words are discussed in their sense relations.[58] The Louw-Nida semantic domain lexicon marked a major step forward in New Testament lexicography by re-conceptualizing the Greek lexicon. This semantic domain lexicon moved away from thinking of words as placeholders for multiple meanings, arranged alphabetically, toward thinking of lexemes as categorized according to their semantic domains. Polysemy is readily seen in the fact that a word may be found in more than one domain or sub-domain. There are numerous shortcomings with the Louw-Nida lexicon, as has been indicated by others. These include the basis of the 93 semantic categories, the use of componential analysis to define words, and the basis for establishing the various sense relations, among others, including simply disagreement on the meanings of various words and how they are expressed.[59] There is another issue, however, and that is the basic question of whether, in fact, words have multiple discrete meanings—as seems to be assumed in much New Testament lexicography—or whether they have a single meaning. There have always been a few in New Testament studies who have suggested or weighed the idea that words have a central meaning.[60] However, it is only recently that a number of New Testament scholars have more rigorously pursued the notion that a better approach to meaning is not to assume polysemy but to take what has been called a "monosemic bias."[61] The monosemic bias states essentially that, rather than an individual lexeme contributing maximal meaning, the lexeme contributes minimal meaning. What is often confused with lexical meaning—that is, the meaning of the word—is contributed by cotextual (linguistic) or contextual (extralinguistic) factors. Other ways of stating this are that there is a difference between the meaning of a word gained through knowledge of its range of uses and the additional or instrumental meaning gained from its particular usage. There are various ways of conceptualizing this meaning of a word, whether it is a singular abstract meaning or whether it is a singular meaning that captures the lexeme's diverse functions.[62] There have been several studies of

---

58. Lyons, *Semantics*.

59. See Porter, *Greek New Testament*, 63–71, for discussion of the criticism.

60. E.g., Thiselton, "Semantics and New Testament Interpretation," 83–84; Porter, *Greek New Testament*, 54.

61. See Ruhl, *On Monosemy*, 3 and throughout. I have actively pursued the monesemic bias in Porter, "Matthew and Mark," 97–119, esp. 105–9; Porter, "Greek Linguistics and Lexicography," 19–61, esp. 27–37; Porter, "Θαυμάζω in Mark 6:6 and Luke 11:38," 75–79; and Porter, *Linguistic Analysis*, 47–59, esp. 51–53.

62. Porter, *Linguistic Analysis*, 52, citing Ruhl, *On Monosemy*, vii.

words within New Testament Greek that utilize the monosemic bias, with the promise of many more.[63]

The most significant implication of monosemy is reconceptualizing the Greek lexicon and how lexicons themselves are fashioned. There are several factors to consider. The first is how to arrive at the broad or unitary meaning of a given lexeme, when so much of what we typically think of as the meaning of a word is its cotextual or contextual (pragmatic) meaning. However, we must recognize that lexemes do have meanings (wherever we get them from, and this is debated) and that these meanings must be able to be expressed. The second is the issue of how one decides when a word has two or more distinct meanings. Most New Testament lexicography assumes polysemy, but monosemy assumes that a lexeme has a single meaning, even if broadly conceived and minimal in its contribution, unless this is seen to be impossible to sustain (in which case we have homophones or homographs). The third factor is to adjust to the notion that individual lexemes make a minimal semantic contribution to the discourse, rather than a maximal one. Much theological lexicography, all too often seen in a variety of commentaries, takes a maximalist view of lexicographical meaning, in which the individual word maximally contributes to the meaning and becomes a cipher for an entire, developed theology. The minimalist semantic contribution requires the harder work of analyzing more than simply individual words to arrive at meaning, even on a small scale and at lower ranks. Fourth and finally, monosemy requires a re-thinking of the organization of the Greek lexicon itself as an encapsulation of Greek lexical meaning. The semantic domain lexicon may still prove to be the most functional, with the semantic domains themselves proving to be useful heuristic devices for differentiating genuine polysemy.

Regarding rhetoric, Black treats rhetoric as essentially style. Since the time of his writing, there has been a veritable explosion in interest in ancient rhetoric in New Testament studies. This has resulted in numerous conferences with their publications, a variety of individual volumes, and articles too numerous to mention on particular New Testament books or issues.[64] Whereas Black could offer his discussion of rhetoric as style as a sub-area of semantics, such is not possible today for several reasons. One of these reasons is that few of the rhetorical studies over the last thirty years have

---

63. The challenge of monosemy has been taken up by Fewster, *Creation Language* from a Systemic Functional Linguistics perspective, and Lappenga, *Paul's Language of* Ζῆλος from a Relevance Theory perspective.

64. For a recent volume, see Porter and Dyer, *Paul and Ancient Rhetoric*, with essays by many of the leading figures in New Testament rhetorical study.

concerned themselves with style.⁶⁵ They are instead concerned with other areas of rhetoric, such as genre/type, arrangement, and invention, all of them treated in a non-linguistic fashion. Style is the only one of these elements that has a place within a discussion of linguistics, at least as the subject is currently discussed. Instead rhetoric is often treated as if it has a special claim to interpretive significance, ostensibly because it was an interpretive framework used by the ancients themselves. This is a questionable claim at best, as there is very little evidence that the principles of rhetoric taught to the elite in specialist education became a part of the everyday rhetoric of writers such as those who constructed the New Testament. However, there are still a few scholars who have continued to think that style is probably the only major area within contemporary rhetorical studies that has a legitimate claim to use within New Testament study, although even these rarely treat the topic within a linguistic framework. The reason for this is possibly found in the fact that various types of discourse analysis seem to be much more highly developed and linguistically grounded attempts to accomplish the same purpose, without the limitations of the ancient conceptual framework. Some of these models of discourse analysis make provision for rhetoric.

Discourse analysis has burgeoned since the publication of Black's work in 1988. Black identifies J. P. Louw's colon analysis with discourse analysis for New Testament scholars.⁶⁶ However, Louw's South African colon analysis, which identifies individual colons (consisting of a subject and predicate), and then analyzes their meaning relations, is only one form of discourse analysis that has become popular within New Testament studies. The other types of discourse analysis are: Systemic Functional Linguistics motivated discourse analysis, Continental discourse analysis or textlinguistics, Summer Institute of Linguistics discourse analysis often motivated by Tagmemics, and an eclectic form of discourse analysis that draws upon various models, especially recent literary interpretation.⁶⁷ Louw's colon analysis, developed in South Africa and widely used there (and elsewhere), made early inroads into New Testament studies, but has since not found many who have utilized it.⁶⁸ This is probably because of its lack of rigor in establishing its meaningful relations. Continental discourse analysis, which comes in a variety of forms, has also continued to be used, but not apparently as

65. An exception is Hellholm, "Amplificatio," 123–51.
66. Black, *Linguistics for Students*, 138, citing Louw, *Semantics*.
67. This typology is from Porter and Pitts, "New Testament Greek Language and Linguistics," 214–55, esp. 235–41, an expansion of Porter, "Discourse Analysis and New Testament Studies," 14–35.
68. See Louw, "Ephesians 1.3–14," 308–15 (in a volume with a wide variety of types of discourse analysis represented); and Louw, "Reading a Text as Discourse," 17–30.

frequently as at one time. The two major forms of Continental discourse analysis include Scandinavian and German forms. What they have in common in general is their emphasis upon the semantics/pragmatics divide, use of communications theory, and employment of rhetorical theory.[69] The Summer Institute of Linguistics continues to develop as a major venue for discourse analysis. Early on, the Institute's linguists were heavily influenced by Kenneth Pike's Tagmemics, especially as found in the work of Robert Longacre.[70] However, in more recent times a variety of other approaches have been incorporated, including those inspired by various functional models such as found in the eclectic cognitive-functional work of Stephen Levinsohn and Steven Runge[71] and Relevance Theory.[72] This approach remains localized in interest, in terms of both corpus and rank of analysis. The two most widely used types of discourse analysis are probably those either inspired by Systemic Functional Linguistics or focused upon various eclectic models. Systemic Functional Linguistics, especially in its use of register analysis (see below), has seen much productive research. This model sees language as a meaning-making device, and begins not with forms but with meanings and their realizations in forms. In some ways, Systemic Functional Linguistics, even though it was most broadly theorized on English, has categories that can be adapted and re-thought for the treatment of ancient Greek.[73] This type of discourse analysis shows every sign of expanding its scope of study. The eclectic method includes a variety of approaches, as the name implies. Its strength is its combinatorial ability, which is also its greatest weakness. It draws, often favorably, upon various other types of discourse analysis, as well as upon elements of literary criticism. The question that inevitably arises with this form of discourse analysis is methodological regarding the possibilities and advisability of creating such an eclectic method. George Guthrie was one of the first to utilize such an approach, and he has been followed by others.[74] It appears at this point that discourse

---

69. Cook, *Structure and Persuasive Power*; Holmstrand, *Markers and Meaning*; Schenk, "The Testamental Disciple-Instruction," 197–222.

70. Longacre, "Narrative Analysis," 140–68; Longacre, "Mark 5.1–43," 169–96; Booth, *Selected Peak Marking Features*; Capshaw, *Textlinguistic Analysis*; Kellum, *Unity of the Farewell Discourse*; and many of the essays in Black et al., *Linguistics and New Testament Interpretation*.

71. Levinsohn, *Discourse Features*; Runge, *Discourse Grammar*. See also Runge, *Discourse Studies and Biblical Interpretation*, for some essays that follow Levinsohn.

72. Pattemore, *Souls*; Pattemore, *People of God*; Fantin, *Lord of the Entire World*.

73. See Reed, *Philippians*; Klutz, *Exorcism Stories*; Van Neste, *Cohesion and Structure*; Westfall, *Hebrews*; Porter, *Romans*.

74. Guthrie, *Structure of Hebrews*; Cheung, *Genre, Composition and Hermeneutics*; Becker, *Letter Hermeneutics*; Taylor, *Text-Linguistic Investigation*; Peng, *Hate the Evil*.

analysis will continue to be one of the growth areas in linguistic study of the New Testament. Whereas Black devoted two to three pages to this topic in his 1988 volume, there are numerous different types of discourse analysis being done on the New Testament. This seems to indicate, if not a full acceptance, at least a begrudging acknowledgment, that study of Greek must proceed at the level of the clause and above. This represents a major shift in Greek language study from a previous era, which was dominated by study of various phenomena up to the level of the clause. If this kind of analysis can find its way into all areas of Greek textual study, especially commentaries but also monographs and articles, this would bode well for the future of New Testament studies.

There is also a further area that Black does not consider in more than passing fashion under his title "Semantics," and that is the area of semantics outside of lexical semantics.[75] This is not the place to try to define the notion of meaning, except to note that a number of linguistic models have defined meaning in different ways. Many linguists would today recognize not only lexical semantics, but meaning beyond or outside the word, such as grammatical semantics, sentential semantics, pragmatics, and discourse semantics, or some configuration of them. In other words, there are definable categories of meaning that can be found and should be discussed at each of these levels. Many linguistic models differentiate semantics and pragmatics, and there has been some work that has pursued the pragmatic side of the divide through speech-act theory.[76] As mentioned above, one of the distinguishing features of Systemic Functional Linguistics is that it stratifies language into three major levels: context, content, and expression. The content stratum consists of semantics and lexicogrammar. There is no formal distinction made between semantics and pragmatics, but what is often labeled as pragmatics (even if it is not pragmatics in a formal sense) is part of semantics. For Systemic Functional Linguistics, context is realized by semantics is realized by lexicogrammar is realized by expression. There are other, though not fully developed, discourse models that have also been proposed. Despite the apprehensions of some regarding discourse analysis, a significant amount of work has been done in this area that has helped interpreters to understand meaning at higher levels, especially beyond the meanings of words.

---

75. His brief treatment of grammatical semantics mostly occurs within his chapter on morphology, in recognizing the meaning of inflections.

76. E.g., Botha, *Jesus and the Samaritan Woman*; Neufeld, *Reconceiving Texts*; Upton, *Hearing Mark's Endings*.

HISTORICAL AND COMPARATIVE LINGUISTICS

Historical and comparative linguistics is the topic of the final chapter in Black's book. In some ways, this represents a look back to the period that preceded the rise of so-called modern linguistics and harks back to the comparative linguistics of the nineteenth century. However, even with the rise of the synchronic method, most good linguists want to recognize that there is a complex interplay between the synchronic and the diachronic. Black's tracing the history of Koine Greek in relation to other periods of Greek and in relation to other Indo-European languages helps to offset so much of the study of the Greek of the New Testament that has tended to see it as either unique (to the point of being a unique or even divinely inspired form of Greek) or as a creole language with an admixture of Greek and Semitic elements.[77]

In the light of subsequent developments within Greek linguistics, however, perhaps a better way to frame this discussion today would be in terms of the distinction sometimes made between varieties of language.[78] Black hints at the issue of varieties when he traces the history of the Koine in relation to classical Greek, seeing Koine not as a decayed form of language but as a developed form suitable for its purpose as the use of Greek was extended geographically over a much wider scope. Another way of examining varieties of language is to compare language according to user and language according to use.[79] Language according to user refers to dialect, and can be extended to include idiolect as well. Dialects are various varieties based upon a variety of social, cultural, geographical and other factors (e.g., economic level, education, etc.), and idiolects reflect the individual variety of a given user. Another type of variety, however, is language according to use. Language according to use is another way of speaking of the highly productive notion of register, as used within Systemic Functional Linguistics. The notion of register is that within a given context—a context of situation—in which language is used, there are typical ways in which language can be employed. These types of language use are called registers. As Michael Halliday states:

---

77. Black, *Linguistics for Students*, 143–69. Cf. Porter, *Language of the New Testament*, for discussion of some of these issues. There has been some analysis of the history of Greek from a linguistic perspective since 1988. See, for example, Watt, "Ancient Greek," 225–42; Porter, "New Testament," 497–500.

78. Land, "Varieties of the Greek Language," 243–60.

79. See Porter, "Dialect and Register," 190–208, used throughout this section, here 197, referring to Halliday, in Halliday and Hasan, *Language, Context, and Text*, 41.

> The notion of register is at once very simple and very powerful. It refers to the fact that the language we speak or write varies according to the type of situation . . . What the theory of register does is to attempt to uncover the general principles which govern this variation so that we can begin to understand *what* situational factors determine *what* linguistic features.[80]

The contextual configuration can be expressed in terms of the three major conceptual components of field, tenor, and mode. The field is realized by the ideational metafunction of language, the tenor by the interpersonal metafunction, and the mode by the textual metafunction. The register of a discourse is the sociolinguistic characterization of the language event in a typical situational context, and attempts to characterize typical uses of language on the basis of the configuration of its situational contextual features. It is not that the context of a situation determines or dictates the lexicogrammatical realizations, but that it constrains the semantic or functional components available so as to limit the linguistic parameters that may be realized.

There have been a number of register analyses of the Greek of the New Testament, including some of those above that have been characterized as discourse analyses (I believe that register analysis constitutes a type of discourse analysis, in which the focus is examination of the register of the discourse and its realization in the content stratum).[81] Register analysis has provided the means for examination of the functions of language individually and typically, on the basis of how individual contextual elements are realized within the various metafunctions. Through this register analysis, we have gained several important insights into the language of the New Testament. First, we have been able to utilize a linguistic model that differentiates its meaningful components on the basis of both strata or levels of language use and the various ranks at which various meaningful elements are expressed. As a result, more variegated conclusions about the Greek of the New Testament can be made regarding such components as the context of situation (not to be confused with a material situation), semantics, and lexicogrammar. Second, register analysis, functioning within the Systemic Functional Linguistics context, provides a reciprocal process of analysis that moves from meaning to instantiation, and then from lexicogrammar to context of situation, moving up and down the linguistic strata. Whereas many of the types of language study examined above function at either a single level

---

80. Halliday, *Language as Social Semiotic*, 31–32.

81. See, for example, Martín-Asensio, *Transitivity-Based Foregrounding*; Land, *2 Corinthians*, 24–35.

or invariably move from form to meaning, Systemic Functional Linguistics incorporates both movements within its purview. Third, register analysis provides a means of uniting text with context, and thus helps to bridge one of the major hermeneutical gaps of biblical interpretation. Register analysis recognizes the social function of language and that situations provide the context for the exchange of meanings and hence the use of language.[82] As a result, register analysis defined in this way entails formal structures through analysis of the lexicogrammar, functional specificity through analysis of the semantics of the language, and situational generalization through analysis of the context of situation within which the register is a configuration.

CONCLUSION

At the outset of this article, I asked the question of what we have learned in the last thirty years of Greek linguistic study. My friend David Alan Black in many ways set the stage for such a discussion by writing a very helpful book that went into surprisingly great detail on a number of topics that were important and current at the time. He provided a snapshot of his understanding of our state of linguistic knowledge of the Greek New Testament at the time. Since then, our knowledge of various linguistic dimensions of the Greek New Testament has continued to grow and develop, as well as expanding into further areas, some of them indicated above. However, as I have attempted to show, we have not proceeded in all areas at a similar pace. In some ways, David was clearly at the forefront of the discussion and has continued to be there, while in others there has been a wealth of understanding that has taken discussion to entirely new areas of investigation. What I have attempted to do here is to use David's encapsulation of the state of play as a bottom line for discussing what we have learned since the publication of his book in 1988. My survey of at least some of the major discussions of the variety of topics has made clear that much has been accomplished in the last thirty years, but that there is much that still remains to be done. I wish to thank David for the significant part that he has played in ensuring that this journey has not only continued but that it was able to begin from such a strong initial position.

---

82. Other efforts in sociolinguistics, a topic not directly covered by Black, are Watt, *Code-Switching*; Porter, *Diglossia and Other Topics*; Lee, *Jesus and Gospel Traditions*; Snyder, *Language and Identity*; Lamb, *Text, Context and the Johannine Community*; Ong, *Multilingual Jesus*. Not all of the studies define or treat sociolinguistics in the same way, but all show developments in understanding the relationship between language and social context.

BIBLIOGRAPHY

Anderson, Stephen R. *Phonology in the Twentieth Century: Theories of Rules and Theories of Representation*. Chicago: University of Chicago Press, 1985.

Barr, James. *The Semantics of Biblical Language*. Oxford: Oxford University Press, 1961.

Becker, Eve-Marie. *Letter Hermeneutics in 2 Corinthians: Studies in Literarkritik and Communication Theory*. Translated by Helen S. Heron. JSNTSup 279. London: T. & T. Clark, 2004.

Black, David Alan. *Linguistics for Students of New Testament Greek: A Survey of Basic Concepts and Applications*. Grand Rapids: Baker, 1988.

———, with Katharine Barnwell and Stephen Levinsohn, eds. *Linguistics and New Testament Interpretation: Essays on Discourse Analysis*. Nashville: Broadman, 1992.

Black, Stephanie L. *Sentence Conjunctions in the Gospel of Matthew: καί, δέ, τότε, γάρ, οὖν and Asyndeton in Narrative Discourse*. JSNTSup 216. Sheffield: Sheffield Academic, 2002.

Booth, Steve. *Selected Peak Marking Features in the Gospel of John*. New York: Peter Lang, 1996.

Botha, J. Eugene. *Jesus and the Samaritan Woman: A Speech Act Reading of John 1:1–42*. NovTSup 65. Leiden: Brill, 1991.

Buth, Randall. *Living Koiné Greek*. 2 vols. Fresno, CA: Biblical Language Center, 2007.

Caird, G. B. *The Language and Imagery of the Bible*. Philadelphia: Westminster, 1980.

Campbell, Constantine. *Advances in the Study of Greek: New Insights for Reading the New Testament*. Grand Rapids: Zondervan, 2015.

———. *Verbal Aspect and Non-Indicative Verbs: Further Soundings in the Greek of the New Testament*. SBG 15. New York: Peter Lang, 2008.

———. *Verbal Aspect, the Indicative Mood, and Narrative: Soundings in the Greek of the New Testament*. SBG 13. New York: Peter Lang, 2007.

Capshaw, Jeffrey L. *A Textlinguistic Analysis of Selected Old Testament Texts in Matthew 1–4*. New York: Peter Lang, 2004.

Caragounis, Chrys C. *The Development of Greek and the New Testament*. WUNT 167. Tübingen: Mohr Siebeck, 2004.

———. "The Error of Erasmus and Un-Greek Pronunciations of Greek." *Filología Neotestamentaria* 8 (1995) 151–85.

Carson, D. A. *Exegetical Fallacies*. Grand Rapids: Baker, 1984.

Cheung, Luke L. *The Genre, Composition and Hermeneutics of James*. Carlisle: Paternoster, 2003.

Chomsky, Noam, and Morris Halle. *The Sound Pattern of English*. Reprint ed. Cambridge, MA: MIT Press, 1991.

Cirafesi, Wally V. *Verbal Aspect in Synoptic Parallels: On the Method and Meaning of Divergent Tense-Form Usage in the Synoptic Passion Narratives*. LBS 7. Leiden: Brill, 2013.

Cook, John G. *The Structure and Persuasive Power of Mark: A Linguistic Approach*. Atlanta: Scholars, 1995.

Cotterell, Peter, and Max Turner. *Linguistics and Biblical Interpretation*. London: SPCK, 1989.

Croft, William. *Verbs: Aspect and Causal Structure*. Oxford: Oxford University Press, 2012.

Danove, Paul L. *A Grammatical and Exegetical Study of New Testament Verbs of Transference: A Case Frame Guide to Interpretation and Translation.* LNTS 329. London: T. & T. Clark, 2009.

———. *Linguistics and Exegesis in the Gospel of Mark: Applications of a Case Frame Analysis and Lexicon.* JSNTSup 218. Sheffield: Sheffield Academic, 2001.

———. *New Testament Verbs of Communication: A Case Frame and Exegetical Study.* LNTS 520. London: Bloomsbury, 2015.

Decker, Rodney J. *Temporal Deixis of the Greek Verb in the Gospel of Mark with Reference to Verbal Aspect.* SBG 10. New York: Peter Lang, 2001.

de Saussure, Ferdinand. *Course in General Linguistics.* Edited by Charles Bally and Albert Sechehaye with Albert Reidlinger. Translated by Wade Baskin. London: Fontana/Collins, 1959.

Ellis, Nicholas J., Michael G. Aubrey, and Mark Dubis. "The Greek Verbal System and Aspectual Prominence: Revising Our Taxonomy and Nomenclature." *Journal of the Evangelical Theological Society* 59/1 (2016) 33–62.

Fanning, Buist M. *Verbal Aspect in New Testament Greek.* OTM. Oxford: Clarendon, 1990.

Fantin, Joseph D. *The Greek Imperative Mood in the New Testament: A Cognitive and Communicative Approach.* SBG 12. New York: Peter Lang, 2010.

———. *The Lord of the Entire World: Lord Jesus, a Challenge to Lord Caesar?* NTM 31. Sheffield: Sheffield Phoenix, 2011.

Fewster, Gregory P. *Creation Language in Romans 8: A Study in Monosemy.* LBS 8. Leiden: Brill, 2013.

Foley, Toshikazu S. *Biblical Translation in Chinese and Greek: Verbal Aspect in Theory and Practice.* LBS 1. Leiden: Brill, 2009.

Gibson, Arthur. *Biblical Semantic Logic: A Preliminary Analysis.* Oxford: Blackwell, 1981.

Gignac, Francis T. *A Grammar of the Greek Papyri of the Roman and Byzantine Periods.* Vol. 1, *Phonology.* Milan: Istituto Editoriale Cisalpino—La Goliardica, 1976.

Guthrie, George H. *The Structure of Hebrews: A Text-Linguistic Analysis.* Leiden: Brill, 1994.

Halliday, Michael A. K. *Language as Social Semiotic: The Social Interpretation of Language and Meaning.* London: Edward Arnold, 1978.

Halliday, Michael A. K., and Ruqaiya Hasan. *Language, Context, and Text: Aspects of Language in a Social-Semiotic Perspective.* Geelong: Deakin University Press, 1985.

Hellholm, David. "Amplificatio in the Macro-Structure of Romans." In *Rhetoric and the New Testament: Essays from the 1992 Heidelberg Conference,* edited by Stanley E. Porter and Thomas H. Olbricht, 123–51. JSNTSup 90. Sheffield: Sheffield Academic, 1993.

Holmstrand, Jonas. *Markers and Meaning in Paul: An Analysis of 1 Thessalonians, Philippians and Galatians.* ConBNT 28. Stockholm: Almqvist & Wiksell, 1997.

Howe, Bonnie. *Because You Bear This Name: Conceptual Metaphor and the Moral Meaning of 1 Peter.* BINS 81. Leiden: Brill, 2006.

Howe, Bonnie, and Joel B. Green, eds. *Cognitive Linguistic Explorations in Biblical Studies.* Berlin: de Gruyter, 2014.

Huffman, Douglas S. *Verbal Aspect Theory and the Prohibitions in the Greek New Testament.* SBG 16. New York: Peter Lang, 2014.

Kellum, L. Scott. *The Unity of the Farewell Discourse: The Literary Integrity of John 13.31—16.3*. JSNTSup 256. Sheffield: Sheffield Academic, 2004.

Klutz, Todd. *The Exorcism Stories in Luke–Acts: A Sociostylistic Reading*. SNTSMS 129. Cambridge: Cambridge University Press, 2004.

Kroeger, Paul R. *Analyzing Syntax: A Lexical-Functional Approach*. Cambridge: Cambridge University Press, 2004.

Kwong, Ivan Shing Chung. *The Word Order of the Gospel of Luke: Its Foregrounded Messages*. LNTS 298. London: T. & T. Clark, 2005.

Lamb, David A. *Text, Context and the Johannine Community: A Sociolinguistic Analysis of the Johannine Writings*. LNTS 477. London: Bloomsbury, 2014.

Lamb, Sidney. *Outline of Stratificational Grammar*. Washington, D.C.: Georgetown University Press, 1966.

Land, Christopher D. *The Integrity of 2 Corinthians and Paul's Aggravating Absence*. NTM 36. Sheffield: Sheffield Phoenix, 2015.

———. "Varieties of the Greek Language." In *The Language of the New Testament: Context, History, and Development*, edited by Stanley E. Porter and Andrew W. Pitts, 243–60. ECHC 3. LBS 6. Leiden: Brill, 2013.

Lappenga, Benjamin J. *Paul's Language of Ζῆλος: Monosemy and the Rhetoric of Identity and Practice*. BINS 137. Leiden: Brill, 2016.

Lee, Jae-Hyun. *Paul's Gospel in Romans: A Discourse Analysis of Rom 1:16—8:39*. LBS 3. Leiden: Brill, 2010.

Lee, Sang-Il. *Jesus and Gospel Traditions in Bilingual Context: A Study in the Interdirectionality of Language*. BZNW 186. Berlin: de Gruyter, 2012.

Lepschy, G. C. *A Survey of Structural Linguistics*. New ed. London: André Deutsch, 1980.

Levinsohn, Stephen H. *Discourse Features of New Testament Greek: A Coursebook on the Information Structure of New Testament Greek*. 2nd ed. Dallas: SIL, 2000.

Longacre, Robert E. "Mark 5.1–43: Generating the Complexity of a Narrative from Its Most Basic Elements." In *Discourse Analysis and the New Testament: Approaches and Results*, edited by Stanley E. Porter and Jeffrey T. Reed, 169-96. JSNTSup 10. Sheffield: Sheffield Academic, 1999.

———. "A Top-Down, Template-Driven Narrative Analysis, Illustrated by Application to Mark's Gospel." In *Discourse Analysis and the New Testament: Approaches and Results*, edited by Stanley E. Porter and Jeffrey T. Reed, 140-68. JSNTSup 10. Sheffield: Sheffield Academic, 1999.

Louw, Johannes P. "A Discourse Reading of Ephesians 1.3–14." In *Discourse Analysis and the New Testament: Approaches and Results*, edited by Stanley E. Porter and Jeffrey T. Reed, 308-15. JSNTSup 10. Sheffield: Sheffield Academic, 1999.

———. "Reading a Text as Discourse." In *Linguistics and New Testament Interpretation: Essays on Discourse Analysis*, edited by David Alan Black with Katharine Barnwell and Stephen Levinsohn, 17–30. Nashville: Broadman, 1992.

———. *Semantics of New Testament Greek*. Philadelphia: Fortress, 1982.

Louw, Johannes P., and Eugene A. Nida. *Greek-English Lexicon of the New Testament Based on Semantic Domains*. 2 vols. New York: United Bible Societies, 1988.

Lyons, John. *Semantics*. Cambridge: Cambridge University Press, 1977.

Martín-Asensio, Gustavo. *Transitivity-Based Foregrounding in the Acts of the Apostles: A Functional-Grammatical Approach to the Lukan Perspective*. JSNTSup 202. Sheffield: Sheffield Academic, 2000.

Mathewson, David L. *Verbal Aspect in the Book of Revelation: The Function of Greek Verb Tenses in John's Apocalypse*. LBS 4. Leiden: Brill, 2010.
Matthews, P. H. *Syntax*. CTL. Cambridge: Cambridge University Press, 1981.
McKay, K. L. *A New Syntax of the Verb in New Testament Greek: An Aspectual Approach*. SBG 5. New York: Peter Lang, 1994.
Mel'čuk, Igor A. *Dependency Syntax: Theory and Practice*. Albany: SUNY Press, 1988.
Mounce, William D. *The Morphology of Biblical Greek*. Grand Rapids: Zondervan, 1994.
Neufeld, Dietmar. *Reconceiving Texts as Speech Acts: An Analysis of 1 John*. BINS 7. Leiden: Brill, 1994.
O'Donnell, Matthew Brook. *Corpus Linguistics and the Greek of the New Testament*. NTM 6. Sheffield: Sheffield Phoenix, 2005.
O'Donnell, Matthew Brook, et al. "OpenText.org and the Problems and Prospects of Working with Ancient Discourse." In *A Rainbow of Corpora: Corpus Linguistics and the Languages of the World*, edited by Andrew Wilson et al., 109–21. Munich: Lincom, 2003.
O'Grady, William, and John Archibald. *Contemporary Linguistic Analysis: An Introduction*. 6th ed. Toronto: Pearson Longman, 2009.
Olsen, Mari Broman. *A Semantic and Pragmatic Model of Lexical and Grammatical Aspect*. New York: Garland, 1997.
Ong, Hughson T. *The Multilingual Jesus and the Sociolinguistic World of the New Testament*. LBS 12. Leiden: Brill, 2016.
Palmer, Micheal W. *Levels of Constituent Structure in New Testament Greek*. SBG 4. New York: Peter Lang, 1995.
Pang, Francis G. H. *Revisiting Aspect and Aktionsart: A Corpus Approach to Koine Greek Event Typology*. LBS 14. Leiden: Brill, 2016.
Park, Yoon-Man. *Mark's Memory Resources and the Controversy Stories (Mark 2:1–3:6): An Application of the Frame Theory of Cognitive Science to the Markan Oral-Aural Narrative*. LBS 2. Leiden: Brill, 2010.
Pattemore, Stephen. *The People of God in the Apocalypse: Discourse, Structure and Exegesis*. SNTSMS 128. Cambridge: Cambridge University Press, 2004.
———. *Souls under the Altar: Relevance Theory and the Discourse Structure of Revelation*. UBS Monograph 9. New York: United Bible Societies, 2003.
Peng, Kuo-Wei. *Hate the Evil, Hold Fast to the Good: Structuring Romans 12.1—15.1*. LNTS 300. London: T. & T. Clark, 2006.
Pitts, Andrew W. "Greek Word Order and Clause Structure: A Comparative Study of Some New Testament Corpora." In *The Language of the New Testament: Context, History, and Development*, edited by Stanley E. Porter and Andrew W. Pitts, 311–46. ECHC 3. LBS 6. Leiden: Brill, 2013.
Porter, Stanley E. "Commentaries on the Book of Romans." In *On the Writing of New Testament Commentaries: Festschrift for Grant R. Osborne on the Occasion of His 70th Birthday*, edited by Stanley E. Porter and Eckhard J. Schnabel, 365–404. TENT 8. Leiden: Brill, 2013.
———. "Dialect and Register in the Greek of the New Testament: Theory." In *Rethinking Contexts, Rereading Texts: Contributions from the Social Sciences to Biblical Interpretation*, edited by M. Daniel Carroll R., 190–208. JSOTSup 299. Sheffield: Sheffield Academic, 2000.
———, ed. *Diglossia and Other Topics in New Testament Linguistics*. JSNTSup 193. Sheffield: Sheffield Academic, 2000.

———. "Discourse Analysis and New Testament Studies: An Introductory Survey." In *Discourse Analysis and Other Topics in Biblical Greek*, edited by Stanley E. Porter and D. A. Carson, 14–35. JSNTSup 113. Sheffield: JSOT, 1995.

———. "Greek Linguistics and Lexicography." In *Understanding the Times: New Testament Studies in the 21st Century; Essays in Honor of D. A. Carson on the Occasion of His 65th Birthday*, edited by Andreas J. Köstenberger and Robert W. Yarbrough, 19–61. Wheaton, IL: Crossway 2011.

———. *Idioms of the Greek New Testament*. BLG 2. Sheffield: Sheffield Academic, 1992.

———, ed. *The Language of the New Testament: Classic Essays*. JSNTSup 60. Sheffield: Sheffield Academic, 1991.

———. *The Letter to the Romans: A Linguistic and Literary Commentary*. NTM 37. Sheffield: Sheffield Phoenix, 2015.

———. *Linguistic Analysis of the Greek New Testament*. Grand Rapids: Baker, 2015.

———. "The Linguistic Competence of New Testament Commentaries." In *On the Writing of New Testament Commentaries: Festschrift for Grant R. Osborne on the Occasion of His 70th Birthday*, edited by Stanley E. Porter and Eckhard J. Schnabel, 33–56. TENT 8. Leiden: Brill, 2013.

———. "Matthew and Mark: The Contribution of Recent Linguistic Thought." In *Mark and Matthew: Comparative Readings*. Part 1, *Understanding the Earliest Gospels in Their First-Century Settings*, edited by Eve-Marie Becker and Anders Runesson, 97–119. WUNT 271. Tübingen: Mohr Siebeck, 2011.

———. "New Testament." In *Encyclopedia of Ancient Greek Language and Linguistics*, edited by Georgios K. Giannakis, 2:497–500. Leiden: Brill, 2014.

———. *Studies in the Greek New Testament: Theory and Practice*. SBG 6. New York: Peter Lang, 1996.

———. "Studying Ancient Languages from a Modern Linguistic Perspective: Essential Terms and Terminology." *Filología Neotestamentaria* 2 (1989) 147–72.

———. *Verbal Aspect in the Greek of the New Testament, with Reference to Tense and Mood*. SBG 1. New York: Peter Lang, 1989.

———. "Word Order and Clause Structure in New Testament Greek: An Unexplored Area of Greek Linguistics Using Philippians as a Test Case." *Filología Neotestamentaria* 6 (1993) 177–206.

———. "Θαυμάζω in Mark 6:6 and Luke 11:38: A Note on Monosemy." *Biblical and Ancient Greek Linguistics* 2 (2013) 75–79.

Porter, Stanley E., and Andrew W. Pitts. "New Testament Greek Language and Linguistics in Recent Research." *Currents in Biblical Research* 6/2 (2008) 214–55.

Porter, Stanley E., and Bryan R. Dyer, eds. *Paul and Ancient Rhetoric: Theory and Practice in the Hellenistic Context*. Cambridge: Cambridge University Press, 2016.

Reed, Jeffrey T. *A Discourse Analysis of Philippians: Method and Rhetoric in the Debate over Literary Integrity*. JSNTSup 136. Sheffield: Sheffield Academic, 1997.

Robins, R. H. *A Short History of Linguistics*. 3rd ed. London: Longman, 1990.

Robinson, Ian. *The New Grammarians' Funeral: A Critique of Noam Chomsky's Linguistics*. Cambridge: Cambridge University Press, 1975.

Ruhl, Charles. *On Monosemy: A Study in Linguistic Semantics*. New York: SUNY Press, 1989.

Runge, Steven E. *Discourse Grammar of the Greek New Testament: A Practical Introduction for Teaching and Exegesis*. Peabody, MA: Hendrickson, 2010.

———, ed. *Discourse Studies and Biblical Interpretation: A Festschrift in Honor of Stephen H. Levinsohn*. Bellingham, WA: Logos Bible Software, 2011.
Schenk, Wolfgang. "The Testamental Disciple-Instruction of the Markan Jesus (Mark 13): Its Levels of Communication and Its Rhetorical Structures." In *Discourse Analysis and the New Testament: Approaches and Results*, edited by Stanley E. Porter and Jeffrey T. Reed, 197–222. JSNTSup 10. Sheffield: Sheffield Academic, 1999.
Silva, Moisés. *Biblical Words and Their Meaning: An Introduction to Lexical Semantics*. Grand Rapids: Zondervan, 1983.
———. *God, Language, and Scripture: Reading the Bible in the Light of General Linguistics*. Grand Rapids: Zondervan, 1990.
Sim, Margaret G. *Marking Thought and Talk in New Testament Greek: New Light from Linguistics on the Particles ἵνα and ὅτι*. Eugene, OR: Pickwick, 2010.
Snyder, Julia A. *Language and Identity in Ancient Narratives*. WUNT 2.370. Tübingen: Mohr Siebeck, 2014.
Stovell, Beth M. *Mappping Metaphorical Discourse in the Fourth Gospel: John's Eternal King*. LBS 5. Leiden: Brill, 2012.
Stump, Gregory T. *Inflectional Morphology: A Theory of Paradigm Structure*. CSL 93. Cambridge: Cambridge University Press, 2001.
Taylor, Mark Edward. *A Text-Linguistic Investigation into the Discourse Structure of James*. LNTS 311. London: T. & T. Clark, 2006.
Thiselton, Anthony C. "Semantics and New Testament Interpretation." In *New Testament Interpretation: Essays on Principles and Methods*, edited by I. Howard Marshall, 75–104. Grand Rapids: Eerdmans, 1977.
Upton, Bridget Gilfillan. *Hearing Mark's Endings: Listening to Ancient Popular Texts through Speech Act Theory*. BINS 79. Leiden: Brill, 2006.
Van Neste, Ray. *Cohesion and Structure in the Pastoral Epistles*. JSNTSup 280. London: T. & T. Clark, 2004.
Wallace, Daniel B. *Granville Sharp's Canon and Its Kin: Semantics and Significance*. SBG 14. New York: Peter Lang, 2009.
———. *Greek Grammar Beyond the Basics: An Exegetical Syntax of the New Testament*. Grand Rapids: Zondervan, 1996.
Watt, Jonathan M. "A Brief History of Ancient Greek with a View to the New Testament." In *The Language of the New Testament: Context, History, and Development*, edited by Stanley E. Porter and Andrew W. Pitts, 225–42. ECHC 3. LBS 6. Leiden: Brill, 2013.
———. *Code-Switching in Luke and Acts*. Berkeley Insights in Linguistics and Semiotics 31. New York: Peter Lang, 1997.
Westfall, Cynthia Long. *A Discourse Analysis of the Letter to the Hebrews: The Relationship between Form and Meaning*. LNTS 297. London: T. & T. Clark, 2005.
Wierzbicka, Anna. *What Did Jesus Mean? Explaining the Sermon on the Mount and the Parables in Simple and Universal Human Concepts*. Oxford: Oxford University Press, 2001.
Wong, Simon. *A Classification of Semantic Case-Relations in the Pauline Epistles*. SBG 9. New York: Peter Lang, 1997.

2

Prepositions and Exegesis
What's in a Word?

CONSTANTINE R. CAMPBELL
Trinity Evangelical Divinity School

INTRODUCTION

GREEK PREPOSITIONS ARE IMPORTANT, but poorly understood. This is not a good combination. While most prepositional usage in biblical Greek is straightforward and unremarkable, there are instances in which the meaning of a preposition is open to interpretation, and in some cases a preposition finds itself at the center of an exegetical or theological debate.

Until relatively recently, we have not had the benefit of much substantial research into Greek prepositions. Emily Helen Dutton's treatise of 1916 and P. F. Regard's 1919 contribution (written in French)[1] were the last monograph-length treatments of the subject before Sylvia Luraghi's 2003 publication, *On the Meaning of Prepositions and Cases: The Expression of Semantic Roles in Ancient Greek.*[2] For eighty-four years, the only published

---

1. Dutton, *Greek Prepositional Phrases*; Regard, *Contribution à l'étude des prepositions.*
2. Luraghi, *Prepositions and Cases.*

treatments of Greek prepositions were to be found in lexicons, grammars, theological dictionaries, and occasional journal articles. Luraghi's work was followed by Pietro Bortone's 2010 monograph, *Greek Prepositions: From Antiquity to the Present*,[3] and Murray Harris's 1978 dictionary appendix has been expanded into the 2012 book, *Prepositions and Theology in the Greek New Testament*.[4]

THE USE OF TOOLS

Of the recent contributions, Harris provides the most useful practical tool for exegesis, while Luraghi and Bortone provide essential linguistic and philological discussions. For most exegetes, Harris' volume, alongside standard lexicons such as BDAG and Louw-Nida will be the most important "go-to" resource. Compared to lexicon entries, which are necessarily brief, Harris' work offers explanatory discussions that exegetes will find helpful. The lexicons, however, offer a comprehensive summary of the potential senses of each preposition, and in that respect they remain essential tools.

While our lexicons are extremely useful for the range of potential senses of any given preposition, they are not always reliable insofar as the categorization of particular instances. Editors of lexicons list particular occurrences of prepositions under certain functions by observation of context and through exegesis. Most serious exegetes, however, will want to reproduce those steps for themselves.

As such, this paper offers some reflections on how we might proceed in the exegesis of prepositions. I will discuss the following: (1) the semantic nature of prepositions; (2) prepositions and case; (3) context (or co-text); (4) lexical factors; and (5) theological exegesis.

THE SEMANTIC NATURE OF PREPOSITIONS

We turn first to the semantic nature of prepositions. Pietro Bortone identifies the nub of the issue: "Prepositions are described as semantically poor, but very dense . . . a way of saying that their meaning is ill-defined but its nuances are manifold: not only is the basic sense (if any) unclear, but the semantic ground covered can be vast and cannot easily be predicted."[5]

---

3. Bortone, *Greek Prepositions*.
4. Harris, *Prepositions and Theology*.
5. Bortone, *Greek Prepositions*, 41–42.

Polysemy

Bortone notes that many scholars have treated prepositions as inherently meaningless, and exhibit a mere relational function with cases; "the multiple and unpredictable meanings of prepositions and cases are often highlighted as proof."[6] Some have held the view that the variety of potential meanings are unrelated and simply happen to be expressed by the same form.[7]

Rather than abandoning the notion of semantic meaning, however, Bortone argues for a principled polysemy, which casts doubt on the notion that multiplicity of sense is random and accidental.[8] Polysemy describes "our tendency to re-apply images to new concepts, to graft the structure of one semantic field onto other (especially abstract) domains."[9]

> [T]here are clear and demonstrable links between, for example, locative, comitative, and instrumental/model meanings. The "localistic" interpretation of this is that the various non-spatial senses of cases or adpositions are related in a chain of semantic extensions which starts from a spatial notion.[10]

Following the principles of Cognitive Linguistics, Bortone posits a principled sequence for polysemy. The starting point is a concrete spatial notion, with "subsequent grafting of the structure of the spatial semantic field onto abstract domains."[11] There is a chain of semantic developments, all of which related to a spatial meaning.[12] According to the "family relations" model, new meanings may co-exist with old ones, and the result may be that "distant relatives may seem to have nothing in common."[13] While the traditional understanding of the lack of common traits between two uses of the same word has been taken as proof for homonymity, an understanding of the diachrony of prepositions permits polysemy.

Being semantically poor, but very dense, some prepositions are capable of wildly different exegetical possibilities, depending on context. Such elasticity means that prepositions are particularly susceptible to the whims of theological interpretation. This can create scenarios in which certain prepositions may even be understood in exactly *opposite* ways, depending

---

6. Ibid., xiii.
7. Ibid., 71.
8. Ibid.
9. Ibid., 72.
10. Ibid., xiii.
11. Ibid., xiv.
12. Ibid., 47.
13. Ibid., 74.

on exegetical and theological convictions brought to the texts in which they are found.

Localist Theory

Underpinning prepositional polysemy, Bortone endorses a "localist hypothesis" in which the concrete spatial meanings of prepositions are the earliest ones, and that "spatial meanings evolve into non-spatial ones but not vice-versa."[14] This is in keeping with the principles of Cognitive Linguistics.[15] Growing out of such spatial meanings, there are "plenty of other 'abstract' meanings that can be brought within the scope of localism."[16] Indeed, a preposition "may have different, even incompatible meanings synchronically, or may develop them diachronically."[17]

Sylvia Luraghi also identifies an original spatial meaning for Greek prepositions. However, "to say that the abstract meaning of grammatical forms derives from an original spatial meaning does not mean that the spatial meaning is synchronically available as their 'basic' meaning."[18] Rather, the original spatial meaning reaches into more abstract notions through the diachronic development of prepositional forms. According to Luraghi,

> Semantic extension proceeds from abstraction based on two common procedures of human cognition, metaphor and metonymy. Through metaphor a concrete relation is mapped onto a less concrete one ... Through metonymy a certain concept can be used in reference to another, related one ... .[19]

---

14. Ibid., xii.

15. "It is not surprising, although it is an over simplification, that the basic approach of Cognitive Linguistics has been dubbed 'generalized neo-localism' (Rastier 2006: 93); localists such as Anderson (1992: 71) indeed had argued that 'abstract situations are conceptualized in these spatial terms.... Abstract domains are structured linguistically by space-based metaphor, including its ego-centric orientation'. Localists had preceded Cognitive Linguists also in interpreting transitivity (in line with the etymology of the term) as a flow of the energy or action (cf. Cienki 1995: 151–4). Cognitive Linguistics, in turn, has built upon localist scholarship, exploring extensively the pervasiveness of metaphorization, noticing the role played by other elements of our perceptual world besides location, such as animacy, and drawing upon the idea of meanings being structured around a prototype, a theory which was explored in the 1970s (cf. Dahl 1979: 18)" (ibid., 56–57).

16. Ibid., 70.

17. Ibid., 42.

18. Luraghi, *Prepositions and Cases*, 12.

19. Ibid.

In a localist theoretical framework, "space is considered the source domain for the conceptualization of reality."[20] Spatial notions provide access to understand more complex, abstract relations. But in synchronic terms, "the expression of spatial relations usually constitutes only one of the functions of a given preposition or case form."[21]

As with Bortone, Luraghi states that the direction of development from spatial to abstract is unidirectional and is assumed to be irreversible.[22]

PREPOSITIONS AND CASE

Grammarians have long said that prepositions govern particular cases, but Porter is probably correct to say that "a preposition is governed by its case, in some way helping the case to manifest its meaning to perform more precisely its various functions."[23] Through the Hellenistic period, we see an increase in the use of prepositions, probably due to the greater specificity that they add to case, in order to aid second and third language users who may not grasp the subtleties of various case meanings. Prepositions make explicit what Greek could generally convey through case.

For the exegesis of prepositions, Robertson proposed beginning with case: "The scientific method of studying the Greek preposition is to begin with the case-idea, add the meaning of the preposition itself, then consider the context."[24] Harris, however, resists this starting point, citing Bortone's point that in Hellenistic Greek, "the meaning of the case governed by a preposition fades,"[25] and the observation of P. F. Regard that the growing role of prepositions corresponds to the decreasing role of case.[26]

The decreasing role of case, however, does not mandate a methodological *ordo salutis*, in which case is considered further down the pecking order of relevant factors. While case is found at point 2 of Harris' four principles for the exegesis of prepositions (see below), it is also folded into point 1. In fact, consideration of preposition and case are likely too intertwined to separate them out into distinct steps in a process of analysis.

---

20. Ibid., 20.
21. Bortone, *Greek Prepositions*, 71.
22. Luraghi, *Prepositions and Cases*, 18.
23. Porter, *Idioms*, 140.
24. Robertson, *Grammar*, 568.
25. Bortone, *Greek Prepositions*, 183.
26. Harris, *Prepositions and Theology*, 31–32.

CONTEXT

In every useful treatment of prepositions, the role of context comes to the fore. Since there is very little formal information that can be used to discern between senses, context remains by far the most important consideration.

Harris outlines four principles for interpreting prepositions:

1. the primary meaning of the preposition itself (i.e., the local/spatial sense) and then its range of meanings when used with the particular case involved
2. the basic significance of the case that is used with the preposition
3. the indications afforded by the context as to the meaning of the preposition
4. the distinctive features of prepositional usage in the New Testament that may account for seeming irregularities[27]

Of these four principles, point 3—addressing context—is where most ambiguity steps in. Considering the primary meaning of the preposition, and the case with which it operates, is necessary, but basic. In the case of the preposition ἐν, for example, after addressing points 1 and 2, we are still left to sift through twelve major categories of interpretation listed in BDAG, not to mention the several subcategories under each of those twelve. Leaving principle 4 to the side, since it only affects a handful of instances, we are left with principle 3 to decide between the twelve possible categories and multiple subcategories in understanding any particular use of the preposition ἐν.

Robertson suggests that "the only way to know the resultant meaning of ἐν is to note carefully the context. It is so simple in idea that it appears in every variety of connection."[28] Harris concurs: "Sometimes all the exegete can do is to reduce the number of possible meanings of *en* by examining the context."[29] The role of context in understanding the various functions of ἐν is of utmost importance.

It is also reasonable to regard the spatial sense of the preposition to be primary, and this should be our first consideration when analyzing each instance. As Oepke points out: "The spatial sense is always the starting-point, but we have to ask how far there is an intermingling of other senses, esp. the

---

27. Ibid., 31.
28. Robertson, *Grammar*, 589.
29. Harris, "Appendix," 1191. Indeed, "any sensible exegete will hesitate to dogmatize"; Kennedy, "Two Exegetical Notes," 322.

instrumental."³⁰ Even when moving to figurative uses of ἐν, it is generally agreed that a spatial understanding of figurative senses is to be preferred where possible.

Beyond that, we are left to work out which sense is most likely in any given context. In my work of analyzing all occurrences in Paul's letters of the prepositional phrases ἐν Χριστῷ, εἰς Χριστόν, σὺν Χριστῷ, διὰ Χριστοῦ, and all the variations of those phrases using personal or relative pronouns, I did not detect any useful patterns that might aid in interpretative predictability.³¹

As for ἐν Χριστῷ, it is capable of "a broad range of expressions, owing to the flexibility of the preposition ἐν and determined by context."³² The idiom can express instrumentality, close association, agency, recognition, cause, kind and manner, locality, specification or substance, circumstance or condition, the object of faith, incorporation, union, reference or respect, and participation. Only context can establish which of these is meant.

LEXICAL FACTORS

A significant element within context is the presence of lexemes that can narrow the possible senses of a preposition in usage. Luraghi acknowledges the crucial role of lexical factors for understanding prepositions:

> Lexical meaning of the NPs [Noun Phrases] that actually occur with specific cases or adpositions is often crucial to the understanding of the semantic function expressed. In many cases, one can say that a certain lexical feature 'activates' a specific meaning of the relevant grammatical form, which is polysemous in isolation.³³

The role of contingent lexical factors is perhaps the most neglected in consideration of prepositional exegesis. As for the phrase ἐν Χριστῷ, a good example is found in Colossians:³⁴

---

30. Oepke, "ἐν," 538.
31. See my *Paul and Union with Christ*, chs. 3–6.
32. Ibid., 198.
33. Luraghi, *Prepositions and Cases*, 13.
34. The following discussion is based on my *Paul and Union with Christ*, 106–8.

Col 1:28

> ὃν ἡμεῖς καταγγέλλομεν νουθετοῦντες πάντα ἄνθρωπον καὶ διδάσκοντες πάντα ἄνθρωπον ἐν πάσῃ σοφίᾳ, ἵνα παραστήσωμεν πάντα ἄνθρωπον τέλειον <u>ἐν Χριστῷ</u>.
>
> "We proclaim him, warning and teaching everyone with all wisdom, so that we may present everyone mature <u>in Christ</u>."

Under BDAG's locative category for ἐν, a subcategory is listed in which ἐν is rendered as "before, in the presence of," and can be understood in a forensic sense: "in someone's court or forum."[35] Read this way, ἐν Χριστῷ means "before Christ" or "in the presence of Christ," such that Paul's desire is to present everyone mature before Christ. The key to this reading is found with the phrase ἵνα παραστήσωμεν. The verbal lexeme παρίστημι can be found in legal contexts, meaning "to bring before a judge."[36] Thus the use of this lexeme in connection with the forensic potential of ἐν is suggestive of a legal situation, in which Christ is portrayed as judge.

Further confirmation of this reading is found earlier in the same chapter:

Col 1:22

> νυνὶ δὲ ἀποκατήλλαξεν ἐν τῷ σώματι τῆς σαρκὸς αὐτοῦ διὰ τοῦ θανάτου παραστῆσαι ὑμᾶς ἁγίους καὶ ἀμώμους καὶ ἀνεγκλήτους <u>κατενώπιον αὐτοῦ</u>.
>
> "But now he has reconciled you by his physical body through his death, to present you holy, faultless, and blameless <u>before him</u>."

Here we see the same verbal lexeme (παραστῆσαι), and in this context it is clear that the *presenting* has forensic overtones since people are presented "before Him" (κατενώπιον αὐτοῦ). Insofar as v. 22 uses παρίστημι in connection with κατενώπιον αὐτοῦ, it is possible to conclude that in v. 28 παρίστημι in connection with ἐν Χριστῷ conveys a similar notion.[37] Since we have already established the possibility of ἐν Χριστῷ here meaning "before Christ," the apparent parallel with v. 22 provides confirmation. Thus, the most appropriate manner in which to understand ἵνα παραστήσωμεν πάντα

---

35. BDAG, 327.
36. BDAG, 778.
37. The connection between the two verses is noted by several commentators. See O'Brien, *Colossians, Philemon*, 89; Wright, *Colossians and Philemon*, 92; Thompson, *Colossians and Philemon*, 46.

ἄνθρωπον τέλειον ἐν Χριστῷ is "so that we may present everyone mature before Christ."

THEOLOGICAL EXEGESIS

In some instances, we find prepositions at the center of theological debate. More than that, a preposition may on occasion be the hinge upon which certain theological positions rest. In such cases, it is nigh impossible to separate the exegesis of a preposition from theological concerns—and so we must include "theological exegesis" as one of the factors that inform the exegesis of (at least some) prepositions.

An excellent example is found in Rom 4:25: "He was delivered up for our trespasses and raised for our justification." In this verse are two instances of the preposition διά ("delivered up *for* [διά] our trespasses" and "raised *for* [διά] our justification"). Both instances are relevant to this discussion, though the function of the second is our primary interest. It is important first to outline the theological issues surrounding this verse.

Theological Issues Surrounding Romans 4:25

There is of course a long history of connecting justification with the *death* of Christ, but also some reluctance to acknowledge a relationship between justification and his *resurrection*. This reluctance has caused a problem for interpreters of Rom 4:25, which seems to draw such a connection quite tightly. According to Fitzmyer, in the Latin Fathers the common solution to this problem has been to treat the final phrase of 4:25 as an appendage, or as "an exemplary confirmation of Jesus' death, which they considered to be the real cause of forgiveness of sins and justification."[38] While the trend to associate justification with the death of Jesus—and *not* his resurrection—has a long history, this has no doubt been exacerbated by the crucicentrism of the modern Evangelical movement, since its Awakening in Britain in the 1730s and following.[39] Adding to the traditional reluctance to connect justification to resurrection is current resistance against some exponents of the so-called New Perspective on Paul, N. T. Wright in particular. Since Wright draws a strong connection between resurrection and justification, that very idea can become guilty by association in the minds of those who reject Wright's approach to justification in Paul.

---

38. Fitzmyer, *Romans*, 389. See also Lowe, "Oh διά!," 149.
39. Bebbington, *Evangelicalism*.

The Preposition διά in Romans 4:25

According to Robertson, the etymology of διά begins with the word δύο ("two"), and developed into the concept of "by-twain, be-tween, in two, in twain."[40] Thus the notion of "*interval* (be-tween) is frequent in the N. T. both in composition and apart from composition."[41] Furthermore, the idea of interval-between leads to the notion of passing between two objects.[42] As such, according to Robertson, "'Through' is thus not the original meaning of διά, but is a very common one."[43] With the accusative case, διά can function as a "marker of extension through an area," or as a "marker of someth[ing] constituting cause."[44] The latter function, which pertains to 4:25, is clearly an abstraction derived from the localist origin of the preposition, as per Bortone's expectation.

More precisely, as has been acknowledged by a number of interpreters, the key issue in understanding the use of διά in Rom 4:25 is whether it is to be regarded as *retrospective* or *prospective*. That is, does it mean "he was raised *because of* our justification" (retrospective) or "he was raised *for* our justification" (prospective). This question must be evaluated with respect to the other use of διά in the previous clause in the same verse: "He was delivered up for our trespasses." It is often assumed that the parallel uses of διά in both clauses of 4:25 indicates that they both must be taken the same way—both are either retrospective or prospective. Michael Bird rejects this assumption and points to the fact that in the two preceding verses, 4:23–24, the same preposition is also used in parallel: "In v. 23 it says 'these things were not written (διά) *because* of him only' (retrospective) and in v. 24 it states 'but also (διά) *for* us' (prospective)."[45] Bird therefore makes the case that, grammatically, "the juxtaposition of the retrospective and prospective

---

40. Robertson, *Grammar*, 580. See also Harrison, *Greek Prepositions*, 187; Dutton, *Greek Prepositional Phrases*, 14.

41. Robertson, *Grammar*, 580.

42. Ibid., 581.

43. Ibid., 581. BDAG regard the fundamental idea that is expressed by this preposition to be that of separation; BDAG, 223.

44. BDAG, 225–26. Dutton, *Greek Prepositional Phrases*, outlines several other uses of the preposition within Ancient Greek that are not commonly recognized: within idiomatic phrases (18–19); within proverbial phrases (20); with technical terms pertaining to the military, legal proceedings, the field of rhetoric, and the field of games (20–21); with verbs of motion, creating a periphrasis for the action or state described by the verb indicated by the noun in the phrase (29–30); in a distributive use (31); in pregnant expressions (32); and as plastic and picturesque expressions (32).

45. Bird, "Raised for Our Justification," 43.

uses of the preposition διά is continued on in v. 25."[46] In other words, interpreters are not incorrect to read the second διά of 4:25 in parallel; it's just that the parallel is usually not comprehensive enough.[47] It is not parallel to the first διά of 4:25, but both uses of διά in 4:25 are parallel to the double use in 4:23–24. Thus, there is grammatical and rhetorical support for the retrospective-prospective reading of the two instances of διά in 4:25.

Having established the grammatical plausibility of the prospective reading of διά in the phrase "he was raised for our justification" in Rom 4:25, we turn now to consider the second matter for consideration, which is how well this fits Paul's biblical theology of the resurrection and justification.

Reading Romans 4:25 in Light of Pauline Biblical Theology

There are several layers of analysis to be considered when ascertaining the best theological reading of Rom 4:25. First, its background in Isaiah 53 must be taken into account.[48] Second, the role of 4:25 with respect to the rest of chapter four is to be considered.[49] Third, how 4:25 fits into the entire sweep of the argument from 1:3–4:25 is of significance.[50] Finally, the proposed connection between resurrection and justification must be evaluated with respect to Paul's biblical theology. Is it a connection that makes sense in his theological world?

There is not enough space to do justice to these four layers of analysis, though each contributes to the question at hand. On the first three layers, there is plenty of discussion to be found in commentaries and other sources, from which a strong case can be made for the prospective reading of διά in 4:25. Rather than rehash those here, I will merely explore the broadest layer of analysis, namely whether or not the connection between resurrection and justification makes sense in Paul's biblical theological framework.[51]

---

46. Ibid., 43.

47. "Almost universally, discussion of the meaning of διά in v. 25b has been reduced to a comparison with the διά clause in the first part of the same verse. In spite of the fact that all four prepositional phrases are διά + accusative, the first two (vv. 23–4), are usually overlooked. The emphasis in these two occurrences, however, is highly instructive for the emphasis that should be read in v. 25" (Lowe, "Oh διά!," 150).

48. See Bird, "Raised for Our Justification," 32–35.

49. Lowe, "Oh διά!," 152–55; Kirk, *Unlocking Romans*, 82–83.

50. Bird, "Raised for Our Justification," 35–38.

51. With minor alterations, the following three paragraphs are based on my *Paul and Union with Christ*, 397–98.

Several scholars have drawn a connection between justification and resurrection in Paul's thought.[52] Jewish eschatology anticipated resurrection for the righteous on the last day, and Paul likely drew on this expectation for his understanding of the theological significance of Christ's resurrection.[53] The resurrection of Christ signals his vindication in God's sight; he has been declared righteous through his resurrection from the dead.[54] As Kirk states, "the resurrection is Jesus' justification."[55]

If the justification of Christ occurs through his resurrection, it can be argued that the justification of believers occurs by their participation with him.[56] So Burger describes, "Just as Christ participated in our unrighteousness, we now participate in his vindication and become justified. Our justification is a gracious participation of the ungodly in the vindication of Christ."[57] Believers share in the vindication of Christ's resurrection by dying and rising with him; they are declared righteous by virtue of their participation in these events.[58] Gaffin endorses such logic: "[I]n view of the solidarity involved, being raised with Christ has the same significance for

---

52. For instance, Kirk, *Unlocking Romans*, 14–32; Burger, *Being in Christ*, 250; Bird, *Saving Righteousness*, 40–59. This is by no means taken for granted, however. Wright laments that "[t]here seems to be something about the joining together of resurrection and justification which some of our Western traditions have failed to grasp" (Wright, *Justification*, 219).

53. Powers says that while Paul probably developed most of his understanding of believers' eschatological resurrection as a participation in Jesus' resurrection, "one should not too readily dismiss the possibility that Paul borrowed the principal elements of this conception from Jewish tradition. Indeed, in the Assumption of Moses, there are certain eschatological motifs which seem to parallel, and perhaps even underlie, Paul's understanding of the believers' eschatological resurrection as a participation in Jesus' resurrection" (Powers, *Salvation*, 215).

54. Ibid., 82–83; Hooker, *From Adam to Christ*, 40.

55. Kirk, *Unlocking Romans*, 78.

56. So Hooker, "Christ's death and resurrection lead to 'justification' for many precisely because he himself is 'justified' by God and acknowledged as righteousness" (Hooker, *From Adam to Christ*, 31).

57. Burger, *Being in Christ*, 248. Also Bird, "Jesus' resurrection is his justification and believers are justified in so far as they have union with the justified Messiah" (Bird, *Saving Righteousness*, 2); and "Consequently, union with Christ is union with the justified Messiah and the now Righteous One. Jesus by fact of his resurrection is the locus of righteousness and redemption and believers are justified only because they have been united with the justified Messiah" (ibid., 56).

58. So Hooker, again: "To be in Christ is to be identified with what he is. It is not surprising, then, if his resurrection and vindication as the righteous one lead both to the acknowledgement of believers as righteous, and to their resurrection" (Hooker, *From Adam to Christ*, 37).

believers that his resurrection has for Christ."[59] In fact, Gaffin goes much further; he argues that whenever Paul speaks of the believer's justification, adoption, sanctification, glorification, or any other benefit connected to them, in such instances the underlying consideration is resurrection with Christ.[60]

After his death for sin, the righteousness of Christ is declared by his resurrection, which is the sign of his vindication. As Bird states, "Christ's death constitutes the verdict against sin for justification to proceed, whilst resurrection 'enacts' or 'executes' the verdict both now and in the future."[61] Believers are regarded as having died with Christ, having been raised with him, and likewise therefore as being righteous with him. The justification of believers is the result of their death and resurrection with Christ, just as the righteousness of Christ results from his own death and resurrection.[62] Thus Gorman correctly states that "for Paul justification is an experience of participating in Christ's resurrection life that is effected by co-crucifixion with him."[63]

In conclusion, there is strong biblical-theological warrant for acknowledging the relatedness of justification and resurrection, and thus also for reading the second διά in 4:25 as prospective. Christ was raised *for* our justification.

Romans 4:25 demonstrates the necessity of considering theological concerns in the exegesis of *some* prepositions. Rather than driving exegesis by a top-down theological agenda, however, this is simply another way of considering context. Understanding an author's theological concerns helps us to determine likely ways of reading prepositions as they intersect such concerns. Considering theological likelihood is, in fact, part of reading the text well.

---

59. Gaffin, *Resurrection*, 129: "To be more exact, the notion that the believer has been raised with Christ brings into view all that now characterizes him as a result that he has been justified, adopted, sanctified, and glorified with Christ, better, that he has been united with the Christ, who is justified, adopted, sanctified, and glorified, and so by virtue of this (existential) union shares these benefits" (129).

60. Gaffin, *Resurrection*, 129. So Powers: "Paul views reconciliation, justification, and the non-reckoning of sins to the believer as being the result of the mutual participation and identification of Christ with the believer and the believer with Christ" (Powers, *Salvation*, 83–84).

61. Bird, "Raised for Our Justification," 46.

62. So Gaffin: "For Christians, then, Christ's justification, given with his resurrection, becomes theirs, when united, by faith, to the resurrected Christ, that is, the justified Christ, his righteousness is reckoned as theirs or imputed to them" (Gaffin, "Justification and Eschatology," 6).

63. Gorman, *Inhabiting the Cruciform God*, 40.

CONCLUSION

There are no simple answers when it comes to exegeting Greek prepositions, but a few guidelines should be kept in mind. The points listed below are similar to Harris's exegetical principles, but are supplemented with some additional advice.

1. The original local/spatial sense of the preposition is likely never too far away, even for the more abstract senses that have developed from it.
2. The use of standard lexica, such as BDAG and Louw-Nida, is essential for understanding the range of possible senses of any preposition. However, caution should be employed when consulting their categorization of any particular use of a preposition. It is generally preferable to reproduce this step of analysis for oneself.
3. Case must be considered, since prepositions function to specify which case function is meant. Case, then, remains a key factor for the interpretation of prepositions even though cases are losing their potency in the Hellenistic period.
4. Context remains the most determinative criterion by which to judge prepositional usage. There are no ready patterns to predict which sense is intended with the use of any given preposition.
5. A factor within the context that can significantly affect the function of a preposition is lexical usage. Certain lexical items found in the context will narrow the field of potential senses of a preposition. This step requires study of the preposition *and* the other lexeme(s) in question.
6. Theological factors may come into play. Prepositions lie at the center of some exegetical and theological concerns, and it would be silly to ignore "theological context" in determining how an author may use a preposition in certain contexts.

BIBLIOGRAPHY

Bebbington, David W. *Evangelicalism in Modern Britain: A History from the 1730s to the 1980s*. London: Routledge, 1989.

Bird, Michael F. "Raised for Our Justification: A Fresh Look at Romans 4:25." *Colloquium* 35/1 (2003) 31–46.

———. *The Saving Righteousness of God: Studies on Paul, Justification and the New Perspective*. Milton Keyes: Paternoster, 2006.

Bortone, Pietro. *Greek Prepositions: From Antiquity to the Present*. Oxford: Oxford University Press, 2010.

Burger, Hans. *Being in Christ: A Biblical and Systematic Investigation in a Reformed Perspective*. Eugene, OR: Wipf & Stock, 2009.
Campbell, Constantine R. *Paul and Union with Christ: An Exegetical and Theological Study*. Grand Rapids: Zondervan, 2012.
Dutton, Emily Helen. *Studies in Greek Prepositional Phrases: διά, ἀπό, ἐκ, εἰς, ἐν*. Chicago: University of Chicago Press, 1916.
Fitzmyer, Joseph A. *Romans*. Anchor Yale Bible Commentary. New Haven, CT: Yale University Press, 1993.
Gaffin, Richard B. *The Centrality of the Resurrection: A Study in Paul's Soteriology*. Grand Rapids: Baker, 1978.
———. "Justification and Eschatology." In *Justified in Christ: God's Plan for Us in Justification*, edited by K. Scott Oliphant, 1–21. Fearn, Scotland: Mentor, 2007.
Gorman, Michael J. *Inhabiting the Cruciform God: Kenosis, Justification, and Theosis in Paul's Narrative Soteriology*. Grand Rapids: Eerdmans, 2009.
Harris, Murray J. "Appendix: Prepositions and Theology in the Greek New Testament." In *New Interational Dictionary of New Testament Theology*, edited by Colin Brown, 3:1171–1215. Carlisle: Paternoster, 1976.
———. *Prepositions and Theology in the Greek New Testament*. Grand Rapids: Zondervan, 2012.
Harrison, Gessner. *A Treaty on the Greek Prepositions, and on the Cases of Nouns with Which These Are Used*. Philadelphia: Lippincott, 1858.
Hooker, Morna D. *From Adam to Christ: Essays on Paul*. Reprint ed. Eugene, OR: Wipf & Stock, 2008.
Kennedy, H. A. A. "Two Exegetical Notes on St. Paul." *Expository Times* 28 (1916–1917) 322–23.
Kirk, J. R. Daniel. *Unlocking Romans: Resurrection and the Justification of God*. Grand Rapids: Eerdmans, 2008.
Lowe, Bruce A. "Oh διά! How is Romans 4:25 to be Understood?" *Journal of Theological Studies* 57/1 (2006) 149–57.
Luraghi, Silvia. *On the Meaning of Prepositions and Cases: The Expression of Semantic Roles in Ancient Greek*. Amsterdam: John Benjamins, 2003.
Oepke, Albrecht. "ἐν." In *Theological Dictionary of the New Testament*, edited by Gerhard Kittel, 2:537–44. Translated by Geoffrey W. Bromiley. Grand Rapids: Eerdmans, 1964.
O'Brien, Peter T. *Colossians, Philemon*. Word Biblical Commentary 44. Nashville: Thomas Nelson, 1982.
Porter, Stanley E. *Idioms of the Greek New Testament*. 2nd ed. Sheffield: Sheffield Academic Press, 1994.
Powers, Daniel G. *Salvation through Participation: An Examination of the Notion of the Believers' Corporate Unity with Christ in Early Christian Soteriology*. Leuven: Peeters, 2001.
Regard, P. F. *Contribution à l'étude des prepositions dans la langue du Nouveau Testament*. Paris: Gabalda, 1919.
Robertson, A. T. *A Grammar of the Greek New Testament in the Light of Historical Research*. 4th ed. Nashville: Broadman, 1934.
Thompson, Marianne Meye. *Colossians and Philemon*. Two Horizons New Testament Commentary. Grand Rapids: Eerdmans, 2005.

Wright, N. T. *Colossians and Philemon*. Tyndale New Testament Commentaries. Leicester: InterVarsity, 1986.

———. *Justification: God's Plan and Paul's Vision*. London: SPCK, 2009.

3

Reclaiming Γάρ
Correcting the Conjunctive Errors of New Testament Lexicography

MICHAEL RUDOLPH

INTRODUCTION

"RECLAIMING ΓΆΡ" IS A curious title for scholars oblivious to the fact that the meaning of γάρ has been lost. In fact, γάρ is but one of several conjunctive signals of Koine Greek that continues to elude the grasp of the modern interpreter. In the study of the Greek New Testament, the significance of the conjunction is usually regarded as syntactical minutiae, better suited for detail-oriented grammarians but of minor importance in the larger forum of theological debate. The oversight is unfortunate. Robertson once described these words as "the hinges of speech, the joints of language."[1] While his metaphor is ill-chosen (see further below), he is correct to highlight the inherent significance of these words. Their abuse by scholars is not without consequence in the interpretation of the text.

---

1. Robertson, *Grammar*, 1144, also 1177. Robertson, however, struggled to define γάρ. He states, "The precise relation between clauses or sentences is not set forth by γάρ. That must be gathered from the context if possible" (1191).

This study is not the first to draw attention to this issue. In the nineteenth century, Winer sharply criticized his contemporaries for their abuse of these important signals, accusing them of treating Scripture like a waxen nose that could be twisted however one pleased.[2] He stated:

> The use of all these conjunctions, devised for the expression of the *various relations* in sentences, would be set aside again in its regularity, if it were really the practice of N. T. writers . . . to use one conjunction for another, so as frequently to make δέ equivalent to γάρ, γάρ to οὖν, ἵνα to ὥστε, etc. . . . [H]ow absurd would it be to think that the apostles could actually write 'for' where they intended 'but' or 'but' where they should have written 'for'. Any child can distinguish *such relations* as these . . . As purely fictitious as this canon of "unlimited interchange" is the doctrine of the "weakening" of conjunctions, which teaches that even particles with a sharply defined meaning, such as *for*, *but*, are in many cases altogether redundant, or are mere particles of transition.[3]

Sadly, little has changed since Winer's era. Even today scholars continue to tolerate in their New Testament exegesis what they would never tolerate in their own native languages.[4] Considering the role of these markers in communication, it is little wonder that consensus is rarely reached regarding the structural analysis of most New Testament books.[5] Yet, if one cannot rightly divide the text, one cannot rightly claim to understand the text.[6]

---

2. Winer, *Idiom of the New Testament*, vi.

3. Ibid., 563–65. In the final comment noted above, Winer is expressly referencing the use of γάρ, cf. p. 568. Regarding *"various . . . [or] such relations"* (emphasis mine), Winer demonstrates what would become known as a *coherence-based approach* (i.e., the view that conjunctive markers serve to *connect* the text in a series of logical relationships). Unfortunately, Winer was ultimately unsuccessful in resolving this issue. For his own difficulty in distinguishing γάρ and δέ in his discussion of Luke 13:35 as compared with Matt 23:39, see p. 571.

4. See e.g., Wallace, *Greek Grammar*, who on the basis of a coherence-based approach (668), posits both a causal and inferential γάρ (673–74).

5. Osborne, *Matthew*, 40, states, "Most biblical books have almost as many positions on structure as there are scholars working on them." The status of research on Hebrews is perhaps most telling. Westfall states, "The structure of the book of Hebrews has been the subject of an ongoing debate. While on the one hand many have declared it to be the only literary masterpiece in the New Testament, on the other hand there is little consensus on the nature of its design. There is no agreement on the major and minor divisions of the book or the development of its argument. This is a paradox, because by definition, a literary masterpiece would require an identifiable argument or a clear train of thought" (Westfall, *Hebrews*, xi).

6. Brown and Yule, *Discourse Analysis*, 94, state, "[O]ur interpretation of *what*

Thus, a radical re-thinking of New Testament conjunctive lexicography is needed.

This study seeks to point scholars in a more productive direction. First, the dynamics that led to the current state of conjunctive lexicography and the extent of the problem will be uncovered. Second, through an examination of failed linguistic theories, the underlying communicative issue and a new pragmatic perspective will emerge. Finally, a closer look at the best available source regarding the meaning of γάρ will not only expose a serious lexicographical error, it will provide historical credibility to a new communicative paradigm that offers a compelling resolution to the issues plaguing New Testament conjunctive lexicography. Ultimately, γάρ is not a conjunction having various meanings (i.e., causal, explanatory, or transitional, etc.), but a discourse marker signaling the author's (or speaker's) response to a perceived (i.e., implied, but inescapable) question or objection.

THE ROOT OF THE PROBLEM

Modern New Testament lexicons are not reliable sources of conjunctive lexicography.[7] If one retraces the recent lexicographical survey of John Lee, focusing specifically upon conjunctive markers, the issue becomes immediately apparent. The semantic distinctions of New Testament conjunctive markers were lost at an early stage in the transmission of the text long before any significant lexicographical work was undertaken (i.e., the sixteenth century). The critical issue, as Lee notes, was this: "[T]ranslations . . . not the lexicons, led the way in presenting a statement of the meaning of the Greek text in another language."[8]

Each step in this translational process became an opportunity to blur and eventually lose the intended semantic distinctions of these markers.[9] When faced with a conjunctive marker, non-native translators, who lacked

---

a speaker is talking about is inevitably based on *how* he structures what he is saying" (emphasis Brown and Yule's). Blass (*Relevance Relations in Discourse*, 12), however, demonstrates that discerning *how* a text is structured is not itself sufficient. The foundational, and more critical, issue is *why* a text is structured in a particular way.

7. For a broader discussion of this issue, see Lee, *New Testament Lexicography*, xi, who states, "After five centuries of accumulation and refinement, the content of major lexicons of our day might be expected to be highly reliable. It is not."

8. Ibid., 36.

9. The state of Latin translations greatly multiplied this effect. Metzger notes, "[V]arious people, at various times and in various places, with varying degrees of success, had translated various parts of the Bible into Latin. The result was chaos" (Metzger, *Early Versions*, 330–31).

a full understanding of the situational context or the cognitive assumptions of the original participants, had little recourse but to translate these words on the basis of a perceived semantic connection between presumably conjoined propositions that best coincided with their interpretive expectations. Being separated from the original context by time and culture, as well as ignorant of the subtle, situational nuances reflected in the statement, these scholars could easily misjudge the intended signal and choose the wrong translational equivalent if, in fact, a translational equivalent even existed in the target language. In time, this dynamic eventually justified several, conflicting definitions.

A survey of sixteenth- through eighteenth-century conjunctive lexicography highlights the extent of this semantic crisis. As scholars scoured ancient translational sources, the list of Latin glosses utilized to *define* these markers exploded. The lexicon of Mintert was perhaps the worst in this respect. Twenty-five glosses were found for οὖν, thirty for δέ, forty-two for γάρ, and sixty-one for καί! Of these glosses, six were included as equivalents for each of these conjunctive markers: *autem, igitur, inquam, nam, porro,* and *vero*.[10] The eighteenth-century transition from a list of glosses to semantic classifications further exposed the logical inconsistencies of this approach. Both adversative and continuative as well as causal and illative (inferential) meanings were simultaneously attributed to γάρ, δέ, καί, and οὖν. Schleusner, for example, described δέ as the same as (*idem quod*) καί, γάρ, ἤ, and τοτέ.[11] It was little wonder that eventually lexicographers could offer nothing more than vague descriptions, rather than definitions, for these communicative signals.[12]

Two flawed conclusions eventually emerged: first, conjunctive markers appeared to have multiple meanings and, second, semantic overlap between conjunctive markers was viewed as normative. While modern lexicographers no longer stress *idem quod*, the issue has not been resolved, the semantic overlap and logical inconsistencies remain, and the sharp criticism of Winer is no less appropriate. Most scholars continue to assume the

---

10. Mintert, *Lexicon Graeco-Latinum*, s.v., οὖν, δέ, γάρ, and καί. Seventeen glosses were shared by γάρ and δέ, seventeen glosses were shared by γάρ and καί, and fifteen glosses were shared by γάρ and οὖν.

11. Schleusner, *Novum Lexicon Graeco-Latinum*, s.v., δέ.

12. See e.g., Stock, *Clavis Linguae Sanctae Novi*, s.v., γάρ: "[E]st particula variae significationis." Translation: "It is a particle of various meanings." S.v., δέ: "Est [c]onjunctio varii usus & significationis." Translation: "It is a conjunction with various uses and meanings." S.v., καί: "[E]xprimit . . . omnes sere conjunctionum species, pro varietate contextus vix determinandi." Translation: "It expresses almost all species of conjunctions, for a variety of connections, scarcely confined." S.v., οὖν: "[E]xprimit . . . conjunctiones varii generis." Translation: "It expresses . . . conjunctions of various classes."

accuracy of the lexicons and to remain oblivious to the significance of this issue, willingly appropriating their misguided definitions when their own interpretations have gone astray. There has always been, however, a few scholars who sought at least to provide an explanation.

THE SEARCH FOR AN EXPLANATION

The dictum noted by Falla, "[S]ound lexicography requires sound linguistic theory," correctly points toward the resolution of this problem; it also highlights, however, why the problem remains.[13] Nineteenth-century philology and twentieth-century Saussurean linguistics each brought new hope for scientific advancements in the study of ancient Greek. Both were a product of, and therefore shaped by, the unique and prevailing theories of the scholarly environments from which they arose. Yet both, being constrained by these underlying assumptions, would also ultimately fail. Unfortunately, the majority of New Testament scholars, who notoriously lag far behind their secular counterparts, still work from within one of these two perspectives.[14]

---

13. Falla, "Series Preface," xxiii.

14. Note, for example, the work of the classical Greek scholar, Denniston, *Greek Particles*. This work relied heavily upon the nineteenth-century philology of Hartung, Klotz, Bäumlein, and Kühner (Denniston, *Greek Particles*, vii). First published in 1934, twenty years after the paradigmatic revolution of Saussure, this work has always been obsolete. Nevertheless, the editors of Bauer first cite this reference in BDAG (2000). Denniston's own words in his preface should have alerted later scholars to be skeptical of its worth. He states, "I have cited more examples than previous writers have done. The reader should be enabled to *bathe* in examples . . . The more I study the Greek particles . . . the more I feel the ultimate decision in each case rests with instinctive judgment . . . I regard explanation . . . as less important than illustration" (Denniston, *Greek Particles*, vi; emphasis original). Three concerns immediately arise: the subjectivity of "instinctive judgment," the danger of concealing weak analysis with multiplied illustration, and the reliance upon the flawed theories of nineteenth-century philologists (see further below). Forcing an overwhelming deluge of examples into a flawed semantic framework merely led to an excessively microscopic division of semantic classifications in order to explain apparent exceptions. Denniston's exhaustive work was convenient and provided the appearance of legitimacy, yet, in reality, his discussion was misguided and imbued scholars with a false confidence in its semantic insights. Most troubling is his statement, "We have seen (and the pages of this book will prove it abundantly) that few Greek particles possess one meaning and one alone. New uses develop out of old, and the old, though they sometimes wither and die, more frequently prolong their existence, often in altered forms, by the side of the new. *The meaning of particles, more than those of any other part of speech, are fluid*" (Denniston, *Greek Particles*, lvi; emphasis mine). In reality, the meaning of particles, more than those of any other part of speech, are fixed (see further below). For a summary and critique of Denniston's work, see Rijksbaron, "Introduction," 2.

Nineteenth-century philology was a diachronic quest to discover the *Ursprache*. Having been freed from an undue reverence for the Hebrew language, these, primarily German, scholars sought to justify their own nationalistic, cultural, and philosophical concerns by identifying this most ancient language and by tracing their own relationship to it.[15] This compulsion emphasized an etymological approach that sought to chart the semantic progression of words throughout the centuries and, eventually, as philology progressed to comparative philology, how multiple languages interacted with one another. By this methodology, it was thought, one might hypothesize the original meaning of a word, trace how divergent meanings arose from it, and illuminate a specific author's meaning by charting its use along this chronological progression.[16] The impact of this monumental and, most often, tedious research was occasionally enlightening, often speculative, and ultimately irrelevant—as Saussure would show.[17] With respect to γάρ, two conflicting studies were written based upon the assumption that γάρ was formed from the combination of γε and ἄρα.[18] Yet, in spite of their attractive hypotheses, no consensus was ever reached and their theories eventually discarded, because the evidence would simply not support their claims.[19]

With Saussure, the study of language, including ancient Greek, took a decidedly synchronic shift. Two factors seem to have driven Saussure's paradigmatic revolution: first, the prevailing movement in the larger scientific community to affirm the primacy of socially-derived, systemic relationships as an ordering principle and, second, Saussure's personal desire to establish linguistics as a distinct, scientific (i.e., definable) field of inquiry. Regarding this first factor, scholars diverged from their predecessors by asserting that human behavior, including language, exists and is best studied within a social framework rather than historically as a series of postulated cause-and-effect events. Society was the primary reality that dictated human behavior rather than the sum total of individual acts.[20] Regarding the scientific study of language, Saussure postulated the existence of *langue* and *parole*. The

---

15. For a discussion of the factors driving German philological research in the nineteenth century, see Benes, *In Babel's Shadow*.

16. Winer, *Grammar of New Testament Greek*, 9–10.

17. Harris and Taylor, *Linguistic Thought*, 182.

18. See Hartung, *Lehre von den Partikeln der griechischen Sprache*, 1:457–80; and Klotz, *Adnotationes Continens* 2:232. For a similar view to Klotz, see Bäumlein, *Untersuchungen über griechische Partikeln*, 68.

19. For a history of the etymological discussion of γάρ and reasons to reject these theories, see Misener, "TAP," 7–11.

20. For a discussion of this issue, see Culler, *Ferdinand de Saussure*, 15–16, 85–94; or Harris and Taylor, *Linguistic Thought*, 180–81.

hypothetical *langue* was an abstract concept of language—a system of interrelated sub-systems having, at least theoretically, distinct boundaries. *Parole* was defined as *language in use*—allowing for the possible introduction of (presumably insignificant) variation. In defining *langue* as the only proper (i.e., scientific) focus of linguistic study, Saussure, in effect, eliminated the exercise of the human will from the discussion.[21] He argued that since meaning was arbitrarily assigned to phonetic sounds represented by written symbols, the meaning attached to a word was not inherent in the word itself. Rather, it was defined by its distinction from related concepts as established by this societal collective. These definitions were imprinted upon the minds of each member in the form of an identical dictionary (or fixed code), which allowed for (and constrained) the transmission of meaning between communicative partners, a process described as telementation.[22]

Saussure's linguistic paradigm is no more relevant than the comparative philology that he replaced. The boundaries of *langue* cannot be defined, nor even statistically approximated.[23] Even scholars working within this paradigm admit that language is distinct to the level of the idiolect and, in fact, can be subdivided further by the *apparent* exercise of diglossia.[24] The assumed irrelevant variations of the Saussurean era are now glaring anomalies in the present-day diversity of a multi-ethnic society. Yet the fatal flaw of the Saussurean paradigm as a meaningful interpretive paradigm lies not in its inability to establish *langue* as a verifiable entity, but rather in its elimination by definition, or minimization through statistical analysis, of

---

21. Joseph, "Saussurean Tradition," 7:3665, states, "The human will remains in exile from linguistics, and *langue* (naturally somewhat evolved from Saussure's original conception of it) continues to be the object of study of virtually every approach to which the name of 'linguistics' is accorded."

22. For a discussion of the various metaphors that have been applied to the concept of telementation as well as evidence of its unifying constraint on seemingly *divergent* linguistic schools, see Blackburn, *Code Model*, 12–91, 132–67. See also Harris, "On Redefining Linguistics," 20–21, 25. Harris also notes the foundational role of a fixed code for Saussurean linguistics. He states, "The fixed code is essential to the concept of a synchronic system. Once change is introduced we are no longer dealing with the original synchronic system but with its diachronic successor" (Harris, "On Redefining Linguistics," 29).

23. *Contra* Halliday, "Language as System and Language as Instance," 66. Halliday's weather analogy does not avoid the problems inherent in the Saussurean paradigm. See further below.

24. See e.g., Wardhaugh, *Sociolinguistics*, 5, who, although affirming the *langue/parole* distinction, acknowledges this issue. Wardhaugh's solution is to suggest diglossia (87–94) and code-switching (100–114). His remedy, however, only compounds the problem.

the human will.²⁵ This hypothetical societal collective at best distorts and may, in fact, entirely miss the intent of the individual mind. Since meaning is imperfectly shared, even at the smallest, most intimate, social levels, it must transcend language itself. Thus, if an act of communication is to be understood, it must be examined for what it is—an individual act of the human will—and for this, a new paradigm is required.²⁶

It is unfortunate that New Testament scholars largely missed the point when Grice's foundational work in pragmatics was written. New Testament scholars commonly reference his conclusions (the conversational maxims), but ignore what prompted his research, what phenomenon he was

---

25. Harris ("On Redefining Linguistics," 22) states, "[T]he fundamental error in contemporary linguistics is still the fundamental error of Saussure's original thesis. It involves a crude process of abstraction by which certain phenomena are segregated from the continuum of human communication, and these segregated phenomena are then, rather capriciously, set up for academic purposes as constituting the *linguistic* part of communication."

26. For an attempt to delineate New Testament Greek conjunctive markers from a Saussurean perspective, see Porter and O'Donnell, "Conjunctions, Clines and Levels of Discourse," 3–14. Porter and O'Donnell hypothesize a system of non-logical markers having "low semantic specificity" (Ibid., 7n17) that, on the basis of frequency of use and certain undefined "markedness factors and semantics" (Ibid., 10), are arranged along a cline from unmarked continuity to marked discontinuity. They suggest that δέ, μέν, οὖν, and γάρ serve as "mid-level markers of discontinuity" (Ibid., 10). In effect, they have drained these markers of semantic significance, obscured their communicative purpose, and arbitrarily reduced their *meaning* to these subjectively chosen features. If Porter and O'Donnell were correct, one would expect these markers to be used almost interchangeably. The evidence of the New Testament, however, shows that they are not. In fact, the use of δέ defies this proposed cline since it covers the full range of discontinuity—from the level of marking words (Eph 4:11) to the highest divisions of the text (John 13:1). (Δέ *is* a marker of discontinuity—nothing more, nothing less, and nothing else. This does not mean, however, that all markers should be measured according to this meaning.) In contrast, μέν, γάρ, and οὖν are more restricted. One should also note the use of δέ and γάρ to mark both successive and parenthetical statements—features lacking in μέν and οὖν. On the other hand, οὖν, *but also* δέ, can mark the resumption after a parenthetical statement—μέν and γάρ do not. Porter and O'Donnell fail to explain these distinctions. One cannot rightly claim to understand the meaning of these markers unless one's analysis can explain why the author's choice of a particular marker in a specific setting is not only appropriate but distinctly appropriate. See also Black, *Sentence Conjunctions*, who, although working from the same linguistic perspective (23–40), was forced to borrow the pragmatic definition of γάρ from the earlier work of Regina Blass (265; cf. 280), because of the limited sample of γάρ-propositions included in her chosen corpus (ten uses, 254). Blass, who affirms Relevance Theory, states, "The function of γάρ is not only to mark a proposition as a premise, but that this premise backwards confirms and therefore strengthens a conclusion. It always follows the conclusion." Blass, "Constraints on Relevance," 5–7. Note, the definition affirmed here is more precise than Blass offers and rests upon historical evidence rather than the broad pragmatic generalizations of Relevance Theology (see further below).

seeking to explain, and, most importantly, where his research has led.[27] Grice was wrestling with the realization that what a person says (or writes) is unavoidably less than, or even different from, what that person means. This phenomenon was first observed in exploring the apparent differences between natural and logical language, i.e., specifically, between *and* and *&*. The meaning of these two, he concluded, was the same; the difference in what was communicated, however, was indicative of implied propositions (implicatures) that communicative partners understood by following his suggested conversational maxims.[28] This failure to distinguish between the semantics of a conjunctive marker from the pragmatics of implicit communication, along with the confusion of gloss for meaning, has played a large role in the current, chaotic state of New Testament conjunctive lexicography.[29] Resolving the issue of conjunctive lexicography requires a model of communication capable of addressing implicit propositions, beyond what Grice suggested, while also acknowledging the true role conjunctive markers play.

Two issues lie at the heart of the paradigmatic revolution of pragmatics: underdeterminacy and the fallacy of mutual understanding. Regarding the first issue, speakers (and writers) unavoidably verbalize less than what they mean and yet communication most often proceeds successfully because of an innate, cognitive process allowing recipients to draw the correct inferences from the explicit message received.[30] This presents a further issue for Saussurean linguistics: not only is the existance, and thus the systemic, constraining force, of *langue* a myth, the issue is further complicated by the unique experiences and beliefs of each communicative participant from which these inferences are drawn. Sperber and Wilson have demonstrated

---

27. See e.g., Cotterell and Turner, *Linguistics and Biblical Interpretation*, 260–62, 287; Vanhoozer, *Meaning in This Text?*, 337–50. The conversational maxims of Grice were rightfully criticized—most notably because they were inadequate to exclude all but a single interpretation. See Sperber and Wilson, *Relevance*, 21–38. For a discussion of the development of Relevance Theory and its distinction from Grice's original maxims, see Clark, *Relevance Theory*, 43–89.

28. Grice, "Meaning," 377–88. Grice, "Logic and Conversation," 113–28. This work was originally given as part of the William James Lectures at Harvard University in 1967.

29. While New Testament scholars accept multiplied, and even contradictory, meanings for καί, secular scholars have long recognized that *and* is monosemic. For a more recent discussion of this issue that corrects the analysis of Grice, see Wilson and Sperber, "Pragmatics and Time," 277–98. Clark, *Relevance Theory*, 55, notes that this same phenomenon is found in other languages where the same range of meanings are commonly, but illegitimately, attributed to *and*—illustrating once again the dictum of Falla, noted above.

30. See Carston, *Thoughts and Utterances*.

that this process is possible because of the cognitive search for relevance. In searching for positive cognitive effects (the addition of new information, or the confirmation, clarification, or correction of old information) with a minimization of cognitive effort, recipients are able to draw the correct conclusions when their expectations of relevance are satisfied. If not, the communication is abandoned (a point critical to a proper understanding of γάρ, as noted below).[31]

The emerging pragmatic paradigm of the twenty-first century involves a necessary shift in the underlying model of communication. Meaning is not shared; it is negotiated as speakers (or writers) use words, according to their own history of use, to recreate a mental image of their own communicative intent in the minds of the recipients.[32] Communication is dialogical, even in written forms, in that the speaker (or writer) is constantly monitoring the perceived (or assumed) reaction to the message and adjusting its ongoing presentation accordingly.[33] Discourse markers (including what New Testament scholars classify as conjunctions) are critical to this process though not in the sense of conjoining explicit (or even implicit) propositions (as per the coherence-based theory). Rather, discourse markers serve as *procedural* signals indicating to the receptor how the following proposition(s) is (are) to be interpreted or processed in light of how the speaker (or writer) assumes the message has to this point been received.[34] Procedural meaning is not only monosemic, it is rigid. In other words, it is obligatory. It cannot be adjusted, modified, or cancelled by the context. Rather, it takes precedence over conceptual and contextual information. In other words, where contextual or conceptual propositions suggest alternative meanings for discourse markers to non-native speakers, the rigidity of procedural meaning alerts

---

31. For several resources beyond Sperber and Wilson's foundational work, *Relevance Theory*, see Yus, "Relevance Theory." In recent years, Relevance Theory has appropriately begun to make inroads into biblical studies. See e.g., Brown, *Scripture as Communication*, 35–38; Green, "Relevance Theory and Biblical Interpretation," 217–40; Gutt, *Translation and Relevance*; Jobes, "Relevance Theory and the Translation of Scripture," 773–97; and Levinsohn, "Relevance of Greek Discourse Studies to Exegesis," 11–21.

32. Blackburn, *Code Model*, 218–31.

33. Hasan states, "The present emphasis on the private nature of writing and reading tends to obscure the fact that both are a form of dialogue, in which the turns are separated by the social import of time and place. In dialogue you are never free to say just what you like; the nature of the other's turn acts upon the nature of your [own]" (*Linguistics, Language, and Verbal Art*, 103).

34. For further discussion of procedural meaning, see Blakemore, *Relevance and Linguistic Meaning*, 82–8; Clark, *Relevance*, 323–26.

native speakers that it is their own interpretation of the context or concepts that must be adjusted.[35]

THE DISCUSSION OF APPOLONIUS

Reclaiming γάρ rests securely upon the historical witness of the source best-suited to clarify its meaning and to highlight its *pragmatic* significance: Appolonius Dyscolus.[36] An examination of his work, Περὶ Συνδέσμων, provides the added benefit of exposing Bauer's error. In 1853, Arthurus von Velsen compiled a collection of *fragments* of the writings of the Greek grammarian, Trypho (1st c. B.C.).[37] Confronted by situations where he would have preferred to see γάρ replaced by δέ, Bauer seized upon one fragment noted by Velsen to support his case. His discussion, expanded somewhat by later editors, now states in the most recent edition of the lexicon:

> Akin to [the] explanatory function is the use of γάρ as a narrative marker to express continuation or connection (in later G[ree]k writers, where more recent users of the texts, not finding the causal force they expect, would often prefer to see it replaced by δέ; unnecessarily, since the grammarian Trypho Alex. [I BC], fgm. 54 ed. AvVelsen 1853 shows clearly that γάρ under certain circumstances εἴς οὖν ἐστὶν ἀντὶ τοῦ δέ = is one and the same thing as δέ). Indeed, in many instances γάρ appears to be used adverbially like our "now" (in which the temporal sense gives way to signal an important point or transition), "well, then," "you see."[38]

This statement represents the misquotation of a secondary source taken out of context. As such it is a better indicator of the sad state of New Testament conjunctive lexicography than an accurate assessment of the meaning of γάρ.

---

35. Escandell-Vidal and Leonetti, "Procedural Meaning," 81.

36. Dickey, *Ancient Greek Scholarship*, 73. Dickey states, "The works of Apollonius Dyscolus are the most important and influential of surviving grammatical treatises. In antiquity and the Byzantine world Apollonius was considered the greatest grammarian, and it is no coincidence that far more remains of his work than of any other Greek grammarian before the Byzantine period."

37. For fragments related to this discussion, see Velsen, *Tryphonis*, 40–42.

38. BDAG, s.v., γάρ. See also Louw and Nida, *Greek-English Lexicon*, 1:811n2, who suggest that as a marker of transition γάρ is "perhaps best left untranslated, since [it] serve[s] more to indicate merely a new sentence or a new paragraph rather than to carry significant features of coordinate or subordinate relations."

The work of Appolonius is frequently noted for arguing both sides of an issue and thus presents a challenge for the modern interpreter—especially where reference is made to an isolated comment.³⁹ In his discussion of γάρ, from which four Trypho *fragments* are noted by Velsen, Appolonius draws a much different conclusion than the claim made by Bauer. His discussion can be divided into three sections.⁴⁰ In the first section (239, 9–21a), Appolonius presents the accepted understanding of γάρ as a postpositive causal conjunction—specifically that the proposition introduced by γάρ, the *cause*, must follow the proposition relating the effect. In the second (239, 21b–240, 19) and third sections (240, 20–241, 29), he discusses what appear to be exceptions (but, in fact, are not): i.e., γάρ marking the initial proposition and, finally, the possibility of a pleonastic γάρ in combination with other conjunctions.

In section two of his discussion of γάρ (239, 21b–240, 19), Appolonius clarifies the meaning of this conjunctive marker and notes its distinction from δέ. He acknowledges that γάρ sometimes appears *with the apparent cause* in the first proposition rather than in the second (postpositive) proposition, and, even more troubling, sometimes it appears in the first proposition *separated from the apparent cause* in the second proposition, as in this example:

> O Circe, γάρ who will lead the way on this journey?
>
> To Hades δέ no one has yet gone (*Od.* 10.501–502).

Without comment, Appolonius inverts the two phrases.

> O Circe, to Hades δέ no one has yet gone;
> γάρ who will lead the way on this journey?

The result, however, is no better since γάρ is still separated from the *apparent* cause.

It is here that the comments of Trypho, and also Velsen, are first introduced. Velsen, who has summarized the preceding text, noting the postpositive placement of γάρ and the suggested transposition of phrases, presents the argument of Trypho as an opposite interpretation.⁴¹

---

39. Sluiter, *Ancient Grammar*, 106–7.

40. The notations utilized here for marking the text of Apollonius reflect the edition of Schneider and were also adopted by Dalimier. Schneider, "Περί Συνδέσμων," 213–64; cf. Dalimier, *Apollonius Dyscole*.

41. Velsen states, "[C]ontratiam tradit a Tryphone propositam horum versuum Homericorum interpretationem." Translation: "Trypho gives the opposite interpretation of these verses of Homer set before us" (*Tryphonis*, 40).

Τρύφων μέντοι φησὶν ἐπὶ τοῦ τοι<ού>του συνδέσμους ἀντιπαρειλῆφθαι,

τὸν γὰρ ἀντὶ τοῦ δέ καὶ τὸν δέ ἀντὶ τοῦ γάρ·

Τίς δὲ ταύτην τὴν ὁδὸν ἡγεμονεύσει;

εἰς Ἅϊδος γὰρ οὔ πώ τις ἀφίκετο (240, 4–7).[42]

The interpretation of Trypho, however, does not truly represent the *opposite* position, but rather a different set of parameters. Trypho is suggesting an *interchange* of conjunctions rather than an inversion of propositions, as per the previous discussion. The original issue (γάρ introducing a proposition in the initial position) remains and has not yet truly been answered, yet now an additional question has also been raised regarding the relationship of γάρ and δέ.

The text recorded by Velsen continues, presenting a further argument by Trypho. He states, καὶ οὐκ ἔστιν ἀσύνηθες τὸν δέ εἰς τὸν γάρ μεταλαμβάνεσθαι ("the use of δέ *instead of* γάρ is not unusual"). He offers evidence to support his argument from the work of Homer: a series of statements each marked by δέ relating a succession of events, within which one proposition, presenting a possible cause for another, suggests that δέ has been substituted for γάρ.

> The horse leapt on high,
> δέ [γάρ, or *because*, as per Trypho] the arrow entered the brain
> (*Il.* 8.85).[43]

This example is preceded by narrative describing the results of battle: only Nestor remained ... and not of his own will ... his horse was wounded. After a statement explaining the vulnerability of horses at the crown of their heads, Homer (*Il.* 8.85–86) switches to a slow-motion flashback of the events, focused specifically upon the horse:

ἀλγήσας δ' ἀνέπαλτο,	[δέ] feeling pain, he sprung up,
βέλος δ' εἰς ἐγκέφαλον δῦ,	[δέ] [the] arrow into [the] brain plunged,
σὺν δ' ἵππους ἐτάραξε	[δέ] with [the] horses he was confused,
κυλινδόμενος περὶ χαλκῷ.	writhing upon the bronze.

---

42. Translation: "Trypho, however, says regarding this example, 'The conjunctions have been interchanged, the γάρ in place of the δέ and the δέ in place of the γάρ:
   'Δέ who will be the guide on this journey?
   Γάρ to Hades no one has yet gone.'"

43. Trypho continues, "αἰτία γάρ ἐστι τοῦ ἀναπαλῆναι τὸν ἵππον" (240, 9). Translation: "This is the reason the horse sprang up."

Logically and chronologically, the arrow entered the brain first and caused the subsequent actions. However, the text is poetic and the author is relating the unfolding realization of the horse—pain, an arrow, confusion—without the explicit intention of specifying cause and effect.[44] This text illustrates the point argued by Sicking, who states, "[T]he form of a text is never determined directly by the events recounted or states of affairs described in the statements making up the text, but always by the author presenting these data and placing them in some particular light for reasons of his own."[45] The logical precision preferred by the scientific grammarian does not transcend the rhetorical effect intended by the author. Γάρ could be exchanged for δέ, but the resulting meaning and certainly the rhetorical impact would be much different.[46]

In the conclusion of this section (240, 12b–19), Appolonius not only resolves the apparent exception of γάρ in the initial proposition, he also identifies the meaning of γάρ and simultaneously marks its distinction from δέ. Appolonius notes in these cases, as Trypho also admits, that γάρ appears to be pleonastic (i.e., redundant) because of antapodosis (i.e., *the response to a question unformulated, but apparently inescapable*).[47] The example noted above is sufficient to illustrate this point (*Od.* 10.496–502). Upon hearing the words of Circe that he must go to Hades, Ulysses reacted with great emotion. His spirit was broken. He wept on his bed. He had no desire to live. The proposition marked by γάρ ("who will be the guide on this journey?") justifies his reaction and appeal to Circe, in effect, answering the unstated,

---

44. See Pulleyn, *Iliad Book One*, 15–16, who notes Homer's economical use of words, allowing the speech and actions of the characters to speak for themselves.

45. Sicking, "Text Articulation," 46; cf. 45.

46. A second example (*Il.* 199–200), given by Trypho (240, 10–11), should likewise be interpreted in these same terms. For the correct interpretation of one debated element within this text, see Robertson, "Achilleus," 1–7.

47. Dalimier, *Apollonius Dyscole*, 339, states, "[D]ans tous les cas cités, l'énoncé avec γάρ être considéré comme compensatoire, non pas d'un énoncé précis, mais d'une prise de parole, prévenant ainsi la surprise de l'interlocuteur: *ce serait la réponse à une question non formulée mais qui paraît inéluctable*" (emphasis mine). Translation: "[I]n all the cited cases, the statement with γάρ could be considered as compensatory, not a clear statement, but a 'taking the floor', thereby preventing the surprise of the dialogue partner: *it would be the response to a question unformulated, but apparently inescapable*." Cf. Sicking, "Text Articulation," 24–25, who states, "Those who consider that γάρ by itself introduces a reason or cause are regularly faced with the need to supply (in thought) from the context the statement which is supposed to call for such causal explanation . . . To arrive at an adequate interpretation it is more helpful to make explicit which *question* the γάρ-sentence is supposed to answer, than to assume an ellipse and supply a 'suppressed' or 'missing' *statement*" (emphasis original). See also "Devices for Text Articulation," 21–25, 45–46.

but inescapable question of the goddess, "Why are you reacting in this manner?" The following proposition relates a fact well-known to both the goddess and Ulysses: "to Hades δέ no one has yet gone *in a black ship.*"⁴⁸ While its content gives a possible cause for the preceding question, its presence in the text is more appropriately interpreted as parenthetical. This statement prepares the reader for the following comment of the goddess: μή τί τοι ἡγεμόνος γε ποθὴ παρὰ νηὶ μελέσθω . . . τὴν δέ κέ τοι πνοιὴ Βορέαο φέρησιν.⁴⁹ This comment would seem abrupt and misplaced if not for the preceding parenthetical statement. Thus, the suggested interchange of conjunctions by Trypho is not only unnecessary, it would cause one to miss the interaction of the implied dialogue.⁵⁰

In the final section of his discussion of γάρ (240, 20–241, 29), Apollonius addresses the apparent pleonastic use of γάρ in combination with other conjunctions. Appolonius acknowledges, in partial agreement with Trypho, that two words, conjunctions or otherwise, may combine to have the effect of one meaning. He states, however, that Trypho's thesis is not always true. Each word may also retain their own respective force. Appolonius specifically notes his disagreement with Trypho as he introduces the text misquoted by Bauer. The entire fragment, along with this introductory comment (omitted by Velsen), is as follows (the words noted by Velsen are italicized):

οὐκ ἐκεῖνο μέντοι παραδεξόμεθα, ἐφ' οὗ φησι τὸν μενγάρ <ἕνα> εἶναι σύνδεσμον, ἰσοδυναμοῦντα τῷ δέ, ἐν ὑποδείγματι τοιούτῳ·

<<ἐγὼ μὲν καὶ Διονύσιος ἐδειπνοῦμεν,

σὺ μενγὰρ οὐ παρεγένου.>>

Οὔτε γάρ, φησιν, ὁ μέν δεόντως <ἔ>χει, οὔτε ὁ γάρ ἐπ' αἰτίας τινὸς παραλαμβάνεται. Εἷς οὖν ἐστιν ἀντὶ τοῦ δέ (241, 1–7).⁵¹

---

48. This final phrase (*Od.* 10.502b), while critical to understand the role of the conjunctions in this text, is not included in the fragment of Trypho, or the explicit discussion of Apollonius.

49. *Od.* 10.505–7. Translation: "Do not be concerned for a pilot to guide your ship ... the breath of the North Wind will bear her onward."

50. See Dalimier, *Apollonius Dyscole*, 339, who notes that γάρ functions in this same manner in other examples noted in the discussion (*Il.* 3.226; 4.189; and *Od.* 17.251).

51. Translation: "However, we will not accept that [the thesis] of which he [Trypho] speaks, 'the μενγάρ is one conjunction, equivalent to δέ', as in this example:

'Dionysios and I were dining
μενγάρ you did not come'.

For neither, he [Trypho] says, is the μέν placed as it should be, nor is the γάρ [used] with reference to a certain cause. Therefore, this one [unique conjunction] is [used] in

What Velsen illegitimately separates (μὲν γάρ), Dalimier properly joins (μενγάρ) to reflect the point argued by Trypho, namely that μενγάρ is one conjunction equivalent to δέ. Trypho's intention to speak of both words as one is evident from the following words which Velsen also fails to note: καὶ ὁ τύπος τῆς φωνῆς καὶ ἔτι ὁ τόνος αἴτιοί εἰσι τοῦ μὴ δοκεῖν τὸν μέν καὶ γάρ ἕνα εἶναι (241, 7–8).[52] On this basis alone the statement of Bauer should be rejected since the conjunction equated with δέ (ἰσοδυναμοῦντα τῷ δέ) by Trypho is μενγάρ rather than γάρ. Apollonius concludes that while the combination suggested by Trypho is possible, his solution is unnecessary since γάρ may be considered pleonastic, as noted in section two, and μέν may be used in place of μήν (i.e., to mark emphasis).

Once again, Apollonius illustrates his point from the works of the Poet (*Il.* 3.453; 241, 27–28) and, in so doing, marks both a similarity and, in such cases, the distinction between δέ and γάρ. In this context (*Il.* 3.450–453), Menelaus is searching "throughout the throng like a wild beast" to find his Trojan enemy, Alexander, but none of the Trojans could find Alexander for him. This statement raises the obvious, but unstated question, "Why would the Trojans betray Alexander, one of their own, to Menelaus?" The author's parenthetical answer (γάρ) is in two parts: first, indirectly, but emphatically (μέν) by denying the expected reason for the opposite reaction ("not for love would they hide [him]"), and, second, by answering (γάρ) once again, this time directly, with an emphatic metaphor: "for he was hated of all even as black death." The use of δέ in this example, instead of μὲν γάρ, while appropriate to mark the *discontinuity* of a parenthetical statement, would have failed to achieve the intended rhetorical effect of *engaging the recipients* (γάρ) at this critical juncture in the text.

EVIDENCE FROM THE NEW TESTAMENT

An examination of New Testament texts confirms the analysis of γάρ noted above. Both γάρ and δέ, for example, mark parenthetical statements. The procedural signal that they communicate, however, is much different. The fourth chapter of the Gospel of John provides an opportunity to highlight this difference. In this text the author interrupts the flow of thought four

---

place of the δέ." Cf. Velsen, *Tryphonis*, 41.

52. Translation: "Both the type of sound and emphasis [of the word] are reasons that μέν and γάρ would not seem to be one [unique conjunction]." Note also the subsequent text (241, 9b–28) in which Appolonius offers specific reasons to reject the thesis of Trypho—e.g., the use of μενγάρ by Trypho is incorrect, being properly accented μένγαρ (as also αὔταρ and other words ending with ρ and having a final short syllable).

times to provide information necessary for understanding the narrative. The first two statements are introduced by δέ: first, in leaving Judea to travel to Galilee, "(δέ) it was necessary that he pass through Samaria," and later, upon arriving in Sychar, "(δέ) Jacob's well was there." These facts would be relevant and apparent to Palestinian Jews early in the first century, but would not be so well known and could not be assumed of the recipients of the Gospel of John. The author needed to pause, filling in these details with a parenthetical statement, in order to *prepare readers for the following narrative*. Two additional parenthetical statements are introduced by γάρ: "(γάρ) his disciples had gone away into the city to buy food" and "(γάρ) Jews have no dealings with Samaritans." These statements reflect *answers to questions likely raised in the minds of the recipients by the preceding text* (i.e., respectively: "Why would Jesus ask the woman to give him a drink if he was traveling with his disciples?" and "Why did the Samaritan woman react with surprise when spoken to by Jesus?"). In the statements marked by γάρ one finds antapodosis, not with the participants of the narrative, but with the author and the readers of the text.[53]

Statements marked by γάρ also provide a glimpse into the situational context of a text. Consider the example, noted above, that troubled Winer. In the parallel passages, Matt 23:39 and Luke 13:35, a direct statement, λέγω ὑμῖν, is introduced by γάρ and δέ respectively. In this context, Jesus mourns the repeated rejection and murder of the prophets by the city of Jerusalem and pronounces judgment: your house is left to you desolate (Matt 23:38; Luke 13:35a). The phrase noted above follows, introducing the prophetic statement, οὐ μή με ἴδητε . . . ἕως . . . εἴπητε· εὐλογημένος ὁ ἐρχόμενος ἐν

---

53. The tenets of Relevance Theory raise the question of what purpose parenthetical statements serve in discourse. Their presence in spoken, spontaneous discourse is not unexpected. Distractions and interruptions happen. They are, however, also not uncommon in planned, written discourse. As Blakemore notes, parentheticals in written discourse "are the result of a deliberate stylistic choice . . . made on the basis of assumptions about the audience's contextual and processing resources [i.e., on the basis of what the author perceives would be the reaction of the recipients to the text]" ("And-Parentheticals," 1167–68). Parentheticals, of course, increase the processing costs experienced by the recipients. There must therefore be sufficient cognitive effects to justify the expenditure. Blakemore continues, "[T]hese parentheticals . . . contribute their own cognitive effects, but in a context of assumptions made accessible by the interpretation of the host . . . [specifically by] *providing an answer to a question which the speaker assumes is raised by the interpretation . . . of the host*" ("And-Parentheticals," 1684–85). A troubling question or sudden resistance left in the mind of a recipient represents an insurmountable hurdle to relevance. The author/speaker cannot afford to have the mental processing of the recipients come to a standstill. To incorporate such vital information into the original proposition is to add unnecessary costs and thus cloud the processing of the core message. On the other hand, to answer the questions of the recipient *as they arise* achieves greater effect—ultimately for less effort.

ὀνόματι κυρίου. The difference between a Jewish audience (Matthew's Gospel) and Gentile audience (Luke's Gospel) explains the choice of conjunctive marker. The rejection of the house of Israel is a personal issue for Jewish recipients who are directly involved and thus impacted by this statement. Demanding a response (γάρ, "What do you mean by this statement?") is therefore appropriate. For a Gentile audience, the desolation of the house of Israel is merely one more detail that may be observed with a certain detachment. In Luke's Gospel, signaling the following proposition as a response (γάρ) would be awkward and misplaced.

Finally, scholars who resort to a transitional γάρ marking the next main point demonstrate only that their interpretation is skewed. The statement introduced by γάρ in 1 Thess 2:1, for example, is not the opening statement for the body of this epistle. Rather, it is the second in a series of five successive γάρ-propositions in which the author demonstrates why there is no need for him to defend himself before his detractors.[54] Hebrews 5:1 is also typically misunderstood. The backbone of this text is hortatory. Its divisions are clearly marked and not overlapping. Having finally specified the point of the first section (Heb 3:1–4:15) in Heb 4:14 and having announced the parallel second point in Heb 4:16, introducing the next section (Heb 4:16–10:18), the author appropriately signals his intention to answer: "What is it that you have to say?" with what has been described as an inchoative γάρ. This use, as one might expect in a text known for the quality of its Greek, follows a pattern also found in Classical Greek.[55]

CONCLUSION

Γάρ is not transitional; it does not mark the next main point. Rather, it indicates that, from the author's perspective, something more must be said so that the previously stated main point will be more readily accepted or understood. The implications of this conclusion for New Testament scholarship should not be missed. Γάρ reflects the dialogical nature of the text and thus serves as a window into the situational context. Furthermore, several widely accepted structural divisions are misplaced (e.g., Rom 1:18; 1 Thess

---

54. Note the parallels between 1 Thess 1:9–10 and 1 Thess 2:1 (αὐτοί γάρ, a verb related to knowledge, εἴσοδον, and evidence describing the legitimacy of the apostle's ministry among the recipients). Note also, the Nestle-Aland text fails to divide 1 Thess 1:8 into two sentences, as is correct in light of the οὐ μόνον . . . ἀλλά construction. Romans 1:18 (the third in a series of six γάρ-propositions) is also often inappropriately marked as the inception of the body of that text.

55. See de Jong, "TAP," 181. See also *Il.* 2.284, noted by Appolonius (239, 26), as an example of this same use.

2:1; Heb 5:1). Even text critics must rethink the process by which they evaluate conjunctive variants in light of the influence of non-native scribes. Finally, this problem is not limited to γάρ. There is no adversative καί, no copulative δέ, no causal καθώς. Many of the convenient definitions offered by the current lexicons serve not to prove exegetical conclusions, but rather to shape waxen noses. Only a more sound pragmatic and communicative foundation for NT conjunctive lexicography will resolve the issue.

BIBLIOGRAPHY

Bäumlein, W. *Untersuchungen über griechische Partikeln*. Stuttgart: Metzlerschen, 1861.
Benes, Tuska. *In Babel's Shadow: Language, Philology, and the Nation in Nineteenth-Century Germany*. Kritik: German Literary Theory and Cultural Studies. Detroit: Wayne State University Press, 2008.
Black, Stephanie L. *Sentence Conjunctions in the Gospel of Matthew: καί, δέ, τότε, γάρ, οὖν and Asyndeton in Narrative Discourse*. Journal for the Study of the New Testament: Supplement Series 216; Studies in New Testament Greek 9. London: Sheffield Academic Press, 2002.
Blackburn, Perry L. *The Code Model of Communication: A Powerful Metaphor in Linguistic Metatheory*. SIL e-Books 4. N.p.: SIL International, 2007.
Blakemore, Diane. "*And*-Parentheticals." *Journal of Pragmatics* 37 (2005) 1165–81.
———. *Relevance and Linguistic Meaning: The Semantics and Pragmatics of Discourse Markers*. Cambridge Studies in Linguistics 99. Cambridge: Cambridge University Press, 2002.
Blass, Regina. "Constraints on Relevance in Koiné Greek in the Pauline Letters." Paper first presented at the Summer Institute of Linguistics Exegetical Seminar, Nairobi, Kenya, May 29–June 19, 1993, and slightly revised March 1998.
———. *Relevance Relations in Discourse: A Study with Special Reference to Sissala*. Cambridge Studies in Linguistics 55. Cambridge: Cambridge University Press, 1990.
Brown, Gillian, and George Yule. *Discourse Analysis*. Cambridge Textbooks in Linguistics. Cambridge: Cambridge University Press, 1983.
Brown, Jeannine K. *Scripture as Communication: Introducing Biblical Hermeneutics*. Grand Rapids: Baker, 2007.
Carston, Robyn. *Thoughts and Utterances: The Pragmatics of Explicit Communication*. Malden, MA: Blackwell, 2002.
Clark, Billy. *Relevance Theory*. Cambridge Textbooks in Linguistics. Cambridge: Cambridge University Press, 2013.
Cotterell, Peter, and Max Turner. *Linguistics and Biblical Interpretation*. Downers Grove, IL: InterVarsity, 1989.
Culler, Jonathan. *Ferdinand de Saussure*. Rev. ed. Ithaca, NY: Cornell University Press, 1986.
Dalimier, Catherine. *Apollonius Dyscole Traité des Conjonctions*. Histoire des Doctrines de L'Antiquité Classique 25. Paris: Librairie Philosophique J. Vrin, 2001.
Danker, Frederick William. *A Greek-English Lexicon of the New Testament and Other Early Christian Literature*. 3rd ed. Chicago: University of Chicago Press, 2000.

de Jong, Irene J. F. "TAP Introducing Embedded Narratives." In *New Approaches to Greek Particles: Proceedings of the Colloquium held in Amsterdam, January 4–6, 1996, to Honour C. J. Ruijgh on the Occasion of his Retirement*, edited by Albert Rijksbaron, 175–85. Amsterdam Studies in Classical Philology 7. Amsterdam: Gieben, 1997.

Denniston, J. D. *The Greek Particles*. 2nd ed. Oxford: Clarendon, 1954.

Dickey, Eleanor. *Ancient Greek Scholarship: A Guide to Finding, Reading, and Understanding Scholia, Commentaries, Lexica, and Grammatical Treatises, from Their Beginnings to the Byzantine Period*. American Philological Association Classical Resources. Oxford: Oxford University Press, 2007.

Escandell-Vidal, Victoria, and Manuel Leonetti. "On the Rigidity of Procedural Meaning." In *Procedural Meaning: Problems and Perspectives*, edited by Victoria Escandell-Vidal and Manuel Leonetti, 81–102. Current Research in the Semantics/Pragmatics Interface 25. Bingley, UK: Emerald, 2011.

Falla, Terry C. "Series Preface." In *Foundations for Syriac Lexicography III: Colloquia of the International Syriac Language Project*, xxiii–xxiv. Perspectives on Syriac Linguistics 4. Piscataway, NJ: Gorgias, 2008.

Green, Gene L. "Relevance Theory and Biblical Interpretation." In *The Linguist as Pedagogue: Trends in the Teaching and Linguistic Analysis of the Greek New Testament*, edited by Stanley E. Porter and Matthew Brook O'Donnell, 217–40. New Testament Monographs 11. Sheffield: Sheffield Phoenix, 2009.

Grice, H. P. "Further Notes on Logic and Conversation." In *Pragmatics*, vol. 9 of *Syntax and Semantics*, edited by P. Cole. New York: Academic Press, 113–28. Cambridge, MA: Harvard University Press, 1989.

———. "Meaning." *The Philosophical Review* 66 (1957) 377–88.

Gutt, Ernst-August. *Translation and Relevance: Cognition and Context*. 2nd ed. Manchester: St. Jerome, 2000.

Halliday, M. A. K. "Language as System and Language as Instance: The Corpus as a Theoretical Construct." In *Directions in Corpus Linguistics: Proceedings of Nobel Symposium 82 Stockholm, 4–8 August 1991*, edited by Jan Svartvik. Trends, 61–77. Linguistics: Studies and Monographs 65. Berlin: Mouton de Gruyter, 1992.

Harris, Roy. "On Redefining Linguistics." In *Redefining Linguistics*, edited by Hayley G. Davis and Talbot J. Taylor, 18–52. London: Routledge, 1990.

Harris, Roy, and Talbot J. Taylor. *Landmarks in Linguistic Thought: The Western Tradition from Socrates to Saussure*. Routledge History of Linguistic Thought. London: Routledge, 1989.

Hartung, Johann Adam. *Lehre von den Partikeln der griechischen Sprache*. 2 vols. Erlangen: Palm and Enke, 1832–1833.

Hasan, Ruqaiya. *Linguistics, Language, and Verbal Art*. Geelong: Deakin University Press, 1985.

Jobes, Karen H. "Relevance Theory and the Translation of Scripture." *Journal of the Evangelical Theological Society* 50 (2007) 773–97.

Joseph, J. E. "Saussurean Tradition in Twentieth-century Linguistics." *The Encyclopedia of Language and Linguistics*, edited by R. E. Asher and J. M. Y. Simpson, 7:3664–69. Oxford: Pergamon, 1994.

Klotz, Reinhold. *Adnotationes Continens*. Vol. 2 of *Matthaei Devarii Liber de Graecae Linguae Particulis*. Edited by Reinhold Klotz. Leipzig: Baumgaertner, 1842.

Lee, John A. L. *A History of New Testament Lexicography*. Studies in Biblical Greek 8. New York: Lang, 2003.
Levinsohn, Stephen H. "The Relevance of Greek Discourse Studies to Exegesis." *Journal of Translation* 2 (2006) 11–21.
Louw, Johannes, and Eugene A. Nida. *Greek-English Lexicon of the New Testament: Based on Semantic Domains*. 2nd ed. New York: United Bible Societies, 1989.
Metzger, Bruce M. *The Early Versions of the New Testament: Their Origin, Transmission, and Limitations*. Oxford: Clarendon, 1977.
Mintert, Petri. *Lexicon Graeco-Latinum in Novum D.nJesu Christi Testamentum*. Frankfort: Multz, 1728.
Misener, Geneva. "The Meaning of ΓΑΡ." PhD diss., University of Chicago, 1904.
Osborne, Grant R. *Matthew*. Exegetical Commentary on the New Testament 1. Grand Rapids: Zondervan, 2010.
Porter, Stanley E., and Matthew Brook O'Donnell. "Conjunctions, Clines and Levels of Discourse." *Filología Neotestamentaria* 20 (2007) 3–14.
Pulleyn, Simon. *Iliad Book One: Edited with an Introduction, Translation, and Commentary*. Oxford: Oxford University Press, 2000.
Rijksbaron, Albert. "Introduction." In *New Approaches to Greek Particles: Proceedings of the Colloquium held in Amsterdam, January 4–6, 1996 to Honour C. J. Ruijgh on the Occasion of His Retirement*, edited by Albert Rijksbaron, 1–14. Amsterdam Studies in Classical Philology 7. Amsterdam: Gieben, 1997.
Robertson, A. T. *A Grammar of the Greek New Testament in the Light of Historical Research*. 4th ed. Nashville: Broadman, 1934.
Robertson, G. I. C. "The Eyes of Achilleus: *Iliad* 1.200." *Phoenix* 53 (1999) 1–7.
Schleusner, Johann Friedrich. *Novum Lexicon Graeco-Latinum in Novum Testamentum*. 2 vols. 3rd ed. Leipzig: Weidmann, 1808.
Schneider, Richard, ed. "Περὶ Συνδέσμων." In *Apollonii Dyscoli Quae Supersunt: Recensuerunt, Apparatum Criticum, Commentarium, Indices Adiecerunt*, edited by Richard Schneider and Gustav Uhlig, 213–64. Part 2, volume 1. Grammatici Graeci. Leipzig: Teubner, 1878–1910.
Sicking, C. M. J. "Devices for Text Articulation in Lysias I and XII." In *Two Studies in Attic Particle Usage: Lysias and Plato*, edited by C. M. J. Sicking and J. M. Van Ophuijsen, 5–66. Mnemosyne Supplementum 129. Leiden: Brill, 1993.
Sluiter, Ineke. *Ancient Grammar in Context: Contributions to the Study of Ancient Linguistic Thought*. Amsterdam: VU University Press, 1990.
Sperber, Dan, and Deirdre Wilson. *Relevance: Communication and Cognition*. 2nd ed. Malden, MA: Blackwell, 1995.
Stock, Christian. *Clavis Linguae Sanctae Novi Testamenti*. Edited by Johann Friderich Fischer. 5th ed. Leipzig: Weidmann, 1752.
Vanhoozer, Kevin J. *Is There a Meaning in This Text? The Bible, The Reader, and the Morality of Literary Knowledge*. Grand Rapids: Zondervan, 1998.
von Velsen, Arthurus. *Tryphonis Grammatici Alexandrini Fragmenta: Collegit et Disposuit*. Berlin: Friderici Nicolai, 1853.
Wallace, Daniel B. *Greek Grammar Beyond the Basics: An Exegetical Syntax of the New Testament*. Grand Rapids: Zondervan, 1996.
Wardhaugh, Ronald. *An Introduction to Sociolinguistics*. 4th ed. Blackwell Textbooks in Linguistics 4. Malden: MA: Blackwell, 2002.

Westfall, Cynthia Long. *A Discourse Analysis of the Letter to the Hebrews: The Relationship between Form and Meaning*. Library of New Testament Studies 297. London: T. & T. Clark, 2005.

Wilson, Deirdre, and Dan Sperber. "Pragmatics and Time." *University College London Working Papers in Linguistics* 5 (1993) 277–98.

Winer, George Benedict. *A Grammar of the Idiom of the New Testament Prepared as a Solid Basis for the Interpretation of the New Testament*. Translated by J. Henry Thayer. Andover: Draper, 1869. Translation of *Grammatik des neutestamentlichen Sprachidioms als sichere Grundlage der neutestamentlichen Exegese*. Edited by Gottlieb Lünemann. 7th ed. Leipzig: Vogel, 1867.

———. *A Treatise on the Grammar of New Testament Greek Regarded as a Sure Basis for New Testament Exegesis*. Translated by W. F. Moulton. 3rd rev. ed. Edinburgh: T. & T. Clark, 1882. Translation of *Grammatik des neutestamentlichen Sprachidioms als sichere Grundlage der neutestamentlichen Exegese*. Edited by Gottlieb Lünemann. 7th ed. Leipzig: Vogel, 1867.

Yus, Francisco. "Relevance Theory Online Bibliographic Service." http://www.ua.es/personal/francisco.yus/rt/html.

4

Majority Text or Not
Which Criteria Should Be Adopted When Assessing Textual Variation in the Greek New Testament?

J. K. ELLIOTT
The University of Leeds

IN PREPARING THIS CONTRIBUTION to our honoree's Festschrift, I happily recall my stay in his home in North Carolina, my two visits to Southeastern Baptist Theological Seminary (hereafter SEBTS), David's visit to my house in Yorkshire, and his lecturing in Leeds.

I also remember that it was in Basle where he undertook his doctoral research. That famous city was much in evidence among biblical scholars in 2016 as Kanton Baselstadt was commemorating the 500th anniversary of a landmark and pioneering New Testament. The first published Greek New Testament (1516) was edited by Desiderius Erasmus, based on manuscripts he happened upon in Basle. The manuscripts were, in general, those that today would be classified as Byzantine in text-type. They largely conformed to Erasmus' revision of the Latin New Testament that was his main motive in publishing what he originally styled his *Novum Instrumentum*, i.e., a new Latin version differing from the Vulgate, which by then had been corrupted. As a self-proclaimed Jerome *redivivus*, Erasmus sought to gain favour for his revolutionary new Latin translation by accompanying it on each page with a parallel Greek New Testament so that learned readers with knowledge of Greek could assess the accuracy of this new version against the original language. Obviously, as we know, it was his Greek column that was soon to dominate biblical studies, especially when reformers and a nascent Protestantism came to prefer a Bible translated from the original languages, rather than the Latin version, which was exclusively promoted by the Catholic Church.

Erasmus concentrated his Greek text on manuscripts that were not aberrant when compared with the Latin familiar to him and his intended readers. Thus, although he had access to minuscule 1 and had a contact in the Vatican consult majuscule B 03, those witnesses would not have been deemed reliable or familiar for his purposes. Eventually Erasmus' Greek was in large part adopted in subsequent editions of the Greek New Testament, produced by Colinaeus, Stephanus, Beza and the Elzevier family. It was the Elzeviers' edition of 1633 that coined the term *Textus Receptus* in its publishing blurb to imply that this text was being accepted by absolutely everybody. The term has of course subsequently been used to apply to any and all Greek New Testaments from Erasmus' 1516 edition through to 1881 when Westcott and Hort's *New Testament in the Original Greek* finally toppled the Textus Receptus (TR) from the position of pre-eminence that it had held for 350 years.

This preamble is obviously familiar matter especially to our honoree and to all those working in textual criticism. In the academic and church circles frequented by David there is still, however, a residual but strongly maintained adherence to that old TR, and through it to the English version of the Bible whose New Testament is based largely on the TR, namely the Authorised Version, commonly styled in America as the King James Version (KJV). (On entering the car-park at SEBTS, where I was to be thrown among the lions, lecturing on my brand of textual criticism, I vividly recall seeing—with some consternation and apprehension—many car bumpers bearing a transfer reading "If it ain't the KJV, it ain't the Bible.")[1] Significantly it is at SEBTS where David's colleague, Maurice Robinson, is the internationally respected defender of the Byzantine text-type, being the co-editor of a printed edition that repeats Westcott and Hort's title,[2] although in Robinson and Pierpont's case referring to the Byzantine/Majority text type[3]

---

1. An American translation of my British English would refer to "decals on an automobile's fender in the parking lot"—such are the linguistic differences that divide our two cultures!

2. Robinson and Pierpont, *New Testament*.

3. Münster's abandonment of text types in their *Text und Textwert* series and the

and not a text based largely on two "Alexandrian" majuscules, namely ℵ 01 and B 03. David, despite working in the same institution, maintains a more central role in often defending the text of the popular critical Nestle-Aland text, *Novum Testamentum Graece* (NA).

In the third chapter of his little primer on textual criticism,[4] Black (to use the conventional surname only, to conform with academic practice) gives four examples of how to assess textual variation. In most of his arguments for the chosen *Ausgangstext* (the jargon term now used to denote the earliest recoverable text from which most variants may be seen to have descended), using both internal and external grounds, he sometimes favours readings that are *not* Byzantine/Majority text-type.

His examples are Mark 1:2 where he accepts the non-Byzantine reading "in Isaiah the prophet" because it is a reading found in early and diverse witnesses. As it happens, he accepts the Byzantine readings in his other examples not because it is the Majority text as such but because the opposing variant(s) are found in only one strand of the tradition.

He claims, quite wisely, to be "shamelessly neutral"[5] and that intellectual honesty is found in the guidelines offered to students regarding Matt 5:22, which led him to a reading that is supported (but not found exclusively) in Byzantine manuscripts. As a *Post Scriptum* to his discussion it may be worth adding that the disputed word ειχη happens to follow ειπη. The similarity of the two words may have encouraged a scribe to make the addition; conversely the similarity of the two may have created an accidental shortening.[6]

The other two examples he gives are Eph 1:1 where he argues for the originality of εν Εφεσω and John 3:13 (yet another choice between a longer or a shorter reading) in favor of the originality of "which is in heaven." In all these examples I applaud not just his reaction to the external witnesses but his weighing of evidence based on the author's language, style, and theology.

---

editors' refusal to countenance such terminology in the *Editio critica maior* (ECM) makes one hesitate to continue to use these obsolete, historic terms, except without qualification or undue explanation. As far as Münster's new allegiance to its homespun "Coherence-Based Genealogical Method" (CBGM) is concerned, they did adopt it as their *ECM* Catholic Epistles progressed, and I understand it will be applied more consistently in John. I am not privy to how the editorial decision-making processes are affected by CBGM and what consequences it will have on the manifold variation units being selected for inclusion in the printed edition of *ECM* John.

4. Black, *New Testament Textual Criticism*.

5. Ibid., 43.

6. See Houghton, "Latin Fathers," 376, where he notes that Cyprian, *Ad Quirinum* 3.8 knew the qualification "without cause" a century before a corrector added it in the margin of Codex Sinaiticus.

It is refreshing to read that Black, unlike many conservative evangelicals, says that no one text-type is "perfectly trustworthy"[7] and that no one text-type is to be given "automatic preference."[8] It is not for Black to talk about "God-breathed protection" for a given reading, manuscript, or type, nor does he use bizarre terms like "infallibility" of a given stream of tradition. It is clear from the vast array of interwoven readings and influences between manuscripts that any appeal to a supernaturally protected stratum is not only illogical and contrary to the evidence but a blasphemy, implying that the scholar is privy to divine intentions!

Black may be immune from such strange ways of arguing, but I noted with dismay that Harold Greenlee (*ob.* 2015) in his last book on the topic[9] fell foul of these unwelcome influences. He was a respected scholar whose earlier studies were on uncial palimpsests, and whose previous primer was greatly, and justifiably, praised. It was grievous to find him claiming to invoke the providential preservation of the (Holy) Spirit[10] in a way previously alien to his rigorous academic writings. Despite peculiar aberrations such as these, Greenlee, like Black, was, nevertheless, not wedded to any one text-type, such as that of the majority of witnesses; in the many examples of variation he adduces in chapter 8 we find that, by and large, he follows Metzger's reasoned eclecticism and is, in general, apologetic for the critical edition of Nestle-Aland (NA). At 1 Cor 6:20 the long reading is a "pious expansion"; at John 5:3–4 he accepts the shorter text deleting those verses. For Greenlee the Pericope Adulterae is not part of the New Testament, neither is the Comma Johanneum original to 1 John; he accepts the absence of Acts 8:37. It is therefore not surprising that he and Black are on the same and sane side of textual criticism.[11]

But back to Black. He was duly appreciative of Greenlee's (previous) style and his enduring scholarship. Thus he wrote an enthusiastic endorsement for the cover of Greenlee's 2008 primer and had previously edited a Festschrift for Greenlee, published in 1992.[12]

---

7. Black, *New Testament Textual Criticism*, 51.

8. Ibid., 55.

9. Greenlee, *New Testament Textual Criticism*.

10. The Spirit even merits an entry in the Index of People (*sic!*); see pp. 37, 61, 120.

11. See Greenlee's other discussions in his chapter 8: e.g., Matt 1:25: 6:1, 4; 8:25; 12:15; 22:30; Mark 6:22; Luke 2:14; 4:17; 6:1–10; 11:2–4; 15:21; John 3:1; 1 Cor 11:29; 1 Thess 2:3; Gal 1:16 Eph 1:1 Rev 12:18 (not Rev 21:18 as I erroneously wrote in my *RBL* online review [January 2009], reproduced in van der Watt, *Review of Biblical Literature 2009*, 538–43). Most of the variants are decided on the internal considerations. Usually his choice is not the Byzantine (majority) text-type.

12. Black, *Scribes and Scripture*.

My own position as a so-called thoroughgoing text critic (i.e., one who is prepared to print as original those readings that agree with the language, style, and proven usage of the New Testament author or with Koine Greek)[13] means that, occasionally, I argue for a text that may today be read in only a few extant manuscripts that have chanced to survive the centuries since they were first copied out. At other times my findings may indeed encourage me to go with the majority of manuscripts, but certainly not out of a misguided loyalty towards a tempting principle of democracy when one counts noses to opt for a reading found in the bulk of witnesses. Possibly as a result of my occasionally going against the printed text of NA, I became a sleeping partner in the now-defunct "Majority Text Society," which regularly circulated amongst its members text-critical discussions and which, albeit *parti pris*, were recognisably academic in their workings. I, tolerated as a passenger, even contributed a piece to its newsletter. I wrote on John 1:18, a tricky verse with intractable variants, where the Alexandrian witnesses alone support "God" (θεος) and the rest—including Fathers—have "Son" (υιος). "Son," despite its having allusions to Jesus' insubordination (to God), fits Johannine style, usage, and theology (see John 3:16). On the other hand, one may argue that if the beginning of the Prologue refers to God, so too should its closing (if 1:18 is indeed the end). I concluded that the jury is (or should be) still deliberating. In that instance I left the door open. I do not know which reading is original and which secondary. If no decision were forthcoming I suggested in the article that one may do as the editors of the second edition of the *ECM* of the Catholic Epistles do, namely to print *both* alternatives. The prime line of text there is sometimes divided. That is worth considering for those (few) places where an editorial decision is not possible. (One may wish to extend that to other knotty problems such as in the textual cruces in the Parable of the Two Boys [Matt 21:28–32].)

Fortunately, I have never been constrained by having to adhere to any particular party line, such as an acceptance of "inerrancy," which, *pace* fundamentalist scholars, is an illogical and bizarre principle that flies in the face of the history of textual witnesses and refuses to recognise that all manuscripts, however maverick they be branded by modern scholarship, were nonetheless at one time the divine and sacred scriptures of the individuals, churches, and communities that happened to read *and use* each and every copy.

I turn now to nine readings and variants that figure among old favourites. David may well be familiar with my arguments from earlier encounters, but I revisit them and do so now in his honour:

---

13. Elliott, *New Testament Textual Criticism*.

1. 1 Tim. 6:7

οτι ℵ* A F G 048 33 81 1739 1881 Lvt (r) Did
δηλον οτι ℵ² D¹ K L P Ψ 104 365 630 1175 1241 1505 Maj Lvt (f m) Lvg sy
αληθες οτι D* Lvt (ar b) Lvg mss. Ambst Spec

οτι *simpliciter* is likely to be original. It is the *difficilior lectio* and the additions are clarifications to make the two phrases cohere—and, as such, they are secondary.[14] What οτι means precisely is a problem. Marshall in his ICC volume on the Pastorals[15] proffers some nine solutions to its meaning which various exegetes have suggested. Not all are viable.

Other *v.ll.* include:

a) *om.* οτι copt Jer

b) και copt arm eth

c) αλλ' Aug

Concerning the first reading (a), the omission is yet a different way of eliminating the difficulty of οτι here. The last two readings, b and c, are probably inner-versional or free renderings. They may be discounted, other than our noting that the original reading evidently proved itself difficult to understand and translate.

2. Tit. 3:9

ερεις ℵ² A C Maj
εριν ℵ* D F G Ψ
εριδας 241 462
[cf. 1 Tim 6:4 ερις ℵ A K P Maj; ερεις D F G L Lvt Lvg.]

In the New Testament the singular ερις occurs at Rom 1:29; 13:13 (*v.l.* plural); 1 Cor 3:3; 2 Cor 12:20 (*v.l.* plural); Gal 5:20 (*v.l.* plural) but examples from the Pauline Epistles need be of no relevance in a discussion of the Pastoral Epistles.

There are no firm examples of the plural form ερεις in the New Testament.

---

14. In differing circumstances it may be argued that an original δηλον was accidentally omitted by homoioteleuton (κοσμONδηλON).

15. Marshall with Towner, *Pastoral Epistles*, 646–48.

Metzger, *Commentary*[16] accepts the plural because of the surrounding plurals and because of allegedly strong external support. But the plural is more likely to be due to assimilation to those other plurals in this list. Read εριν at Tit 3:9. This was changed to the plural εριδας and subsequently altered yet again by Atticist scribes to ερεις. εριδες is a Hellenistic form of the plural and is found without variant at 1 Cor 1:11.

3. Philm 2

Is Apphia τη αγαπητη with D² K L Maj., τη αδελφη read by ℵ A D* F G et al. or αδελφη τη αγαπητη with 629 and some versional evidence? Most critical editions of the Greek New Testament prefer τη αδελφη and argue that τη αγαπητη has been introduced later by scribes influenced by τω αγαπητω used of Philemon himself in v.1, whereas a change in the opposite direction is thought to be less likely.

A thoroughgoing critic may well favour the longer reading αδελφη τη αγαπητη, despite its being supported by only one Greek minuscule and supported by earlier Latin and Syriac witnesses. That reading has the merit of explaining the origin of the other two texts as accidental shortenings, in one case possibly caused by homoioteleuton (αδελφHτηαγαπητH), in the other case by the deliberate deletion of αδελφη to make the appellation of Apphia balance that of Philemon in verse 1.[17]

Αδελφη, unqualified, occurs in other Pauline letters at Rom 16:1, 15; 1 Cor 7:15; 9:5. αδελφος, unqualified, occurs frequently throughout the Pauline corpus. Thus the author's style may support the shorter reading τη αδελφη in verse 2. However, Pauline usage has αδελφος αγαπητος at 1 Cor 15:58; Eph 6:21; Phil 4:1; Col 4:7, 9 and Philm 16. This combining of αδελφος with αγαπητος in v. 16 should sway us to follow that usage in Philm 2 (and 1!); αγαπη is a particular theme in this little letter (see also vv. 5, 7, 9); the noun and its cognates are to the fore.

4. Heb 11:11

αυτη Σαρρα στειρα 𝔓⁴⁶ D* Ψ
αυτη Σαρρα 𝔓¹³ ℵ A D² Maj
αυτη Σαρρα στειρα ουσα P 104 365 2127

---

16. Metzger, *Textual Commentary*.

17. We may even be prepared to argue for the originality of *v.l.* τω αγαπητω αδελφω with D* (ar) b Ambst in v. 1.

αυτη Σαρρα η στειρα D¹ 1739 1881

Exegesis is affected by our choice of reading here. One assumes, probably naively, that all authors wrote clearly and with sense. That need not be true. Και αυτη Σαρρα (στειρα) may well be original although it fits into the sentence only with difficulty. Σαρρα (as a nominative) makes an unlikely subject of the sentence. Abraham is the most likely subject of this and surrounding sentences. Here he is clearly said to be the one with the ability to procreate despite his age. Attempts to make the euphemism δυναμιν εις καταβολην σπερματος apply to Sarah are unnatural and strained. The words cannot mean that Sarah was "enabled to conceive."[18] The variant adding ετεκεν is likely to be secondary to imply Sarah is the subject of the clause. The reading + εις το τεκνωσαι likewise is intended to make Sarah the subject of the sentence. The variants adding η and ουσα are secondary, to improve the flow of the sentence.

Και αυτη Σαρρα στειρα is unlikely to be a gloss;[19] it is, rather, a clumsy circumstantial clause (a *Zustandsatz*[20]) or dative of accompaniment i.e., a *dativus commodi* (iota subscripts were not always written in manuscripts) giving the parenthesis "together with (the barren) Sarah" in a sentence that shows how *Abraham's* faith was rewarded.

The omission of στειρα may have been due to homoioteleuton: σαρPAστειPA.

Therefore, read και αυτη Σαρρα as a parenthesis within a sentence that maintains Abraham as the subject of vv. 8–12.

5. Heb 12:3

αυτον D² K L Ψ* Maj
εαυτον A P 104 326 1241
αυτους 𝔓¹³ 𝔓⁴⁶ ℵ² Ψᶜ 33 81 1739*
εαυτους ℵ* D*

[Insofar as many manuscripts do not carry breathings or accents, αυτον/ αυτους could imply a rough or smooth breathing, the rough being an accepted alternative spelling of the reflexive.]

---

18. See Black, *Aramaic Approach*, 83–89.
19. As Zuntz implies in *The Text of the Epistles*, 16.
20. See Beyer, *Semitische Syntax*.

Again, these *v.ll.* concern exegesis. Should the sentence read: "Consider him who endured such hostility against himself from sinners" or "Consider him who endured such hostility from sinners against them(selves)"? The latter raises the question whether sinners injure them(selves)?[21]

Metzger's *Commentary ad loc.* betrays its weakness by arguing that the majority of the UBS committee accepted the singular as the "least inadequately" supported reading! According to Zuntz,[22] the plural is meaningless and a "primitive corruption" but, as this is the more difficult of the readings, may we not apply the maxim *praestat lectio ardua?*

Robinson and Pierpont's edition, not unexpectedly, reads αυτον, although it is mistyped twice on page 476.

6. Rev 5:9

τω θεω ημας ℵ.01 209 1006 Maj
ημας τω θεω 2050 2344 (= TR)
ημας θεου 2814
τω θεω A.02 (NA²⁸)
om. τω θεω Lvt (a c)
ημας instead of τω θεω 1 2065*

Metzger, *Commentary ad loc.* argues that the reading of A.02 explains the origin of the other variants. ηγορασας has as an object εκ πασης φυλης... but a more precise object is needed, therefore ημας before or after τω θεω was added or ημας was written instead of τω θεω. However, ημας does not readily agree with αυτους in v.10 (although the TR reads ημας at v.10 too, supported by some versions, including Latin).

7. Rev 13:10

Variants at Rev 13:10 need to be seen in their totality. There are two related issues here. The first is: εις αιχμαλωσιαν¹ 𝔓⁴⁷ ℵ.01 C.04 A.02 MajA. This is the reading often deemed accountable for the other readings; it is read by NA. These are the variants:

a) εχει αιχμαλωσιαν 051* MajK. Probably εχει was due to a misreading of εις.

---

21. The pronoun is not even translated in the Revised English Bible of 1989.
22. Zuntz, *Text of the Epistles*, 120

b) εις αιχμαλωσιαν απαγει 2351 3244. The absence of a verb with the first clause prompted the addition of απαγει or συναγει 2059 2081 (= TR) or the altering to αιχμαλωτιζει 94 104 459 2019.

c) om. εις αιχμαλωσιαν² 𝔓⁴⁷ ℵ.01 C.04 Maj

d) εις αιχμαλωσιαν² A.02 2351

The omission was probably due to homoioteleuton.

The second issue is as follows:

αποκτανθηνει αυτον. A singular reading by A.02 accepted by NA (as either imperatival or elliptical)
αποκτε(ι/ν)νει, δει αυτον ℵ.01 C.04 051* 1006 1611* 1854 2329 MajA
δει αυτον 051^{v.l.} MajK

A verb is needed with the second clause, hence δει was provided by some manuscripts.

Joël Delobel[23] wisely and correctly encourages our examining the rhetorical context and accepts the balance of the phrases as:

10a	ει τις εις αιχμαλωσιαν
10b and	εις αιχμαλωσιαν υπαγει
10c	ει τις εν μαχαιρη αποκτανθηναι
10d	αυτον εν μαχαιρη αποκτανθηναι

This encourages a particular exegesis, again showing the close relationship of text and meaning. It reflects teaching such as Jer 15:2 (and, perhaps, Jer 43:11), indicating the inevitability of God's plans being accomplished. It is not referring to retribution, such as in Matt 26:52 (*lex talionis*). The addition of the verbs in 10a is secondary. In 10c and 10d the infinitive used twice is a Hebraism. Other manuscripts change c and d to: ει τις εν μαχαιρη αποκτενει / δει αυτον εν μαχαιρη αποκτανθηναι thus transforming the meaning to one of retaliation whether one reads αποκτεν(ν)ει future or αποκτεινει present. Once again, a global approach to the variants in the verse does justice to the context in a way that a narrow concentration on the readings of favoured manuscripts would not.

---

23. Delobel, "Le texte de l'Apocalypse," 162–65.

8. Rev 20:2

The inconcinnity of the nominative ο οφις ο αρχαιος read by A.02 1678 1778 2080 virtually alone is a solecism. But it is a characteristic of the author to use the nominative for a title or proper name in apposition to a noun in an oblique case. See 1:5; 2:13 and also with participles at 2:20; 3:12; 8:9; 9:14; 14:12, 14. Pedantic scribes altered this to the grammatically correct τον οφιν τον αρχαιον ℵ.01 046 051 Maj (whence TR).

9. Rev 22:21

These are the last words of the Christian Bible, but there is confusion as to what our author actually wrote and also why his original words were changed. There is no obvious motive in any direction.

μετα παντων with A.02 alone (but with Lvg) is read by NA[28], but this shorter reading is possibly caused by hom: παν*ΤΩΝΤΩΝ*αγι*ΩΝ*

The *v.ll* are:

μετα παντων των αγιων 046 051[supp] 205 209 1006 Maj (cf. 8:3)
μετα των αγιων ℵ.01 2062 2377
μετα παντων των αγιων αυτου 2030
μετα των αγιων σου 2329

μετα παντων (η)μων is reported in NA[27], but Rykle Borger[24] indicates the problems here: he shows that its apparatus has "π. (η)μων 2050 *pc*". What does this mean? The TR has μετα παντων ημων. Such a reading may have come from 2 Cor 13:13; 2 Thess 3:18. The reading is not in UBS but Metzger, *Commentary*, has this as the reading of 296, which is a handwritten copy of a printed edition. Is that one of the "*pc.*"? What others can *pc.* conceal? And which witnesses read υμων? Tischendorf's apparatus shows the apparent absences of Greek manuscripts behind the TR with a stigma + cum? (and sometimes with "*sine teste/ sine codice*" (e.g., Rev 2:2).[25] Significantly, the newly drafted apparatus in NA[28] gives only 2050.

Of the fifteen New Testament books that end with a salutation six (Romans [16:20b = 16:24], 1, 2 Corinthians, 2 Thessalonians, Titus, Hebrews) conclude with μετα παντων υμων. (The conclusion in 2 Thessalonians in particular is very similar to that in Revelation.)

---

24. Borger, "Nestle-Aland 26," 56f.
25. Ibid., 57 omits a reference to 22:16.

Ross[26] argues in favour of μετα των αγιων σου read by only 2329[27] (this *v.l.* is not in NA, despite this manuscript's being included as "consistently cited" there, nor is it in the United Bible Society's apparatus in its *The Greek New Testament*, but see Metzger, *Commentary*). This occurs in a rewritten verse that seems to have been composed later and was probably liturgical, beginning as it does with αμην ερχου κυριε and omitting η χαρις του κυριου.

Here ends our few examples, conclusions in which are independent of a blind following of the Majority text-type. I trust David approves!

To conclude: We now convey our hearty congratulations to David, not least for his successes over many years, encouraging generations of students to take the minutiae of textual criticism seriously. On the occasion of this milestone we wish him Ad multos annos!

BIBLIOGRAPHY

Beyer, Klaus. *Semitische Syntax im Neuen Testament*. Göttingen: Vandenhoeck and Ruprecht, 1961.

Black, David Alan. *New Testament Textual Criticism: A Concise Guide*. Grand Rapids: Baker, 1994.

———. *Scribes and Scripture: New Testament Essays in Honor of J. Harold Greenlee*. Winona Lake, IN: Eisenbrauns, 1992.

Black, Matthew. *An Aramaic Approach to the Gospels and Acts*. 3rd ed. Oxford: Clarendon, 1967.

Borger, Rykle. "Nestle-Aland 26 und die neutestamentliche Textkritik." *Theologische Rundschau* 52 (1987) 1–58, 326.

Delobel, Joël. "Le texte de l'Apocalypse: Problèmes de la méthode." In *L'Apocalypse johannique et l'Apocalyptique*, edited by Jan Lambrecht, 151–66. BETL 43. Leuven: Leuven University Press, 1980.

Elliott, J. K. *New Testament Textual Criticism: The Application of Thoroughgoing Principles; Essays on Manuscripts and Textual Variation*. NovTSup160. Leiden: Brill, 2010.

Greenlee, J. Harold. *Introduction to the New Testament Textual Criticism*. Rev. ed. Peabody, MA: Hendrickson, 1995.

Houghton, H. A. G. "The Use of the Latin Fathers for New Testament Textual Criticism." In *The Text of the New Testament in Contemporary Research: Essays on the Status Quaestionis*, edited by Bart D. Ehrman and Michael W. Holmes, 375–405. 2nd ed. NTTSD 46. Leiden: Brill, 2013.

Marshall, I. Howard, with Philip H. Towner. *A Critical and Exegetical Commentary on the Pastoral Epistles*. Edinburgh: T. & T. Clark, 1999.

Metzger, Bruce M. *A Textual Commentary on the Greek New Testament*. 2nd ed. Stuttgart: Deutsche Bibelgesellschaft, 1994.

---

26. Ross, "Apocalypse," 338–44.
27. See Hoskier sub 200, i.e., his number for 2329.

Robinson, Maurice A., and William G. Pierpont, eds. *The New Testament in the Original Greek: Byzantine Textform 2005*. Southborough: Chilton, 2005.

Ross, J. M. "The Ending of the Apocalypse." In *Studies in New Testament Language and Text*, edited by J. K. Elliott, 337–44. Supplements to Novum Testamentum 44. Leiden: Brill, 1976.

Van der Watt, Jan, ed.. *Review of Biblical Literature*. Atlanta: SBL, 2009.

Zuntz, Günther. *The Text of the Epistles: A Disquisition upon the Pauline Corpus*. London: Oxford University Press, 1953.

5

A Short Textual Commentary on the Lucan Travel Narrative (Luke 9:51—19:46)

TOMMY WASSERMAN
Ansgar Teologiske Høgskole

INTRODUCTION

THE MOST WIDELY USED contemporary translation of the New Testament in Swedish was published in 1981 by the Swedish Bible Society.[1] In 2014, the Society took the first steps towards a new translation by commissioning a trial translation of two New Testament texts, the Lucan Travel Narrative (Luke 9:51—19:46) and Paul's Letter to the Galatians. In this connection, I was asked to be one of the consultants for the project. My task was to discuss significant textual problems relevant to the translation and to supply footnotes pertaining to these textual problems, a selection of which will accompany the new translation. In this essay, I present a part of this material in the form of "a short textual commentary on the Lucan Travel Narrative."[2]

---

1. *Nya Testamentet* (Stockholm, 1981).

2. I have published a revised version of my textcritical commentary to Galatians as "A Short Textual Commentary on Galatians," 345–71.

In this selection of passages I will give particular attention to textual problems where I prefer a reading that differs from at least one of the following two influential editions: (1) the twenty-eighth edition of Nestle-Aland, *Novum Testamentum Graece* (NA[28]); (2) the *Society of Biblical Literature Greek New Testament* (SBLGNT) edited by Michael W. Holmes.[3] Further, I will discuss a number of passages where words are printed in square brackets in NA[28] reflecting "a great degree of difficulty in determining the text" on the part of the editors.[4] Finally, I will note the text underlying three major English translations: the NASB, NIV, and NRSV.

The method I apply represents reasoned eclecticism, the dominant force in contemporary textual criticism, which takes into account external and internal evidence.[5] External evidence pertains to the physical textual witnesses, their date, source, and relationship to other textual witnesses, whereas internal evidence depends partly on considerations of the habits of scribes and various palaeographical features in the manuscripts (transcriptional evidence), and partly on considerations of what the author was likely to have written (intrinsic evidence).[6]

The editors of Nestle-Aland (the Alands et al.) and of SBLGNT (Holmes) use the same general approach, but with some differences, in particular with regard to the evaluation of external evidence, which is affected by the editors' particular view of the history of the New Testament text. The current text of Luke in NA[28] has remained unchanged since the twenty-sixth edition (identical to the UBS[3]), and the editors behind it were largely influenced by the views of B. F. Westcott and F. J. A. Hort.[7] In practice, this means that they assigned the greatest weight to witnesses affiliated to the Alexandrian, or "Neutral" text-type, to use the term of Westcott and Hort,

3. Aland et al., *Novum Testamentum Graece*; Holmes, *Greek New Testament*.

4. Aland et al., *Novum Testamentum Graece*, 54* (introduction).

5. See Holmes, "Reasoned Eclecticism," 771–802 (including the bibliography on p. 778n33). Alternative approaches rely primarily on either internal evidence (generally referred to as "thoroughgoing eclecticism"), or external evidence ("historical documentary," "Majority text" or "Byzantine priority" approaches). See Elliott, "Thoroughgoing Eclecticism," 745–70; and Robinson, "New Testament Textual Criticism," pars. 1–113. For a survey of methodological questions and a debate between the proponents of these different approaches, see the important volume edited by Black, *Rethinking New Testament Textual Criticism*.

6. For a detailed discussion of these criteria, see Wasserman, "Criteria," 579–612.

7. Westcott and Hort, *The New Testament in the Original Greek*. As Metzger explains, "The international committee [including Kurt Aland] that produced the *United Bible Societies* Greek New Testament, not only adopted the Westcott and Hort edition as its basic text, but followed their methodology in giving attention to both external and internal consideration" ("Westcott and Hort Greek New Testament," 75). For the significance of Westcott and Hort's edition, see Birdsall, "Recent History."

whereas they viewed the "Western" text and its representatives as an early but largely corrupt text, and the Byzantine textual tradition, reflected in the majority of MSS (mostly minuscules), as a late secondary text that cannot independently preserve the earliest text. The approach is best reflected in the accompanying *Textual Commentary* produced by Bruce M. Metzger on behalf of the UBS/NA editorial committees.[8]

In the introduction to the *Textual Commentary*, the UBS Committee divides the textual witnesses (in the epistles) into: Primary Alexandrian: 𝔓⁶⁶ 𝔓⁷⁵ ℵ B Sahidic (in part), Clement of Alexandria, Origen (in part) and most of the papyrus fragments; and Secondary Alexandrian: (C) L T W (Luke 1:1—8:12) (X) Z Δ Ξ Ψ (partially in Luke) 33 579 892 1241 Bohairic. The chief witnesses of the "Western" text in Luke are: 𝔓⁶⁹ D 0171, the Old Latin, (syrˢ and syrᶜ in part), and early Latin Fathers. Finally, the Byzantine text in Luke is represented by: A E F G H K P S V W (Luke 8:13—24:53) Π Ψ (partially in Luke) Ω and most minuscules.[9]

Unfortunately, Holmes has not yet produced an equivalent textual commentary for his edition, explaining in detail his textual decisions in critical passages. However, he has acknowledged that his version of reasoned eclecticism, as reflected in the SBLGNT, is particularly influenced by the views of Günther Zuntz.[10]

As for the textual base of the three English translations, the New American Standard Bible (NASB) of 1995 was based on NA²⁶ "in most instances."[11] The Greek text behind the New International Version (NIV)

---

8. Metzger, *Textual Commentary*. Metzger was the secretary of the committee (the other members were Kurt Aland, Matthew Black, Carlo M. Martini, and Allen Wikgren) in a selection of signficant passages.

9. Ibid., 15*.

10. See Zuntz, *Epistles*. Holmes states the following concerning those passages where the SBLGNT deviates from other major editions: "In all cases, a decision as to which variant reading to print was made on the basis of a reasoned evaluation of the available evidence, utilizing the reasoned eclectic approach I have long advocated in conjunction with a view of the history of the transmission of the New Testament texts influenced in particular by Zuntz and by Wachtel . . . Edited using a methodology similar to that of the NA/UBS Editorial Committee but influenced by a different view of the history of the transmission of the text, the SBLGNT offers in many instances an alternative assessment of the textual data, one that takes into account as much of the available data as possible, reflects developments and advances in the discipline's understanding of the history of the text, as one editor sees them" (Holmes, "SBL Greek New Testament," 6–7).

11. The NASB preface says: "Consideration was given to the latest available manuscripts with a view to determining the best Greek text. In most instances the 26th edition of Eberhard Nestle's *Novum Testamentum Graece* was followed." For this and other NASB translation principles, see the publisher's website: http://www.lockman.org/nasb/nasbprin.php.

of 1973 mostly follows the Nestle-Aland text too; it deviates from the NA²⁸/UBS⁵ at 231 places in the New Testament.[12] Finally, the New Revised Standard Version (NRSV) of 1990 also follows the text of NA²⁸/UBS⁵, which is not surprising since Bruce Metzger served in both the NRSV and UBS editorial committees.

TEXTUAL COMMENTARY

For each variation-unit, reading A is the text printed in NA²⁸. Right below the textual apparatus I indicate the reading of SBLGNT and the reading I prefer (Wasserman).[13] My own judgment includes a symbol reflecting my general view of the "balance of probabilities," i.e., the state of the external and internal evidence for each variation-unit, which is reflected in the subsequent commentary.[14]

The following symbols are used:

{e+i}	External and internal evidence unequivocally support a variant reading.
{e>i}	External evidence favors a variant reading, whereas internal evidence is ambiguous.
{e<i}	External evidence is ambiguous, whereas internal evidence favors a variant reading.
{e=i}	External and internal evidence are balanced or, alternatively, external evidence favors one variant reading, internal evidence another.

At the end of the article, there is a comparative table showing the differences between the printed text in NA²⁸ and SBLGNT, the readings I prefer, and the readings reflected in the English versions as far as they can be determined.

---

12. The Greek text behind the NIV has been reconstructed by Goodrich and Lukaszewski, *Reader's Greek New Testament*, and they calculate 231 deviations from the Nestle-Aland text (ibid., 10n6).

13. The textual apparatus for each variation-unit is based on NA²⁸ unless otherwise is noted.

14. I proposed this as a new "rating system" in Wasserman, *Jude*, 236–37, where I compared it to earlier systems, most notably the one used by the UBS committee in Metzger's textual commentary. That rating system has been abandoned in UBS⁵, after severe critique. I still think a brief description of the state of evidence in regard to a variation-unit can be useful insofar as it stimulates readers to engage with the evidence for themselves.

9:62a

My apparatus:
A. εἶπεν δὲ πρὸς αὐτὸν ὁ Ἰησοῦς ℵ L Ξ f^1 33. 1241. 2542. lat sy[s.c.p]
B. εἶπεν δὲ ὁ Ἰησοῦς πρὸς αὐτόν A C K N W Γ Θ Ψ f^{13} 565. 579. 892. 1424 𝔐 q sy[h]
C. ὁ δὲ Ἰησοῦς εἶπεν αὐτῷ D
D. εἶπεν δὲ ὁ Ἰησοῦς 𝔓[45.75] B 0181. 700 sa[mss]
E. εἶπεν δὲ πρὸς αὐτόν Δ

SBLGNT: D
Wasserman: D {e<i}
NASB: A/B/C ("But Jesus said to him")
NIV: D
NRSV: A/B/C ("Jesus said to him")

Did Luke use the prepositional object πρὸς αὐτόν or was it added later, and which is the initial word order? Significantly, the prepositional object apparently has a wide support in the textual tradition (readings A-B). On the other hand, Bruce Metzger points out that it is difficult to say which reading best explains the rise of the others; the words are enclosed in square brackets in the UBS/NA text.[15]

The unique reading of Codex Sangallensis 48 (Δ 037), omitting the subject, can be disregarded. The reading of Codex Bezae (reading C) has been assigned to reading A in NA[28] (within parenthesis), although it could have developed out of a different reading or independently as a harmonization to 9:60. On the other hand, the object follows after the verb, as in reading A, which is supported by the whole Latin tradition with a single exception (q). Reading A is probably older than reading B.

It is very difficult to argue for or against the object from Lukan style or scribal tendencies in specific manuscripts. On the one hand, we know that some early scribes tended to omit small words, which did not have any significant effect on the meaning of the text. On the other hand, scribes could have added the object to give more emphasis to the conclusion of the pericope, or in order to harmonize it to the immediate context where there is an object each time Jesus speaks: εἶπεν δὲ πρὸς αὐτὸν ὁ Ἰησοῦς (9:50); καὶ εἶπεν αὐτῷ ὁ Ἰησοῦς (9:58); Εἶπεν δὲ πρὸς ἕτερον (9:59); εἶπεν δὲ αὐτῷ (9:60). In addition, the fact that the object is attested in three distinct variants

---

15. Metzger, *Textual Commentary*, 125.

(reading A-C) may suggest that it has been added independently by different scribes as different times.

In sum, I prefer reading D.

9:62b

A. οὐδεὶς ἐπιβαλὼν τὴν χεῖρα ἐπ' ἄροτρον καὶ βλέπων εἰς τὰ ὀπίσω B f^1 (επιβαλλων $\mathfrak{P}^{75}$ 0181)

B. οὐδεὶς ἐπιβαλὼν (επιβαλλων A L W Θ) τὴν χεῖρα αὐτοῦ ἐπ' ἄροτρον καὶ βλέπων (στραφεις 892) εἰς τὰ ὀπίσω ℵ A C K L N W Γ Δ Θ Ξ Ψ f^{13} 33. 565. 579. 700. 892. 1241. 1424. 2542 $\mathfrak{M}$ vg sy

C. οὐδείς εἰς τὰ ὀπίσω βλέπων καὶ ἐπιβαλὼν τὴν χεῖρα αὐτοῦ ἐπ' ἄροτρον $\mathfrak{P}^{45vid}$ D it; Cl

SBLGNT: A
Wasserman: B {e+i}
NASB: B
NIV: A
NRSV: A

Reading C has an unexpected word order which could be translated, "No one who looks back and puts his hand to the plow . . . ." Metzger suggests that the reading does not make sense, and is probably the result of "scribal inadvertence."[16] Nevertheless, this reading and reading B attest to the possessive pronoun αὐτοῦ, "his" (hand). The UBS Committee regarded this textual problem as difficult, but preferred reading A without the pronoun because they were "impressed by the weight of the witnesses" (mainly $\mathfrak{P}^{75}$ B). The longer reading, however, has both stronger and wider support in the textual tradition, and in this case it is more likely that the pronoun has been omitted early on by one or several scribes who regarded it as superfluous. I clearly prefer reading B, as reflected in the NASB: "No one, after putting his hand to the plow and looking back, is fit for the kingdom of God."

10:1

A. ἑβδομήκοντα δύο $\mathfrak{P}^{75}$ B D 0181 lat sy$^{s.c}$ sa bo^{ms}; Ad

B. ἑβδομήκοντα ℵ A C K L N W Γ Δ Θ Ξ Ψ $f^{1.13}$ 565. 579. 700. 892. 1241. 1424. 2542 $\mathfrak{M}$ f q sy$^{p.h}$ bo; Ir^{lat} Cl Or

---

16. Ibid., 125–26.

SBLGNT: A
Wasserman: A/B {e=i}
NASB: B
NIV: A
NRSV: B

The choice here is between "seventy" or "seventy-two," depending on whether the numeral δύο is included. The external evidence is almost evenly divided. In fact, the text types traditionally labeled as "Alexandrian" and "Western" are divided between the two readings, whereas the Byzantine text supports "seventy."[17] It is somewhat surprising that the Committee does not take into account the external evidence of 10:17 where the same variation occurs. The situation is similar, but one additional important witness is extant in 10:17, 𝔓[45], which, contrary to what NA[28] indicates, supports the shorter reading, ἑβδομήκοντα and probably had the same reading in 10:1 where it is now lacunose.[18]

Further, in regard to internal evidence, the Committee thought that none of the two numbers was more suitable than the other to express a symbolism if such was intended.[19] A majority of the UBS Committee therefore decided that the word δύο should be included in square brackets in order to represent the balance of both external and internal evidence.

At the same time, Kurt Aland objected to the decision.[20] He listed a number of examples of "70" from the Old Testament (70 in the house of Jacob; 70 elders; 70 sons, 70 priests, 70 in several chronological references), in order to demonstrate that the number has large symbolic significance in the LXX and in Christian tradition, whereas the number 72 is of less signifi-

---

17. For a contemporary survey of text types (or textual clusters) in New Testament textual criticism, see Epp, "Textual Clusters," 519–78.

18. Metzger ("Seventy or Seventy-Two?," 299) states that he had examined the passage in 𝔓45 "under natural and artificial light, and has assured himself that the Greek character which follows the letter omicron (standing for '70') is . . . merely the diple, or space-filler (>)," i.e., not the β with overbar (= δύο). This judgment can be confirmed by new images of 𝔓45 provided by the CSNTM (see http://www.csntm.org/manuscript/View/GA_P45). This author has notified the editors of NA[29].

19. In this connection, the evidence of Origen, which is discussed by Metzger elsewhere, is illustrative of the "stalemate" in that Origen, rather typically, supports both readings. "In his homily 7, 3 in Exod. (preserved only in Latin) he argues on the basis of the seventy palm trees that there were seventy disciples. On the other hand, in his homily 27, 11 in Num. he finds the seventy-two palms a type of Jesus' seventy-two disciples" (Metzger, "Seventy or Seventy-Two,?" 302).

20. Metzger, *Textual Commentary*, 126–27.

cance. He thinks that it is therefore surprising that the reading ἑβδομήκοντα δύο in 10:1 and 10:17 has such strong support—it is easier to see how scribes would have omitted δύο (Aland speaks of "ecclesiastical normalizing"). Aland and the Committee only discuss the symbolic significance of the numbers. Whereas the number 70 may have been more attractive for scribes, it is possible from historical (and practical) point of view that each apostle had oversight over six other disciples, i.e., the number 72 is divisible by seven.

In regard to transcriptional evidence, I would finally like to add one specific observation that relates to another textual problem in the immediate context of this verse: Just a few words later where the text reads ἐπέστειλεν αὐτοὺς ἀνὰ δύο δύο and where some MSS omit δύο, written as *beta* (β) with overbar. The presence of this figure in the same verse, perhaps written at the same place on the successive line in a papyrus exemplar, is a potential cause for adding it to the earlier figure. In my view, both external and internal evidence is evenly balanced and the two variants are of equal value for establishing the initial text. This applies to the similar variation in 10:17 as well.

10:15

A. καταβήσῃ 𝔓⁷⁵ B D 579 sy^{s.c}
B. καταβιβασθήσῃ 𝔓⁴⁵ ℵ A C K L N W Γ Δ Θ Ξ Ψ 0115 f^{1.13} 33. 565. 700. 892. 1241. 1424. 2542 𝔐 lat sy^{p.h} co

SBLGNT: B
Wasserman: B {e+i}
NASB: B
NIV: A
NRSV: B

The verb form καταβιβασθήσῃ (of καταβιβάζω) has causal force, as reflected in the NRSV, "No, *you will be brought down* to Hades" (NRSV; my italics). The reading is well attested (𝔓⁴⁵ ℵ A C L W f^{1.13} *al*) and it is plausible that scribe(s) replaced it with the more common καταβήσῃ (of καταβαίνω), "No, you will go down to Hades" (NIV). The latter reading may also be the result of harmonization to Isa 14:15 (LXX: νῦν δὲ εἰς ᾅδου καταβήσῃ), which the passage alludes to. The UBS Committee, however, prefers reading A "impressed by the superior external testimony of 𝔓⁷⁵ B D *al*)" and Metzger further points to the possibility that scribes could have provided the causal form in order to "heighten the sense of the saying."[21]

The textual problem should be treated with attention to the parallel in Matt 11:23, where one can note that the "Western" textual tradition (Codex Bezae, Old Latin MSS and the Vulgate) support καταβήσῃ in Matt 11:23, whereas Codex Bezae (both Greek and Latin columns), known for its tendency to harmonize to Synoptic parallels, here in Luke 10:15 goes against the Latin tradition which reflects καταβιβασθήσῃ.[22] Thus, it is likely that Bezae here reflects a harmonization to Matt 11:23.

On the one hand, I prefer καταβήσῃ in Matt 11:23, but, on the other hand, I prefer the more rare form καταβιβασθήσῃ here, since it has better textual support and differs from both the Synoptic parallel and Isa 14:15 (LXX)—passages which may have caused scribes to harmonize.

10:41–42

My apparatus:[23]

A. Μάρθα, Μάρθα, μεριμνᾷς καὶ (θορυβάζῃ) περὶ πολλά, ἑνὸς δέ ἐστιν χρεία· Μαριὰ(μ) δέ/γάρ 𝔓⁴⁵·⁷⁵ A C* W Θ Σ Ψ f¹³ 𝔐 aur f q vg sa sy^{c.p.h} Chr Nil Aug

B. Μάρθα, Μάρθα, μεριμνᾷς καὶ θορυβάζῃ περὶ πολλά, ὀλίγων δέ ἐστιν χρεία ἢ ἑνός· Μαριὰ(μ) γάρ 𝔓³ ℵ² [ℵ* om. χρεια] B [χρεια εστιν] C² L 070^{vid} f¹ 33 (579) (sy^{hmg}) bo eth^{pp} Or Bas Cyr Hier Cn

C. Μάρθα, Μάρθα, μεριμνᾷς καὶ τυρβάζῃ περὶ πολλά, ὀλίγων δέ ἐστιν χρεία· Μαρία δέ (formerly 38) sy^{pal} arm geo bo^{ms} eth^{TH}

D. Μάρθα, Μάρθα· Μαρία D (+ θορυβαζη) a b (d) e ff2 i l r1 Amb Poss

SBLGNT: B
Wasserman: B {e=i}
NASB: A
NIV: B
NRSV: A

---

21. Ibid., 127 (see also 25).

22. For this point on methodology, see Holmes, "Text of the Matthean Divorce Passages," 651–64.

23. The apparatus in NA²⁸ is difficult to overview and lacks Origen's attestation. My apparatus is a revised version of Gordon Fee's apparatus in "'One Thing Is Needful'?," 61–63.

There are four basic text forms in this variation-unit, which relates to Jesus' reply to Martha.[24] The shortest reading (D), attested by some few "Western" witnesses, may be the result of a haplography caused by homoeoarcton (Μαρ-).[25] Reading C has very weak textual support, so the choice is between readings A and B, both of which have strong external support. The two alternative readings are reflected in the NASB and NIV, respectively:

> But the Lord answered and said to her, "Martha, Martha, you are worried and bothered about so many things; but {only} one thing is necessary (ἑνὸς δέ ἐστιν χρεία), for Mary has chosen the good part, which shall not be taken away from her." (NASB)

> "Martha, Martha," the Lord answered, "you are worried and upset about many things, but few things are needed—or indeed only one (ὀλίγων δέ ἐστιν χρεία ἢ ἑνός). Mary has chosen what is better, and it will not be taken away from her." (NIV)

The question is which reading gave rise to the other readings in the variation-unit. The UBS Committee, which preferred the shorter reading (A), explained their view on this matter:

> Most of the other variations seem to have arisen from understanding ἑνός to refer merely to the provisions that Martha was then preparing for the meal; the absoluteness of ἑνός was softened by replacing it with ὀλίγων (preserved today only in 38 and several versions); and finally in some witnesses (including 𝔓3 ℵ B L ƒ1 33) the two were combined, though with disastrous results as to sense.[26]

In a Festschrift for Bruce M. Metzger from 1981, Gordon D. Fee published a full-scale defence of the longer reading (B).[27] His contribution was important for two reasons. First, he exposed a particular weaknesses in the above explanation: the shorter reading can hardly explain the presence of the other readings; the scenario described by Metzger of an original ἑνός ("only one thing") regarded as the *lectio difficilior*, replaced with ὀλίγων ("few things"—a softer, less categorical reading) and, eventually, conflated

---

24. Nestle-Aland 28 does not list the third reading because of its slim support, and the fourth reading is simply represented by Codex Bezae (D05), which reads Μάρθα, Μάρθα, θορυβάζῃ· Μαρία. UBS⁵ lists these readings but splits the fourth reading in two (the Greek and Latin reading of Codex Bezae is presented separately).

25. It should be noted that the "Western text" is divided between readings A and D with Codex Bezae D (05), which includes the verb θορυβάζῃ ("you are worried") stands midway.

26. Metzger, *Textual Commentary*, 153–54.

27. Fee, "'One Thing Is Needful'?," 61–75.

to ὀλίγων . . . ἢ ἑνός is unlikely because of the very weak support of reading C which Fee thought had merely survived in one late Greek miniscule (38) from the thirteenth century and a few versions. In fact, it is not even present in miniscule 38, which actually attests to the Majority text (reading 1).[28] Secondly, Fee presented the textual evidence in a comprehensive and unparalleled way, in particular the patristic evidence, which had only been partially accounted for, or even misrepresented.[29] In fact, the earliest witness to the long reading, Origen, was erroneously listed as a witness to reading 3 (ὀλίγων δέ ἐστιν χρεία) in the apparatuses of the UBS GNT editions 1–3 ("Origen ½"), which then seemed to give early significant support to the proposed scenario.[30]

Origen refers to the passage in two different contexts. First, he comments on the passage in his *Commentary on John*, albeit in an abbreviated form, which does not reflect any known reading in the Greek MSS.[31] From a methodological standpoint, this adaptation cannot be taken as support for reading C.[32] In fact, in the fourth edition of UBS GNT the mistake has been rectified, so that Origen is cited only in support of reading B.[33] Origen cites the passage more extensively in Homilies on Luke (*Homiliae in evangelium secundum Lucam*), where he interprets the paradoxical wording by referring to the ten commandments ("a few necessary things") which ultimately can be summarized in *one* single necessary commandment: to love. Origen's exposition presupposes reading B:

---

28. This error first appeared in J. J. Wettstein's 1751-edition and has continued to influence the discussion of the passage until now.

29. For example, Augsten, "Lukanische Miszelle," 581–83, and Baker, "One Thing Necessary," 127–37, discuss Origen's text without attention to the context, which results in incorrect conclusions about the text he was using (see below).

30. Cf. Dupont, "De quoi est-il besoin (Lc x.42)?," 116, "On se contente parfoise de ce critère pour écarter la seconde leçon contrastée, ὀλιγων; la prudence s'impose cependant, car elle semble ancienne (Origène), et la leçon longue [ὀλίγων δέ ἐστιν χρεία ἢ ἑνός] pourrait en dériver et donc en attester indirectement la diffusion." Augsten even regarded this as the initial reading, since she thought it had the support from Origen in the third century ("Lukanische Miszelle," 582).

31. Origen, *Fr. Jo.* 78 (GCS 10.545): καὶ οὐκ ἀπιθάνως διὰ τὴν ἐν τῷ Μωϋσέως νόμῳ πολιτείαν φήσει εἰρῆσθαι τῇ Μάρθᾳ· "Μάρθα Μάρθα, περὶ πολλὰ "θορυβῇ καὶ περισπᾶσαι, ὀλίγων δέ ἐστι χρεία"· εἰς σωτηρίαν γὰρ οὐ τῶν πολλῶν κατὰ τὸ γράμμα τοῦ νόμου ἐντολῶν χρεία, ἀλλ' ὀλίγων, ἐν οἷς κρέμαται ὅλος ὁ νόμος καὶ οἱ προφῆται, τῶν περὶ ἀγάπης νενομοθετημένων.

32. Fee, "'One Thing Is Needful,'" 65–67. Fee refers to Grant's dictum: "[P]atristic citations are not citations unless they have been adequately analyzed," pointing out that a loose citation where the debated words are missing at the beginning or end cannot be used for text-critical purposes (ibid., 67). See Grant, "Patristic Evidence," 124.

33. United Bible Societies' Greek New Testament.

Martha can also be the synagogue of circumcision, which received Jesus in his own territory, because it was engaged in worship according to the letter of the Law. But Mary is the Church of the Gentiles, which has chosen the good part, the "spiritual law," which is not to be taken from her and cannot be destroyed, like the glory upon the face of Moses. From the Law she takes the few beneficial things—or rather, she sums all of them up in one commandment: "You shall love." And, corresponding to the expression "one thing is necessary", you will understand, "you shall love your neighbor as yourself." And, to the expression, "there is need of few things", "you understand the commandments: You shall not commit adultery. You shall not murder", and what follows.[34]

It is apparent that Origen supports reading B, and yet, this early and important attestation is missing from the NA[28] apparatus. Moreover, a survey of a number of recently published commentaries of Luke, shows that the explanation of the UBS Committee has prevailed—the long reading is still regarded as a conflation of two readings which does not make any sense.[35]

What then is the possible meaning of the long reading, "but few things are necessary, or only one"? Fee followed Frédéric Godet's explanation: "few

---

34. Origen, *Fragment on Luke* 171 (trans. Joseph Lienhard; FC 94:192–93) = Origen, *Fr. Luc.* 39 (GCS 49.298): δύναται δὲ Μάρθα μὲν εἶναι καὶ ἡ ἐκ περιτομῆς συναγωγὴ εἰς τὰ ἴδια ὅρια δεξαμένη τὸν Ἰησοῦν, περισπωμένη περὶ τὴν ἐκ τοῦ γράμματος τοῦ νόμου πολλὴν λατρείαν, Μαρία δὲ ἡ ἐξ ἐθνῶν ἐκκλησία "τὴν ἀγαθὴν" τοῦ "πνευματικοῦ νόμου" "μερίδα" ἐκλεξαμένη ἀναφαίρετον καὶ μὴ "καταργουμένην" ὡς ἡ ἐπὶ τοῦ προσώπου Μωυσέως δόξα, ὀλίγα τὰ χρήσιμα ἐκ τοῦ νόμου ἐπιλέξασα ἢ πάντα ἀναφέρουσα εἰς ἓν τὸ "ἀγαπήσεις". καὶ εἰς μὲν τό· "ἕνός ἐστι χρεία" χρήσῃ τό· "ἀγαπήσεις τὸν πλησίον σου ὡς σεαυτόν", εἰς δὲ τό· "ὀλίγων ἐστὶν" "τὰς ἐντολὰς οἶδας· οὐ μοιχεύσεις· οὐ φονεύσεις" καὶ τὰ ἑξῆς. The authenticity of the Greek fragments has been discussed, i.e., whether they can be attributed to Origen. I judge them as authentic since they attest to a very similar interpretation of the passage as in Origen's *Commentary on John*.

35. See e.g., Fitzmyer, *Luke X–XXIV*, 894: "The best reading is now *henos de estin chreia* . . . One ms. (38) reads *oligōn* instead of *henos* . . . However, a number of mss . . . have combined the two readings: *oligōn de estin chreia ē henos* . . ."; Green, *Gospel of Luke*, 433n133: "This [shorter] reading is probably original, but the starkness of ἑνός has given rise to several alternative readings—especially (1) substituting ὀλίγων for ἑνός . . . and (2) conflating these two readings"; Johnson, *The Gospel of Luke*, 174: "[S]ome copyists replaced 'one' with 'a few,' and still others combined the two phrases to accomplish total confusion"; Bovon, *Luke 2*, 74: "The third textual variant [the long reading] appears to be an awkward conflation, for the 'few things' suggests the idea of material possessions, while the '(only) one thing' refers to spiritual commitment to God . . . The transformation of 'only one thing' into 'few things' in the course of the transmission of the textual tradition may be explained as a misunderstanding. Some scribes believed that Jesus was still talking about Martha's preparations." Cf. Augsten, "Lukanische Miszelle," 581: "Vermutlich aus der Kontamination von I und II enstanden."

things are necessary," that is, for the body, "or only one," that is, for the soul. This interpretation has been criticized. For example, John Nolland says that it requires "neccesary" (χρεία) to function in two quite different senses.³⁶ Fee admits that the meaning is subtle, but not intolerable and refers to its "long and worthy tradition."³⁷ This is another strength in Fee's argumentation, taking into account the history of interpretation of the passage when making the text-critical decision.

In contrast, François Bovon, in his Hermeneia commentary on Luke, first makes a textual decision in favor of reading A, while dismissing the long reading B as an "akward conflation."³⁸ Then he provides an extensive excursus on the history of interpretation where he concludes that Origen's interpretation of the passage "was to have a long and lasting success."³⁹ Probably, Bovon did not realize that Origen's influential interpretation presupposes the long reading.

In my opinion, the longer reading is the *lectio difficilior* that best explains the presence of the other readings. At some point, one or several scribes clarified the text by omitting the perplexing reference to a "few things," because ultimately only one thing is necessary and that is what Mary chose. Finally, Fee points to another detail which speaks in favor of this scenario—the variation between γάρ and δέ among manuscripts attesting to reading A (γάρ is strongly supported by $\mathfrak{P}^{3.75}$ ℵ B L Ψ f^1 892. 1241. 1424. 2542. L2211 sa bo^{pt}), which is another sign that reading A arose from reading B.⁴⁰

11:10

A. ἀνοιγήσεται $\mathfrak{P}^{45}$ ℵ C L Θ Ψ $f^{1.13}$ 33. 579. 700. 892. 1241. 2542 *pm*
B. ἀνοιχθήσεται A K W Γ Δ 565. 1424 *pm*
C. ἀνοίγεται $\mathfrak{P}^{75}$ B D

SBLGNT: A
Wasserman: A {e>i}
NASB: A
NIV: A
NRSV: A

36. Nolland, *Luke 9:21—18:34*, 600; cf. Green, *Gospel of Luke*, 433n133.
37. See esp. Csányi (who preferred the longer reading), "Optima pars," 5–78.
38. Bovon, *Luke 2*, 74.
39. Ibid., 75–77 (75).
40. This was noted by Weiss, *Die Evangelien*, 485.

All editions and translations choose to read the verb in the future indicative passive, ἀνοιγήσεται (A), "(the door) will be opened." Reading B, ἀνοιχθήσεται, is an alternative form of the same tense and indirectly supports reading A, which has superior attestation.[41] However, the verb is printed in square brackets in NA[28], ἀνοιγ[ήσ]εται, because the UBS Committee thought it was difficult to decide between the first and the third reading.[42] Three very important textual witnesses, representing the Alexandrine text (𝔓[75] B) and the "Western" (D) text, respectively, attest to reading C, ἀνοίγεται, in the present tense, "(the door) opens." The future form may represent a harmonization to the same verb in v. 9. On the other hand, the present form may be the result of harmonization to the present forms in v. 10.

It is surprising that the UBS Committee did not take into account the Synoptic parallel in Matt 7:8 where the same logion appears. Apparently, only Codex Vaticanus (B 03) attests to the present tense there (𝔓[75] and Codex Bezae are not extant), whereas Codex Koridethi (Θ 38) attests to ἀνοιχθήσεται—the intrinsic evidence speaks in favor of ἀνοιγήσεται in the Synoptic tradition as a whole. The textual problem is very difficult. Since internal criteria are ambiguous, my decision is based mainly on external criteria: The "Western" text supports the future tense with one MS as exception (Codex Bezae), which is known for its tendency to harmonize. The Alexandrian text is split (𝔓[75]-B are closely related and represent an early textual stream), whereas the Byzantine majority unequivocally supports reading A.

11:33

A. οὐδὲ ὑπὸ τὸν μόδιον ℵ A B C D K W Δ Θ Ψ f^{13} 700^c. 892. (565. 579. 1424) 𝔐 latt sy$^{(c.p).h}$; (Cl)
B. — 𝔓$^{45.75}$ L Γ Ξ 070 f^1 700*. 1241. 2542 sy^s sa

SBLGNT: A
Wasserman: B {e<i}
NASB: A
NIV: A
NRSV: B

---

41. Codices W Γ 1424 among others have the same form ἀνοιχθήσεται in the preceeding verse.
42. Metzger, *Textual Commentary*, 132.

Metzger points out that Luke apparently did not use μόδιον in the similar passage in Luke 8:16, Οὐδεὶς δὲ λύχνον ἅψας καλύπτει αὐτὸν σκεύει ἢ ὑποκάτω κλίνης τίθησιν, "No one after lighting a lamp hides it under a jar, or puts it under a bed . . ." (NRSV), and that the word here may relfect a harmonization to Matt 5:15 or Mark 4:21 which have the same phrase, ὑπὸ τὸν μόδιον. However, the UBS Committee decided to include the phrase in square brackets on the basis of strong and diversified external evidence.[43]

The only patristic evidence cited in the apparatus of NA[28] is Clement of Alexandria who says in the *Stromata*, "οὐδεὶς ἅπτει λύχνον καὶ ὑπὸ τὸν μόδιον τίθησιν," ἀλλ' ἐπὶ τῆς λυχνίας φαίνειν τοῖς τῆς ἑστιάσεως τῆς αὐτῆς κατηξιωμένοις (*Strom* 1.12.3).[44] Clement's attestation stands in parenthesis in the apparatus, and should be used with caution—it is likely that it reflects a conflation with the passage in Matt 5:15, οὐδὲ καίουσιν λύχνον καὶ τιθέασιν αὐτὸν ὑπὸ τὸν μόδιον ἀλλ' ἐπὶ τὴν λυχνίαν, καὶ λάμπει πᾶσιν τοῖς ἐν τῇ οἰκίᾳ. In fact, the only unique element from Luke is the usage of the verb ἅπτω. Origen cites the saying in a similar form that is even closer to Matthew: Οὐδεὶς λύχνον ἅψας, τίθησιν αὐτὸν ὑπὸ τὸν μόδιον, ἀλλ' ὑπὸ τὴν λυχνίαν, τοῦ φαίνειν πᾶσι τοῖς ἐν τῇ οἰκίᾳ (*Expositio in Proverbia* 1.17.189).[45] On the other hand, the catena preserves a comment by Origen where he clearly cites the passage in Luke 11:33 with the short reading, οὐδεὶς λύχνον ἅψας εἰς τὴν κρύπτην τίθησιν, ἀλλ' ἐπὶ τὴν λυχνίαν (*Fragmenta in Lucam* 1.1.186).[46]

Although, patristic evidence must be used with great caution, here it shows that several different passages were conflated and there is good reason to suspect that scribes in this passage added the phrase ὑπὸ τὸν μόδιον from Matthew 5:15.[47] Further, the shorter reading has strong support including the earliest two wittneses ($\mathfrak{P}^{45.75}$) and important versions (the Old Syriac Sinaiticus and the Sahidic Coptic). External evidence is slightly balanced in favor of the long reading, whereas internal evidence decisively supports the short reading.

13:7

A. οὖν $\mathfrak{P}^{75}$ A L Θ Ψ 070 f^{13} 33. 579. 892 lat sy[h] co

43. Ibid., 134.
44. GCS 52:9.
45. PG 17:192.
46. GCS 49:258.

47. Another passage in Origen reflects a conflation of Matthew and Mark: Οὐδεὶς λύχνον ἅψας καλύπτει αὐτὸν σκεύει, ἢ ὑποκάτω κλίνης τίθησιν, ἀλλ' ἐπὶ λυχνίας, ἵνα οἱ εἰσπορευόμενοι βλέπωσι τὸ φῶς (*Scholia in Lucam*; PG 17.333).

B. — ℵ B D K N W Γ Δ f¹ 565. 700. 1241. 1424. 2542 𝔐 e sy⁽ˢ⁾·ᶜ·ᵖ

SBLGNT: B
Wasserman: A {e<i}
NASB: B
NIV: B
NRSV: B

In the standard editions the inferential particle οὖν ("so"/"therefore") is printed in square brackets since the editors think that external evidence is balanced and internal evidence is inconclusive.[48] In this case, when the variation concerns a small word, whose presence does not affect the meaning much, it is important to take into account the recent research about scribal habits. The "shorter reading" criterion, or *lectio brevior potior*, rests on the assumption that scribes tended to add words to rather than omit words from the text. It is one of the most debated criteria and has proven to be in such need of qualification that some regard it as relatively useless, in particular for the early papyri. James Royse and others have demonstrated that the early scribes of the New Testament tended to omit rather than to add, in particular inessential words.[49] I am not surprised that all the traditional text types, including the Alexandrian text are split in this variation-unit (even 𝔓⁷⁵ and B read differently). I think a number of scribes throughout the history of transmission, deemed the particle οὖν to be superfluous. In my opinion, the transcriptional evidence in favor of its inclusion outweighs external evidence.

14:17

A. ἤδη ἕτοιμά ἐστιν B it
B. ἤδη ἕτοιμά εἰσιν 𝔓⁷⁵ ℵ*·ᶜ L Θ 579
C. ἤδη ἕτοιμά ἐστιν πάντα A (D) K N P W Γ Δ Ψ f¹·¹³ 565. 700. 892. 1241. 1424. 2542 𝔐 lat
D. ἤδη ἕτοιμά εἰσιν πάντα ℵ¹ᵛⁱᵈ

SBLGNT: A

---

48. Metzger, *Textual Commentary*, 137.

49. Royse, *Scribal Habits*, 705–36. Cf. Epp, who reformulates the criterion in order to avoid a simplistic application: [Prefer] "A variant—depending on circumstances—that is the shorter/shortest reading or that is the longer/longest reading in its variation-unit." See Epp, "Traditional 'Canons,'" 106.

Wasserman: A {e<i}
NASB: C
NIV: C
NRSV: C

The printed text in NA²⁸, ἤδη ἕτοιμά ἐστιν, follows Codex Vaticanus (B 03) and the Old Latin version (it), and translates "it is now ready." Luke frequently uses the word πάντα (over 30 times in the Gospel). On the other hand, the parallel in Matt 22:4 reading πάντα ἕτοιμά (without textual variation) may have caused later copyists to harmonize and amplify the text in Luke by adding πάντα. The amplification is all the more significant since the invitation to the banquet, "Come; for everything is ready now" (NRSV; the long reading), has soteriological implications—the meal likely represents salvation, made possible by Jesus on the cross (cf. John 19:28, ἤδη πάντα τετέλεσται). Further, readers and copyists may have heard the liturgical overtones of the passage as an implicit invitation to come to the Lord's Supper (where everything is prepared at the table).

Both of the readings A and B support an initial text without the word πάντα. Finally, there is wider support for ἐστιν than εἰσιν in Alexandrian, "Western" and Byzantine witnesses (both variants are possible from syntactical viewpoint). In my opinion, reading A best explains the rise of all other readings in the variation-unit.

15:16

A. χορτασθῆναι ἐκ 𝔓⁷⁵ ℵ B D L f¹·¹³ 579. 1241. 2542 (e f sa)
B. χορτασθῆναι ἀπό 1241
C. γεμίσαι τὴν κοιλίαν αὐτοῦ ἀπό A K N P Q Γ Δ Θ Ψ 565. 700. 892. 1424. ℓ 844. ℓ 2211 𝔐 lat sy^{p.h} bo
D. γεμίσαι τὴν κοιλίαν καὶ χορτασθῆναι ἀπό W

SBLGNT: C
Wasserman: A {e>i}
NASB: C
NIV: C
NRSV: A

The majority of text witnesses (A Ψ 𝔐 al) replace χορτασθῆναι (A), "have filled himself" (NRSV), with γεμίσαι τὴν κοιλίαν αὐτοῦ ἀπό (C), "fill his stomach" (NIV), whereas one witness Codex Washingtonianus (W 032) conflactes the two. The Nestle-Aland apparatus treats the variation between the prepositions ἐκ and ἀπό separately, although the usage is related to the choice of verb (but does not affect the translation).

Reading A has wide and superior external support, which is why the UBS Committee preferred it.[50] Further, it is congruent with Luke's style; the poor Lazarus, Luke says, "longed to satisfy his hunger with (χορτασθῆναι ἀπό) what fell from the rich man's table" (Luke 16:21). On the other hand, this passage in 16:21 may have caused scribes to harmonize and simplify the longer phrase, γεμίσαι τὴν κοιλίαν αὐτοῦ, which has no equivalent in the New Testament.[51] If this is a harmonization, however, then the preposition ἐκ is quite unexpected (only 1241 ἀπό and can be disregarded).

If reading A is the initial reading, then the colorful expression (reading C) represents a heightening paraphrase by copyist(s).[52] Ultimately, my decision in favor of reading A is based on the superior external evidence, and the presence of ἐκ, which speaks against a harmonization to the Matthean parallel.

17:24

A. ἐν τῇ ἡμέρᾳ αὐτοῦ ℵ A K L N W Γ Δ Θ Ψ $f^{1.13}$ 565. 579. 700. 892. 1241. 1424. 2542 𝔐 lat sy bo
B. — 𝔓^{75} B D it sa

SBLGNT: A
Wasserman: B {e<i}
NASB: A
NIV: A
NRSV: A

This textual problem is very difficult as reflected in NA^{28} where the phrase ἐν τῇ ἡμέρᾳ αὐτοῦ is included in square brackets. The shorter reading B has strong support in early and important witnesses representing the

---

50. "On the basis of age and diversity of text-type of witnesses, the committee preferred the reading χορτασθῆναι ἐκ" (Metzger, *Textual Commentary*, 139).

51. So Grundmann, *Lukas*, 312n23, who thinks that scribes corrected the strong, almost crude expression.

52. Cf. Westcott and Hort, "Notes on Select Readings," 2:62: "But the Western reading may as easily be a paraphrastic exposition of the supposed meaning of χορτασθῆναι. It misses the true point however, for the Prodigal Son could easily fill his 'belly' with the 'husks,' though he could not 'be satisfied' with them. The documentary evidence here is in any case decisive" [in favor of χορτασθῆναι].

Alexandrian and "Western" text types, which apparently impressed the UBS Committee, whereas the longer reading A is also widely attested by representatives of all the major textual clusters.[53] Internal evidence is ambiguous too: The shorter reading may reflect a haplography due to homoioteleuton (-ου).

Alternatively, it may represent a harmonization to Matt 24:27. However, none of the attesting Greek MSS have added παρουσία from the parallel in Matthew,[54] and 𝔓⁷⁵ and B are not known for harmonistic tendencies (as opposed to D). On the other hand, the longer reading may be influenced by the way Jesus introduces the saying, "The days are coming when you will long to see *one of the days of the Son of Man*, and you will not see it" (NRSV; my italics).

Whereas external evidence is rather balanced, I prefer the shorter reading because it is the *lectio difficilior*—if original it would have left a gap for scribes to provide an adverbial phrase of time correlating to v. 22, "one of the days of the Son of Man."

18:11

A. πρὸς ἑαυτὸν ταῦτα προσηύχετο A K N Q W Γ Δ f^{13} 565. 700. 1424 𝔐 syʰ
B. ταῦτα πρὸς ἑαυτὸν (αυτον L) προσηύχετο 𝔓⁷⁵ ℵ² B L T Θ Ψ f^1 579. 892. 1241. ℓ 844ᶜ lat
C. ταῦτα προσηύχετο ℵ* ℓ 844* (it) sa
D. καθ' ἑαυτὸν ταῦτα προσηύχετο D 2542

SBLGNT: A
Wasserman: A {e<i}
NASB: B
NIV: A
NRSV: A

The main question here is whether the prepositional phrase πρὸς ἑαυτόν (/καθ' ἑαυτόν) goes with the participle σταθείς as in reading A (cf. NIV: "The Pharisee stood by himself and prayed"), or with the main verb προσηύχετο (prayed) as in reading B (cf. NASB: "The Pharisee stood and was praying this to himself").

---

53. Metzger, *Textual Commentary*, 142.
54. Some versional and patristic witnesses reflect harmonization to the Matthean reading, οὕτως ἔσται ἡ παρουσία τοῦ υἱοῦ τοῦ ἀνθρώπου (see UBS⁵).

Reading D supports reading A indirectly. Reading C may be the result of a haplography due to homoioarchton arising from reading B (ΠΡΟΣΕΑΥΤΟΝ . . . ΠΡΟΣΗΥΧΕΤΟ). The UBS Committee, however, thinks that scribe omitted the phrase altogether because of the "difficulty of construing πρὸς ἑαυτόν (especially when the words stood next to σταθείς)."[55] Indeed, reading A is the more difficult reading, which led some scribes to replace substitute the more natural καθ' ἑαυτόν (by himself).

External evidence is rather evenly balanced, since reading D supports reading A and C is ambiguous. Internal criteria, on the other hand, speak decisively in favor of reading A, which is the *lectio difficilior*.

18:24

A. περίλυπον γενόμενον A (D) K N P W Γ Δ Θ Ψ 078 *f*[13] 33[vid]. 565. 700. 892. 1424 𝔐 latt sy

B. — ℵ B L *f*[1] 579. 1241. 2542 co

SBLGNT: B
Wasserman: B {e=i}
NASB: B
NIV: B
NRSV: B

The words περίλυπον γενόμενον, ([seeing] that he had become sad), is printed in square brackets in NA[28]/UBS[5], which reflects the difficulty. A number of important MSS omit the words. Possibly some scribes misunderstood the phrase as referring to Jesus himself (cf. ESV, "Jesus, looking at him with sadness")—an interpretation which actually requires the nominative case, περίλυπος γενόμενος. Perhaps the need to avoid such a misunderstanding resulted in the unique word order in Codex Bezae (D 05): αὐτὸν περίλυπον γενόμενον εἶπεν ὁ Ἰησοῦς.

On the other hand, the phrase may have been added under influence of the expression in the previous verse, περίλυπος ἐγενήθη, "he became sad." Metzger points out that this argument is ambiguous since Luke is fond of repeating a word or phrase in this way.[56] Possibly, the shorter reading Ἰδὼν δὲ αὐτὸν ὁ Ἰησοῦς, "Jesus looked at him and said" (NRSV) may have led a scribe to repeat the man's reaction from v. 23, in order to clarify more specifically

---

55. Metzger, *Textual Commentary*, 143.
56. Ibid.

what it was that made Jesus say, "How hard it is for those who have wealth to enter the kingdom of God!" (NRSV).

In sum, I prefer the shorter reading without the participle phrase, because it has slightly better external and internal attestation.

Table 1. Comparison between NA[28], SBLGNT, Wasserman, NASB, NIV, and NRSV.

NA[28] (always reading A)	SBLGNT	Wasserman	NASB	NIV	NRSV
9:62a εἶπεν δὲ [πρὸς αὐτὸν] ὁ Ἰησοῦς	εἶπεν δὲ ὁ Ἰησοῦς (reading D)	εἶπεν δὲ ὁ Ἰησοῦς (reading D) {e<i}	But Jesus said to him (reading A/B/C)	Jesus replied (reading D)	Jesus said to him (reading A/B/C)
9:62b οὐδεὶς ἐπιβαλὼν τὴν χεῖρα ἐπ' ἄροτρον καὶ βλέπων εἰς τὰ ὀπίσω	οὐδεὶς ἐπιβαλὼν τὴν χεῖρα ἐπ' ἄροτρον καὶ βλέπων εἰς τὰ ὀπίσω (reading A)	οὐδεὶς ἐπιβαλὼν τὴν χεῖρα αὐτοῦ ἐπ' ἄροτρον καὶ βλέπων εἰς τὰ ὀπίσω (reading B) {e+i}	No one, after putting his hand to the plow and looking back, is fit for the kingdom of God. (reading B)	No one who puts a hand to the plow and looks back is fit for service in the kingdom of God. (reading A)	No one who puts a hand to the plow and looks back is fit for the kingdom of God. (reading A)
10:1 ἑβδομήκοντα [δύο]	ἑβδομήκοντα δύο (reading A)	ἑβδομήκοντα / ἑβδομήκοντα δύο (reading A/B) {e=i}	seventy (reading B)	seventy-two (reading A)	seventy (reading B)
10:15 καταβήσῃ	καταβιβασθήσῃ (reading B)	καταβιβασθήσῃ (reading B) {e+i}	You will be brought down (reading B)	you will go down (reading A)	you will be brought down (reading B)
10:41–42 Μάρθα Μάρθα, μεριμνᾷς καὶ θορυβάζῃ περὶ πολλά, ἑνὸς δέ ἐστιν χρεία	Μάρθα, Μάρθα, μεριμνᾷς καὶ θορυβάζῃ περὶ πολλά, ὀλίγων δέ ἐστιν χρεία ἢ ἑνός (reading B)	Μάρθα Μάρθα, μεριμνᾷς καὶ θορυβάζῃ περὶ πολλά, ὀλίγων δέ ἐστι χρεία ἢ ἑνός (läsart B) {e=i}	you are worried and bothered about so many things; but {only} one thing is necessary (reading A)	you are worried and upset about many things, but few things are needed—or indeed only one (reading B)	you are worried and distracted by many things; there is need of only one thing (reading A)

11:10 ἀνοιγ[ήσ]εται	ἀνοιγήσεται (reading A)	ἀνοιγήσεται (reading A) {e=i}	it will be opened (reading A)	the door will be opened (reading A)	the door will be opened (reading A)	
11:33 εἰς κρύπτην τίθησιν [οὐδὲ ὑπὸ τὸν μόδιον]	εἰς κρύπτην τίθησιν οὐδὲ ὑπὸ τὸν μόδιον (reading A)	εἰς κρύπτην τίθησιν (reading B) {e<i}	in a cellar nor under a basket (reading A)	in a place where it will be hidden, or under a bowl (reading A)	in a cellar (reading B)	
13:7 ἔκκοψον [οὖν]	ἔκκοψον (reading B)	ἔκκοψον οὖν (reading A) {e<i}	Cut it down! (reading B)	Cut it down! (reading B)	Cut it down! (reading B)	
14:17 ὅτι ἤδη ἕτοιμά ἐστιν	ὅτι ἤδη ἕτοιμά ἐστιν (reading A)	ὅτι ἤδη ἕτοιμά ἐστιν (reading A) {e<i}	Come; for everything is ready now. (reading C)	Come, for everything is now ready. (reading C)	Come; for everything is ready now. (reading C)	
15:16 χορτασθῆναι ἐκ	γεμίσαι τὴν κοιλίαν αὐτοῦ ἀπό (reading C)	χορτασθῆναι ἐκ (reading A) {e>i}	filled his stomach with (reading C)	to fill his stomach with (reading C)	have filled himself with (reading A)	
17:24 οὕτως ἔσται ὁ υἱὸς τοῦ ἀνθρώπου [ἐν τῇ ἡμέρᾳ αὐτοῦ]	οὕτως ἔσται ὁ υἱὸς τοῦ ἀνθρώπου ἐν τῇ ἡμέρᾳ αὐτοῦ (reading A)	οὕτως ἔσται ὁ υἱὸς τοῦ ἀνθρώπου (reading B) {e<i}	so will the Son of Man be in His day (reading A)	For the Son of Man in his day will be like (reading A)	so will the Son of Man be in his day (reading A)	
18:11 ὁ Φαρισαῖος σταθεὶς πρὸς ἑαυτὸν ταῦτα προσηύχετο·	ὁ Φαρισαῖος σταθεὶς πρὸς ἑαυτὸν ταῦτα προσηύχετο· (reading A)	ὁ Φαρισαῖος σταθεὶς πρὸς ἑαυτὸν ταῦτα προσηύχετο· (reading A) {e<i}	The Pharisee stood and was praying this to himself: (reading B)	The Pharisee stood by himself and prayed: (reading A)	The Pharisee, standing by himself, was praying thus (reading A)	
18:24 ἰδὼν δὲ αὐτὸν ὁ Ἰησοῦς [περίλυπον γενόμενον]	Ἰδὼν δὲ αὐτὸν ὁ Ἰησοῦς (reading B)	Ἰδὼν δὲ αὐτὸν ὁ Ἰησοῦς (reading B) {e=i}	And Jesus looked at him and said (reading B)	Jesus looked at him and said (reading B)	Jesus looked at him and said (reading B)	

CONCLUSION

In 2014, the Swedish Bible Society took the first steps towards a new Swedish translation of the New Testament by commissioning a trial translation of two New Testament texts, the Lucan Travel Narrative (Luke 9:51—19:46) and Paul's Letter to the Galatians. This article presents parts of the result of my text-critical work as a consultant for the new translation. It includes a selection of thirteen textual problems in Luke (9:62 [x2]; 10:1, 15, 41–42; 11:10, 33; 13:7; 14:17; 15:16; 17:24; 18:11, 24), where in most cases there is some variation between the critical texts of NA[28], SBLGNT, Wasserman, or any of the three major Bible translations (NASB, NIV, NRSV).

The treatment of each passage includes an apparatus and a textual commentary the new translation, a suggested footnote for the general readership, a critical apparatus, and a textual commentary. I have applied reasoned ecclecticism taking into account both external and internal evidence. My text-critical decisions are reflected in a rating given to each passage providing the reader with my overall evaluation of the balance of external and internal evidence. In one case, where the evidence is balanced between two readings, I have left the decision open (Luke 10:1). In an extended discussion of Luke 10:41–42 I have proposed a Greek text as reflected in the NIV, where Jesus replies to Martha, "You are worried and upset about many things, but few things are needed—or indeed only one. Mary has chosen what is better, and it will not be taken away from her."

A table of comparison (Table 1) displays the thirteen passages in the various critical texts and versions. The table shows that my text (Wasserman) deviates from NA[28] in 7/12 passages. Further, my text is closest to the SBLGNT (7/12; with four common deviations from the NA[28]).[57] The SBLGNT in turn agrees very often with the NIV in this particular selection (11/13). The NIV is the translation closest to NA[28] (7/13). Only in one case, in Luke 11:10, all the included critical texts and translations agree with NA[28] in preferring the reading ἀνοιγήσεται (however, the verbform is printed in square brackets). In one other variation-unit, all deviate from NA[28] by omitting περίλυπον γενόμενον in Luke 18:24 (which is printed in square brackets).

BIBLIOGRAPHY

Aland, Kurt, et al., eds. *Novum Testamentum Graece*. 28th rev. ed. Stuttgart: Deutsche Bibelgesellschaft, 2012.

Augsten, Monika. "Lukanische Miszelle." *New Testament Studies* 14 (1967-1968) 581–83.

Baker, A. "One Thing Necessary." *Catholic Biblical Quarterly* 27 (1965) 127–37.

Birdsall, J. Neville. "The Recent History of New Testament Textual Criticism (from Westcott and Hort, 1881, to the present)." *ANRW* II.26.1:99–197. Edited by H. Temporini and W. Haase. Berlin: de Gruyter, 1992.

---

57. One passage is left undecided (Luke 10:1).

Black, David Alan. *Rethinking New Testament Textual Criticism*. Grand Rapids: Baker, 2002.
Bovon, François. *Luke 2: A Commentary on the Gospel of Luke 9:51—19:27*. Hermeneia. Minneapolis: Fortress, 2013.
Clement of Alexandria. *Stromata*. Edited by Otto Stählin et al. GCS 52 (Buch I–VI). Berlin: Akademie, 1985.
Csányi, Daniel A. "Optima pars: Auslegungsgeschichte von Lk 10,38-42 bei den Kirchenvätern der ersten vier Jahrhunderte." *Studia monastica* 2 (1960) 5–78.
Dupont, Jacques. "De quoi est-il besoin (Lc x.42)?." In *Text and Interpretation: Studies in the New Testament Presented to Matthew Black*, edited by E. Best and R. M. Wilson, 115–20. Cambridge: Cambridge University Press, 1979.
Ehrman, Bart D., and Michael W. Holmes, eds. *The Text of the New Testament in Contemporary Research. Essays on the Status Questionis*. 2nd ed. NTTSD 46. Leiden: Brill, 2013.
Elliott, J. K. "Thoroughgoing Eclecticism in New Testament Textual Criticism." In *The Text of the New Testament in Contemporary Research: Essays on the Status Questionis*, edited by Bart D. Ehrman and Michael W. Holmes, 745–70. 2nd ed. NTTSD 46. Leiden: Brill, 2013.
Epp, Eldon J. "Textual Clusters: Their Past and Future in New Testament Textual Criticism." In *The Text of the New Testament in Contemporary Research: Essays on the Status Questionis*, edited by Bart D. Ehrman and Michael W. Holmes, 519–78. 2nd ed. NTTSD 46. Leiden: Brill, 2013.
———. "Traditional 'Canons' of New Testament Textual Criticism: Their Value, Validity, and Viability—or Lack Thereof." In *The Textual History of the Greek New Testament: Changing Views in Contemporary Research*, edited by Klaus Wachtel and Michael W. Holmes, 79–128. Atlanta: Society of Biblical Literature, 2011.
Fee, Gordon D. "'One Thing Is Needful'? Luke 10:42." In *New Testament Textual Criticism: Its Significance for Exegesis: Essays in Honour of Bruce M. Metzger*, edited by Eldon J. Epp and Gordon Fee, 61–75. Oxford: Clarendon, 1981.
Fitzmyer, Joseph A. *The Gospel According to Luke X-XXIV*. AB 28A. New York: Doubleday, 1985.
Goodrich, Richard J., and Albert L. Lukaszewski. *A Reader's Greek New Testament*. Grand Rapids: Zondervan, 2003.
Grant, R. M. "The Citation of Patristic Evidence in an Apparatus Criticus." In *New Testament Manuscript Studies: The Materials and the Making of a Critical Apparaus*, edited by M. M. Parvis and A. P. Wikgren, 117–24. Chicago: University of Chicago Press, 1950.
Green, Joel B. *The Gospel of Luke*. NICNT. Grand Rapids: Eerdmans, 1997.
Grundmann, Walter. *Das Evangelium nach Lukas*. THKNT 3. 4th ed. Berlin: Evangelische Verlagsanstalt, 1966.
Holmes, Michael W., ed. *The Greek New Testament: SBL Edition*. Atlanta: Society of Biblical Literature; Bellingham, WA: Logos Bible Software, 2010.
———. "Reasoned Eclecticism in New Testament Textual Criticism." In *The Text of the New Testament in Contemporary Research: Essays on the Status Questionis*, edited by Bart D. Ehrman and Michael W. Holmes, 771–802. 2nd ed. NTTSD 46. Leiden: Brill, 2013.

———. "The SBL Greek New Testament. Papers from the 2011 SBL Panel Review Session." *TC: A Journal of Biblical Textual Criticism* 17 (2012) 6–7. http://purl.org/TC.

———. "The Text of the Matthean Divorce Passages: A Comment on the Appeal to Harmonization in Textual Decisions." *JBL* 109/4 (1990) 651–64.

Images of 𝔓⁴⁵. Centre for the Study of New Testament Manuscripts. http://www.csntm.org/manuscript/View/GA_P45.

Johnson, Luke Timothy. *The Gospel of Luke*. Sacra Pagina 3. Collegeville, MN: Liturgical, 1991.

Metzger, Bruce M. "Seventy or Seventy-Two Disciples?" *NTS* 5 (1959) 299–306.

———. *A Textual Commentary on the Greek New Testament*. Corr. ed. London: United Bible Societies, 1975.

———. *A Textual Commentary on the Greek New Testament*. 2nd ed. Stuttgart: Deutsche Bibelgesellschaft, 1994.

———. "The Westcott and Hort Greek New Testament—Yesterday and Today." *The Cambridge Review* 103 (1981) 71–76.

NASB (preface). http://www.lockman.org/nasb/nasbprin.php.

Nolland, John. *Luke 9:21—18:34*. WBC 35b; Nashville: Thomas Nelson, 1993.

Nya Testamentet. Bibelkommissionens utgåva 1981. Stockholm: Swedish Bible Society, 1981.

Origen. *Expositio in Proverbia*, edited by J.-P. Migne. Patrologia cursus completus. Series graeca 17:161–252. Paris, 1857.

———. *Fragmenta in evangelium Johannis*. Edited by Erwin Preuschen. GCS 10. Leipzig: Hinrichs, 1903.

———. *Fragmenta in Lucam*. Edited by Max Rauer. 2nd ed. GCS 49. Berlin: Akademie, 1959.

———. *Homilies on Luke*. Translated by Joseph T. Lienhard. FC 94. Washington, D.C.: Catholic University of America Press, 1996.

———. *Scholia in Lucam*. Edited by J.-P. Migne. Patrologia cursus completus. Series graeca 17:312–69.. Paris, 1857.

Robinson, Maurice A. "New Testament Textual Criticism: The Case for Byzantine Priority." *TC: A Journal of Biblical Textual Criticism* 6 (2001) pars. 1–113. http://purl.org/TC.

Royse, James R. *Scribal Habits in Early Greek New Testament Papyri*. NTTSD 36. Leiden: Brill, 2008.

United Bible Societies' Greek New Testament. Edited by Barbara Aland et al. 4th rev. ed. Stuttgart: Deutsche Bibelgesellschaft/United Bible Societies, 2001.

Wasserman, Tommy. "Criteria for Evaluating Readings in New Testament Textual Criticism." In *The Text of the New Testament in Contemporary Research: Essays on the Status Questionis*, edited by Bart D. Ehrman and Michael W. Holmes, 579–612. 2nd ed. NTTSD 46. Leiden: Brill, 2013.

———. *The Epistle of Jude: Its Text and Transmission*. CBNTS 43. Stockholm: Almqvist & Wiksell, 2006.

———. "A Short Textual Commentary on Galatians." In *Studies on the Text of the New Testament and Early Christianity: Essays in Honor of Michael W. Holmes*, edited by Daniel M. Gurtner et al., 345–71. NTTSD 50. Leiden: Brill, 2015.

Weiss, Bernhard, *Die Evangelien des Markus und Lukas*. KEK 1. 9th ed. Göttingen: Vandenhoeck & Ruprecht, 1901.

Westcott, B. F., and F. J. A. Hort. *The New Testament in the Original Greek*. 2 vols. London: Macmillan, 1881–1882.

Zuntz, Günther. *The Text of the Epistles: A Disquisition upon the Corpus Paulinum*. The Schweich Lectures of the British Academy, 1946. Oxford: The British Academy, 1953.

6

"It's All About Variants"—Unless "No Longer Written"[1]

Maurice Robinson
Southeastern Baptist Theological Seminary

> "It's amazing how many textual critics can carry on a discussion of a variant unit in total ignorance of how the mass of manuscripts read. And why? Because it's not mentioned in their trusted apparatus."[2]

INTRODUCTION

ALTHOUGH A SMALL-FORMAT EDITION (*Handausgabe*) of the Greek New Testament is a valuable commodity for utilization by the exegetical and translational researcher, it is also well-known that the particular format of such editions restricts the quantity of textual variation that might otherwise be presented in more extensive apparatuses, such as those of Tischendorf,

---

1. This title intentionally invokes those utilized by Epp, "It's All About Variants," 275–308, and Wettlaufer, *No Longer Written*.

2. Daniel Buck, post on a NT Textual Criticism discussion list, April 9, 2015 <www.facebook.com/groups/302249746528699/>.

von Soden, or the currently progressing *Editio Critica Maior* (ECM) of the Greek New Testament.³

The commonly used UBS Greek New Testament,⁴ for example, claims to limit its citation of textual variants to those considered "significant for translators," therefore including only approximately 1500 variant units. In contrast, the other prevailing edition in general use—particularly for text-critical, exegetical, and hermeneutical purposes—is the Nestle-Aland *Novum Testamentum Graece* (NA$^{27/28}$, cited as NA when distinction is unnecessary) which by its own admission is *not* to be considered a "final" authoritative form of the text, but only a "working edition," from which other researchers are free to depart on the basis of the variant readings cited in its more extensive apparatus.⁵ As stated in the NA^{27} "Introduction":

> The 27th edition . . . intends to provide the user with a well-founded working text together with the means of verifying it or alternatively of correcting it. Correspondingly, the edition contains all the variants necessary for this purpose in as complete a form as possible within its limitations. The variants included are important either for their content or for their historical significance. The user can also gain an accurate impression of the amount of variation in the New Testament textual tradition, as well as of the general character of these variants, and of the motives and origins they reflect.⁶

---

3. Tischendorf, *Novum Testamentum Graece*; von Soden, *Die Schriften des Neuen Testaments* (vol. 2, *Text und Apparat*); Aland et al., *Novum Testamentum Graecum: Editio Critica Maior, IV, Die Katholischen Briefe*: 1, Der Jakobusbrief; 2, Die Petrusbriefe; 3, Der Erste Johannesbrief; 4, Der Zweite und Dritte Johannesbrief; Der Judasbrief (Stuttgart: Deutsche Bibelgesellschaft, 1997–2005).

4. Aland et al. (eds.), *Greek New Testament*.

5. Aland et al. (eds.), *Nestle-Aland Novum Testamentum Graece*. The main text of the UBS and Nestle-Aland volumes remains identical according to their corresponding editions (UBS$^{4/5}$ = NA$^{27/28}$). Aside from minor variations in punctuation and diacriticals, the primary difference between the two editions is the level of variant citation in their respective apparatuses.

6. Aland and Aland, "Introduction," NA^{27}, 45*–46*. For text-critical study, the apparatus of the NA^{27} remains superior to that found in NA^{28}, due to a more specific citation of support by minority groups categorized as either *pc* (*pauci* = few) or *al* (*alii* = some); such designations have been eliminated in the NA^{28} edition, as noted in its "Introduction," xiii: "The notes *pauci (pc)* and *alii (al)* indicating that, apart from the witnesses cited explicitly, there are a few or more additional witnesses for a variant, have been abandoned" on the presumption that "these notes could easily lead to a mistaken conclusion that apparatus entries without *pc* or *al* were exclusively supported by the witnesses cited" and that possibly "full collation of all the manuscripts would yield more witnesses for known variants" (of course, how such *actually* would impact the *pc* or *al* designations remains puzzling).

A sticker affixed to a copy of the NA[27] reads, "The Nestle-Aland Greek New Testament with Complete Apparatus. 'The Standard in Greek Textual Study'"—yet one has to wonder how "complete" the apparatus actually might be, especially in view of the clear qualification in the same volume:

> No manual edition of the Greek New Testament can offer the full spectrum of textual variants or cite all the witnesses significant for the history of the text . . . A manual edition is therefore of limited usefulness for specialized studies of the history of the text or of individual manuscripts. The present edition provides the reader primarily with the basis for studying the text and evaluating the most important variants.[7]

A major problem that tends to slip by unnoticed is that those who use either the NA or UBS edition are often convinced that *only* the variants appearing in the respective apparatuses of those editions are of any real significance for exegesis, translation, or interpretation, and that any alternative variants legitimately can be ignored for most purposes. Thus, readers easily can be misled to presume that all major translatable variants representing the three major text types (Alexandrian, Western, Byzantine) are cited in its apparatus, while the actual situation is tellingly different, as Michael Holmes has noted:

> The standard text [NA/UBS] is viewed by some of those who use it as a "final" text to be passively accepted rather than a "working" text subject to verification and improvement . . . The exegetical habits of some scholars and students seem to reflect a belief that all the important text-critical work has already been completed, that one can more or less equate the standard Greek New Testament with the "original" text. With a mindset such as this, it is not surprising that entire commentaries have been written that simply take the standard text as printed and scarcely discuss textual matters.[8]

The same concern is expressed by Bill Warren:

> Most scholars are too quickly assuming the United Bible Societies (UBS) *Greek New Testament* (GNT) or the Nestle-Aland (NA) *Novum Testamentum* text as being solid without addressing the

---

7. Aland and Aland, "Introduction," 50*. A similar statement appears in NA[28], "Introduction," xix: "A hand edition like the Nestle-Aland cannot comprehensively document the textual history of the Greek New Testament and list all significant witnesses with all their variants . . . The present edition provides the reader primarily with the basis for studying the text and evaluating the most important variants."

8. Holmes, *Greek New Testament*, vii–viii.

questions being debated in the text-critical field . . . Certain NT texts warrant deeper text-critical analyses in order to ascertain the importance of the various textual readings for the overall meaning of the passage.[9]

The current state of affairs is further illustrated by John Piper's early anecdotal experience that even today remains reflective of current scholarly opinion:[10]

> When I was doing my doctoral studies in Germany . . . I decided to present my first paper on . . . text-critical issues . . . Dr. Goppelt thanked me for the work I had done and then said as gently as he could, "Mr. Piper . . . this will not be necessary for the rest of the texts you deal with. You may simply take your starting point from the established critical edition of the Greek text. We are assured that the text-critics have provided us with a reliable text." That was, and is, the general view of mainline biblical scholarship. It is not a uniquely conservative or evangelical view.[11]

Although those utilizing the Nestle-Aland editions may be aware of its stated limitations and relative deficiency in variant unit citation, they often remain peculiarly unaware that numerous significant and even translatable variant readings are skirted by without notice—particularly readings characteristic of the Byzantine Textform.[12] As a result, the readers become convinced that all one really needs to know about textual variation, significant or otherwise, is contained in the more extensive apparatus of the Nestle-Aland edition. As a result, the overall perception is exactly what Epp described as supposedly "evident" to most people:

> In the final analysis, variants not selected for the critical text of the Nestle-Aland and the United Bible Societies' Greek New Testaments (that is, are not part of the original text) have little further, independent worth . . . Indeed, whenever a critical text

---

9. Warren, "Remembered Jesus," 164.

10. A prospective doctoral student in Austria recently had his text-critical dissertation proposal rejected, on one count because he suggested that a theoretical alternative to the current critical text might be preferable (the present writer was in attendance at the student's committee hearing).

11. Piper, *Peculiar Glory*, 80. Piper himself accepts the "mainline" position as described.

12. In fact, the *SQE*—published under the same editorial auspices as the UBS and NA editions—offers even more variant unit data for the Gospels than otherwise is available in the UBS$^{4/5}$ or NA$^{27/28}$ editions. Aland and Aland, *Synopsis Quattuor Evangeliorum*.

> is identified with "the original text" the variants to that text are by nature *rejected readings* and therefore distinctly of second-class status.[13]

Such an opinion, of course, strays far from the truth.

Years ago, Ernest C. Colwell addressed this issue, noting that even though "all critical apparatuses suffer some limitation . . . the minimum intention must be to enable the user to evaluate the variant readings."[14] His primary theme was that the restricted citation of variants and their witnesses actually *obscures* the history of the development of the text—regardless of what textual theory might be followed or advocated.[15] Yet as Colwell particularly noted, "Without a knowledge of groups, the history of the text cannot be illuminated. Without a knowledge of the history of the text the original reading cannot be established."[16] As a result, "these editions . . . do not make it possible for the reader to use the 'external evidence of manuscripts' in judging variant readings . . . The number of variations cited is too limited to permit a sound appraisal of manuscript evidence."[17] It is precisely this that has become the locus of current misapprehension regarding the presumed sufficiency of the major apparatus in current use, the Nestle-Aland in its various editions. In actuality, numerous variants found within the MSS representing the Byzantine form of the text are summarily excluded without mention, this in part leading to Eldon J. Epp's lament that

> [t]extual variants . . . not only deserve a position of greater respect, but also of more immediate access and visibility. Such enhanced visibility would insure that the narrative quality of variants would be recognized more readily and would provide insightful occasions for enriching our understanding . . . Readers need to be confronted by these variants, not protected from them.[18]

---

13. Epp, "It's All About Variants," 286, 290.

14. Colwell, "Greek New Testament," 31, 36. Although Colwell wrote regarding NA^{25} (1963–1978), his statements apply equally to the later editions of NA^{26} (1979–1992), NA^{27} (1993–2007), and NA^{28} (2012–present).

15. Ibid., 35–36, specifically notes that "The disproportionate frequency with which such mss. as W, P66 and P75 are cited misrepresents their status in relation to other witnesses which are more frugally cited" and that such "listing . . . cannot help but mislead the student."

16. Ibid., 37.

17. Ibid., 37, 40.

18. Epp, "It's All About Variants," 307.

Nevertheless, it appears clear that various biblical scholars, students, exegetes, and translators—whose tasks necessarily involve variant readings—are concerned primarily with the readings of the Alexandrian, Western, and Caesarean MSS, and not with all significant or translatable Byzantine readings that vary from the NA editorial preferences or apparatus decisions.[19]

Whatever might have been the NA criteria for selection of apparatus units — and Rosario Pierri observes that in some cases "the criteria . . . are unclear or not altogether coherent"[20]—there is really no good reason to include a number of nearly meaningless variants such as the presence or absence of the definite article found among favored witnesses while totally ignoring many far more significant and meaningful variants that happen to have a Byzantine connection. As Günther Zuntz stated over 80 years ago,

> We must know the hay before we can pick out the gold . . . The reconstruction of the Byzantine text is a necessary preliminary to the production of a thesaurus exhibiting, within surveyable limits, the whole material for the criticism of the New Testament . . . *In an apparatus based on a "neutral" text the Byzantine readings would have to be included* . . . In the future, as in the past, scholars advancing new textual theories will support them by an appropriate selection of the evidence. But *the repertory from which the student draws his information should remain intact* . . . Such a thesaurus . . . would never become obsolete . . . The critic of the future would at last be provided with an instrument supplying the complete data for his work without prejudicing its results.[21]

Even when "manuscripts must be weighed rather than counted"—a frequently repeated maxim that is applicable to a certain degree[22]—it appears quite illegitimate to exclude meaningful variants merely because they occur

---

19. As stated by Komoszewski et al., *Reinventing Jesus*, 295 n. 39, "A good guide on the more meaningful and viable variants in the New Testament is the textual apparatus of the Nestle-Aland, *Novum Testamentum Graece*, 27th ed. . . . This is the standard Greek New Testament used today."

20. Pierri, "Codex B e Nestle-Aland XXVIII," 183–196; an English summary is found in *New Testament Abstracts* 58 (2014) 481, entry 1507. Pierri specifically "identifies a series of readings that are not noted in the critical apparatus of NA^{28}."

21. Zuntz, "Byzantine Text," 27–30; emphasis added.

22. Wettlaufer, *No Longer Written*, 18: "The single most important principle of modern textual criticism is that manuscripts must be weighed not counted"; restated at 33, 117. The same principle is repeatedly stated in numerous sources, e.g., Aland and Aland, *Text of the New Testament*, 280; Metzger, *Textual Commentary*, 12*; Clarke, *Textual Optimism*, 37, 44, 51, 162, 174; Wegner, *Textual Criticism*, 132, 212, 240, 248; Holmes, "Reconstructing the Text," 83–84; Mounce, *Greek for the Rest of Us*, 266.

in a particular texttype, whether numerically dominant or not. Over a century ago, J. J. Lias rightly observed, "The weight of the MSS. simply depends upon the fact that they are the representatives of a tradition very much older than themselves."[23] If so, translatable variants that are clearly representative of a particular transmissional tradition indeed *should* be included in any *apparatus criticus* intended to serve the needs of scholars, exegetes, and translators.

PASSAGES IN THE TEXT OR APPARATUS

> "A critical apparatus is a critically important tool for any serious student of the Bible."[24]

Almost all who utilize the Greek New Testament for exegetical purposes recognize that the main text of a critical edition should not be accepted blindly as representing a definitive form of the autographs. Such at best might represent a reasonable approximation to the original text, with further fine-tuning dependent on the testimony of various other witnesses: documents, versional readings, patristic quotations, manuscript families, and text types in general.[25] To facilitate the textual evaluation, witnesses that differ from (and often transcend) the published main text generally are cited in the apparatus of a particular critical edition. As noted online by Logos Bible Software:

> The apparatus ... does a few things: 1. Points out that there is, in fact, a variant. 2. Gives a history of significant textual witnesses on all sides, with information on the dates of the textual witnesses involved. 3. Allows the reader to weigh this evidence and make a decision ... A commentary may pick and choose among the stuff the writer finds most interesting, or, perhaps, more germane to prove a particular point. Having access to the apparatus lets the user dig into this detail independently.[26]

The primary misperception facing the student or researcher is the presumption that the commonly utilized NA apparatus is sufficient for all text-critical

---

23. Lias, *Biblical Criticism*, 160.

24. www.accordancebible.com/buzz/articles/critapp.php.

25. One must remember that approximately 94 percent of the entire text in the various Greek NT editions is considered to reflect the autographs accurately, regardless of the many variations scattered throughout the otherwise accepted preponderance of text.

26. Logos Bible Software, "Critical Apparatuses: What and Why," www.logos.com/products/info/apparatuses.

purposes, and thus everything one needs to know regarding text and variation for establishing the New Testament text is available therein.[27] Such a perception is directly promulgated by the German Bible Society (publishers of the NA) at their online "Scholarly Bible Portal":

> With its extensive, differentiated apparatus, above all the Novum Testamentum Graece by Nestle-Aland enables its readers to reach their own judgments in matters of New Testament textual research.[28]

Thus the all-too-common misperception that, regardless of textual theory, the original text can be established from the data presented either in the NA main text or its apparatus. Craig Blomberg and Jennifer Foutz Markley present a typical misinterpretation of the issue:

> Interpreting the [Nestle-Aland] text-critical apparatus has given us the necessary [!] external evidence to begin making a decision on . . . variant reading[s] . . . Even if the text established by the preferred readings of the critical editions of the Greek New Testament or chosen by the translator or exegete does not always perfectly represent the originals, *the odds are exceedingly high that the original reading is represented among the textual variants.* The person trained in textual criticism is therefore at least aware of the original reading, even if he or she is not certain which one of several options it is.[29]

Even less restrained expressions of this concept find frequent assertion—particularly in online utterance, as demonstrated by the following examples:

> David Alan Black: "I'm not always sure whether the correct reading is printed in the text of my Greek New Testament or in

---

27. The UBS apparatus, even though prepared under the same auspices as the Nestle-Aland texts, is limited only to variant units considered significant for translators, thus representing a separate issue.

28. German Bible Society, www.academic-bible.com/en/home/scholarly-editions/greek-new-testament/text-and-textual-apparatus/. The same point is restated elsewhere on the same website: "The Nestle-Aland Novum Testamentum Graece . . . puts its readers in a position to make their own judgments in matters of New Testament textual research," www.academic-bible.com/en/ home/scholarly-editions/greek-new-testament/nestle-aland/.

29. Blomberg and Markley, *New Testament Exegesis*, 15, 16, 17, 18–19; emphasis added. That that NA text and apparatus is in view is clearly stated in the same section: "NA proves handy for the interpreter who . . . is still interested in seeing if and how manuscript traditions diverge from one another in that particular text, even if in more minor ways" (17).

> the apparatus, but it's my humble opinion that we haven't lost a single word of the New Testament."[30]
>
> Scott Sanjay Hayes: "There's a very high degree of confidence that the original said either what's in the text or in the footnotes and very little else. So always read the footnotes."[31]
>
> James White: "Pick up a copy of the Nestle-Aland text... Look at the text, and look at the bottom of the page... *Any* reading that is in *any* of the tradition is found in the text or the footnote."[32]

So also in published material, even Daniel B. Wallace repeatedly has expressed the same presumption:

> Reasoned eclectics simply do not resort to conjectural emendation—there is textual basis for the readings they select. Consequently, *it is certain* [!] *that the original wording is found either in the text or in the apparatus.*[33]
>
> What we have in our hands today is the original NT; we just do not know in all cases if it is in the text or in the apparatus.[34]
>
> When one looks at the Nestle-Aland *Novum Testamentum Graece,* he or she is looking at the original text—either in the text or in the apparatus... We *have* the original somewhere on the page of the Greek New Testament.... The words of the original text are evident—in either the text or the variants... Pragmatically the wording of the original is to be found either in the text *or the apparatus* of the Nestle-Aland Greek New Testament. We have the original in front of us; we're just not sure at all times whether it is above the line or below it.[35]

Although nearly everyone should acknowledge that "[t]he 'apparatus'... contains some (not all) of the more significant variants,"[36] the leap from that position to the more absolute claims expressed above is unwarranted and overly optimistic. Even Bill Warren overstates the case in his claim that

---

30. See www.daveblackonline.com/march_2010_blog_archives.htm.
31. See www.facebook.com/groups/11404207692/; posted Dec 21, 2015.
32. White, "New Age Bible Versions Refuted," www.sermonaudio.com/playpopup.asp? SID=529152352572 (Nov 1, 1993), timemark 28:55; emphasis added.
33. Wallace, "Majority Text," 155 n. 15; emphasis added.
34. Wallace, "Challenges," 95.
35. Wallace, "Inerrancy," 217, 219; emphasis original.
36. Stewart, "Introduction," 188 n. 7.

> [i]n the Nestle-Aland *Novum Testamentum* . . . we have enough data to . . . evaluate the variants we find, that we can know that there is no 'cover up' within the field of textual criticism that might emerge that will surprise us about the text.[37]

Yet, the NA *non*-citation of numerous significant variant readings—particularly those pertaining to the major Byzantine textual tradition—thereby *does* become a *de facto* "cover-up," whether deliberate or unintentional, even if such variant units are not considered significant for translation, exegesis, or interpretation.

PASSAGES *NOT* IN THE APPARATUS

> "The greatest value in a critical edition is . . . in the manuscript evidence provided in the apparatus."[38]

The recognition that certain significant variant units are *not* mentioned in the NA apparatus often comes as an eye-opening experience, as James Snapp recently noted:

> In the course of collating the text of 2425, I noticed a significant variant-unit in Second Timothy 4:1 that is not in the Nestle-Aland apparatus. The words "the Lord"—του Κυριου in Greek—are not in the Alexandrian Text, but . . . του Κυριου is included in the Byzantine Text . . . To put this another way: a variant in Second Timothy 4:1 that has an impact on translation, and which is found in the majority of Greek manuscripts, is not in the Nestle-Aland *Novum Testamentum Graece* at all. It's not in the text of NA-27 and it's not in the apparatus . . . I conclude that the claim that "it is certain that the original wording is found either in the text or in the apparatus" may be an overly optimistic assessment when applied to the Nestle-Aland *Novum Testamentum Graece*.[39]

Similarly, James White comments on another theologically important substitution also not mentioned at all in the NA apparatus: Acts 22:16, where the NA main text reads επικαλεσαμενος το ονομα αυτου and the Byzantine majority read επικαλεσαμενος το ονομα του κυριου:

---

37. Warren, "Who Changed the Text and Why?," 110.

38. Posted on the ETC Blogsite by "Tim," evangelicaltextualcriticism.blogspot.com/2016/01/tc-journal-vol-20-packed-with-articles.html#comments, January 11, 2016.

39. Snapp, "Lessons." http://www.thetextofthegospels.com/2015/11/lessons-from-medieval-fragment-of.html. Snapp quotes Wallace, "Majority Text and the Original Text," 155 n. 15, online at: bible.org/article/majority-text-and-original-text-are-they-identical.

One will search in vain through the Nestle-Aland 25th, 26th, and 27th editions ... for the slightest indication that this variant [unit] even exists, despite 'the name of the Lord' being the reading of the majority of Greek manuscripts ... Surely such a reading, despite it being probably secondary, should at least be noted for the sake of all those who wish to do textual studies.[40]

To further illustrate the problem, consider the following examples where the NA apparatus fails to display significant Byzantine (𝔐) readings[41] (the manuscript evidence for these examples comes from Swanson's display of manuscript data):[42]

Matt 27:28 — transposition of phrases:

περιεθηκεν αυτω χλαμυδα κοκκινην   - 𝔐

χλαμυδα κοκκινην περιεθηκεν αυτω   - NA ℵ B (D) L Q 69 124 788 1346

Acts 3:11a — major translatable substitution:*

* In Luke-Acts, a genitive absolute with αυτου serving as subject is rare (Luke 15:14; 18:40; Acts 14:20 [NA]; 21:40; 25:7, 17; 28:17). Far more typical for Luke is the use of a *non*-pronominal subject (Luke 4:42; 7:24; 12:36; 22:55; Acts 2:6; 5:2; 12:18; 14:20 (𝔐); 15:2; 21:17, 20; 23:12; 27:9, 13; 28:3, 9, 17).

κρατουντος δε του ιαθεντος χωλου τον πετρον   - 𝔐

κρατουντος δε αυτου τον πετρον   - NA 𝔓74vid ℵ A B C E Ψ 057 81 88 323 945 1175 1611 1739 1891

Acts 3:11b — transposition later in the same verse:*

* The NA apparatus cites only two variants at this point: the substitution of τε for δε (𝔓74vid A) and a convoluted restructuring in D (h mae) encompassing both the 3:11a and 3:11b segments (εκπορευομενου δε του πετρου και ιωαννου συνεξεπορευετο κρατων αυτους· οι δε θαμβηθεντες εστησαν).

συνεδραμεν προς αυτους πας ο λαος επι   - 𝔐

---

40. White, *King James Only Controversy*, 223–224. White particularly notes that "older Greek texts [and apparatuses], such as von Soden and Tregelles, note the variant" (223).

41. The 𝔐 designation in NA27/28 represents the "*Mehrheitstext*" (i.e., "majority text"), inclusive of the Byzantine Textform and any non-Byzantine MSS agreeing with such.

42. Swanson, *New Testament Greek Manuscripts*. Swanson's 𝔐 designation primarily represents the majority of MSS collated for his edition; in most instances such agrees with 𝔐 as cited in NA27/28.

| συνεδραμεν <u>πας ο λαος προς αυτους</u> επι | - NA 𝔓^74vid ℵ A B C Ψ 057 81 88 323 1175 |

Acts 4:12 — omission of phrase:*

* Cited by David Robert Palmer as an "example of limitations of the NA²⁸ footnote apparatus—In Acts 4:12 you would not know that the Robinson-Pierpont [main] text omits υπο τον ουρανον" <www.facebook.com/groups/NTTextualCriticism/> (accessed October 2015).

| ετερον το | - 𝔐^pt (RP2005^txt) |
| ετερον <u>υπο τον ουρανον</u> το | - NA/𝔐^pt (RP2005^mg) 𝔓^74vid? ℵ A B D E Ψ 0165 33 88 104 (226^c) 323 927 945 1175 1505 |

Acts 8:18 — substitution of a more common synonym (the rarer and "more difficult" 𝔐 reading occurs only at John 1:38; 6:5, while the "easier" NA form occurs 58x in the NT [62x in 𝔐]):

| <u>θεασαμενος</u> | - 𝔐 |
| <u>ιδων</u> | - NA 𝔓^74 ℵ A B C D E Ψ 33 81 88 323 440 614 927 1175 1611 1646 1739 1891 |

Acts 23:10a — substitution affecting translation and exegesis:

| <u>ευλαβηθεις</u> | - 𝔐 |
| <u>φοβηθεις</u> | - NA 𝔓^74 (ℵ) A B C E Ψ 33 81 614 945 1175 1505 1611 1739 1891 (2344) |

Acts 23:10b — another translatable difference within the same verse:*

* Ironically, even while the two more substantial variant units within this verse are absent from the NA apparatus, in the same verse that apparatus does cite the extremely minor omission of τε, supported only by B 69—a variant apparently *never* considered original by anyone. The only other variant unit cited by NA for this verse involves the single-letter shift distinguishing the aorist and present participle of γινομαι (NA γενομενης vs. 𝔐 γινομενης).

| <u>καταβηναι και</u> | - 𝔐 |
| <u>καταβαν</u> | - NA 𝔓^74 ℵ A B C E Ψ 33 81 945 1175 1739 2344 |

Acts 23:20 — mid-verse word order:

| <u>εις το συνεδριον</u> <u>καταγαγης</u> <u>τον Παυλον</u> | - 𝔐 |
| <u>τον Παυλον</u> <u>καταγαγης</u> <u>εις το συνεδριον</u> | - NA 𝔓^74vid ℵ A B E Ψ 33 69 81 547 945 1175 1739 1891 2344 |

128 Getting into the Text

Acts 24:13 — word order, plus alteration of pronoun and case:*
* Again ironically, the NA apparatus in this verse cites two extremely minor variant units involving insignificant interchanges (NA ουδε / 𝔐 ουτε and NA νυνι / 𝔐 νυν), even while ignoring the more substantial variation cited below.

με δυνανται   - 𝔐

δυνανται σοι   - NA 𝔓⁷⁴ᵛⁱᵈ ℵ A⁽*⁾,ᶜ B E Ψ 33 69 81 88 104 323 927
                                945 1175 1270 1739 2344

The NA apparatus thus displays a selectivity that tends to favor inclusion of numerous less essential variants while totally ignoring many more substantial Byzantine readings, generally due to an editorial preference for readings found primarily in particular favored MSS; this even while J. Keith Elliott has stated, "It is desirable to seek to have as full a representation of manuscripts in our apparatus as possible."⁴³ Such obviously has *not* been the case in relation to the popular NA editions that contain the text and apparatus most commonly used with authority by modern students and scholars alike.

AN ILLUSTRATIVE POINT: EIGHTY-NINE VERSES WITHOUT "JESUS" IN MARK

> "Decisions about readings . . . can rarely be made without assessing each reading to determine its sense, its significance, and its story in the context of its variation-unit. In the final analysis, exegesis is the arbiter in a text-critical decision." ⁴⁴

The absence of pertinent variant information in the NA apparatus is best exemplified by an example significant for exegesis and thematic interpretation. On multiple occasions Daniel Wallace has claimed that a particular interpretative point within the Gospel of Mark supposedly demonstrates the superiority of the NA critical text against the Byzantine majority.

The point at issue involves the absence of the proper name Ιησους from the critical text of Mark over an extended section spanning 89 consecutive verses (Mark 6:31—8:26) including "the so-called Bethsaida section, Mark 6:45—8:26, which corresponds to Luke's 'great omission.'"⁴⁵ The Byzantine

---

43. Elliott, "What Should Be in an *Apparatus Criticus*?," 136.

44. Epp, "It's All About Variants," 297.

45. Carlson, "Origin(s)," 18. Carlson continues, "Further limiting the role of synoptic harmonization, this section includes a lengthy pericope not paralleled by Matthew (Mark 8:22–26) and a fair number of sentences completely lacking in Matthew (e.g.,

Textform within that same segment includes the name Ιησους in four locations (Mark 6:34; 7:27; 8:1; 8:17). From at least 2006 onward, Wallace has claimed that these majority Byzantine inclusions are secondary and due to lectionary influence upon the mass of Byzantine continuous-text MSS. Beginning with the claim that "[l]ectionaries contributed heavily to the expansion of the New Testament," Wallace applies this to the Markan segment in question:

> Lectionaries are manuscripts that have assigned Scripture readings for various days of the week. The assigned reading for a particular day could not very well begin with, "Now, when he was teaching by the seashore." Who is the *he*? The lectionaries added clarification to the text precisely because they pulled passages out of their larger contexts—passages that often used only pronouns to identify the main characters. The scribes knew the Scriptures well, especially because of constant use and memorization of the lectionaries. *They would often import the added words from the lectionaries into the biblical text.* For example, in the heart of Mark's Gospel, for the space of eighty-nine verses (Mark 6:31—8:26), Jesus is *never* identified by name or title. He is not called "Jesus," "the Lord," "teacher," or "rabbi." The pronouns are the only indications to go on that tell who is in view. *Because of the influence from the lectionaries, most manuscripts add nouns here and there to identify the person in view.* In these eighty-nine verses in Mark, for example, the majority of later manuscripts add "Jesus" in 6:34; 7:27; 8:1, and 17. These variants certainly affect the translation, but the referent (Jesus) is still the same either way.[46]

Obviously Wallace considers this issue important for the exegetical and interpretative study of Mark's Gospel[47]—he repeats essentially the same claim on various occasions, although not identifying the precise span of Markan verses or the locations where Ιησους is found in most MSS.

Mark 7:2–5)."

46. Komoszewski, Sawyer, and Wallace, *Reinventing Jesus*, 58–59; emphasis added. The issue again is referenced later in the book: "We noted that Mark described Jesus only with the use of pronouns through eighty-nine consecutive verses... Scribes would naturally want to add the name of Jesus to clarify who is in view. In such instances, the original reading is both shorter and harder... The shorter reading is usually to be preferred. We have already discussed the addition of the name *Jesus* in several places in the Gospels where it was not originally used" (91–92).

47. So also Price, *Original Bible*, 116. Although Price at this point clearly is dependent upon *Reinventing Jesus*, he does not mention Greek lectionary practice as the proximate cause of Byzantine variation.

In *The Case for the Real Jesus* (2008) interview by Lee Strobel, Wallace stated the following:

> In the Gospel of Mark, there are 89 verses in a row where the name of Jesus isn't mentioned once. Just pronouns are used, with "he" referring to Jesus. Well, if you excerpt a passage for a daily lectionary reading, you can't start with "When he was going someplace . . ." The reader wouldn't know to whom you were referring. So it was logical for the scribe to replace "he" with "Jesus" in order to be more specific in the lectionary. *But it's counted as a variant every single time.*[48]

Also in 2008, on the Dallas Seminary blogsite, Wallace raised the same issue:

> Scribes also were prone to clarify passages, especially for liturgical reasons. For example, 89 successive verses in Mark do not mention the name of Jesus once nor refer to him by any noun at all. But in the lectionary cycle, a portion of Mark's Gospel would be read for the assigned day. It would be a bit confusing if the passage began with, "And he went out from Galilee." Who is the 'he'? The lectionaries would add the name of Jesus (and they did so in three [four!] well-placed locations in these 89 verses) to give a little context to the reader. *The lectionaries exercised a great influence on the later manuscripts especially.* What was part of the prescribed reading of scripture became so ingrained in the scribes' minds that *they naturally added the words that they knew from such recitations.*[49]

Given Wallace's emphasis on the significance of the absence of the proper name Ιησους from the critical text at the four Byzantine inclusionary locations, one would presume those important points of variation would be noted in the NA apparatus—yet in three of the four instances (Mark 6:34; 7:27; 8:1), the NA apparatus is silent regarding the Ιησους variants, thereby leaving the reader uninformed on what Wallace considers an essential text-critical matter (only at Mark 8:17 is the Ιησους majority variant actually cited in the NA apparatus, with the NA main text supported only ℵ¹ B Δ 892* aur

---

48. Strobel and Vogel, *Real Jesus: Student Edition*, 65; ellipses original; emphasis added. A shorter form of the same material appeared a year earlier in the initial study, Strobel, *Real Jesus*, 88—the quotation there prefaced with "Here's what happened": but lacking the final three sentences (from "The reader wouldn't know" through "every single time").

49. Wallace, "Scribal Corruptions," www.bible.org/article/significance-scribal-corruptions-new-testament-text (April 16, 2008); emphasis added. In order to agree with his previous statement, Wallace's *"three* well-placed locations" should read "four."

i sa^{mss} bo [2427]).⁵⁰ Even the more detailed *SQE* apparatus remains deficient in these particular variant units: the variant units at Mark 6:34 and 7:27 are cited negatively (listing only readings and MSS that *differ* from the NA main text), and at Mark 8:1 the Ιησους variant is ignored entirely. Only at Mark 8:17 does *SQE* fully cite the variant at issue (with main text support identical to that displayed in the NA apparatus).

In contrast, Reuben Swanson's collation material (displayed below) does cite the more important MSS that support the NA main text in the three Markan locations ignored by the NA apparatus. The majority reading in each case is followed by Swanson's data regarding exclusion of Ιησους in the NA main text):⁵¹

Reference	𝔐	NA	Greek MSS Supporting NA Main Text
Mark 6:34	ο Ιησους	—	ℵ B L W Θ f¹ f¹³ 28 33 565 700
Mark 7:27	ο δε Ιησους ειπεν	και ελεγεν	ℵ B D L Θ 579 700
Mark 8:1	ο Ιησους	—	ℵ A B D K L M N W Δ Θ Π f¹ 28 33 565 579 700 788 1071 1424

Basically, the evidence supporting the NA main text in these three uncited variant units is similar to what appears in comparable units.⁵² Contrary to Wallace, however, the NA non-inclusion of majority Ιησους readings is hardly restricted to these units: *Nine* additional locations in Mark also find the NA main text not including a majority Ιησους reading, with three of these locations again *not* mentioned in the NA apparatus. The thirteen Markan occurrences are charted as follows (the four instances cited by Wallace are shaded):

---

50. Although MS 2427 is cited from the NA²⁷ apparatus, that MS definitively has been shown to be a ninteenth-century forgery, and no longer is cited in the NA²⁸ apparatus. Citation in the present essay is due to its consistent citation in the NA²⁷ apparatus of Mark.

51. Swanson, *Mark*, 94, 113, 118, 124.

52. The consistently common support for these three readings happens to be only ℵ B L Θ 700.

MARKAN PASSAGES WHERE ΙΗΣΟΥΣ OR Ο ΙΗΣΟΥΣ IS PRESENT IN 𝔐 BUT ABSENT OR SUBSTITUTED IN THE NA MAIN TEXT

Reference	𝔐	NA	Greek MSS Supporting NA Main Text
Mark (13)			
Mark 1:41	ο δε Ιησους	και	ℵ B D 892 [2427] it sa^{mss} bo^{pt}
Mark 5:13	ο Ιησους	—	ℵ B C (D) L W Δ Θ f^1 28 (565) (579) (700) 892* 2542 [2427] b e sy^{s,p} bo Epiph
Mark 5:19	ο δε Ιησους	και	Not in NA apparatus (SQE negative)
Mark 6:34	ο Ιησους	—	Not in NA apparatus (SQE negative)
Mark 7:27	ο δε Ιησους ειπεν	και ελεγεν	Not in NA apparatus (SQE negative)
Mark 8:1	ο Ιησους	—	Not in NA apparatus or SQE
Mark 8:17	ο Ιησους	—	ℵ^1 B Δ 892* [2427] aur i sa^{mss} bo
Mark 10:52	τω Ιησου	αυτω	ℵ A B C D L W Δ Ψ f^1 f^{13} 28 565 579 700 892 1241 1424 2542 *al* latt sy^{s,hmg} cop
Mark 11:11	ο Ιησους και	—	Not in NA^{27} apparatus (SQE negative)
Mark 11:14	ο Ιησους	—	Not in NA apparatus or SQE
Mark 11:15	ο Ιησους	—	Not in NA^{27} apparatus (NA^{28} negative; so also SQE)
Mark 12:41	ο Ιησους	—	ℵ B L Δ Ψ 892 [2427] *pc* a k sa^{ms} bo
Mark 14:22	ο Ιησους	—	ℵ^1 B D W f^{13} 565 [2427] it sy^s sa (NA^{28} does not include sy^s)

This complete Markan table demonstrates that NA main text exclusions of Ιησους are more common than noted by Wallace. Further, the *only* witness common to *all* cited exclusions (whether noted in NA or Swanson)[53] is Co-

---

53. For reasons of space, the corroborating Swanson data is not displayed within the

dex Vaticanus (B), with Codex Sinaiticus (ℵ) following close behind. The remaining witnesses at best offer varying levels of support, some only in a single instance.

Beyond Mark, instances where Ιησους is present in the majority of witnesses but absent from the NA main text occur 33 additional times in the remaining Gospels, with nine of these instances (shaded) again ignored by the NA apparatus:

THE 33 REMAINING LOCATIONS WHERE ΙΗΣΟΥΣ OR Ο ΙΗΣΟΥΣ IS PRESENT IN 𝔐 BUT ABSENT OR SUBSTITUTED IN THE NA MAIN TEXT[54]

Reference	𝔐	NA	Greek MSS Supporting NA Main Text
Matthew (18)			
Matt 4:12	ο Ιησους	—	ℵ B C*vid D Z 33 700 1241 *pc* ff¹ k vg^st sy^s sa mae bo^pt Or
Matt 4:23	ο Ιησους	—	B (k) sy^c sa mae
Matt 8:3	ο Ιησους	—	ℵ B C* *f*¹ *f*¹³ 33 82 *al* k sa^mss bo Cyr
Matt 8:7	ο Ιησους	—	ℵ B 892 *pc* k sy^s bo
Matt 9:12	Ιησους	—	ℵ B D 0233* 0281 892 *l*-844 *pc* sy^s sa mae
Matt 12:25	ο Ιησους	—	𝔓²¹ ℵ B D 892* (k) sy^s,c sa bo
Matt 13:36	ο Ιησους	—	ℵ B D *pc* lat sy^s,c cop (αυτου *f*¹ 1424)
Matt 13:51	λεγει αυτοις ο Ιησους	—	ℵ B D *pc* lat sy^s sa bo

---

table; see the various locations in Swanson, *New Testament Greek Manuscripts: Mark*, for complete verification. This also applies to the tables that follow, for the same reason.

54. The data presented is from NA²⁷. The NA²⁸ apparatus differs in seven places from NA²⁷ primarily due to omission of various witnesses, noted as follows: Matt 9:12 (0233* 844); Matt 14:14 (a b ff² sy^s,c); Matt 15:16 (579); Matt 17:11 (sy^c); Luke 9:43 (sy^s,c). Beyond these, John 4:16, where NA²⁸ reads 33 without "vid" and replaces ac² (= Subakhmimic) with the typographically more problematic designation "ly" (= Lycopolitanic). The same ac²/ly replacement occurs at John 8:21 in this table.

Getting into the Text

Matt 14:14	ο Ιησους	—	ℵ B D Θ f^1 f^{13} 33 700 892* pc a b ff² sy^{s,c} lat cop	
Matt 14:22	ο Ιησους	—	Not in NA apparatus	
Matt 14:25	ο Ιησους	—	Not in NA apparatus	
Matt 15:16	Ιησους	—	ℵ B D Z 0281 33 579 892 1424 pc lat sy^{s,c,p} cop	
Matt 16:20	Ιησους	—	ℵ* B L Δ Θ f^1 f^{13} 565 700 1424 al it sy^{c,p} sa Or	
Matt 17:11	Ιησους	—	ℵ B D L W Z f^1 33 579 892 1424 pc lat ^{syc} cop	
Matt 18:2	ο Ιησους	—	ℵ B L Z 078* 0281 f^1 700 892* 1241 bo	
Matt 22:37	Ιησους	—	ℵ B L 33 892 pc sa bo	
Matt 24:2	Ιησους	—	Not in NA apparatus	
Matt 26:38	ο Ιησους	—	Not in NA apparatus	

Luke (7)				
Luke 7:22	ο Ιησους	—	Not in NA apparatus	
Luke 8:38	ο Ιησους	—	Not in NA apparatus	
Luke 9:43	ο Ιησους	—	$\mathfrak{P}^{75}$ ℵ B D L Ξ f^1 579 700 1241 2542 pc lat sy^{s,c} cop	
Luke 9:60	ο Ιησους	—	Not in NA apparatus	
Luke 10:21	ο Ιησους	—	$\mathfrak{P}^{45}$ $\mathfrak{P}^{75}$ ℵ B D Ξ 1241 pc lat sy^{s,c} sa bo^{pt}	
Luke 13:2	ο Ιησους	—	$\mathfrak{P}^{75}$ ℵ B L 070 1241 pc lat sa^{mss} bo^{pt}	
Luke 24:36	ο Ιησους	—	$\mathfrak{P}^{75}$ ℵ B D L 1241 it sy^{s,c} sa bo^{mss}	

John (8)				
John 4:16	ο Ιησους	—	$\mathfrak{P}^{66}$ $\mathfrak{P}^{75}$ B C* 33^{vid} pc a sa^{mss} ac² bo^{mss}	

John 4:46	ο Ιησους	—	𝔓⁶⁶ 𝔓⁷⁵ ℵ B C D L Wˢ 086 33 1241 *al* lat syᶜ
John 6:14	ο Ιησους	—	𝔓⁷⁵ ℵ B D W 091 *pc* a it vgˢᵗ syˢ,ᶜ cop Didˡᵉᵐ
John 8:20	ο Ιησους	—	Not in NA apparatus
John 8:21	ο Ιησους	—	𝔓³⁹ᵛⁱᵈ 𝔓⁶⁶* 𝔓⁷⁵ ℵ B D L T W *pc* b (e) ac² pbo
John 11:45	ο Ιησους	—	Not in NA apparatus
John 13:3	ο Ιησους	—	𝔓⁶⁶ 𝔓⁷⁵ ℵ B D L W 1241 *pc* lat pbo
John 18:5	ο Ιησους	—	𝔓⁶⁰ B D *pc* it syˢ pbo

Again, the *only* manuscript common to all remaining exclusions of a Ιησους majority reading (at least where NA provides evidence) happens to be Codex Vaticanus (B), making it strongly appear that the primary driving force in this matter is not some presumed "Markan proclivity" that supposedly has been corrupted by the Byzantine majority of MSS (as claimed by Wallace), but instead the questionable "cult of the best MS."

REGARDING ALLEGED LECTIONARY INFLUENCE

> "Occasional small textual modifications in non-lectionary manuscripts have arisen from the presence of the incipit at the beginning of a passage."[55]

The issue does not end here, however, since Wallace additionally claimed that Ιησους was added four times between Mark 6:31 and 8:26 in the Byzantine MSS due to Greek Orthodox lectionary practice. Although Wallace is quite correct that lectionary MSS often do adjust the opening and closing portions of various lections, his particular assertion is readily falsified.

Metzger correctly notes that "[i]n addition to the presence of the incipit, often the proper name is introduced for a person who may be referred to simply by a pronoun in the continuous text manuscripts";[56] and Colwell is even more specific: "Especially is 'Jesus' (ο Ιησους) added after a verb of saying."[57] Yet limitations to this practice are determinative; as Colwell

---

55. Metzger, "Greek Lectionaries," 495.
56. Ibid., 483.
57. Colwell, "Gospel Lectionary," 2.

further notes, "Most of these changes are *made in the first clause of the opening sentence* of the lection; *it is only rarely that any change of this sort is made after the opening clause.*"[58] So also Metzger: "Such adaptation, however, rarely extends to more than half a dozen words."[59] Thus, although proper names, titles, or phrases often are inserted at the commencement of a lection so that the hearer correctly will comprehend the person introduced into a particular setting, *almost all* lectionary-based insertions remain *limited* to the opening words—and this among *lectionary* MSS, with hardly any influence upon continuous-text MSS, and especially *not* upon the overwhelming majority of MSS. As Allen P. Wikgren notes, "The difference between the typical Byzantine MS and the typical lectionary is apparent," since "[l]ectionaries were as a rule copied from lectionaries."[60]

To illustrate, consider the following:

1. Matt 9:36, where the lection for β/γ Matt (spanning Matt 9:36—10:8)[61] adds Ιησους in the opening verse for identification (Τω καιρω εκεινω, ειδεν ο Ιησους πολυν οχλον). In contrast, *both* NA and 𝔐 lack ο Ιησους, reading only Ιδων δε τους οχλους. The *only* continuous-text MSS reflective of lectionary intrusion that insert ο Ιησους in this verse are C G N f^{13} *al* and the versional witnesses (g¹ vg^{mss}) sy^{p,h**} mae.[62]

2. Matt 12:9, where the lectionary text for β/ε Matt begins with ηλθεν ο Ιησους εις, while NA/𝔐 read και μεταβας εκειθεν ηλθεν εις. Among the continuous-text MSS, only C N Σ *al* a g¹ h sy^p add ο Ιησους—and then *following* and not *preceding* εκειθεν.[63]

3. Matt 9:1, where the lectionary text for κυ/ς Matt begins εμβας ο Ιησους εις while NA/𝔐 have only και εμβας εις. Only C³ F Θ^c f^{13} *al* vg^s among the continuous-text MSS add ο Ιησους *post* εμβας.[64]

4. John 9:1, where the lectionary text for κυ/ς John begins παραγων ο Ιησους ειδεν, while NA/𝔐 read και παραγων ειδεν. Again, only C³ F G

---

58. Ibid., 157 n. 4; emphasis added.
59. Metzger, "Greek Lectionaries," 453; emphasis added.
60. Wikgren, "Chicago Studies," 103, 121.
61. Lection designations reflect the day/week and primary Gospel segment as displayed in the Orthodox Greek Lectionary, Θειον και Ιερον Ευαγγελιον· Ομοιον κατα παντα προς το αναγινωσκομενον εν ταις Εκκλησιαις (Αθηναι: Αποστολικη Διακονια της Εκκλησιας της Ελλαδος, 1979).
62. The insertion appears after τους οχλους in C N f^{13} *al*, and after δε in G *pc*.
63. SQE cites E G c as additional witnesses to the minority reading.
64. C* *pc* insert ο Ιησους following πλοιον.

Η Θ f¹³ 1006ᶜ ᵛⁱᵈ 1424 al a l vgᶜˡ boᵐˢ among the continuous-text MSS insert ο Ιησους at this point (cited in SQE but not in the NA apparatus).

5. Luke 7:31, where the lectionary text for παρ/γ Luke begins ειπεν ο κυριος, found among continuous-text MSS (as ειπεν δε ο κυριος) only in (Mᵐᵍ) pc (f) vgᶜˡ.⁶⁵

6. Similarly, Metzger cites Matt 25:31, where the lectionary phrase ειπεν ο κυριος appears in Γ, and Luke 13:10, where G H Γ Ω 59 440 474 475 478ᶜ 481 al insert ο Ιησους after διδασκων.⁶⁶

Numerous additional examples could be cited, where Ιησους or κυριος is inserted at the beginning of a lection with no serious affect upon NA or 𝔐; but space does not permit a detailed presentation.⁶⁷

A similar example of the limited effect of lectionary-based intrusion upon continuous-text MSS is illustrated at the *conclusion* of various lections where such hardly affects any continuous-text MSS. As Colwell notes, these occur only "occasionally and in much slighter degree" and "are relatively rare and unimportant,"⁶⁸ having only limited effect upon continuous-text MSS. Thus, "He that has an ear, let him hear," is added to Matt 25:29 or 30 in C³ H Γ f¹³ 892ᵐᵍ pc; to Luke 13:9 in Γ al; to Luke 12:21 in U f¹³ 579 892ᶜ al; and to Luke 21:4 in Γ f¹³ 892ᵐᵍ al. The same principle applies to lectionary-based verse relocations, such as the insertion of Luke 22:43–44 following Matt 26:39, found among continuous-text MSS only in Cᵐᵍ f¹³ pc.

Beyond this, however, Wallace seriously errs in his claim that the four Byzantine inclusions of Ιησους at Mark 6:34; 7:27; 8:1; 8:17 represent alteration based on the *commencement* of a lection as opposed to the normally untouched central portion of such. Demonstrable proof of this error is clearly at hand.

The lections relating to the Markan passages under question are the following:⁶⁹

65. The Luke 7:31 minority variant properly is ignored by the NA apparatus, although cited in SQE. Ironically, the TNIV and NIV 2011—based on a form of the critical text—begin Luke 7:31 with "Jesus went on to say" (*absent* from earlier NIV editions).

66. Metzger, "Greek Lectionaries," 495.

67. From just the first 105 pages of the 550-page Orthodox Greek Lectionary (Θειον και Ιερον Ευαγγελιον), the following instances (cited in lectionary order) of Ιησους insertion appear against the absence of such in NA/𝔐: John 3:2 (ε/α John); John 2:12 (παρ/α John); John 4:5 (κυ/ε John); John 11:47 (β/ς John); John 12:19 (γ/ς John); Matt 8:23 (ε/β Matt); Matt 9:14 (παρ/β Matt); Matt 4:18 (κυ/β Matt); Matt 12:46 (ε /ε Matt); Matt 8:28 (κυ/ε Matt); Matt 13:10 (β/ς Matt); Matt 9:18 (σα/ς Matt); Matt 13:54 (β/ζ Matt).

68. Colwell, "Gospel Lectionary," 2.

69. Lection data from Gregory, "Die kirchlichen Lesestücke," 343–86; Scrivener,

Day/Week	Segment	Lection Commences	Lection Ends	Location of Ιησους Variant
ε/ιε	Matthew	Mark 6:30	Mark 6:45	Mark 6:34
ε/ις	Matthew	Mark 7:24	Mark 7:30	Mark 7:27
παρ/ις	Matthew	Mark 8:1	Mark 8:10	Mark 8:1
β/ιγ	Luke	Mark 8:11	Mark 8:21	Mark 8:17

Contrary to Wallace's claim, three of these four lections do *not* begin with the verse containing the presumed insertion of Ιησους; rather, the Ιησους variant appears well into the *center* of those lections.

At Mark 6:30 both NA and the Byzantine Textform read προς τον Ιησουν in the opening verse of the lection—this, however, has *no bearing* on the later presence or absence of ο Ιησους at Mark 6:34 in the middle of that lection. Also, the Mark 6:34 lectionary text reads και εξελθων ο Ιησους, ειδεν πολυν οχλον, whereas the Byzantine continuous-text MSS transpose (και εξελθων ειδεν πολυν οχλον ο Ιησους). Had the lectionary text *actually* affected the continuous-text MSS at this point, such transposition would have been highly unlikely.

In the Mark 7:24 lection, the lectionaries clearly *do* insert Ιησους at the beginning of the lection (ηλθεν ο Ιησους εις τα μεθορια)—*but* the continuous-text MSS at that location read απηλθεν εις τα μεθορια, and do *not* include Ιησους at all. At Mark 7:27, however, both the lectionaries and continuous-text MSS retain Ιησους in a central portion of text *not* subject to lectionary adjustment (ο δε Ιησους ειπεν αυτη). At Mark 8:11, the lectionaries again insert Ιησους, reading ηλθον οι Φαρισαιοι προς τον Ιησουν, και, but there the continuous-text MSS do *not* include Ιησους, but read only και εξηλθον οι Φαρισαιοι, και. The middle of the lection at Mark 8:17 finds both the lectionaries and continuous-text Byzantine MSS reading και γνους ο Ιησους λεγει αυτοις), at a central location where lectionary-based adjustment does *not* occur.

Mark 8:1, however, does find both the lectionaries and the continuous-text Byzantine MSS including Ιησους while NA omits such (προσκαλεσαμενος ο Ιησους τους μαθητας αυτου).[70] This is the *only* example from Wallace that

---

"Synaxarion and Eclogadion, 1:80–89; and the actual readings of the Orthodox Greek Lectionary, Θειον και Ιερον Ευαγγελιον, 156, 163, 241.

70. The *actual* lectionary adjustment at the commencement of the Mark 8:1 lection involves *only* the opening phrase: the continuous-text MSS read εν εκειναις ταις ημεραις, παμπολλου οχλου οντος, while the lectionaries alter this into παλιν πολλου οχλου οντος. The remaining text of this verse, with the subsequent inclusion of Ιησους appearing

possibly could support his claim; but given the lack of lectionary-related influence in the three other instances and among the continuous-text MSS overall, the likelihood of *actual* lectionary influence causing a later majority insertion of Ιησους is no more probable than in other Markan or New Testament passages where Ιησους happens to be absent from the NA main text. Simply put, lectionary usage is seen to have had *no serious influence* upon continuous-text MSS, particularly in relation to the presence or absence of Ιησους and especially regarding such within the 89-verse segment cited by Wallace.

CONCLUSION

> "Enhanced visibility would insure that the narrative quality of variants would be recognized more readily and would provide insightful occasions for enriching our understanding."[71]

The NA edition has a definite tendency to exclude from its apparatus dozens of Byzantine readings that are significant for exegesis, translation, and hermeneutics. In any given chapter many important and translatable Byzantine variants might be absent; these excluded readings involve what Epp terms "meaningful variants that so often, when rejected in the text-critical process, have been discarded like chaff."[72]

Although the more extensive apparatuses such as Tischendorf, von Soden, *SQE*, ECM and the like contain most of these neglected variants, the use of the Nestle apparatus as a primary source of data by most scholars, students, commentators, exegetes (and even many textual critics) results in a systematic deprivation of meaningful evidence that contrasts with the NA critical text. Yet even Klaus Wachtel from the Münster INTF provides a rationale for apparatus inclusion of additional Byzantine readings:[73]

> The mainstream text form in the Byzantine empire . . . has its headwaters in pre-Byzantine times, in fact in the very first phase of our manuscript tradition . . . and ended up in a largely uniform text characterized by readings attested by the majority of all Greek manuscripts.[74]

in the latter portion, remains identical in both the Byzantine and lectionary lines of transmission.

71. Epp, "It's All About Variants," 307.
72. Epp, "Critical Editions," 47.
73. The Münster Institut für neutestamentliche Textforschung (INTF) is editorially responsible for the UBS and NA editions, as well as the SQE and ECM.
74. Wachtel, "Byzantine Text," 1; emphasis added.

> The Byzantine text as found in the majority of Greek manuscripts ... *was not steered and controlled by a central institution like the Patriarchate of Constantinople* ... *There was a growing pool of majority readings*, i.e. readings shared by the majority of manuscripts *in all phases of the transmission history.*[75]

The NA critical apparatus is deficient in its failure to include numerous Byzantine variants that are meaningful for textual criticism, exegesis, hermeneutics, and translation. Those who claim that the original reading can be found in either the NA main text or its apparatus should recognize that such an assertion is clearly false; this suggests a needed improvement for the Nestle-Aland apparatus.

Future NA apparatuses should include *all* significant or translatable variants representing the dominant Byzantine consensus. Similarly, excision of numerous less meaningful variants (those that have little impact on exegesis, interpretation, or translation), such as the presence or absence of a definite article before a personal name would increase its usefulness, as well as allow more space for inclusion of more significant alternative readings. Already the NA[28] edition has improved its apparatus by eliminating numerous conjectural citations; so also it should eliminate less significant variants that apparently are included solely due to a presence in certain preferred manuscripts as opposed to making any real contribution to scholarly study.

At the very least, the deficiencies of the NA apparatus must be made clear to students and scholars who authoritatively utilize that critical edition. Even if one presumes the NA critical text more nearly to approach the autograph or *Ausgangstext*, one also must consider and account for the rise and dominance of the many Byzantine readings that tend to dominate the transmissional history of any particular New Testament book.[76]

The presentation of variant readings from individual printed editions presented in the SBLGNT apparatus (albeit without citation of manuscript evidence) readily suggests the template for future NA apparatuses. As the editor Michael Holmes states,

> The textual apparatus provides information about a wide range of textual variants. It records all differences between the text of the SBLGNT and the texts of WH, Treg, NIV, RP, and NA except for those differences that fall in the category of "orthography and

---

75. Ibid., 7–8; emphasis added.

76. Those who consider the dominant Byzantine text more nearly to approach the autograph or *Ausgangstext* are equally obligated to account for the various minority deviations from the majority consensus, including the failure of minority readings to perpetuate consistently throughout transmissional history.

related matters... This means that the apparatus includes nearly all the variant or alternative readings noted in the margins or notes of most recent major English translations and numerous translations into other languages as well.[77]

Notably, the Holmes SBLGNT cites Byzantine readings from the published RP2005 edition[78] as "a text that is a reliable representative of the Byzantine textual tradition."[79] Such similarly should become the norm in future Nestle-Aland editions.

APPENDIX: A SAMPLING OF SIGNIFICANT BYZANTINE VARIANT UNITS IN THE GOSPELS THAT ARE NOT CITED IN THE NA APPARATUS

The following tables list significant Byzantine variants that are not cited in the NA apparatus as found in the (randomly selected) chapters 3 and 4 of the Gospels and Acts. Those most seriously affecting English translation are shaded. Excluded from the tables are non-essential differences involving orthography, word division, various forms of proper nouns, adverbial differences, or identical parsings of various verbs.[80]

Table 1. Chapter 3 Gospel References.

Reference	𝔐	NA
Matthew		
Matt 3:3	υπο	δια
Matt 3:4	αυτου ην	ην αυτου
Matt 3:11	βαπτιζω υμας	υμας βαπτιζω
Matt 3:11	πνευματι αγιω	πνευματι αγιω και πυρι
Matt 3:16	και βαπτισθεις	βαπτισθεις δε

---

77. Holmes, *SBL Greek New Testament*, xv; xv n. 18. Details regarding the editions cited by abbreviation (Westcott-Hort, Tregelles, The New International Version, Robinson-Pierpont, and Nestle-Aland) appear on pp. ix–xi.
78. Robinson and Pierpont, *New Testament*.
79. Holmes, *SBL Greek New Testament*, xi.
80. Excluded from the data tables are non-meaningful variations such as the following: Λυδδης/Λυδδας, ευθεως/ευθυς, γνω/γνοι, ειδον/ειδαν, ειπον/ειπαν, ελεουντος/λεωντος, πειν/πιειν, συνεχυννεν/συνεχυνεν, βλαστα/βλασταυη, παραδω/παραδοι.

Mark		
Mark 3:3	εγειραι	εγειρε
Mark 3:5	υγιης ως η αλλη	—
Mark 3:7	ανεχωρησεν μετα των μαθητων αυτου	μετα των μαθητων αυτου ανεχωρησεν
Mark 3:8	ακουσαντες	ακουοντες
Mark 3:16	τω Σιμωνι ονομα	ονομα τω Σιμωνι
Mark 3:25	δυναται	δυνησεται
Mark 3:27	διαρπαση	διαρπασει
Mark 3:28	τα αμαρτηματα τοις υιοις των ανθρωπων	τοις υιοις των ανθρωπων τα αμαρτηματα
Mark 3:28	και βλασφημιαι	και αι βλασφημιαι
Mark 3:28	αν	εαν
Mark 3:31	φωνουντες	καλουντες
Mark 3:32	οχλος περι αυτον	περι αυτον οχλος
Mark 3:32	ειπον δε	και λεγουσιν
Mark 3:34	κυκλω τους περι αυτον	τους περι αυτον κυκλω

Luke		
Luke 3:4	λεγοντος	—
Luke 3:10, 12, 14	ποιησομεν	ποιησωμεν
Luke 3:16	ο Ιωαννης απασιν λεγων	λεγων πασιν ο Ιωαννης
Luke 3:20	εν τη φυλακη	εν φυλακη
Luke 3:22	λεγουσαν	—
Luke 3:23	ωσει ετων τριακοντα αρχομενος	αρχομενος ωσει ετων τριακοντα
Luke 3:26	Σεμει του Ιωσηφ του Ιουδα	Σεμειν του Ιωσηχ του Ιωδα
Luke 3:29	Ιωση	Ιησου
Luke 3:31	Μαιναν	Μεννα

John		
John 3:2	ταυτα τα σημεια δυναται	δυναται ταυτα τα σημεια

Acts		
Acts 3:7	αυτου αι βασεις	αι βασεις αυτου
Acts 3:9	αυτον πας ο λαος	πας ο λαος αυτον
Acts 3:10	τε	δε
Acts 3:11	του ιαθεντος χωλου	αυτου
Acts 3:11	προς αυτους πας ο λαος	πας ο λαος προς αυτους
Acts 3:13	ηρνησασθε αυτον	ηρνησασθε
Acts 3:18	αυτου παθειν τον χριστον	παθειν τον χριστον αυτου
Acts 3:26	παιδα αυτου Ιησουν	παιδα αυτου

Table 2. Chapter 4 Gospel References.

Matthew		
Matt 4:4	ανθρωπος	ο ανθρωπος
Matt 4:9	παντα σοι	σοι παντα
Matt 4:16	ειδεν φως	φως ειδεν

Mark		
Mark 4:1	συνηχθη	συναγεται
Mark 4:1	πολυς	πλειστος
Mark 4:5	αλλο δε	και αλλο
Mark 4:6	ηλιου δε ανατειλαντος	και οτε ανετειλεν ο ηλιος
Mark 4:9	ο εχων	ος εχει
Mark 4:10	οτε δε εγενετο καταμονας ηρωτησαν	και οτε εγενετο κατα μονας ηρωτων
Mark 4:11	δεδοται γνωναι το μυστηριον	το μυστηριον δεδοται
Mark 4:18	ακουοντες	ακουσαντες
Mark 4:19	αιωνος τουτο	αιωνος
Mark 4:20	ουτοι	εκεινοι
Mark 4:21	ο λυχνος ερχεται	ερχεται ο λυχνος
Mark 4:21	επιτεθη	τεθη

Mark 4:22	ο εαν μη	εαν μη ινα
Mark 4:22	εις φανερον ελθη	ελθη εις φανερον
Mark 4:25	αν εχη	εχει
Mark 4:30	τίνι ομοιωσωμεν	πως ομοιωσωμεν
Mark 4:30	ποια	τίνι
Mark 4:31	μικροτερος	μικροτερον ον
Mark 4:31	σπερματων εστιν	σπερματων
Mark 4:34	μαθηταις αυτου	ιδιοις μαθηταις
Mark 4:37	ανεμου μεγαλη	μεγαλη ανεμου
Mark 4:37	τα δε	και τα
Mark 4:37	αυτο ηδη γεμιζεσθαι	ηδη γεμιζεσθαι το πλοιον
Mark 4:38	επι τη	εν τη

Luke		
Luke 4:1	πνευματος αγιου πληρης	πληρης πνευματος αγιου
Luke 4:2	υστερον επεινασεν	επεινασεν
Luke 4:3	και ειπεν	ειπεν δε
Luke 4:4	Ιησους προς αυτον	προς αυτον ο Ιησους
Luke 4:4	αυτον λεγων	αυτον
Luke 4:9	και ηγαγεν	ηγαγεν δε
Luke 4:9	αυτον επι	επι
Luke 4:20	εν τη συναγωγη οι οφθαλμοι	οι οφθαλμοι εν τη συναγωγη
Luke 4:22	ουχ ουτος εστιν ο υιος Ιωσηφ	ουχι υιος εστιν Ιωσηφ ουτος
Luke 4:27	επι Ελισσαιου του προφητου εν τω Ισραηλ	εν τω Ισραηλ επι Ελισσαιου του προφητου
Luke 4:29	αυτων ωκοδομητο	ωκοδομητο αυτων
Luke 4:34	λεγων, Εα	Εα
Luke 4:35	μεσον	το μεσον
Luke 4:38	εκ	απο

John		
John 4:9	ουσης γυναικος Σαμαρειτιδος	γυναικος Σαμαριτιδος ουσης
John 4:20	δει προσκυνειν	προσκυνειν δει
John 4:27	εθαυμασαν	εθαυμαζον
John 4:51	απηντησαν	υπηντησαν
John 4:53	οτι ο	ο

Acts		
Acts 4:2	των	την εκ
Acts 4:5	πρεσβυτερους και γραμματεις	τους πρεσβυτερους και τους γραμματεις
Acts 4:6	Ανναν τον αρχιερεα και Καιαφαν και Ιωαννην και Αλεξανδρον	Αννας ο αρχιερευς και Καιαφας και Ιωαννης και Αλεξανδρος
Acts 4:7	μεσω	τω μεσω
Acts 4:11	οικοδομουντων	οικοδομων
Acts 4:12	ουτε	ουδε
Acts 4:12*	το	υπο του ουρανον το
* The NA reading reflects one portion of the Byzantine Textform ($\mathfrak{M}^{pt}$); the alternative is supported by a different major segment of the Byzantine tradition.		
Acts 4:14	δε	τε
Acts 4:16	ποιησομεν	ποιησωμεν
Acts 4:16	αρνησασθαι	αρνεισθαι
Acts 4:17	απειλησομεθα	απειλησωμεθα
Acts 4:18	παρηγγειλαν αυτοις	παρηγγειλαν
Acts 4:19	προς αυτους ειπον	ειπον προς αυτους
Acts 4:21	κολασονται	κολασωνται

As a further sampling, Table 3 lists significant Byzantine variants not cited in the NA apparatus that occur in chapter 9 locations throughout the New Testament (with the same exclusions regarding non-significant orthographic or other minor variation):

Table 3. Chapter 9 New Testament References.

Reference	𝔐	NA
Matthew		
Matt 9:5	εγειραι	εγειρε
Matt 9:13	ελεον	ελεος
Matt 9:17	απολουνται	απολλυνται
Mark		
Mark 9:3	εγενοντο	εγενετο
Mark 9:3	ως χιων	—
Mark 9:3	λευκαναι	ουτως λευκαναι
Mark 9:9	διηγησωνται α ειδον	α ειδον διηγησωνται
Mark 9:13	ηθελησαν	ηθελον
Mark 9:14	αυτοις	προς αυτους
Mark 9:15	ιδων αυτον εξεθαμβηθη	ιδοντες αυτον εξεθαμβηθησαν
Mark 9:16	τους γραμματεις	αυτους
Mark 9:18	αν	εαν
Mark 9:18	αυτου	—
Mark 9:19	αυτω	αυτοις
Mark 9:20	ευθεως το πνευμα	το πνευμα ευθυς
Mark 9:21	παιδιοθεν	εκ παιδιοθεν
Mark 9:22	αυτον και εις το πυρ	και εις πυρ αυτον
Mark 9:24	κυριε	—
Mark 9:25	πνευμα το αλαλον και κωφον	αλαλον και κωφον πνευμα
Mark 9:26	κραξαν	κραξας
Mark 9:26	σπαραξαν αυτον	σπαραξας
Mark 9:27	αυτον της χειρος	της χειρος αυτου
Mark 9:28	εισελθοντα αυτον	εισελθοντος αυτου
Mark 9:28	επηρωτων αυτον κατ ιδιαν	κατ ιδιαν επηρωτων αυτον
Mark 9:33	προς εαυτους	—

Mark 9:37 (2x)	εαν	αν
Mark 9:38	τω	εν τω
Mark 9:41	ου	οτι ου
Mark 9:42	εαν	αν
Mark 9:42	λιθος μυλικος	μυλος ονικος
Mark 9:43	σοι εστιν	εστιν σε
Mark 9:43	εις την ζωην εισελθειν	εισελθειν εις την ζωην
Mark 9:45	σοι	σε
Mark 9:47	σοι	σε
Mark 9:50	αλας και	αλα και

Luke		
Luke 9:3	ραβδους	ραβδον
Luke 9:5	εαν μη δεξωνται	αν μη δεχωνται
Luke 9:5	αποτιναξατε	αποτινασσετε
Luke 9:9	και ειπεν	ειπεν δε
Luke 9:10*	καλουμενης	καλουμενην
* The NA apparatus includes this variant unit, but fails to note the case difference of the participle.		
Luke 9:11	δεξαμενος	αποδεξαμενος
Luke 9:12	απελθοντες	πορευθεντες
Luke 9:15	ανεκλιναν	κατεκλιναν
Luke 9:20	αποκριθεις δε ο Πετρος	Πετρος δε αποκριθεις
Luke 9:21	ειπειν	λεγειν
Luke 9:23	ελθειν	ερχεσθαι
Luke 9:24	εαν	αν
Luke 9:27	ωδε εστωτων	αυτου εστηκοτων
Luke 9:36	εωρακασιν	εωρακαν
Luke 9:37	εν	—
Luke 9:38	εστιν μοι	μοι εστιν
Luke 9:48	εαν εμε	αν εμε
Luke 9:50	και ειπεν	ειπεν δε

Getting into the Text

Luke 9:57	αν	εαν
Luke 9:60	ο Ιησους	—

John		
John 9:6	τον	αυτου τον
John 9:11	δε	ουν
John 9:16	ουτος ο ανθρωπος ουκ εστιν παρα του θεου	ουκ εστιν ουτος παρα θεου ο ανθρωπος
John 9:17	τω	ουν τω
John 9:18	τυφλος ην	ην τυφλος
John 9:24	εκ δευτερου τον ανθρωπον	τον ανθρωπον εκ δευτερου
John 9:25	και ειπεν	—
John 9:26	δε	ουν
John 9:30	γαρ τουτω	τουτω γαρ το
John 9:40	οντες μετ αυτου	μετ αυτου οντες

Acts		
Acts 9:3	και εξαιφνης περιηστραψεν αυτον φως απο	εξαιφνης τε αυτον περιηστραψεν φως εκ
Acts 9:5	κυριος ειπεν	—
Acts 9:8	τε	δε
Acts 9:10	ο κυριος εν οραματι	εν οραματι ο κυριος
Acts 9:12	ονοματι Ανανιαν	Ανανιαν ονοματι
Acts 9:13	εποιησεν τοις αγιοις σου	τοις αγιοις σου εποιησεν
Acts 9:15	μοι εστιν	εστιν μοι
Acts 9:15	και	τε και
Acts 9:19	ο Σαυλος	—
Acts 9:20	χριστον	Ιησουν
Acts 9:21	εληλυθεν	εληλυθει
Acts 9:24	παρετηρουν τε	παρετηρουντο δε και
Acts 9:26	ο Σαυλος εν Ιερουσαλημ επειρατο	εις Ιερουσαλημ επειραζεν

Acts 9:28	και παρρησιαζομενος	παρρησιαζομενος
Acts 9:28	Ιησου	—
Acts 9:29	αυτον ανελειν	ανελειν αυτον
Acts 9:33	Αινεαν ονοματι	ονοματι Αινεαν
Acts 9:33	κραββατω	κραββατου
Acts 9:38	οκνησαι	οκνησης
Acts 9:38	αυτων	ημων
Acts 9:40	θεις	και θεις
Acts 9:42	πολλοι επιστευσαν	επιστευσαν πολλοι

Romans		
Rom 9:3	γαρ αυτος εγω αναθεμα ειναι	γαρ αναθεμα ειναι αυτος εγω
Rom 9:15	γαρ Μωυση	Μωυσει γαρ
Rom 9:19	ουν μοι	μοι ουν
Rom 9:32	προσεκοψαν γαρ	προσεκοψαν

1 Corinthians		
1 Cor 9:1	χριστον	—
1 Cor 9:3	αυτη εστιν	εστιν αυτη
1 Cor 9:6	του	—
1 Cor 9:8	ουχι	—
1 Cor 9:8	λεγει	ου λεγει
1 Cor 9:10	επ ελπιδι οφειλει	οφειλει επ ελπιδι
1 Cor 9:12	εξουσιας υμων	υμων εξουσιας
1 Cor 9:12	εγκοπην τινα	τινα εγκοπην
1 Cor 9:15	ουδενι εχρησαμην	ου κεχρημαι ουδενι
1 Cor 9:16	δε	γαρ
1 Cor 9:22	τα	—

2 Corinthians		
2 Cor 9:5	προκατηγγελμενην	προεπηγγελμενην

| 2 Cor 9:15 | δε | — |

Hebrews		
Heb 9:13	ταυρων και τραγων	τραγων και ταυρων
Heb 9:24	αγια εισηλθεν ο	εισηλθεν αγια
Heb 9:26	νυν	νυνι

Revelation		
Rev 9:11	βασιλεα επ αυτων	επ αυτων βασιλεα τον
Rev 9:11	εν δε	και εν
Rev 9:19	οφεων	οφεσιν

BIBLIOGRAPHY

Aland, Barbara, et al., eds. *Novum Testamentum Graecum: Editio Critica Maior, IV, Die Katholischen Briefe*: 1, Der Jakobusbrief; 2, Die Petrusbriefe; 3, Der Erste Johannesbrief; 4, Der Zweite und Dritte Johannesbrief; Der Judasbrief. Stuttgart: Deutsche Bibelgesellschaft, 1997–2005.

———, and Kurt Aland, et al., eds. *Nestle-Aland Novum Testamentum Graece*. Stuttgart: Deutsche Bibelgesellschaft, [27]1993–2007, [28]2012.

———, et al., eds. *The Greek New Testament*. Stuttgart: Deutsche Bibelgesellschaft, [4]1994, [5]2014.

Aland, Kurt, ed. *Synopsis Quattuor Evangeliorum*. 15th corr. ed. Stuttgart: Deutsche Bibelgesellschaft, 1997.

———, and Barbara Aland. *The Text of the New Testament: An Introduction to the Critical Editions and to the Theory and Practice of Modern Textual Criticism*. 2nd rev. enlg. ed. Grand Rapids: Eerdmans, 1989.

Blomberg, Craig L., and Jennifer Foutz Markley. *A Handbook of New Testament Exegesis*. Grand Rapids: Baker, 2010.

Carlson, Stephen. "The Origin(s) of the 'Caesarean' Text." SBL Seminar Paper, San Antonio, November 20, 2004.

Clarke, Kent D. *Textual Optimism: A Critique of the United Bible Societies' Greek New Testament*. JSNTSS 18. Sheffield: Sheffield Academic Press, 1997.

Colwell, Ernest Cadman. "The Contents of the Gospel Lectionary." In *Prolegomena to the Study of the Lectionary Text of the Gospels*, edited by Ernest Cadman Colwell and Donald W. Riddle, 1–5. Studies in the Lectionary Text of the Greek New Testament 1. Chicago: University of Chicago Press, 1933.

———. "The Greek New Testament with a Limited Critical Apparatus: Its Nature and Uses." In *Studies in New Testament and Early Christian Literature: Essays in Honor of Allen P. Wikgren*, edited by David Edward Aune, 31–40. SNT 33. Leiden: Brill, 1972.

Elliott, J. Keith. "What Should Be in an *Apparatus Criticus?* Desiderata to Support a Thoroughgoing Eclectic Approach to Textual Criticism." In *The Textual History of the Greek New Testament: Changing Views in Contemporary* Research, edited by Klaus Wachtel and Michael W. Holmes, 129–39. Atlanta: Society of Biblical Literature, 2011.

Epp, Eldon J. "Critical Editions and the Development of Text-Critical Methods, Part 2: From Lachmann (1831) to the Present." In *The New Cambridge History of the Bible, Volume 4: From 1750 to the Present*, edited by John Riches, 13–48. Cambridge: Cambridge University Press, 2015.

———. "It's All About Variants: A Variant-Conscious Approach to New Testament Textual Criticism," *HTR* 100 (2007) 275–308.

Gregory, C. R. *Textkritik des Neuen Testamentes: Erster Band*. Leipzig: J. C. Hinrichs'sche Buchhandlung, 1900.

Holmes, Michael, ed. *The Greek New Testament: SBL Edition*. Atlanta: Society of Biblical Literature, 2010.

———. "Reconstructing the Text of the New Testament." In *The Blackwell Companion to the New Testament*, edited by David E. Aune, 77–89. Oxford: Wiley, 2010.

Θειον και Ιερον Ευαγγελιον· Ομοιον κατα παντα προς το αναγινωσκομενον εν ταις Εκκλησιαις. Αθηναι: Αποστολικη Διακονια της Εκκλησιας της Ελλαδος, 1979.

Komoszewski, J. Ed, M. James Sawyer, and Daniel B. Wallace. *Reinventing Jesus: What* The Da Vinci Code *and other Novel Speculations Don't Tell You*. Grand Rapids: Kregel, 2006.

Lias, J. J. *Principles of Biblical Criticism*. London: Eyre and Spottiswoode, 1893.

Metzger, Bruce M. "Greek Lectionaries and a Critical Edition of the Greek New Testament." In *Die Alten Übersetzungen des Neuen Testaments, die Kirchenväterzitate und Lektionare: Der gegenwärtige Stand ihrer Erforschung und ihre Bedeutung für die Griechische Textgeschichte*, edited by Kurt Aland, 479–97. ANTF 5. Berlin: Walter de Gruyter, 1972.

———. *A Textual Commentary on the Greek New Testament*, 2nd ed. Stuttgart: Deutsche Bibelgesellschaft, 1994.

Mounce, William D. *Greek for the Rest of Us: Using Greek Tools without Mastering Biblical Greek*. Grand Rapids: Zondervan, 2003.

Pierri, Rosario. "Codex B e Nestle-Aland XXVIII a confronto: il Vangelo di Marco." *Studium Biblicum Franciscanum Liber Annuus* 63 (2013) 183–196. [An English summary is found in *New Testament Abstracts* 58 [2014] 481, entry 1507.]

Piper, John. *A Peculiar Glory: How the Christian Scriptures Reveal their Complete Truthfulness*. Wheaton, IL: Crossway, 2016.

Price, Randall. *Searching for the Original Bible*. Eugene, OR: Harvest, 2007.

Robinson, Maurice A., and William G. Pierpont, eds. *The New Testament in the Original Greek: Byzantine Textform 2005*. Southborough, MA: Chilton, 2005.

Scrivener, H. A. *A Plain Introduction to the Criticism of the New Testament*. 4th ed. Revised by Edward Miller. 2 vols. London: George Bell, 1894.

Snapp, James. "Lessons from a Medieval Fragment of Second Timothy and Titus." http://www.thetextofthegospels.com/2015/11/lessons-from-medieval-fragment-of.html.

Stewart, Robert B. "Introduction: Why New Testament Textual Criticism Matters: A Non-Critic's Perspective." In *The Reliability of the New Testament: Bart D. Ehrman* and Daniel B. Wallace in Dialogue, edited by Robert B. Stewart, 1–12. Minneapolis: Fortress, 2011.

Strobel, Lee. *The Case for the Real Jesus: A Journalist Investigates Current Attacks on the Identity of Christ*. Grand Rapids: Zondervan, 2007.

———, and Jane Vogel. *The Case for the Real Jesus: Student Edition. A Journalist Investigates Current Challenges to Christianity*. Grand Rapids: Zondervan, 2008.

Swanson, Reuben J., ed. *New Testament Greek Manuscripts: Variant Readings Arranged in Horizontal Lines against Codex Vaticanus; Acts*. Sheffield: Sheffield Academic Press, 1998.

———, ed. *New Testament Greek Manuscripts: Variant Readings Arranged in Horizontal Lines against Codex Vaticanus; Mark*. Sheffield: Sheffield Academic Press, 1995.

———, ed. *New Testament Greek Manuscripts: Variant Readings Arranged in Horizontal Lines against Codex Vaticanus; Matthew*. Sheffield: Sheffield Academic Press, 1995.

Tischendorf, Constantine, ed. *Novum Testamentum Graece: Editio Octava Critica Maior*. 2 vols. Leipzig: Giesecke and Devrient, 1869.

von Soden, Hermann Freiherr. *Die Schriften des Neuen Testaments in ihrer ältesten erreichbaren Textgestalt*. Vol. 2, *Text und Apparat*. Göttingen: Vandenhoeck und Ruprecht, 1913.

Wachtel, Klaus. "The Byzantine Text of the Gospels: Recension or Process?" Paper prepared for the NTTC session 23-327 at SBL (2009).

Wallace, Daniel B. "Challenges in New Testament Textual Criticism for the Twenty-First Century." *Journal of the Evangelical Theological Society* 52 (2009) 79–100.

———. "Inerrancy and the Text of the New Testament: Assessing the Logic of the Agnostic View." In *Evidence for God: 50 Arguments for Faith from the Bible, History, Philosophy, and Science*, edited by William A. Dembski and Michael R. Licona, 211–19. Grand Rapids: Baker, 2010.

———. "The Majority Text and the Original Text: Are they Identical?" *Bibliotheca Sacra* 148 (1991) 151–69.

———. "The Significance of the Scribal Corruptions to the New Testament Text." https://bible.org/article/significance-scribal-corruptions-new-testament-text.

Warren, William. "The Transmission of the Remembered Jesus: Insights from Textual Criticism." In *Memories of Jesus: A Critical Appraisal of James D. G. Dunn's Jesus Remembered*, edited by Robert B. Stewart and Gary R. Habermas, 159–72. Nashville: Broadman and Holman, 2010.

———. "Who Changed the Text and Why? Probable, Possible, and Unlikely Explanations." In *The Reliability of the New Testament: Bart D. Ehrman and Daniel B. Wallace in Dialogue*, edited by Robert B. Stewart, 105–24. Minneapolis: Fortress, 2011.

Wegner, Paul D. *A Student's Guide to Textual Criticism of the Bible: Its History, Methods, and Results*. Downers Grove IL: InterVarsity, 2006.

Wettlaufer, Ryan D. *No Longer Written: The Use of Conjectural Emendation in the Restoration of the Text of the New Testament, the Epistle of James as a Case Study*. NTTSD 44. Leiden: Brill, 2013.

White, James R. *The King James Only Controversy: Can You Trust The Modern Translations?* Minneapolis: Bethany, 2009.

Wikgren, Allen P. "Chicago Studies in the Greek Lectionary of the New Testament." In *Biblical and Patristic Studies in Memory of Robert Pierce Casey*, edited by J. Neville Birdsall and Robert W. Thomson, 96–121. Freiburg: Herder, 1963.

Zuntz, Günther. "The Byzantine Text in New Testament Criticism." *JTS* 43 (1942) 25–30.

7

L'origine de la parole de Jésus sur la réunion du masculin et du féminin

Christian-B. Amphoux
CPAF, Aix-Marseille Université

INTRODUCTION

La parole sur la réunion du masculin et du féminin est-elle bien de Jésus ? Elle lui est clairement attribuée dans une homélie du début du 2e siècle, la *Deuxième épître* de Clément de Rome[1], le tout premier Père de l'Église[2]; or, elle ne figure pas dans les collections de paroles de Matthieu et de Luc, mais seulement dans un écrit non canonique, l'*Évangile selon Thomas*, que nous connaissons par sa version copte et qui daterait de la fin du 2e siècle[3]. D'où vient donc cette parole, absente du Nouveau Testament, mais authentifiée au début du 2e siècle comme venant de Jésus ? Faisait-elle partie de la première collection de paroles de Jésus, écrite par Matthieu en araméen, selon

---

1. Funk, *Die apostolischen Väter*. Les deux « épîtres » de Clément ont comme premier témoin le Codex Alexandrinus (A), bible grecque du début du 5e siècle contenant, après l'Apocalypse, *1 Clément* en entier et *2 Clément*, jusqu'à 12,5.
2. Reynard, « Premières homélies chrétiennes », 533–541.
3. Meynard, *Thomas*.

le témoignage de Papias datant précisément aussi du début du 2ᵉ siècle[4] ? Si oui, pourquoi ne fait-elle pas partie des deux collections de Matthieu et de Luc ? Et sinon, d'où vient-elle ?

Nous avons reconstitué le parcours de cette parole et découvert la raison pour laquelle elle ne figure ni dans Matthieu ni dans Luc ; et dans le cadre de cet hommage à notre collègue David Alan Black, nous proposons au lecteur un survol de ce parcours, qui va de la première collection des paroles de Jésus jusqu'aux témoignages du début du 2ᵉ siècle, selon l'histoire de la collection des paroles de Jésus que nous avons d'abord rétablie. Notre plan suivra donc la chronologie : (1) L'historique de la collection des paroles de Jésus ; (2) Le cheminement de la parole sur la réunion du masculin et du féminin ; (3) Les traces matthéennes de la réunion du masculin et du féminin ; (4) La désunion du masculin et du féminin ; (5) Conclusion.

L'HISTORIQUE DE LA COLLECTION DES PAROLES DE JÉSUS

La théorie des deux sources distingue pour les synoptiques une source de paroles de Jésus, qui comprendrait l'ensemble des passages communs à Matthieu et Luc et absents de Marc (la « double tradition »), et une source narrative, qui serait Marc ou un écrit très proche de Marc (la « triple tradition »). Mais cette théorie n'envisage ni la différence d'organisation des paroles dans Matthieu et Luc, ni la source araméenne attestée par Papias, ni l'existence de l'*Évangile selon Thomas*, dont les fragments grecs et la version copte ont été découverts après la mise au point de la théorie.

J'ai proposé, dans une précédente étude[5], de reconstituer l'histoire de la collection des paroles de Jésus en distinguant quatre étapes, qui jalonnent la première génération chrétienne. Voici le rappel de ces étapes.

1) *La collection primitive (perdue)*. Au printemps de l'an 30, Jésus est jugé, condamné à mort et crucifié ; et de la foi en sa résurrection naît une communauté nouvelle au sein du judaïsme, à Jérusalem, dont la direction est confiée aux disciples. Ceux-ci demandent alors à un scribe, Matthieu, de réunir les paroles de Jésus ; et une collection est rédigée en araméen.

2) *L'évangile des Hellénistes*. En 32, avant la conversion de Paul qui aura lieu la même année[6] (Ac 9), la communauté primitive se divise à l'initiative

---

4. Eusèbe de Césarée, *Hist. eccl.* 3, 39,16 : « Le premier, Matthieu a mis par écrit en araméen les paroles (*logia*), et chacun les a ensuite traduites comme il en était capable. »

5. Amphoux, « Pour une approche documentaire », 1–13.

6. D'après Galates 1,18 et 2,1, il s'écoule dix-sept ans entre la conversion de Paul et la conférence de Jérusalem (Ac 15), qui est fixée précisément en 49.

d'un groupe qui se nomme les « Hellénistes » et s'oppose aux disciples qu'il appelle les « Hébreux » (Ac 6). À leur tête, Philippe quitte bientôt Jérusalem, valorise le salut par la connaissance et le renoncement à la sexualité (Ac 8) et part vers le sud (8,26), autrement dit vers Alexandrie, d'où Apollos se rendra à Éphèse, instruit dans la Septante et les paroles de Jésus (Ac 18,24–25). L'*Évangile selon Thomas*, qui professe cette même idéologie, est le témoin de l'adaptation en grec par les Hellénistes de la collection primitive, transformée en un écrit philosophique, peu après le départ de Jérusalem.

Paul à Éphèse, en 56, s'oppose à l'enseignement apporté par Apollos, qu'il qualifie d'« évangile qui n'en est pas un » (Gal 1,6–7), et il rejette la collection en traitant les paroles brèves (*logia*) de στοιχεῖα τοῦ κόσμου[7], à cause de leur contenu philosophique (Gal 4,3.9), et en associant au nom d'Apollos[8] plusieurs jeux de mots dépréciatifs : il serait « destructeur » (1 Co 1,12, Ἀπολλῶς / 1,19 ἀπολῶ, « je détruirai »), l'opposé de Paul (1 Co 3,5, Ἀπολλῶς / Παῦλος, soit *a-pwl / pwl*) et associé à une unité à connotation négative (1 Co 4,6 Ἀπολλῶς / 4,15 οὐ πολλούς, « pas plusieurs »). Le message de ces jeux de mots est que les Hellénistes, à travers Apollos, sont porteurs d'une sagesse humaine opposée à celle dont Paul se fait le porte-parole, et marquée par une connotation négative de l'unité. Paul élabore alors la christologie, dans l'esprit de compléter l'enseignement des apôtres[9].

3) *Une traduction grecque fidèle à l'enseignement des apôtres* a été entreprise, entre-temps, à Jérusalem, elle est attestée comme l'œuvre de Jacques, frère de Jésus, chef de la communauté sous Agrippa 1er, au début des années 40 (Ac 12). Le témoin de cette traduction est la *Synopse* du Pseudo-Athanase, œuvre du 4e siècle, et ce témoignage est repris dans les manuscrits des évangiles, dans les préfaces ou dans la souscription de la fin de l'évangile de Matthieu[10], puis cité par Richard Simon[11] : la collection en plusieurs sections que contient Matthieu correspond à ce témoignage.

Le travail de Jacques a d'abord consisté à fixer le vocabulaire grec de la collection, en étant évidemment plus fidèle à la collection primitive que la version des Hellénistes. Cette traduction est sans doute réalisée avant la fin

---

7. L'expression τὰ στοιχεῖα τοῦ κόσμου, « les éléments du monde », est utilisé chez les philosophes pour désigner les constituants de la matière: la terre, l'eau, l'air et le feu.

8. Sur l'identité de cet Apollos, le texte « occidental » donne une indication: Apollos est appelé Apollonios (18,24), le deuxième élément du mot *-oni-* étant l'anagramme du nom de Jean (*Ioan-*). Apollos serait ainsi le surnom de Jean, comme Céphas celui de Simon (Pierre), le chef des apôtres.

9. Sur la chronologie des lettres de Paul, voir Amphoux, « Les lieux de rédaction », 87–104.

10. von Soden, *Die Schriften des Neuen Testaments*, vol. 1, 297–327.

11. Simon, *Histoire critique du texte du Nouveau Testament*, 94.

des années 30, pour les besoins de la prédication qui se tourne, peu après la conversion de Paul, prioritairement vers les païens[12] : Jacques serait devenu le chef de la communauté de Jérusalem après ce travail.

4) *Jacques à Jérusalem*, vers 60, après l'arrestation de Paul au printemps 58 (Ac 21), met au point une révision de la collection de paroles qu'il a lui-même traduite en grec, en gardant le vocabulaire grec et en disposant les paroles autrement, avec un cadre qui associe à l'enseignement des apôtres le salut par la foi qui vient de Paul : la collection intégrée à Luc, lors de la rédaction finale (10,23—18,14), correspond à cette révision ; et sa diffusion s'accompagne d'une première rédaction de l'épître de Jacques.

Mais Paul à Rome, vers 61, s'oppose à cette nouvelle collection, qui est toujours faite de paroles brèves (*logia*) et dont la lettre d'accompagnement attaque directement sa christologie, en refusant de dissocier foi et œuvres (Jc 2,14-26). Il est donc encore question des « éléments du monde » (Col 2,8.20), et Paul confie à ses disciples d'élaborer l'écrit de référence dont les chrétiens ont besoin : parmi eux, Marc et Luc (Col 4,10-14 ; Phm 24).

Voici donc le schéma historique de la collection de paroles dont je fais l'hypothèse, tout au long de la première génération. Et nous allons voir comment chemine la parole sur la réunion du masculin et du féminin, dans cette histoire et à la génération suivante.

LE CHEMINEMENT DE LA PAROLE

Dans la collection primitive

En *2 Clément*, on lit cette citation de la parole en question :

> En réponse à quelqu'un qui lui demandait quand viendrait le royaume, le Seigneur lui-même a dit : « Lorsque les deux seront un, et l'extérieur comme l'intérieur et le masculin avec le féminin, ni masculin ni féminin. » (12,2)

Puis, l'auteur commente cette parole (12,3-6) :

> « Les deux seront un » : quand nous nous disons la vérité et qu'en deux corps, sans hypocrisie, il y a une seule âme.

---

12. En Ac 9,32-43, juste après la conversion de Paul, Pierre opère deux guérisons, la première étant celle d'un païen (Enée) et la seconde, d'une Juive (Tabitha). Le païen a la préséance.

> « L'extérieur comme l'intérieur » : autrement dit, l'intérieur veut dire l'âme, et l'extérieur veut dire le corps. Donc, de la manière dont ton corps se manifeste, qu'ainsi ton âme se montre dans les bonnes œuvres.
>
> « Le masculin avec le féminin, ni masculin ni féminin » : autrement dit, un frère voyant une sœur ne la désire pas comme un être féminin, ni la sœur ne le désire comme un être masculin.
>
> Quand vous aurez fait cela, dit-il, le royaume de mon père viendra.

Selon ce témoignage, la parole remonte à Jésus, elle fait donc partie de la collection primitive des paroles. Mais nous ne savons pas dans quel contexte elle devait se trouver.

Dans l'évangile des Hellénistes

Dans l'*Évangile selon Thomas*, la réunion du masculin et du féminin est incluse dans la parole dont voici une traduction française :

> EvTh 22 : (a) Jésus vit des petits enfants qui tétaient. Il a dit à ses disciples : « Ces petits enfants qui tètent sont le modèle de ceux qui entrent dans le royaume. » Ils lui ont dit : « Alors, est-ce en devenant des petits enfants que nous entrerons dans le royaume ? » (b) Jésus leur a dit : « Quand vous aurez fait de deux un et que vous aurez fait l'intérieur comme l'extérieur et l'extérieur comme l'intérieur et le haut comme le bas, *quand vous aurez réuni le masculin et le féminin*, afin que le masculin ne soit pas masculin ni le féminin féminin, (c) quand vous aurez fait des yeux au lieu d'un œil et une main au lieu d'une main et un pied au lieu d'un pied, une image au lieu d'une image, (b) alors vous entrerez... »

La partie (a) concerne les petits enfants ; la réunion du masculin et du féminin est traitée dans la partie (b) qui indique, en fin de parole, qu'il s'agit d'une voie de salut ; la partie (c), absente de la citation de *2 Clément*, est un complément qui traite un autre sujet.

Cette parole nous est parvenue seulement dans la version copte intégrale retrouvée à Nag Hammadi en 1945 : les fragments grecs découverts au début du 20e siècle à Oxyrhynque[13] ne l'attestent pas. Mais une structure évangélique lie cette parole à plusieurs autres qui correspondent aux sections

---

13. Les papyrus P. Oxy 1, 654, 655 contiennent respectivement EvTh 26-33; 1-7; 36-39.

de l'ensemble commun des synoptiques, à savoir les épisodes disposés dans le même ordre dans les trois livres[14] :

> EvTh 8 (le bon *pêcheur*) correspond à la section du thème de l'eau venant après le baptême : disciples *pêcheurs* / lépreux guéri / paralytique guéri / disciple péager ;

> EvTh 9 (le *semeur*) correspond à la section du thème de la semence venant avant la multiplication des pains : épis froissés / main sèche / le *semeur* / son explication ;

> EvTh 13 (confession des *disciples*) correspond à la section sur les disciples, avant la Transfiguration : confession des *disciples* / 1e annonce de la passion / le chemin de la croix ;

> EvTh 22a (les *enfants*) correspond à la section sur les enfants, après la Transfiguration : fils guéri / 2e annonce de la passion / accueil des *enfants*, en deux parties dissociées ; entre ces deux parties, dans Mt et Mc on trouve la parole de Jésus sur l'union et la désunion ; et dans Lc, toute la collection de paroles, dont celle sur la désunion ; par sa place, la *réunion* du masculin et du féminin (EvTh 22b) correspond à la parole sur la *désunion* ;

> EvTh 63 (les *riches*) correspond à la section sur les riches, en antithèse avec celle des enfants : le jeune homme riche et les riches en danger, en deux parties conjointes / 3e annonce de la passion / aveugle guéri ;

> EvTh 65 et 66 (les *vignerons* / la *pierre angulaire*) correspondent à la section du messie sacerdotal qui suit l'entrée dans Jérusalem : purification du temple / Jean messie sacerdotal / les *vignerons* / la *pierre angulaire* ;

> EvTh 100 et 102 (le *tribut à César* / les *enseignants* récusés) correspondent à la section du messie royal qui suit celle du messie sacerdotal : le *tribut à César* / sur la résurrection / David messie royal / les mauvais *enseignants*.

Au total, ce sont neuf paroles de l'EvTh comptées dix, la parole 22 étant double, et formant une proportion du simple au double dont le centre est la parole 22b sur la réunion du masculin et du féminin :

---

14. Je distingue deux sources narratives des synoptiques, voir Amphoux, « Réponse à E. Nodet », 179-204.

> 3 paroles simples : EvTh 8 / EvTh 9 / EvTh 13 ;
> centre de la structure : EvTh 22b ;
> 3 couples de paroles : EvTh 22a et 63 / EvTh 65 et 66 / EvTh 100 et 102.

Dans cette structure, qui est commune à l'EvTh et à l'ensemble commun des synoptiques, la réunion du masculin et du féminin occupe la position centrale pour l'EvTh, tandis que dans les synoptiques c'est la Transfiguration qui occupe cette place ; de plus, l'association entre la réunion du masculin et du féminin et les enfants suggère un parallèle avec la parole sur la désunion, qui est associée aux enfants dans Mt et Mc.

Ainsi, selon cette analyse, la réunion du masculin et du féminin est, dans la collection des paroles revue par les Hellénistes, le principe philosophique central de leur enseignement, qui

> renvoie au terme grec μοναχός, qui n'est pas à prendre au sens de 'moine' (qu'il aura à partir du 4e siècle), mais de 'celui qui est réduit à l'unité', avec une référence à l'unité primordiale propre au monde pléromatique ou à l'homme issu de la première création, avant le péché originel et la séparation des sexes, qui en fut la conséquence[15].

Mais cette position centrale n'est pas confirmée par les collections de Matthieu et de Luc, puisque la parole sur la réunion ne s'y trouve pas.

Dans la traduction des paroles par Jacques

La collection de paroles de Matthieu ne contient pas la parole sur la réunion du masculin et du féminin, mais on y trouve celle sur la désunion (Mt 5,32), insérée dans la présentation de la loi actualisée comme chemin de salut (5,17–48). Or, cette présence est ambiguë : la parole est insérée entre deux développements, le premier sur deux commandements du Décalogue, le meurtre et l'adultère—déjà sous-jacents dans la loi noachique (Gn 9)—, et le second sur trois prescriptions des lois de sainteté du Lévitique, le faux serment, le talion et l'amour du prochain. L'articulation des deux parties se fait par πάλιν, « de nouveau », au début de la seconde (v. 33) ; et chaque partie commence par se référer aux « anciens » (v. 21 et 33). La parole sur la désunion se réfère à une règle qui n'est pas au niveau des commandements, elle prolonge la question de l'adultère, introduite par un simple : « il a été dit », au lieu de la formule : « vous avez appris qu'il a été dit ». On voit donc,

---

15. Gianotto, « Thomas », 7.

par cet indice des introducteurs, que la parole sur la désunion a été ajoutée à un état plus ancien.

La présence de cette parole ne s'explique donc pas comme venant de la collection primitive et conservée dans la traduction de Jacques ; mais elle se comprend plutôt comme une reprise de la parole que Paul dit inspirée par le Seigneur (1 Co 7,10-11). C'est donc Paul, vers 56, quand il est à Éphèse, qui aurait l'initiative de cette parole, et les évangiles l'auraient intégrée ensuite comme venant de Jésus.

On voit, par cet exemple, que la collection des paroles de Matthieu ne se confond pas toujours avec la traduction en grec par Jacques de la collection primitive. Qu'en est-il, dans ces conditions, de la parole sur la réunion du masculin et du féminin ? Si Jacques a traduit et conservé cette parole de la collection primitive, qu'est-elle devenue ? A-t-elle été remplacée par celle sur la désunion ou a-t-elle simplement disparu et pour quelle raison ?

Le plus probable est que Jacques ne conserve pas cette parole, en raison de l'importance qu'elle a prise dans l'évangile des Hellénistes. La raison de la traduction en grec de la collection primitive est sans doute d'abord de lutter contre l'interprétation philosophique des paroles de Jésus et de limiter la diffusion de cet « évangile » dans le monde romain hellénophone au nom de Jésus. Nous n'avons aucune évidence de la présence de cette parole dans l'enseignement en grec fidèle à la collection primitive ; pour autant, nous allons voir que la rédaction finale de Matthieu n'ignore pas l'idée de la réunion du masculin et du féminin.

Mais il revient à Paul, vers 56 à Éphèse, d'avoir contesté la parole sur la réunion du masculin et du féminin et de l'avoir remplacée de deux manières: d'une part, en introduisant au nom du Seigneur la parole sur la désunion ; et d'autre part en lui substituant le principe de la double relation à Dieu, par la foi, et à l'humanité, par l'amour du prochain. Les deux éléments se trouvent dans la même épître, écrite depuis Éphèse :

> 1 Co 7,10-11 : Je recommande aux gens mariés—non pas moi, mais le Seigneur—que la femme ne se sépare pas de son mari ; ou si elle se sépare, qu'elle reste seule ou se réconcilie avec lui ; et que le mari ne renvoie pas sa femme.

> 1 Co 13,2 : Si j'ai le don de prophétie et toute la connaissance et si j'ai toute la foi à déplacer des montagnes, mais que je n'ai pas l'amour, je ne suis rien.

Paul fait ainsi de la désunion une règle de vie et de la foi associée à l'amour le nouveau principe central de la christologie, rejetant la tendance à l'αὐτάρκεια, « l'auto-suffisance » des Hellénistes, et s'ouvrant au monde, contre le désir de s'en abstraire. Paul met en place les conditions de la rupture avec les Hellénistes.

Dans la révision des paroles par Jacques, vers 60

Mais Jacques voit les choses autrement. Certes, il donne à la collection de paroles réorganisée un cadre joignant l'enseignement des apôtres, représenté par deux paroles :

> Lc 10,27 : Tu aimeras le Seigneur ton Dieu ... et ton prochain comme toi-même ;

> Lc 11,2-4 : Notre Père ...[16]

et celui de Paul, représenté par deux autres :

> Lc 16,18 : Tout homme qui renvoie sa femme et en épouse une autre est adultère, et celui qui épouse une femme renvoyée par son mari est adultère ;

> Lc 17,6 [D] : Si vous avez la foi comme une graine de moutarde, vous direz à cette montagne : déplace-toi, et elle se déplacera ...

On retrouve ainsi, d'une part, l'enseignement de Jésus à ses disciples et, d'autre part, l'apport neuf de Paul.

Mais dans l'épilogue de la collection (Lc 17,12—18,14), Jacques ménage une ouverture vers la théologie des Hellénistes :

> Lc 17,21 : Voici, le royaume de Dieu est à l'intérieur de vous.

En somme, Jacques n'est pas loin de penser que plusieurs courants de pensée peuvent coexister dans le jeune christianisme, et il se montre partisan d'en faire une synthèse ouverte au pluralisme[17] et réunissant les seules paroles de Jésus. La réunion du masculin et du féminin, combattue par Paul, ne s'y trouve pas, mais la présence du royaume « à l'intérieur » de chacun n'en est pas très éloignée.

---

16. La forme du Notre Père comprend, dans le texte « occidental », les sept demandes qu'on lit également chez Matthieu et dans la *Didachè*: c'est probablement la forme qu'avait la rédaction finale de Luc; il faut mettre à l'actif de Marcion d'avoir réduit le texte.

17. D'une manière semblable, le corps de l'épître de Jacques (2,1—4,10) rappelle les trois chemins de salut, la loi (2,1-13), la foi (2,14-26) et la sagesse (3,1-18) et propose comme synthèse la grâce (4,1-10).

Il est clair que Paul, réagissant vers 61 à la collection révisée diffusée par Jacques, s'y oppose avec autant de force qu'il a rejeté, quand il était à Éphèse, l'évangile des Hellénistes, centré sur la réunion du masculin et du féminin. L'appel à la rupture avec les Hellénistes est donc réaffirmé, et les disciples de Paul sont appelés à remplacer la synthèse établie par Jacques.

LES TRACES MATTHÉENNES DE LA PAROLE

La parole sur la réunion du masculin et du féminin pouvait se perdre, à la fin de la première génération, après son retrait de la collection traduite, puis révisée par Jacques à Jérusalem. Mais il n'en est rien. On retrouve sa trace au début du 2ᵉ siècle, non seulement dans la citation de 2 *Clément*, mais encore dans l'évangile de Matthieu, plus précisément dans la parabole des dix vierges et au début de la passion.

Le « fiancé » de la parabole (Mt 25,1)

Dans la parabole des vierges (Mt 25,1–13), dix jeunes filles « sortent à la rencontre » d'un personnage : le texte alexandrin (ℵ B) et le texte byzantin (W *Byz*) font mention « du fiancé » (25,1) ; mais dans le texte « occidental » (D), le type de texte « césaréen » ($\Theta\ f^1$) et la plupart des versions anciennes (it, vg, sy$^{s.p.h}$, cop^M, arm, géo)[18], il s'agit « du fiancé *et de la fiancée* », soit du masculin *et du féminin*, encore séparés. L'attente est plus longue que prévu, et l'huile vient à manquer pour les lampes de certaines jeunes filles. Enfin est annoncé (v. 6), puis arrive (v. 10) celui que l'on attend, qui est cette fois, dans toutes les traditions du texte, « le fiancé » : autrement dit, le masculin et le féminin ont été réunis. La variante-source est ici clairement la leçon du texte « occidental » : la mention de la fiancée (v. 1) a été supprimée par abandon du thème de la réunion du masculin et du féminin, mais elle était présente au moment de la rédaction finale[19].

La parabole insiste, d'ailleurs, sur cette réunion du masculin et du féminin par le choix des adjectifs qualifiant les jeunes filles : les « sages »

---

18. Sur ces témoins, voir Amphoux (éd.), *Manuel de critique textuelle*, les chap. 1 (Les manuscrits grecs) et 2 (Les versions anciennes, par Haelewyck). La rédaction finale des quatre évangiles s'opère vraisemblablement vers 120 à Smyrne, sous l'autorité de Polycarpe (*Manuel de critique textuelle*, 282).

19. Sur la variante-source, voir *Manuel de critique textuelle*, 237–238. Les révisions dont sont issus le texte alexandrin et le texte byzantin ont lieu vers 200, puis vers 300 (*Manuel de critique textuelle*, 287–300). Le *Diatessaron*, qui leur est antérieur, atteste encore la mention de la fiancée en Mt 25, 1 (S. C. E. Legg, *Euangelium secundum Matthaeum*, Oxford, 1940).

(φρόνιμοι), celles qui sont « prêtes » (ἕτοιμοι) avec leur réserve d'huile, sont désignées par des adjectifs en -οι, c'est-à-dire par des formes à la fois masculines et féminines, tandis que pour les « folles » (μωραί), les autres (λοιπαί) jeunes filles, les adjectifs ont une terminaison en -αι, spécifiquement féminine. Les premières ont également réuni le masculin et le féminin, pas les secondes.

L'hôte de la dernière Pâque (Mt 26,18)

La deuxième trace de la réunion du masculin et du féminin se trouve au début du récit de la passion, dans Matthieu, quand Jésus envoie ses disciples préparer la Pâque πρὸς τὸν δεῖνα, « chez Untel », en lisant δεῖνα comme l'indéfini indéclinable de la langue classique. Mais le mot δεῖνα est aussi, dans la Septante, le nom de la fille de Jacob, Dina. Or, en Mt 26,18, δεῖνα est précédé de l'article masculin, et cela semble exclure qu'il s'agisse d'un nom féminin ; sauf s'il s'agit, justement, de la réunion du masculin et du féminin. Et la plupart des versions traduisent l'indéfini de la langue classique[20].

Mais, dans le passage parallèle de Marc et Luc[21], on ne lit pas « allez en ville πρὸς τὸν δεῖνα », mais « allez en ville et (étant entrés en ville, Lc) viendra à votre rencontre : ἄνθρωπος κεράμιον ὕδατος βαστάζων, 'un homme portant une cruche d'eau' » : autrement dit, dans Mc et Lc, l'hôte est un être *masculin* portant une cruche d'eau, qui est un signe *féminin*, car, dans la Judée du temps de Jésus, comme dans l'Afrique d'aujourd'hui, c'est la femme qui va chercher l'eau au puits[22]. Et dans ces conditions, Mc et Lc nous invitent à lire, dans la rédaction finale de Mt, le nom *féminin* de Dina, en rendant compte de l'article *masculin* comme le signe qu'en Dina sont réunis le masculin et le féminin, qu'elle est donc prête à entrer dans le royaume. Mais, dans les révisions, cette lecture se perd : comme dans la parabole des dix vierges, le thème de la réunion du masculin et du féminin est abandonné, puis oublié, au profit de la parole introduite par Paul sur la désunion du masculin et du féminin.

---

20. Exception faite de deux manuscrits, l'un latin, l'autre copte, qui attestent « Dina ».

21. Mc 14,13 et Lc 22,10.

22. On lit dans la TOB, à Mc 14,13 : « On peut se demander s'il s'agit d'un signe convenu: habituellement, ce sont les femmes qui vont chercher l'eau. »

LA DÉSUNION DU MASCULIN ET DU FÉMININ

Dans les évangiles synoptiques, la parole sur la désunion a quatre occurrences, deux chez Mt (5,32 / 19,9), une chez Mc (10,11-12) et une chez Lc (16,18). Cette disposition remonte à la rédaction finale des évangiles, où les livres, selon le texte « occidental », se suivent dans l'ordre Mt-Jn-Lc-Mc, liés entre eux notamment par un épisode central, la Femme adultère (Jn 7,53—8,11) et un épilogue commun (Mc 16,9-20). La Femme adultère est alors au centre d'une double proportion, d'égalité (pour les paroles de Jésus) et du simple au double (pour les parties narratives). On trouve, en effet, deux collections de paroles brèves, une avant (Mt) et une après (Lc) la Femme adultère, mais aussi dix entretiens de Jésus dans Jn, cinq avant et cinq après la Femme adultère ; tandis que les récits du ministère sont pour la plupart en trois exemplaires, un avant (Mt) et deux après (Lc, Mc) l'épisode central ; que les récits de naissance relatent une naissance simple (Mt) et une naissance double (Lc) ; et que dans Jn, les récits forment cette même proportion, de part et d'autre de la Femme adultère[23]. Mais cette disposition remarquable disparaît à la fin du 2ᵉ siècle, quand l'ordre des évangiles est modifié. Il convient donc de rétablir cet ordre ancien, pour comprendre la raison des quatre occurrences de la parole sur la désunion.

D'autres paroles, peu nombreuses, ont cette même disposition, à savoir deux occurrences chez Mt, une chez Lc et une chez Mc ; en particulier, l'amour du prochain (Mt 19,19 / 22,39 ; Lc 10,27 ; Mc 12,31), la foi à déplacer des montagnes (Mt 17,20 / 21,21 ; Lc 17,6 [D] ; Mc 11,22-23) et le signe de Jonas[24] (Mt 12,38-42 / 16,4 ; Lc 11,29-32 ; Mc 8,12). La plupart des paroles sont absentes de Mc et ont en tout deux occurrences, une dans Mt et une dans Lc, comme le Notre Père (Mt 6,9-13 ; Lc 11,2-4). Et dans tous ces cas, les paroles sont en proportion d'égalité, de part et d'autre de la Femme adultère, comme les collections de paroles ou les entretiens johanniques : cette disposition est une manière de les authentifier comme venant bien de Jésus. Un petit nombre de paroles, en revanche, a trois occurrences, une dans chaque évangile synoptique, signifiant par là qu'elles sont attachées au cadre narratif. Ainsi, la lampe, le secret et la rétribution finale sont groupées dans le cadre narratif de Mc (4,21-25) et de Lc (8,16-18) et apparaissent

---

23. Amphoux, « Femme adultère », 149-165.

24. Le signe de Jonas repose sur le jeu de mots Jonas / Onias, celui-ci étant le dernier grand-prêtre de la dynastie des Oniades, déposé en—175 par Antiochos IV. Une période troublée s'ensuit, au terme de laquelle une autre dynastie se met en place, celle des Asmonéens, qui n'obtiendront jamais la pleine reconnaissance de leur légitimité. Puis, Hérode crée une dynastie royale, et les grands-prêtres sont dès lors nommés, perdant encore davantage leur légitimité. Le signe de Jonas est, en somme, un retour à la légitimité sacerdotale, un retour de l'élu de Dieu pour diriger le peuple.

séparées dans les sections de paroles de Mt (5,15 / 10,26 / 13,12) ; ou encore l'homme fort et le péché impardonnable sont groupées dans le cadre narratif de Mt (12,29-32) et de Mc (3,27-30) et séparées dans la collection de paroles de Lc (11,21-22 / 12,10).

Selon cette observation, les paroles qui constituent le cadre de la collection de Lc (voir plus haut) sont toutes des paroles venant de Jésus. Mais nous avons vu que la désunion et la foi à déplacer des montagnes se trouvent dans 1 Co avant de devenir évangéliques. La foi associée à l'image du déplacement de la montagne remplace la paix (EvTh 48[25]) et la désunion remplace la réunion du masculin et du féminin (EvTh 22b). Paul exprime ainsi son désir de faire de la foi un nouveau chemin de salut et son rejet de la réunion du masculin et du féminin, au sens que cette parole a pris avec l'évangile prêché par les Hellénistes. La parole sur la réunion disparaît en tant que parole de Jésus ; mais l'idée de réunion subsiste, non pas avec son sens d'αὐτάρκεια, mais avec l'idée d'une préparation à l'entrée dans le royaume, annonçant ainsi le sens que prendra le mot μοναχός, à partir du 4ᵉ siècle (voir plus haut).

CONCLUSION

La parole sur la réunion du masculin et du féminin a sans doute fait partie de la collection primitive des paroles de Jésus, rédigée en araméen dès l'an 30, autrement dit, elle existe au tout début de la constitution de la première communauté chrétienne, elle a le sens d'une préparation à l'entrée dans le royaume, avec la connotation d'une maîtrise de la sexualité. Mais en 32, dans la dissidence des Hellénistes, la parole prend un sens philosophique nouveau et devient le principe central de la collection de paroles qui est la base de l'enseignement. Les apôtres, à Jérusalem, puis Jacques et les frères de Jésus, à partir du début des années 40, n'acceptent pas ce sens nouveau et, dans la traduction grecque de la collection primitive attribuée à Jacques, la parole disparaît.

Puis, vers 55, à la suite d'un incident survenu à Antioche et montrant que la loi comme seul chemin de salut aboutit à séparer dans la communauté les judéo- et pagano- chrétiens, Paul envisage un nouveau chemin de salut, celui de la foi ; mais, découvrant en 56 l'enseignement des Hellénistes à Éphèse, il s'y oppose. Il substitue alors au principe de la réunion du masculin et du féminin la simple règle qui déconseille la désunion et refuse le remariage ; et il propose un nouveau principe, celui de la double relation par

---

25. EvTh 48 : « Jésus a dit: si deux font la paix dans une maison, ils diront à la montagne: déplace-toi, et elle se déplacera. »

la foi à Dieu et par l'amour avec l'humanité. La rupture s'opère alors entre Paul et les Hellénistes. Jacques, à Jérusalem, tente sans succès de résister à la position radicale de Paul en proposant, par une réorganisation de la collection de paroles, une synthèse qui ménage un espace pour les Hellénistes. Paul rejette cette proposition, un courant majoritaire se forme, qui réunit Paul et les apôtres et rejette l'enseignement des Hellénistes. La réunion du masculin et du féminin disparaît comme parole de la collection, mais l'idée subsiste, avec son sens premier. Elle se transmet par la citation de 2 *Clément*; mais sa présence dans deux passages de la fin de Matthieu se perdra, avec les révisions qui sont à l'origine du texte alexandrin et du texte byzantin.

Ces conclusions sont nouvelles et dépendent de plusieurs hypothèses. La première est littéraire : la théorie des deux sources propose de faire venir les paroles de Jésus d'une source Q qui aurait contenu tous les passages communs à Mt et Lc et absents de Mc ; mais cette source n'a jamais existé. Il y a bien une source de paroles de Jésus, mais celle-ci a évolué au cours de la première génération, présentant successivement l'état de l'EvTh, puis celui des sections de Mt, enfin celui de la collection de Lc. Les passages extérieurs à ces états de la collection ont une origine distincte. La deuxième hypothèse est textuelle : le texte alexandrin et le texte byzantin sont des révisions d'une plus ancienne rédaction attestée par le texte « occidental » dont le principal témoin est le Codex de Bèze (D). Au niveau de cette rédaction, les évangiles entrent dans un même projet éditorial dont ils sont les quatre parties, constituées à partir de sources : la tradition d'Antioche, pour les synoptiques, celle d'Éphèse, pour Jn. La troisième hypothèse est historique : il existe trois courants dans l'Église de la première génération, celui des apôtres, celui des Hellénistes et celui de Paul ; et le débat s'organise autour de la collection des paroles de Jésus, à laquelle les apôtres donnent un sens conservateur qui maintient leur communauté dans le judaïsme, tandis que les Hellénistes privilégient le lien avec la philosophie, pour s'adresser à l'élite internationale du monde romain ; quant à Paul, il rejette cette collection et ouvre avec la christologie le chemin d'une nouvelle référence scripturaire fondée sur une trame narrative.

La parole sur la réunion du masculin et du féminin est au cœur du débat entre ces trois courants ; et après 150, quand une orthodoxie ecclésiale se sera mise en place, elle disparaîtra.

BIBLIOGRAPHIE

Amphoux, C.-B. « La place de l'épisode de la Femme adultère ». Dans *Greeks, Jews, and Christians: Historical, Religious, and Philological Studies in Honor of Jesús Peláez del Rosal*, édité par L. Roig Lanzillotta et I. Muñoz Gallarte, 149-65. Córdoba: El Almendro, 2013.

———. « Les lieux de rédaction des lettres de Paul, d'après la tradition manuscrite ». *B.A.B.E.L.A.O.* 2 (2013) 87-104.

———, éd. *Manuel de critique textuelle du Nouveau Testament*. Bruxelles, 2014.

———. « Pour une approche documentaire des paroles de Jésus ». *B.A.B.E.L.A.O.* 1 (2012) 1-13.

———. , « Réponse à E. Nodet ». Dans *Synoptiques et Actes, quel texte original*, 179-204. CahRB 82. Paris: Gabalda, 2014.

Funk, F. X. *Die apostolischen Väter*. Tübingen, 1906².

———, éd. *Les écrits des Pères apostoliques*. Paris, 2006.

Gianotto, C. « Évangile selon Thomas ». Dans *Écrits apocryphes chrétiens*, 33-53. Vol. 1. Bibliothèque de la Pléiade. Paris: Gallimard 1997.

Meynard, J. E. *L'Évangile selon Thomas*. Nag Hammadi Studies 5. Leiden, 1975.

Reynard, J. « Premières homélies chrétiennes: la seconde épître de Clément ». Dans *Histoire de la littérature grecque chrétienne*, édité par B. Pourderon et E. Norelli, 2:533-41. Paris, 2013.

Simon, R. *Histoire critique du texte du Nouveau Testament*. Rotterdam, 1689.

Von Soden, H. *Die Schriften des Neuen Testaments*. Vol. 1. Berlin, 1902.

8

The Definition and Translation of ἀλήθεια in the Gospel According to John[1]

The Case of John 1:14, 17

JESÚS PELÁEZ AND GASCO
Universidad de Córdoba

INTRODUCTION

THE PRESENT STUDY IS an analysis of the lexeme ἀλήθεια using the method of semantic analysis applied by the Semantic Analysis Group of the University of Cordoba (GASCO), which is editing the *Diccionario griego-español del Nuevo Testamento*. The focus of this study is to determine the different meanings of the lexeme ἀλήθεια in the Gospel of John with special atten-

---

1. The research group GASCO (Group of Semantic Analysis of the University of Cordoba) that is drafting the Diccionario Griego-Español del Nuevo Testamento is formed by the following members: Marta Merino, Israel Muñoz, Dámaris Romero, Lautaro Roig, Lourdes García, Pope Godoy, Rufino Godoy, Luis Domingo, José I. Fernández, Juan Guillén, Juan Barreto, PSD or Graduates in Theology, Biblical or Classical Philology. The project is directed by the author of this article.

tion on its uses in John 1:14 and 17, the goal of which is to propose a new interpretation and translation of the expression χάρις καὶ ἀλήθεια.

The following exchange between Jesus and Pilate is found in the Passion Discourse of the Gospel according to John:

> "So you are a king?" Jesus answered, "You say that I am a king. For this I have been born, and for this I have come into the world, to bear witness to the truth. Everyone who is of the truth hears my voice." Pilate replied, "What is truth?" (John 18:37–38)

The following study is a response to Pilate's question from a philological standpoint. First, I will offer a synthesis of the entry for ἀλήθεια in the *Diccionario griego-español del Nuevo Testamento*, presenting the different definitions provided for this lexeme based on their contexts. Second, I will focus on the specific meaning of ἀλήθεια in the expression χάρις καὶ ἀλήθεια found in John 1:14 and 17. Since this expression is made up of two abstract nouns, whose meaning is not easy to ascertain, I will propose a different translation that the one systematically reproduced in Spanish and English Bibles. Hopefully this will open the door for a discussion on the translation of abstract nouns in general based on the contexts in which they occur, perhaps the subject of a paper in the near future.

THE MEANING OR DEFINITION OF ἀλήθεια IN THE GOSPEL ACCORDING TO JOHN

The lexeme ἀλήθεια appears 119 times in the New Testament, 22 of which occur in the Gospel according to John. When each of these occurences are analyzed in their contexts, three different aspects of meaning surface: (1) ἀλήθεια as a known or knowable reality; (2) ἀλήθεια as a reality expressed in words; and (3) ἀλήθεια as a reality exercised (or, put into practice).

In the second fascicle of the *Diccionario griego-español del Nuevo Testamento*, five different definitions are given for ἀλήθεια. Those definitions are provided below, along with an example from the text of John:[2]

1. "A certain reality that is known or knowable by someone."

John 5:53   ὑμεῖς ἀπεστάλκατε πρὸς Ἰωάννην, καὶ μεμαρτύρηκεν <u>τῇ ἀληθείᾳ</u>.
"You sent messengers to John, and he testified <u>to the truth</u>."

---

2. Mateos et al., *Diccionario griego-español*, facsim. 2, ad locum.

The use of ἀλήθεια in this verse clearly refers to the person of Jesus (i.e., truth = Jesus). In other words, to say John "testified to the truth" is the same as saying John "testified about Jesus," as a personal reality, known by John the Baptist.

2. "The divine and human reality that can be known *via* Jesus or that which is revealed by him." John expresses this sense in 14:6 where Jesus bids farewell to his disciples in order to go to the Father and prepare a place for them. Peter and Thomas ask him about the way to the Father and Jesus answers them:

John 14:6
> ἐγώ εἰμι ἡ ὁδὸς καὶ <u>ἡ ἀλήθεια</u> καὶ ἡ ζωή·
> οὐδεὶς ἔρχεται πρὸς τὸν πατέρα εἰ μὴ δι' ἐμοῦ.
> "I am the way, and <u>the truth</u>, and the life.
> No one comes to the Father except through me."

The person of Jesus, defined as "the truth" (ἡ ἀλήθεια) is, therefore, that divine-human reality manifested in Jesus, through which one gains access to the Father.

3. "The reality of God and of his project regarding mankind, that, once known, leads to act in benefit of human beings." This is when the known reality (i.e., truth) leads to a specific behavior. One example is found in John 8:31–32:

John 8:31–32
> ἔλεγεν οὖν ὁ Ἰησοῦς πρὸς τοὺς πεπιστευκότας αὐτῷ
> Ἰουδαίους· ἐὰν ὑμεῖς μείνητε ἐν τῷ λόγῳ τῷ ἐμῷ, ἀληθῶς
> μαθηταί μού ἐστε καὶ γνώσεσθε τὴν ἀλήθειαν, καὶ <u>ἡ ἀλήθεια</u>
> ἐλευθερώσει ὑμᾶς.
> "Then Jesus said to the Jews who have believed in him: if you continue in my word, you are truly my disciples and you will know the truth, and <u>the truth</u> will make you free."

In this passage Jesus speaks to the Jews who have believed in him and therefore know his message, but who are not yet really disciples, because they do not follow him in their behavior; if they did so, then they would know the truth. "To know the truth" is not something theoretical, but means "to undergo/internalize or put into practice the basic contents of Jesus' message." The putting into practice of Jesus' message is the equivalent of "knowing the truth," as the way to freedom.

4. "Reality adequately expressed in words." This meaning of ἀλήθεια appears when it is the object of phrasal lexemes.

John 8:40
νῦν δὲ ζητεῖτέ με ἀποκτεῖναι ἄνθρωπον ὃς <u>τὴν ἀλήθειαν</u> ὑμῖν λελάληκα ἣν ἤκουσα παρὰ τοῦ θεοῦ· τοῦτο Ἀβραὰμ οὐκ ἐποίησεν.

"But now you are trying to kill me, a man who has told you <u>the truth</u>, which I heard from God. This is not what Abraham did."

"The truth, which I heard from God" is the message that Jesus has learned from God and has revealed in words to the Jews, a message they do not want to accept because, according to John 8:44a their father is the devil/ enemy.

5. "The reality of God and of his project regarding mankind, that, once known, leads to actions to benefit human beings." This use is found when ἀλήθεια is the object of verbs of action such as ποιέω. In this case a metonymy is created in relation to the third definition. There are two sub-definitions involved. The first is when ἀλήθεια denotes the way someone acts or behaves: "The way of acting in benefit of human beings that is the consequence of certain knowledge of the reality of God and of his work regarding mankind." Consider the following example:

John 3:21
ὁ δὲ ποιῶν <u>τὴν ἀλήθειαν</u> ἔρχεται πρὸς τὸ φῶς, ἵνα φανερωθῇ αὐτοῦ τὰ ἔργα ὅτι ἐν θεῷ ἐστιν εἰργασμένα.

"But the one who does <u>what is true</u> comes to the light, so that it may be clearly seen that their deeds have been done in God."

The clause ὁ ποιῶν τὴν ἀλήθειαν ("he who does what is true") stands in contrast with ὁ φαῦλα πράσσων "he who does what is evil/vileness" (3:20). Ἀλήθεια appears with the definite article, and it denotes conduct of the opposite nature, prior to knowledge of the gospel; hence, "those who do what is true *come to the light*" (3:21). In this sense, it deals with a type of human behavior, that is, of fair, honest deeds and loyalty to others. A parallelism can be established between John 3:21 ὁ ποιῶν τὴν ἀλήθειαν ("he who does what is true") and John 5:29 οἱ τὰ ἀγαθὰ ποιήσαντες "those who have done good," where "good" can be translated as "goodness," that is, "justice, honesty, loyalty, or love."

THE MEANING OF THE EXPRESSION χάρις καὶ ἀλήθεια

Despite the fact that there appear to be five different definitions corresponding to the lexeme ἀλήθεια, this lexeme is almost always translated, in Spanish and English Bibles, as "truth." However, there are cases in which the context requires a different translation, as will be demonstrated in the second part of this study dealing with the expression χάρις καὶ ἀλήθεια.

For the purposes of the present study, it is necessary to fix the lexical meaning of ἀλήθεια, but since that lexeme is closely joined by καὶ χάρις it is worth paying attention to the expression χάρις καὶ ἀλήθεια, which appears twice in the Gospel according to John:

John 1:14

Καὶ ὁ λόγος σὰρξ ἐγένετο καὶ ἐσκήνωσεν ἐν ἡμῖν, καὶ ἐθεασάμεθα τὴν δόξαν αὐτοῦ, δόξαν ὡς μονογενοῦς παρὰ πατρός, πλήρης <u>χάριτος καὶ ἀληθείας</u>.

"And the Word became flesh and and lived among us. And we have seen his glory, the glory as of a father's only son, full <u>of grace and truth</u>."

John 1:17

ὁ νόμος διὰ Μωϋσέως ἐδόθη, <u>ἡ χάρις καὶ ἡ ἀλήθεια</u> διὰ Ἰησοῦ Χριστοῦ ἐγένετο.

"The law was indeed given through Moses; <u>grace and truth</u> came through Jesus Christ."

A perusal of a number of Spanish translations[3] to see how χάρις καὶ ἀλήθεια is rendered in these two verses shows that it is consistently translated "gracia y verdad" (grace and truth), with the exception of the Nueva Biblia Española (NBE) by L. A. Schökel and Juan Mateos,[4] who translate it as "amor y lealtad" (love and loyalty) and the Biblia del Peregrino (BP),[5] in which it is rendered, incorrectly in my opinion, as "lealtad y fidelidad" (loyalty and faithfulness). And the most common English translations[6] all translate it as "grace and truth."[7]

The translation of χάρις καὶ ἀλήθεια as "grace and truth" is vague and undefined because it is an expression composed of two abstract nouns, whose meaning is difficult to comprehend unless close observation is made of the context in which they appear. Abstract nouns are those that designate

---

3. Nacar-Colunga, Cantera-Iglesias, Sagrada Biblia, Biblia de la Casa de la Biblia, Biblia de la Conferencia Episcopal Española, Biblia Latinoamericana, and La Biblia de Herder, among others.

4. Schökel et al., *Nueva Biblia Española*, ad locum.

5. Schökel et al., *Biblia del Peregrino*, ad locum.

6. See NIV, NRSV, CEB, CEB, NET, HCSB, among others.

7. The commentaries of the Gospel of John translate almost unanimously "grace and truth," although every one explains the specific meaning of this abstract expression. "Grace and truth": O'Day, "John," 515; McHugh, *John 1–4*, 60; Borgen, "Gospel of John and Hellenism," 102; Kanagaraj, *John*, ad locum; Ridderbos, *John*, 54; Bernard, *John*, 27. "Grâce et verité": L'Éplattenier, *Jean*, 30. "La grace de la verité": Léon-Dufour, *Jean* (Spanish translation: *Juan*, 97). "Grazia e verità": Mannuci, *Giovanni*, 272; Segalla, *Giovanni*, 8. "Gnade und Wahrheit": Beutler, *Das Johannesevangelium*, 94; Schlatter, *Der Evangelist Johannes*, 28; Schenke, *Das Johannes Evangelium*, 20.

or name an object or phenomenon that is not materially concrete. The meanings of such nouns, therefore, are left up to the imagination and intellect. They refer to non-material things such as ideas and sentiments. In this sense, abstract nouns are in opposition to concrete ones that refer to objects that are perceptible by way of the senses. We can say that they are often like "stock words," used to express concepts that can only be made concrete or explicit from their context. And a detailed examination of their context is really the only way to unlock or identify their meaning or definition and, as a result, the correct translation. In other words, a careful reader might wonder what is meant by the expression "grace and truth." How should we translate these lexemes so that their meaning is clear at first sight without the need for additional explanation?

Answering this question requires paying careful attention to the contexts in which the expression appears—not only in the Gospel according to John (immediate context), but also to the Hebrew Bible and its translation into Greek, namely the LXX (remote context). As far as the remote context is concerned, the expression χάρις καὶ ἀλήθεια ("grace and truth") is reminiscent of Exod 34:6:

Exod 34:6 (LXX)
καὶ παρῆλθεν κύριος πρὸ προσώπου αὐτοῦ καὶ ἐκάλεσεν κύριος ὁ θεὸς οἰκτίρμων καὶ ἐλεήμων μακρόθυμος καὶ <u>πολυέλεος καὶ ἀληθινός</u>.

"And the Lord passed before him, and proclaimed: 'The Lord, a God merciful and gracious, <u>in steadfast love and faithfulness</u>."

The expression πολυέλεος καὶ ἀληθινός is the translation of the Hebrew expression *rab ḥesed weʾemet*. There is a difference, though, between this expression in Exod 34:6 and John 1:14 and 17. While the Hebrew Bible uses two nouns joined by a copulative conjunction, as does the Gospel according to John (*ḥesed weʾemet*/χάρις καὶ ἀλήθεια),[8] the LXX version has substituted in this case these two nouns by two adjectives also joined by a copulative conjunction (πολυέλεος καὶ ἀληθινός). But this difference is not important because abstract nouns often denote qualities and these are expressed, mainly but not always, with adjectives, so the use of an adjective in the place of a noun does not change the meaning of the expression.[9]

8. In Josh 2:14, the LXX also translates the expression *ḥesed weʾemet* by two nouns: ἔλεος καὶ ἀλήθεια, where ἔλεος is applied to the relationship among men: ὡς ἂν παραδῷ κύριος ὑμῖν τὴν πόλιν ποιήσετε εἰς ἐμὲ ἔλεος καὶ ἀλήθειαν "then when the Lord gives us the land we will deal kindly and faithfully with you."

9. "Almost identical formula recurs in Num 14:18: '"Yahweh is slow to anger, and abounding in merciful love . . ." This too is a prayer used immediately after a national apostasy, when the people tried to stone Moses and Aaron, Joshua and Caleb (Num

The Meaning of χάρις

Consider first the meaning of *ḥesed*, which is translated by ἔλεος (= χάρις)[10] and can vary according to case:[11]

1. In human interaction, *ḥesed* refers to willing love, a good heart, as opposed to cruelty. This concept could be translated as "clemency" or "mercy." The following passage from the Psalms is an example of this meaning:

Ps 109:16   ἀνθ ὧν οὐκ ἐμνήσθη ποιῆσαι ἔλεος. (LXX)
"for he did not remember to show <u>kindness</u>."

The translation *misericordia* for <u>ἔλεος</u> is found in the Vulgate: *eo quo non est recordatus facere misericordiam.*

2. Said of man towards God, *ḥesed* is filial love, compassion shown in deeds, which can be translated as "kindness." An example is found in Jeremiah:

Jer 2:2   τάδε λέγει κύριος 'Εμνήσθην <u>ἐλέους</u> νεότητος σοῦ καὶ ἀγάπης τελειώθεσεώς σου. (LXX)
"thus says the Lord: I remember <u>the devotion</u> of your youth, your love as a bride." (NRSV)

In English, the word "devotion" is defined as "strong attachment (to) or affection (for a cause, person, etc.) marked by dedicated loyalty."[12] The Vulgate translates Jer 2:2 in the following way: *Recordatus sum tui miserans* (ἔλεος) *adulescentiam tuam et caritatem disponsationis tuae . . .*"

14.10). After this second apostasy, however, the MT omits from the prayer the final word *wĕĕmet*, though the full version, with the two nouns, is found in a handful of MSS, in the Samaritan text of Exodus and in the LXX . . . . Other citations of the phrase from Exod 34.6 occur in the two great penitential services of the post-exilic period, at Joel 2.13 and at Neh 9.17 (here again, in both cases, in the truncated form, without the final *wĕĕmet*)" (McHugh, *John 1–4*, 60–61).

10. χάρις occurs only four times in the Fourth Gospel, all in the prologue. The phrase χάρις καὶ ἀλήθεια recurs in John 1:17, after which it is never again found in the Gospel. John establishes the theme of grace in the prologue and then will illustrate it through the Gospel without naming it again. In its place it will appear πνεῦμα and ἀγάπη, cf. Mateos and Barreto, *Juan*, 71; L'Éplattenier, *Jean*, 30. Montgomery, ("Hebrew Hesed and Greek Charis," 97–102) has shown that χάρις is an excellent translation for *ḥesed*. The Syriac version translates both the *ḥesed* and *ĕmet* of the Old Testament and the χάρις καὶ ἀλήθεια of John 1:14 by the same words (*taibutá* and *qushtá*). The Christian Syro-Palestinian dialect renders χάρις by *hasda* (*ḥesed*).

11. See Mateos and Barreto, *Juan*, ad locum.

12. Collins Dictionary, ad locum.

3. Said of God to man, *ḥesed* means "benevolence, inclination to help and save, mercy." An example of this use is also found in the Psalms:

> κύριε ἐν τῷ οὐρανῷ τὸ <u>ἔλεος</u> σου καὶ ἡ <u>ἀλήθειά</u> σου ἕως τῶν νεφελῶν … ὡς ἐπλήθυνας τὸ <u>ἔλεος</u> σου ὁ θεός … (LXX)

Ps 36:6–7 "Your <u>steadfast love</u>, O Lord, extends to the heavens, your <u>faithfulness</u> to the clouds … How precious is your <u>steadfast love</u> …." (ESV)

The Vulgate translates this: *Domine, in caelo* <u>misericordia</u> *tua,* <u>fides</u> *tua usque ad nubes … Quam pretiosa es* <u>misericordia</u> *tua ….*

In summary, *ḥesed*/ἔλεος can be defined as mercy, benevolence of God manifested to man and, in our case, *the love of God manifested in Jesus,* of whom it is said that he is full of *ḥesed*-ἔλεος (kindness, clemency, mercy), concepts which refer one way or another to "love." The expression πλήρης χάριτος can be translated as "full of love," because grace is none other than the love of God that he affords man, which is manifested in Jesus.

The Meaning of ἀλήθεια

Ἀλήθεια corresponds to the second adjective in the expression πολυέλεος καὶ ἀληθινός (LXX). John, instead of using two adjectives, uses two nouns joined by the conjunction καί (χάρις καὶ ἀλήθεια), which form a *hendiadys*. A *hendiadys* is a rhetorical figure that consists of the expression of a sole concept using two coordinated terms, the second of which qualifies the first, allowing the translation of ἀλήθεια (*ĕmet*) by an adjective. In the Hebrew Bible, *ĕmet* (ἀλήθεια) is a noun that denotes "truth, firmness, sureness." In this way the translation of ἀλήθεια could be *firmness, sureness*. But if we translate ἀλήθεια using an adjective that qualifies χάρις we can state that it is χάρις ("love") that is ἀληθινός (*ĕmet*/ "truth/firm/sure")—"loyal/faithful love." And the expression πλήρης χάριτος καὶ ἀληθείας could be translated as "full of loyal/faithful love." In other words, God's loyal/faithful love has been made manifest to us through Jesus, who is "full of grace and truth," or, better stated, "full of loyal/faithful love."

THE MEANING OF THE EXPRESSION χάρις καὶ ἀλήθεια

Having now walked through this lexical analysis, it is now time to turn to John 1:14 and 17, where one can see that the expression becomes far less ambiguous and easier to understand for readers:

John 1:14, 17

Καὶ ὁ λόγος σὰρξ ἐγένετο καὶ ἐσκήνωσεν ἐν ἡμῖν, καὶ ἐθεασάμεθα τὴν δόξαν αὐτοῦ, δόξαν ὡς μονογενοῦς παρὰ πατρός, <u>πλήρης χάριτος καὶ ἀληθείας</u> ... ὅτι ὁ νόμος διὰ Μωϋσέως ἐδόθη, <u>ἡ χάρις καὶ ἡ ἀλήθεια</u> διὰ Ἰησοῦ Χριστοῦ ἐγένετο.

"And the Word became flesh and lived among us, and we have seen his glory, the glory as of a father's only son, <u>full of loyal/ faithful love</u> .... The law indeed was given through Moses; <u>the loyal/faithful love</u> came through Jesus Christ."

In this way such an abstract expression like χάρις καὶ ἀλήθεία, which is difficult to understand because of the presence of two abstract nouns, is translated in such a way that recognizes the author's use of hendiadys—"loyal/ faithful love"—an expression that is more understandable at first sight. This translation will hopefully lead to further studies dealing with the translation of abstract nouns in their respective contexts.

BIBLIOGRAPHY

Bernard, John Henry. *A Critical and Exegetical Commentary on the Gospel according to John*. Vol. 1. Edinburgh: T. & T. Clark, 1967.
Beutler, Johannes. *Das Johannesevangelium. Kommentar*. Freiburg: Herder, 2013.
Borgen, Peter. "The Gospel of John and Hellenism." In *Exploring the Gospel of John in Honour of D. Moody Smith*, edited by R. Alan Culpepper and C. Clifton Black, 98–123. Louisville: Westminster John Knox, 1996.
Kanagaraj, Jey J. *John: A New Covenant Commentary*. Cambridge: Lutterworth, 2013.
Léon-Dufour, Xavier. *Lecture de l' Évangile selon Jean*. Paris: Editions du Seuil, 1987 (translated into Spanish: *Lectura del evangelio de Juan*, [Salamanca: Ed. Sígueme], 1989).
L'Éplattenier, Charles. *L'Évangile de Jean*. Genéve: Labor et Fides, 1993.
Mannuci, Valerini. *Giovanni, il vangelo narrante: Introduzione all' arte narrativa del quarto Vangelo*. Bologna: Ed. Dehoniane, 1993.
Mateos, Juan, and J. Barreto. *El Evangelio de Juan. Análisis lingüístico y comentario exegético*. Lectura del Nuevo Testamento. Madrid: Ediciones Cristiandad, 1979.
Mateos, Juan, et al. *Diccionario griego-español del Nuevo Testamento*. Fascículo 2. Córdoba: Ediciones El Almendro, 2002.
McHugh, John F. *John 1–4*. Edited by Graham N. Stanton. The International Critical Commentary. New York: T. & T. Clark, 2009.
Montgomery, James A. "Hebrew *Hesed* and Greek *Charis*." NTR 32 (1939) 97–102.
O'Day, Gail R. "The Gospel of John: Introduction, Commentary, and Reflections." In *The New Interpreter's Bible*, 9:493–865. Nashville: Abingdon, 1995.
Ridderbos, Herman N. *The Gospel according to John: A Theological Commentary*. Translated by J. Vriend. Grand Rapids: Eerdmans, 1997.
Schenke, Ludger. *Das Johannes Evangelium. Einführung-Text-dramatische Gestalt*. Stuttgart: Kohlhammer, 2013.
Schlatter, Adolf. *Der Evangelist Johannes*. Stuttgart: Calwer, 1960.

Schökel, L. Alonso, et al. *Biblia del Peregrino*. Estella: Ega Mensajero-Verbo Divino, 1997.
———, et al. *Nueva Biblia Española*. Madrid: Ediciones Cristiandad, 1975.
Segalla, Giuseppe. *Vangelo secondo Giovanni. Traduzione strutturatta*. Subsidi Biblici. Padova: Edizioni San Lorenzo, 1997.

9

The Meaning of πίστις in the Framework of the *Diccionario griego-español del Nuevo Testamento*[1]

Israel Muñoz Gallarte
Universidad de Córdoba

INTRODUCTION

THE MEANING OF THE Greek lexeme πίστις remains one of the most controversial questions in semantic-linguistic studies of the New Testament. A number of researchers over the last few decades have engaged in this discussion, such as Desta Heliso (2007), G. van Kooten (2012), and the numerous members of his research group called "Overcoming the Faith-Reason

---

1. This article has been prepared within the framework of the "Diccionario griego-español del Nuevo Testamento" (FFI2011-26124) Research Programme, financed by the Ministry for Science and Innovation. General Directive for Programmes and Knowledge Transfer. The research group that is drafting the *Diccionario griego-español del Nuevo Testamento* is formed by the following members: Jesús Peláez, Marta Merino, Israel Muñoz, Dámaris Romero, Lautaro Roig Lanzillotta, Lourdes García, Pope Godoy, Rufino Godoy, Luis Domingo, José I. Fernández, and Juan Guillén, PSD or Graduates in Theology, Biblical or Classical Philology. I am very grateful to Prof. Black for his friendship and his numerous publications that opened new paths in the field of New Testament studies.

Opposition: Pauline *Pistis* in Contemporary Philosophy."[2] These works have generally focused exclusively on the differences between the fideistic and the philosophical meanings of the term and, consequently, overlooked the need for a previous semantic analysis of πίστις. The present study is an attempt at such an analysis, employing the methodology and categories of the *Diccionario griego-español del Nuevo Testamento* (*DGENT*).[3] The analysis that follows is limited in scope, focusing exclusively on the undisputed letters of Paul (i.e., Romans, 1 and 2 Corinthians, Galatians, Philippians, 1 Thessalonians, and Philemon),[4] primarily because delimiting the study in this way makes it more manageable, not because the methodology is incapable of treating additional material. Of course, the *DGENT* will take into consideration all 245 uses of πίστις in their respective contexts. The study at hand consists of four sections. The first outlines the discussions of πίστις found in other dictionaries, which sort of sets the backdrop for a new proposal of the meaning of πίστις. The second traces the general and secondary (or contextual) meanings of the lexeme. The third will attempt to identify how context impacts the intended meaning of the lexeme. And the fourth section will draw some conclusions.

THE LEXEME πίστις AND PREVIOUS DICTIONARY ENTRIES

It seems safe to say that the major Greek lexicons, such as Liddell-Scott[5] and Adrados,[6] offer a very broad discussion when they treat lexemes, and that is true of πίστις as well. Such resources are valuable, but their value is limited. One handicap is they do not meet the needs of translators and students of the New Testament that are interested on the meaning of a given lexeme in a particular context. It is important, though, to note how some dictionaries treat πίστις and focus on the semantic aspect in order to structure its different uses, even though the methodologies employed are very different than that of the *DGENT*.

---

2. Also about this topic in classical philosophy, see, for example, Lienhard, "Meaning of *Pistis*," 446–54.

3. Mateos et al., *Diccionario griego-español*.

4. See Morgan, *Roman Faith and Christian Faith*, 264, 302.

5. Liddell et al., *A Greek-English Lexicon*, s.v. πίστις.

6. Rodríguez Adrados et al., *Diccionario griego-español*. This is still an ongoing project, whose last volume published in 2010 covers Ἐκπελλεύω–Ἔξαυος.

Louw-Nida

Louw-Nida[7] identify six meanings:

1. "31.85 πιστεύω; πίστις, εως f: to believe to the extent of complete trust and reliance—'to believe in, to have confidence in, to have faith in, to trust, faith, trust.'"[8]

2. "31.102 πιστεύω; πίστις, εως f: to believe in the good news about Jesus Christ and to become a follower—'to be a believer, to be a Christian, Christian faith.'"

3. "31.104 πίστις, εως f: . . . the content of what Christians believe—'the faith, beliefs, doctrine.'"

4. "31.43 πίστις, εως f: that which is completely believable—'what can be fully believed, that which is worthy of belief, believable evidence, proof.'"

5. "31.88 πίστις, εως f: the state of being someone in whom complete confidence can be placed—'trustworthiness, dependability, faithfulness.'"

6. "33.289 πίστις, εως f: a promise or pledge of faithfulness and loyalty—'promise, pledge to be faithful.'"

Louw-Nida correctly describe the meaning of πίστις from a structure based on three main axes. If the context indicates a dynamic substantive, then uses 1 and 2 are in play. If a static noun, then uses 3 and 4. And, finally, the dictionary warns of a third possibility when metonymy is present in the context; in such cases, πίστις would mean the object that receives the trust/faith, rather than faith in itself. It is unfortunate, however, that Louw-Nida do not discuss the contextual factor(s) associated with the different meanings. Readers are left to figure it all out for themselves. Their only hope is to infer whatever they can from the different Scripture references. The use of definitions is the most interesting feature of this resource. But one weakness is these definitions seem to be used in places for more than one sense meaning. The first two meanings mentioned above are a good example of this. Both denote the idea of believing in someone/something; the only difference is a narrowed focus or object of that belief. The same problem emerges

---

7. Louw and Nida, *Greek-English Lexicon*, s.v. πίστις.

8. Against the association of πίστις and πιστεύω here, see Campbell, "False Presuppositions," 715–16. For an overview on this issue, see also Matlock, "Detheologizing the πίστις Χριστοῦ Debate," 14 n. 39.

when we deal with meanings 3 and 4, in which the objects that receive the trust/faith are differentiated, i.e., whether they are Christians or not.[9]

Thayer

Thayer's lexicon[10] reduces πίστις to two distinct meanings:

1. "a *conviction* or *belief* respecting man's relationship to God and divine things, generally with the included idea of trust and holy fervour born of faith and conjoined with it."

2. "*fidelity, faithfulness*, i.e., the character of one who can be relied on."

Thayer attempts to take into an account and systematically quote the different contexts in which πίστις appears, while citing as much material that was available to him at that time. Like Louw-Nida, Thayer tries to organize the lemma by following lexemic-semantic criteria, such as the use of objective or subjective genitive and the nature of the genitive that follows πίστις. However, the result is somewhat confusing, because the lexicon does not clarify which semantic conditions result in a given meaning. And it seems like he raises more theological questions than linguistic ones. A good example is when Thayer warns about when the word πίστις is used in relationship to God. He says it is "the conviction that God exists and is the creator and the ruler of all things, the provider and bestower of eternal salvation through Christ," which packs into the lexeme the meaning or definition of πίστις found in Hebrews 11:6, 12:2, and 13:7.

BDAG

The dictionary of Bauer and Aland (BDAG)[11] offers a more in-depth analysis of this term by identifying (1) forms and where they occur in the New Testament and (2) semantic meanings, along with (3) the lexemes connected to πίστις in the contexts where it occurs. There are three meanings in BDAG:

1. "[T]hat which evokes trust and faith." There are three submeanings under this category: (1) "the state of being someone in whom confidence

---

9. This problem has been already pointed out by Matlock, "Detheologizing the πίστις Χριστοῦ Debate," 12 n. 34. See also Muñoz and Merino, "El campo semántico," 13–14, 24–25.

10. Thayer et al., *Greek-English Lexicon of the New Testament*, s.v. πίστις. See also Muñoz and Merino, "El campo semántico," 12, 23.

11. Bauer et al., *Greek-English Lexicon*, s.v. πίστις.

can be placed, faithfulness, reliability, fidelity, commitment"; (2) "a solemn promise to be faithful and loyal, assurance, oath, troth"; (3) "a token offered as a guarantee of something promised, proof, pledge."

2. "[S]tate of believing on the basis of the reliability of the one trusted, *trust, confidence, faith.*" There are four subcategories with this meaning: (1) God, (2) Christ, (3) objective genitive, and (4) the use without an object. The latter receives much attention since this is the way the word usually appears.

3. "[T]hat which is believed, *body of faith/belief/teaching*."

We mostly agree with the structure laid out in BDAG. The mixture of semantic, aspectual, and contextual factors, though, muddles the discussion. Moreover, most of the definitions are carried over from the dictionary of Erwin Preuschen, and sometimes these definitions are not accurate.[12]

THE PROPOSAL OF THE *DGENT*

What sets the *DGENT* apart from other lexicons is it follows a strict semantic methodology. In the case of πίστις, we would deal with the lexeme by concentrating heavily on the aspectual qualities of the term in the contexts where it occurs. After reading the passages in which πίστις occurs, we uncover its basic meaning using the methodology of the *DGENT*—a frame of mind related to a term with a complex formula.[13] In this sense, we understand that the lexeme would denote a not-permanent State (State) that is manifested (Relation) in the conduct (Act) related (Relation) to an object (Object).[14] The first sememe of πίστις could be defined like "State of intellectual and active adhesion to someone or something." Right after that, the dictionary would propose the following translations: "faith" and

---

12. Preuschen, *Handwörterbuch*. See also Muñoz and Merino, "El campo semántico," 12–13, 23–24.

13. About the relationship of πίστις with other related terms, like θεοσέβεια, εὐσέβεια, θρησκεία, δεισιδαιμονία, ὁσιότης, with which πίστις shares the semantic formula and basic semes, see Muñoz, *Los sustantivos-Hecho*, 176.

14. We agree with J. Mateos's assessment by classifying the lexematic meaning of πίστις as a "relative state" and "agent's disposition with regard to a term"; Mateos, *El aspecto verbal*, 43, 47; Mateos, *Método de análisis semántico*, 25. Since the diachronic point of view, about the contextual factor of this lexeme in Aristotle's corpus, Lienhard, "Meaning of *Pistis*," 453, points out to morphological causes, "when it occurs in the singular, or in a verbal or adjectival form." See also, on this issue, Dunn's commentary (*Romans 1–8*).

"conviction." Then, to highlight the contexts in which πίστις appears, the *DGENT* would distinguish between the following categories:

1.1. related to adhesion to God, Jesus, and their message:

Rom 3:22	δικαιοσύνη δὲ θεοῦ διὰ <u>πίστεως</u> Ἰησοῦ Χριστοῦ εἰς πάντας τοὺς πιστεύοντας.[A] "the righteousness of God through <u>faith</u> in Jesus Christ for all who believe."
Rom 4:20	ἐνεδυναμώθη τῇ <u>πίστει</u>, δοὺς δόξαν τῷ θεῷ. "he grew strong in his <u>faith</u> as he gave glory to God."
Rom 11:20	τῇ ἀπιστίᾳ ἐξεκλάσθησαν, σὺ δὲ τῇ <u>πίστει</u> ἕστηκας. "They were broken off because of their unbelief, but you stand only through <u>faith</u>."
1 Cor 15:14	εἰ δὲ Χριστὸς οὐκ ἐγήγερται, κενὸν ἄρα [καὶ] τὸ κήρυγμα ἡμῶν, κενὴ καὶ ἡ <u>πίστις</u> ὑμῶν. "if Christ has not been raised, then our proclamation has been in vain and your <u>faith</u> has been in vain."
2 Cor 1:24ab	οὐχ ὅτι κυριεύομεν ὑμῶν τῆς πίστεως ἀλλὰ συνεργοί ἐσμεν τῆς χαρᾶς ὑμῶν· τῇ γὰρ <u>πίστει</u> ἑστήκατε. "I do not mean to imply that we lord it over your faith; rather, we are workers with you for your joy, because you stand firm in the <u>faith</u>."
Gal 2:6ab	οὐ δικαιοῦται ἄνθρωπος ἐξ ἔργων νόμου ἐὰν μὴ διὰ <u>πίστεως</u> Ἰησοῦ Χριστοῦ, καὶ ἡμεῖς εἰς Χριστὸν Ἰησοῦν ἐπιστεύσαμεν, ἵνα δικαιωθῶμεν ἐκ <u>πίστεως</u> Χριστοῦ. "a person is justified not by the works of the law but through <u>faith</u> in Jesus Christ. And we have come to believe in Christ Jesus, so that we might be justified by <u>faith</u> in Christ."[B]
Gal 3:8	προϊδοῦσα δὲ ἡ γραφὴ ὅτι ἐκ <u>πίστεως</u> δικαιοῖ τὰ ἔθνη ὁ θεός, προευηγγελίσατο τῷ Ἀβραὰμ. "And the Scripture, foreseeing that God would justify the Gentiles by <u>faith</u>, declared the gospel beforehand to Abraham."
Phil 3:9ab	εὑρεθῶ ἐν αὐτῷ, μὴ ἔχων ἐμὴν δικαιοσύνην τὴν ἐκ νόμου ἀλλὰ τὴν διὰ <u>πίστεως</u> Χριστοῦ, τὴν ἐκ θεοῦ δικαιοσύνην ἐπὶ τῇ <u>πίστει</u>. "may be found in him, not having a righteousness of my own that comes from the law, but one that comes through <u>faith</u> in Christ, the righteousness from God based on <u>faith</u>."[C]

1 Thess 1:3	μνημονεύοντες ὑμῶν τοῦ ἔργου τῆς <u>πίστεως</u> καὶ τοῦ κόπου τῆς ἀγάπης καὶ τῆς ὑπομονῆς τῆς ἐλπίδος τοῦ κυρίου ἡμῶν Ἰησοῦ Χριστοῦ. "remembering your work of <u>faith</u> and labor of love and steadfastness of hope in our Lord Jesus Christ."
Phlm 5	ἀκούων σου τὴν ἀγάπην καὶ τὴν <u>πίστιν</u>, ἣν ἔχεις πρὸς τὸν κύριον Ἰησοῦν καὶ εἰς πάντας τοὺς ἁγίους. "because I hear of your love for all the saints and your <u>faith</u> toward the Lord Jesus."

A. For an overview of the Paul's use of the objective/subjective genitive in πίστις Χριστοῦ, see Hultgren, "*Pistis Christou* Formulation," 249–53; also, about the so-called "mystic genitive," proposed by Deissmann (250). We agree mostly with his assertion that in these cases "there is a rich blending of the objective genitive with 'genitive of quality'" (263). See also Dunn, "Once more, *PISTIS CHRISTOU*," 61–81. However, there are currently new voices advocating that the genitive could present both meanings, to wit, Christ's faithfulness to God and human faith in Christ; see Morgan, *Roman Faith and Christian Faith*, 273–74, following the proposal of Hooker, "*PISTIS CHRISTOU*," 321–42.

B. About this verse, see Matlock, "Detheologizing the πίστις Χριστοῦ Debate," 12–13. See also Dunn, "New Perspective on Paul," 299–308; Dunn, "Paul and Justification by Faith," 85–101.

C. About this conception, see Morgan, *Roman Faith and Christian Faith*, 271–72. In her view, here πίστις "captures his sense of the doubly reciprocal relationship of Christ with God and humanity."

This meaning is also found in Rom 1:8; 3:25, 26, 27, 28, 30, 31; 4:5, 9, 11, 12, 13, 14, 16ab, 19; 5:1; 9:30, 32; 10:6; 12:3; 12:6; 14:1; 1 Cor 2:5; 12:9; 13:2, 13; 15:17; 16:13; 2 Cor 4:13; 8:7; 10:15; 13:5; Gal 3:7, 9, 11, 12, 14, 22, 24, 26; 5:5, 6; Phil 1:25; 3:9a; 1 Thess 3:2, 5, 6, 7, 10.

1.2. related to a *conviction* in something else:

Rom 14:22	σὺ <u>πίστιν</u> [ἣν] ἔχεις κατὰ σεαυτὸν ἔχε ἐνώπιον τοῦ θεοῦ "The <u>faith</u> that you have, have as your own conviction before God."

This meaning is also found in Rom 14:23.

1.3. in the figurative sense:

2 Cor 5:7	διὰ <u>πίστεως</u> γὰρ περιπατοῦμεν, οὐ διὰ εἴδους. "for we walk by <u>faith</u>, not by sight."

Gal 2:20	ἐν <u>πίστει</u> ζῶ τῇ τοῦ υἱοῦ τοῦ θεοῦ τοῦ ἀγαπήσαντός με καὶ παραδόντος ἑαυτὸν ὑπὲρ ἐμοῦ.
	"I live by <u>faith</u> in the Son of God, who loved me and gave himself for me."
Phil 2:17	Ἀλλὰ εἰ καὶ σπένδομαι ἐπὶ τῇ θυσίᾳ καὶ λειτουργίᾳ τῆς <u>πίστεως</u> ὑμῶν, χαίρω καὶ συγχαίρω πᾶσιν ὑμῖν.
	"But even if I am being poured out as a libation over the sacrifice and the offering of your <u>faith</u>, I am glad and rejoice with all of you."

This meaning is also found in Gal 3:25; 6:10; 1 Thess 1:8; 5:8.

But πίστις occurs in the certain contexts where it is not related to a human entity, rather to a personality, namely God or Jesus. When it does, the lexeme denotes a second sememe. In this case, πίστις does not denote a non-permanent State like the former, but an intrinsic Attribute. When this occurs, the definition switches to "Quality of personal adhesion to someone or something." The lexeme keeps its basic meaning, but the complex structure denotes an Attribute (A) that is manifested (R) in the conduct (H) related (R) to an object (O). In this case, once we accept this semantic nuance, πίστις should be translated like "fidelity" or "faithfulness," as seen in the following examples:

2.1. related to the faithfulness of God:

Rom 3:3	τί γάρ; εἰ ἠπίστησάν τινες, μὴ ἡ ἀπιστία αὐτῶν τὴν <u>πίστιν</u> τοῦ θεοῦ καταργήσει;
	"What if some were unfaithful? Will their unfaithlessness nullify the <u>faithfulness</u> of God?"

2.2. in the figurative sense:

Gal 5:22	ὁ δὲ καρπὸς τοῦ πνεύματός ἐστιν ἀγάπη, χαρά, εἰρήνη, μακροθυμία, χρηστότης, ἀγαθωσύνη, <u>πίστις</u>.
	"By contrast, the fruit of the Spirit is love, joy, peace, patience, kindness, generosity, <u>faithfulness</u>."[A]

A. About the possibility that Paul here just took over a Hellenistic virtue list, see Morgan, *Roman Faith and Christian Faith*, 277.

In some Pauline passages, especially those containing ὑπακοή and δίκαιος (and their compound forms), a third sememe emerges that changes the inner aspect of πίστις to mark when the state of adhesion is a response to a previous action. In those cases, by following the semantic method of the *DGENT*, the lexeme should be classified as the resultative State (S) as the product (R) of a previous Action (H+D). Therefore, the definition of πίστις would change to "adhesion to someone or something as a result of a previous action,"[15] with "faith" or "faithfulness" as possible translations. This meaning is present in the following verses:

> δι' οὗ ἐλάβομεν χάριν καὶ ἀποστολὴν εἰς ὑπακοὴν πίστεως ἐν πᾶσιν τοῖς ἔθνεσιν ὑπὲρ τοῦ ὀνόματος αὐτοῦ.
>
> Rom 1:5 "through whom we have received grace and apostleship to bring about the obedience of faith among all the Gentiles for the sake of his name."

> ἄρα ἡ πίστις ἐξ ἀκοῆς, ἡ δὲ ἀκοὴ διὰ ῥήματος Χριστοῦ.
>
> Rom 10:17 "So faith comes from what is heard, and what is heard comes through the word of Christ."

This meaning is also found in Rom 1:17; 16:26.

There is one final meaning. When πίστις depends upon an Action in response to verbal communication, we detect a phenomenon of metonymy by treating as an object the state of adhesion to the "group of Christian doctrines."[16] When this occurs, the lexeme has the quality of a quasi-Entity and could be translated as *belief* or *teaching*. πίστις has this meaning in the following verses:

> ἐγγύς σου τὸ ῥῆμά ἐστιν ἐν τῷ στόματί σου καὶ ἐν τῇ καρδίᾳ σου, τοῦτ' ἔστιν τὸ ῥῆμα τῆς πίστεως ὃ κηρύσσομεν.
>
> Rom 10:8 "'The word is near you, on your lips and in your heart' (that is, the word of faith that we proclaim)."

> μόνον δὲ ἀκούοντες ἦσαν ὅτι ὁ διώκων ἡμᾶς ποτε νῦν εὐαγγελίζεται τὴν πίστιν ἥν ποτε ἐπόρθει.
>
> Gal 1:23 "They only heard it said, 'The one who formerly was persecuting us is now proclaiming the faith he once tried to destroy.'"

This meaning also occurs in Rom 1:12; Gal 3:2, 5, 23ab; Phil 1:27; Phlm 6.

---

15. Regarding this meaning also in πιστεύω, see Mateos, *El aspecto verbal*, 58–60.

16. However, see the caveat on this definition in Morgan, *Roman Faith and Christian Faith*, 264–66.

CONCLUSION

Without a doubt there have been numerous and important advances in the field of lexicography in recent years, and these advances have had a positive impact on various philosophical, theological, and translational issues in New Testament studies. Likewise, New Testament lexicons, especially (in my opinion) those of Louw-Nida and BDAG, have stressed the importance of proposing a method of semantic analysis and carrying it out in order to obtain successful results. However, at least in the case of πίστις, we think that the results should be still reviewed.

The *DGENT* proposes a new method of semantic analysis based on the following principles:

1. The systematic distinction in the redaction of lexemes between meaning and translation.
2. The construction of the definition of a given lexeme depending entirely on the text.
3. The explanation of what contextual factor or factors contribute to the change in meaning of a given lexeme.
4. The verification of all contexts where the given lexeme appears in the whole corpus.

By employing this methodology in the study of πίστις within the undisputed letters of Paul, the following four sememes are identified:

1. Basic definition: "The state of intellectual and active adhesion to someone or something," translated "fidelity," "faith," or "devotion."
2. When πίστις is related to a divine entity: "The quality of personal adhesion to someone or something," translated "confidence" or "faithfulness."
3. When πίστις appears in a relationship to a previous action, especially in conjunction with ὑπακοή and δικαιόω, as well as their compound forms: "adhesion to someone or something as a result of a previous action," translated "faith" or "faithfulness."
4. When πίστις depends upon a communicative action: "a group of Christian doctrines," translated "belief" or "teaching."

The present analysis is an attempt to highlight the semantic uses of the lexeme πίστις. While this study only highlighted the Pauline uses of the word, the research involved with the *DGENT* will take into consideration all of the books of the New Testament to provide translators and other students of the New Testament with a useful tool as they study the sacred text.

BIBLIOGRAPHY

Arndt, William, et al. *A Greek-English Lexicon of the New Testament and Other Early Christian Literature*. Chicago: University of Chicago Press, 2000.
Campbell, Douglas. "False Presuppositions in the ΠΙΣΤΙΣ ΧΡΙΣΤΟΥ Debate: A Response to Brian Dodd." *Journal of Biblical Literature* 116 (1997) 713–19.
Dunn, James D. G. "The New Perspective on Paul: Paul and the Law." In *The Romans Debate*, edited by K. P. Donfried, 299–308. Peabody, MA: Hendrickson, 1991.
———. "Once more, PISTIS CHRISTOU." In *Pauline Theology IV: Looking Back, Pressing On*, edited by E. Elizabeth Johnson and David M. Hay, 61–81. Symposium 4. Atlanta: Scholars, 1997.
———. "Paul and Justification by Faith." In *The Road from Damascus: The Impact of Paul's Conversion on His Life, Thought, and Ministry*, edited by Richard N. Longenecker, 85–101. Grand Rapids: Eerdmans, 1997.
———. *Romans 1–8*. WBC 38A. Dallas: Word, 1988.
Hooker, Morna D. "*Pistis Christou*." *New Testament Studies* 35 (1989) 321–42.
Hultgren, Arland J. "The *Pistis Christou* Formulation in Paul." *Novum Testamentum* 22/3 (1980) 248–63.
Liddell, H. G., et al., *A Greek-English Lexicon*. Oxford: Clarendon, 1996.
Lienhard, Joseph T. "A Note on the Meaning of Pistis in Aristotle's Rhetoric." *The American Journal of Philology* 87/4 (1966) 446–54.
Louw, Johannes P., and Eugene A. Nida. *Greek-English Lexicon of the New Testament Based on Semantic Domains*. 2 vols. New York: United Bible Societies, 1996.
Mateos, Juan. *El aspecto verbal en el Nuevo Testamento*. Estudios del Nuevo Testamneto 1. Madrid: Ed. Cristiandad e Institución S. Jerónimo, 1977.
———. *Método de análisis semántico aplicado al griego del Nuevo Testamento*. Córdoba: El Almendro, 1989.
Mateos, Juan, et al. *Diccionario griego-español del Nuevo Testamento. Análisis semántico de los vocablos*. Vols. 1–5. Córdoba: El Almendro, 2000–2012.
Matlock, Barry R. "Demythologizing the πίστις Χριστοῦ Debate: Cautionary Remarks from a Lexical Semantic Perspective." *Novum Testamentum* 42/1 (2000) 1–23.
Morgan, Teresa. *Roman Faith and Christian Faith: Pistis and Fides in the Early Roman Empire and Early Churches*. Oxford: Oxford University Press, 2015.
Muñoz Gallarte, Israel. "Los sustantivos-Hecho en el Nuevo Testamento: Clasificación semántica." PhD diss., Universidad Complutense de Madrid, 2008.
Muñoz Gallarte, Israel, and Marta Merino. "El campo semántico de la educación en el Nuevo Testamento: παιδεύω y διδασκαλία." In *Greeks, Jews, and Christians: Historical, Religious, and Philological Studies in Honor of Jesús Peláez del Rosal*, edited by L. Roig Lanzillotta and I. Muñoz Gallarte, 1–26. Córdoba: El Almendro, 2013.
Preuschen, Erwin. *Vollständiges Griechisch-Deutsches Handwörterbuch zu den Schriften des Neuen Testaments und der übrigen urchristlichen Literatur*. Giessen: Töpelmann, 1910.

Rodríguez Adrados, F., et al. *Diccionario griego-español (DGE)*. Madrid: CSIC, 1980–2010.

Thayer, J. H., et al. *Greek-English Lexicon of the New Testament*. Peabody, MA: Hendrickson, 1996.

10

The Infancy Narratives and the Synoptic Problem

Reassessing the Evidence and Arguments

ALEXANDER E. STEWART
Tyndale Theological Seminary

ALTHOUGH THE TWO DOCUMENT Hypothesis (2DH) possibly still remains the consensus solution to the Synoptic problem several minority positions exist. These include: (1) the Two Gospel Hypothesis (2GH; Griesbach Hypothesis; including Bernard Orchard's and David Alan Black's variant Fourfold-Gospel Hypothesis), which posits that Matthew wrote first, Luke used Matthew, and Mark had access to both Matthew and Luke; (2) the Farrer Hypothesis (FH; Mark-Without-Q Hypothesis), which posits that Mark wrote first, Matthew used Mark, and Luke had access to both Mark and Matthew; (3) and the Matthew Conflator Hypothesis (MCH), which posits that Mark wrote first, Luke used Mark, and Mathew had access to both Mark and Luke. These minority positions hold that either Luke used Matthew or Matthew used Luke while the 2DH insists that Matthew and Luke both wrote independently with access to Mark and some other source or sources (Q, M, L).

Any assessment of the literary relationship between Matthew and Luke must give some explanation of their widely divergent infancy narratives.

192   Getting into the Text

This is important because these narratives are lacking in Mark and have been less discussed in source critical research.¹ On the surface the striking differences between the infancy narratives in Matthew and Luke seem to provide strong evidence that Matthew and Luke wrote independently and would seem to support the 2DH. "Such differences are more drastic than anywhere in the canonical Gospels—the synoptics *versus* the Fourth Gospel included."² This article will reassess the infancy narratives in Matthew and Luke in light of the four positions on the Synoptic problem noted above and argue that the differences between the infancy narratives do not preclude the possibility of literary dependence. The argument will proceed in three stages: (1) an overview of the content of the infancy narratives, (2) a discussion of how each solution to the synoptic problem explains the infancy narratives, and (3) an assessment of some of the implications of a literary relationship between the infancy narratives in Matthew and Luke.

THE INFANCY NARRATIVES: AN OVERVIEW

The similarities between the infancy narratives in Matthew and Luke are as follows:³

1. The names of the parents are Mary and Joseph. They are legally engaged (μνηστεύω in both) but have not yet had sexual relations (Matt 1:18; Luke 1:27, 34). Mary is a παρθένος (Matt 1:23; Luke 1:27).

2. The conception of the child is not through intercourse (Matt 1:20, 23, 25; Luke 1:34) but through the Holy Spirit (Matt 1:18, 20; Luke 1:31, 34–35). The birth takes place after the parents have come to live together (Matt 1:24–25; Luke 2:5–6).

3. Jesus is born in Bethlehem (Matt 2:1; Luke 2:4–6) during the days of Herod the king (ἐν ἡμέραις Ἡρῴδου τοῦ βασιλέως [Matt 2:1]; ἐν ταῖς ἡμέραις Ἡρῴδου βασιλέως [Luke 1:5]), but raised in Nazareth (Matt 2:23; Luke 2:39).

---

1. This is evident by a quick search of the Scripture index of Paul Foster et al., *Synoptic Problem*, and Bellinzoni, *Two-Source Hypothesis*. References to the infancy narratives are quite sparse.

2. Stendahl, "Quis et Unde?," 70; italics original.

3. This list seeks to condense some points that are generally listed separately and place the items in a relative order of significance. Raymond E. Brown lists eleven points of contact (*Birth of the Messiah*, 34–35), McNicol et al. list eighteen points (*Beyond the Q Impasse*, 47); Robert K. MacEwen lists twenty-five points (*Matthean Posteriority*), 119; Ronald V. Huggins lists twelve points ("Matthean Posteriority," 1–22, 17).

4. Joseph is a descendent of David (Matt 1:16, 20; Luke 1:27, 32; 2:4).

5. There is an angelic announcement of the forthcoming birth of the child (to Joseph in Matt 1:20-23; to Mary in Luke 1:30-35), during which the angel indicates the child's name (τέξεται δὲ υἱόν, καὶ καλέσεις τὸ ὄνομα αὐτοῦ Ἰησοῦν [Matt 1:21]; καὶ τέξῃ υἱὸν καὶ καλέσεις τὸ ὄνομα αὐτοῦ Ἰησοῦν [Luke 1:31]). This is matched by similarity in the fulfillment (ἔτεκεν υἱόν· καὶ ἐκάλεσεν τὸ ὄνομα αὐτοῦ Ἰησοῦν [Matt 1:25]; καὶ ἔτεκεν τὸν υἱὸν αὐτῆς [Luke 2:7] . . . καὶ ἐκλήθη τὸ ὄνομα αὐτοῦ Ἰησοῦς [Luke 2:21])

6. Jesus receives supernaturally guided visitors (Matt 2:1-12; Luke 2:8-20). The context includes χαρὰν μεγάλην (Matt 2:10; Luke 2:10)

7. Jesus is described as Χριστός (Matt 1:18; Luke 2:11) and son of God (υἱόν μου in Matt 2:15; υἱὸς ὑψίστου in Luke 1:32; υἱὸς θεοῦ in Luke 1:35).

8. God's people will receive salvation from their sins (αὐτὸς γὰρ σώσει τὸν λαὸν αὐτοῦ ἀπὸ τῶν ἁμαρτιῶν αὐτῶν [Matt 1:21 regarding Jesus]; τοῦ δοῦναι γνῶσιν σωτηρίας τῷ λαῷ αὐτοῦ ἐν ἀφέσει ἁμαρτιῶν αὐτῶν [Luke 1:77 regarding John]; cf. the use of σωτήρ in Luke 2:11 regarding Jesus).

9. Characters are described as δίκαιος (Joseph in Matt 1:19; Zechariah and Elizabeth in Luke 1:6; Simeon in Luke 2:25).

10. Characters are introspective (Joseph in Matt 1:20; Mary in Luke 2:19, 51).

11. Opposition to Jesus is anticipated (Matt 2:1-22; Luke 2:34-35).[4]

The differences are also striking. Apart from the points noted above Matthew contains no explicit reference to anything contained in Luke's narratives (angelic announcements to Zechariah and Mary, the visit of Mary to Elizabeth, the *Magnificat*, the birth of John the Baptist, the *Benedictus*, the journey from Nazareth to Bethlehem, the manger, the lack of room in the inn/guest house, the shepherds, the presentation in the temple, Simeon, Anna, the boy Jesus in the temple). Luke, on the other hand, contains no explicit reference to Matthew's narratives (the angel's appearance to Joseph, the fulfillment quotations, the wise men, Herod's plot, the flight to Egypt, the slaughter of the innocents, Joseph's decision about where to resettle). There is similarity in structure regarding the angelical annunciation of the

---

4. Other instances of shared or similar vocabulary could be noted: χρηματίζω (Matt 2:12, 22; Luke 2:26); ταράσσω (Herod; Matt 2:3) and διαταράσσω (Zechariah; Luke 1:29); φοβέω/φόβος (Matt 1:20; 2:22; Luke 1:12, 13, 29-30, 65; 2:9).

birth to one of the parents and the arrival of supernaturally guided visitors but the narratives are quite distinct and involve different characters.

Despite the dramatic differences it is interesting how easily the accounts have been harmonized.[5] The narratives are not contradictory; they simply do not overlap in time with each other in the events they are recounting.[6] As will be noted below, some interpreters focus on the similarities of structure and wording to strengthen the case for literary dependence while others focus on the dramatic differences to argue for literary independence.[7]

INDEPENDENT NARRATIVES: THE TWO DOCUMENT HYPOTHESIS (2DH)

For proponents of the 2DH it seems almost self-evident that the stark differences and lack of harmonization, in contrast to how Matthew and Luke treat Mark, indicate that Matthew and Luke are independent. The argument can be presented as Luke's lack of "M" material or Matthew's lack of "L" material.[8] Stein is representative.

---

5. Brown describes the normal harmonizing sequence as "Luke 1; Matt 1; Luke 2:1-38; an unmentioned return to Bethlehem; Matt 2" (*Birth of the Messiah*, 35).

6. France, "Scripture, Tradition and History," 239-66, 241-42. Brown, however, highlights two details that lead him to believe the accounts are "contrary to each other" and cannot both be historical (*Birth of the Messiah*, 36). First, Luke locates Mary in Nazareth (Luke 1:26; 2:39) and uses the census to explain how the birth took place in Bethlehem, while Matthew indicates that the family lived in a house in Bethlehem (Matt 2:11) and spends time explaining why the family moved to Nazareth instead of resettling in Bethlehem (Matt 2:22-23). Second, "Luke tells us that the family returned peaceably to Nazareth after the birth at Bethlehem (2:22, 39); this is irreconcilable with Matthew's implication (2:16) that the child was almost two years old when the family fled from Bethlehem to Egypt and even older when the family came back from Egypt and moved to Nazareth" (*Birth of the Messiah*, 36). Brown's claim is overstated and his examples of irreconcilable contradictions are explicable based on principles discussed by J. Gresham Machen: narratival silence, differences, and omissions of detail due to authorial selectivity are not automatically contradictions (*The Virgin Birth of Christ*, 192-200). Machen's own harmonization depends upon the assumption that Matthew and Luke are two independent narratives (197).

7. Mark Goodacre suggests that "one of the key questions is whether there are any signs of Luke's knowledge of Matthew in the Birth Narrative" (*The Case Against Q*, 56). For FH and 2GH proponents the prior list provides such signs. John Drury argues that the name of Joseph, the connection of the birth to the days of Herod, and the presence of the genealogies are particularly striking "as an acknowledgement of debt" to Matthew (*Tradition and Design*, 125). McNicol et al. argue that "the sheer number of these parallels invites further curiosity as to a possible literary connection" (*Beyond the Q Impasse*, 48).

8. Stein, *Synoptic Gospels*, 111-12; Fitzmyer, *Luke I-IX*, 75.

> Why would Luke have omitted such material as the coming of the wise men (Matt 2:1–12)? Would not the presence of such Gentiles at the birth of Jesus have been meaningful for Luke's Gentile-oriented Gospel? Why would he have omitted the flight to Egypt and return to Nazareth (Matt 2:13–23) . . . ? Added to this is the observation that if Luke had before him Matthew's birth account and genealogy, one wonders if he would not have sought in some way to "harmonize" his version with the Matthean version . . . It would therefore appear that Luke's use of Matthew is improbable, due to the lack of his incorporation of the M material into his Gospel.[9]

If there were a direct literary relationship between Matthew and Luke how can the dramatic differences between their infancy narratives be explained? This seems like such an obvious problem that little argumentation is generally given.[10]

Raymond Brown accepts the independence of the infancy narratives in Matthew and Luke without much discussion and suggests that "agreement between the two infancy narratives would suggest the existence of a common infancy tradition earlier than either evangelist's work."[11] On this common reading the differences are too great to allow for Matthew or Luke to have known the other but the similarities are also striking enough to posit a common earlier infancy tradition or traditions from which both are selectively drawing.[12]

However, drastic changes to a tradition or the failure to include a tradition does not automatically mean that an author does not have access to those traditions.[13] This is evident throughout the Gospels (regarding Luke's use of Mark compare Mark 1:16–20 with Luke 5:1–11, Mark 6:1–6 with Luke 4:16–30, and Mark 14:3–9 with Luke 7:36–50; regarding Matthew and Luke's use of Q compare Matt 22:1–14 with Luke 14:15–24 and Matt

---

9. Stein, *Synoptic Gospels*, 111–12.

10. Marshall, *Luke*, 45; France, *Matthew*, 42–43; Fitzmyer, *Luke I–IX*, 75.

11. Brown, *Birth of the Messiah*, 34.

12. Hagner, *Matthew 1–13*, 14–15; Fitzmyer, *Luke I–IX*, 306–7. In a pointed response, David T. Landry argues that "it strains credibility to imagine (as one must, according to the Two-Source Theory) that there could have existed oral traditions upon which both Matthew and Luke were relying that included all this information, but which (1) escaped the notice of every other New Testament writer; and (2) also reflected the great number of differences between Matthew and Luke ("Luke's Revision," 66).

13. MacEwen, *Matthew Posteriority*, 122.

25:14–30 with Luke 19:11–27).[14] As explored below, the choice not to include certain available traditions can be explained many ways.

The striking differences between the infancy narratives should not automatically be taken to indicate independence without first exploring how and why an author may have treated his source in such a way. Are there reasonable or plausible explanations by which to understand the redactional activity? If not, the case for independence would be strengthened. Kloppenborg wisely cautions that, "our failure to understand the editorial practices implied by a given source-critical solution or our inability to imagine a credible setting for a particular gospel may be a failure of our imagination rather than a defect of the solution itself."[15] It is not always easy to determine plausibility or inplausibility when evaluating why an ancient author may have made particular redactional decisions. Kloppenborg rightly notes that "we have, however, a gauge of what the Synoptic evangelists considered plausible or appropriate in the actual constructions of their gospels."[16] Methodologically, the Gospels themselves are the surest guides to evaluate the possible explanations discussed below.

LUKE'S USE OF MATTHEW: THE FARRER (FH) AND TWO GOSPEL HYPOTHESES (2GH)

Although the FH and 2GH differ in regard to the placement of Mark (first and third respectively) they are united on the question of Luke's use of Matthew. The old saying is proved to be true that the enemy of my enemy is my friend and each of these hypotheses seeks to demonstrate that Luke had access to Matthew. The first argument is that Luke may well have drawn the very idea of beginning his Gospel with a birth narrative from Matthew.[17] As Mark, John, the sermons throughout Acts, and Paul's letters indicate, the Gospel and early Christian proclamation did not need to begin with a birth narrative. This was not a central part of the proclamation of earliest Christianity so its inclusion at all may indicate literary dependence.

If Luke had access to Matthew what possible reasons could he have had to make the changes he did to Matthew's infancy narrative? Arguments here normally focus on general redactional tendencies or preferences related to different audiences and goals.[18]

14. Ibid., 123.
15. Kloppenborg, "Synoptic Problem," 93.
16. Ibid., 95.
17. Goodacre, *The Case Against Q*, 57.
18. A. M. Farrer argues that "St. Matthew's early chapters define a task [demonstrate

The primary justification for the Gospel of Luke seems to have been twofold. First, there was a place for a work that would meet the needs of certain western-oriented gentile churches better than the Gospel of Matthew could. Second, there was available to the author of Luke extremely valuable tradition that could be substituted for a corresponding but, for his purposes, less suitable tradition in Matthew.[19]

David Alan Black agrees and argues that Luke was "a manifesto that would not only respect the essential message of Matthew but would at the same time remove its preoccupation with matters of little interest or relevance to Greeks."[20] Matthew's birth narrative can be viewed as a Jewish apologetic with the first chapter of Matthew responding to the accusation of Jesus' illegitimate and irregular birth and the second chapter responding to the accusation that the Messiah could not have come out of Nazareth.[21] Luke was not concerned with these issues and instead sought to craft his infancy account in a way that would have been more understandable and meaningful to his gentile readers. Austin Farrer memorably uses "Luke-pleasingness" to describe Luke's redactional methodology.[22] This broadly encompasses theological, artistic, literary, and historiographic pleasingness. Luke retains traditional material from Matthew that is pleasing to him because of its usefulness for his purpose and audience and omits or redacts unpleasing material.

This general observation about Luke's redactional preferences can be expanded to explain most of the changes.

1. Luke rejects the way Matthew structures his infancy narrative around explicit fulfillment quotations because the hermeneutics involved with these particular quotations may not have been immediately obvious or meaningful to normal Gentile readers.[23] Luke is not opposed to fulfillment focused quotations elsewhere (Luke 4:16–21; 20:17, 42–43; 22:37; normally in direct speech) but the four fulfillment quotations

---

that Jesus was a Bethlehemite by birth and the Son of God by supernatural generation], which St. Luke takes up and deals with from his own resources, and with his own improvements" ("On Dispensing with Q," 80). Eric Franklin focuses on divergent theology (particularly the relationship of Israel to the church) and argues extensively that "it is wholly likely that Luke used Matthew's infancy narratives and rewrote them in the light of his own parallel but very different theological concerns" (*Luke*, 362).

19. Farmer, *Jesus and the Gospels*, 162.
20. Black, *Why Four Gospels?*, 54–55.
21. Stendahl, "Quis et Unde?," 72–74.
22. Farrer, "On Dispensing with Q," 57.
23. Cf. Landry, "Luke's Revision," 66–67.

in Matthew 2 are all geographically focused to explain and defend Nazareth as the Messiah's hometown while Luke has no need or desire to make that defense.[24]

2. Luke instead structures his narrative around the alternating parallel stories of John and Jesus.[25] This explains the additional material surrounding John's birth.[26] Luke had access to additional traditions and wanted to relate John to Jesus in a way that honored John but put him in his place as less important than Jesus. The extra space provided by John's birth accounts also allowed him room for character development in regard to Zachariah, Elizabeth, and Mary as his representatives of the faithful remnant within Israel.[27]

3. Luke "fixes" Matthew's geneology. As Farrer describes it: "[Matthew's] genealogy has two formal faults: 1. The artificial doubling of two names, as indicated [David and Jeconias]. The omission of several generations from the biblical list between David and Jeconias. Both faults are eliminated in St. Luke's rewriting."[28] Of course, more is going on in Luke's narrative and the changes also relate to the focus in his genealogy on Jesus as God's Son (Luke 3:38) and how that builds upon the baptismal pronouncement (Luke 3:22) and points forward to the temptation (Luke 4:3, 9).

4. Luke omits the conflict between Herod and Jesus because he wants to highlight the peaceful co-existence of Christianity and the civil government. Jesus's kingship is not a threat to Rome.[29]

5. Luke omits the slaughter of the innocents and the flight to Egypt because this would introduce a sense of fear, negativity, and death into a narrative filled with celebration. Despite a brief indication of future opposition (Luke 2:34–35), Luke presents Jesus' birth as a time of unbridled joy at the fulfillment of God's promises to his people. It is also possible that Luke recognized Matthew's typological connection of Jesus to Moses through these events and was not as interested in

---

24. Stendahl, "Quis et Unde?," 71–73.

25. Landry, "Luke's Revision," 66.

26. McNicol et al. argue that the alternating focus on John and Jesus is "the central literary principle that informs the composition of this unit" (*Beyond the Q Impasse*, 49, cf. 54).

27. Landry, "Luke's Revision," 69.

28. Farrer, "On Dispensing with Q," 87. It is also possible that Luke traced the genealogy through Nathan instead of Solomon because of Solomon's association with idolatry (cf. the small slight to Solomon in Acts 7:47–48; Goulder, *Luke*, 288–9).

29. McNicol et al., *Beyond the Q Impasse*, 50, 64; cf. Goulder, *Luke*, 249.

developing this connection (cf. Luke's disregard for the structure of Jesus's five discourses in Matthew).[30]

6. Luke omits mention of the *magoi* because of the wickedness of Simon (Acts 8:9–24), the active opposition of Bar-Jesus (Acts 13:6–12), and the pervasive use of magic in Ephesus (Acts 19:18–20).[31] Luke was determined not to present *magoi* in a positive light. Drury also makes a cogent case that Luke's redactions throughout reduce Jesus's contact with gentiles (the omission of the Syro-Phoenician woman, the journey into gentile territory, the face-to-face discussion with a centurion) in order to present the gentile mission as the activity of the church in Acts.[32] Omission of the *magoi* and focus on the shepherds also "befits his theme of Jesus coming to the humble and poor."[33]

7. Luke focuses on Mary and the lowliness of the birth to further highlight God's care and concern for women and the poor within society.[34] This could also be Luke's way of highlighting his main eyewitness source for the information (cf. Mary's presence in Acts 1:14).

Although the explanations are not all equally convincing, FH and 2GH proponents have demonstrated that there are reasonable ways to explain Matthew's use of Luke and the mere fact of their radically diverse infancy narratives cannot be used to prove literary independence.

MATTHEW'S USE OF LUKE: THE MATTHEW CONFLATOR HYPOTHESIS (MCH)

Although historically not discussed as much, there are several recent energetic advocates of Matthew's use of Mark and Luke.[35] This theory reverses and uses many of the strategies noted above in regard to Luke's use of Matthew. If Matthew had access to Luke, why did he make such drastic changes?

30. Landry, "Luke's Revision," 68.

31. Goulder, *Luke*, 248–49.

32. Drury, *Tradition and Design*, 126. Cf. McNicol et al., *Beyond the Q Impasse*, 50.

33. Ibid., 50, 65.

34. Goulder, *Luke*, 221; Drury, *Tradition and Design*, 127. On this argument it would seem that Luke undermined his goal by dropping Tamar, Rahab, Ruth, and Bathsheba from the genealogy. Franklin suggests that Luke would have recognized that Matthew included these women to develop a pattern of God's activity through irregular births and would have intentionally omitted these "offensive references to the women" (*Luke*, 362).

35. MacEwen, *Matthean Posteriority*; Garrow, "Streeter's 'Other' Synoptic Solution," 207–26; Huggins, "Matthean Posteriority"; Hengel, *Four Gospels*.

Martin Hengel takes Matthew's apologetic motivation as the main explanation for his treatment of Luke. Matthew responds to Jewish accusations about a dishonourable birth by focusing on Joseph's just conduct and obedience to divine instruction in opposition to Luke's focus on Mary and marginalization of Joseph.[36]

Alan Garrow suggests that Matthew had access to Luke's infancy narrative and an infancy narrative from another source.[37] During the process of conflating these accounts "Matthew would retain only those details, from either text, that were most conducive to his project. This would explain why, where they differ, Matthew's version consistently favours the dignity of Jesus and his claim to Messiahship."[38] This appeal to another source for Matthew's infancy narrative is a response to how Matthew seems to conservatively redact Mark throughout his Gospel while radically redacting Luke in the infancy narratives.[39]

Matthew's apologetic purpose and redactional preferences can explain many of his changes to Luke. "[K]ingship is the central thrust of the stories" in Matthew's infancy narratives.[40]

1. The focus on Joseph instead of Mary and the failure to mention Nazareth as the original home of Mary and Joseph can be explained by Matthew's desire to highlight Jesus' connection to David through Joseph and Bethlehem.[41] This explains how Jesus was grafted into the Davidic line through adoption by Joseph.[42]

2. The inclusion of the account of the μάγοι and the omission of the Lukan shepherds can be explained several ways. Shepherds did not

---

36. Hengel, *Four Gospels*, 200. Hengel cites Origin, *Cels.* I, 28, 32.39 ("The craftsman hated her and cast her out") as evidence for the kind of accusation driving Matthew's apologetic.

37. Garrow, "Streeter's 'Other' Synoptic Solution," 223; cf. MacEwen, *Matthean Posteriority*, 130.

38. Garrow, "Streeter's 'Other' Synoptic Solution," 224.

39. Landry (FH), following Goodacre, suggests this is due to editorial fatigue ("Luke's Revision," 70–71; cf. Mark Goodacre, "Fatigue in the Synoptics," 45–58). Garrow (MCH), MacEwen (MCH), and McNicol et al. (2GH) posit the possession of alternative sources more conducive to the evangelist's agenda (Garrow, "Streeter's 'Other' Synoptic Solution," 223; MacEwen, *Matthean Posteriority*, 130; McNicol et al., *Beyond the Q Impasse*, 53). Prior interpreters holding the 2DH were free to assume literary independence in regard to the infancy narratives so this has not been addressed but now that the way is clearing for an appreciation of their literary dependence the question becomes more pointed.

40. Shuler, "Genre Criticism," 476.

41. MacEwen, *Matthean Posteriority*, 125.

42. Stendahl, "Quis et Unde?," 74–75.

properly represent the dignity and status of Jesus while foreign dignitaries pledging some kind of allegiance to a new-born Jewish king highlighted Jesus' kingship as David's heir. The allegiance of Gentiles at his birth also pointed forward to the claim in the conclusion of Matthew's Gospel that Jesus was the ruler of the entire world and was sending his subjects out to spread the message of his kingdom to all the nations (Matt 28:18–20).

3. The conflict with Herod also highlights Jesus' kingly and messianic identity. Herod would not have been bothered by the birth of a peasant but the birth of a rival king was cause for alarm, especially a rival king with potential Parthian support. Herod is well known for his ruthless and deadly treatment of any potential rival.

4. The flight to Egypt serves as the apologetic link to move Jesus out of Bethlehem and to Nazareth. It also supports Matthew's typological connection between Jesus and Israel where Jesus as God's son is reliving, in miniature, the history of God's son Israel.

5. The slaughter of the children anticipates future hostility between Jesus and his followers and the Jewish leadership, which would culminate in Jesus' death.[43]

6. The omission of the presentation in the temple is due to its unsuitability within Matthew's presentation of events. How could Jesus be publically presented in the temple with the threat of death hanging over him?

7. The omission of the material related to John the Baptist can be explained by Matthew's tendency to abbreviate. This is evident in Matthew's treatment of Mark throughout. "For an abbreviator, the stories about John would have been obvious targets for omission, since a Gospel's focus is on Jesus."[44]

8. The omission of the canticles can be explained by Matthew's desire to show fulfillment of Old Testament prophecies directly through fulfillment quotations and not indirectly through allusions and echoes.[45] Matthew often added fulfillment quotations to Markan material so the addition of Isa 7:14 and Mic 5:2 to his Lucan source to more clearly highlight the prophetic fulfillment of the virgin conception and birth in Bethlehem would be expected.[46]

---

43. MacEwen, *Matthean Posteriority*, 126.
44. Ibid., 125.
45. Ibid.
46. Ibid., 126–27.

9. Matthew heavily redacts Luke's genealogy to promote the dignity of Jesus's royal connection to David through Solomon instead of the obscure Nathan.[47] It begins and ends with David and fourteen may intentionally relate to the numerical value of David's name.[48] The inclusion of four gentile women (Tamar, Rahab, Ruth, Uriah's wife) may support Matthew's universal vision or apologetically demonstrate that God has worked in the past through irregular births to preserve the Davidic line.

In addition to these general redactional tendencies, there are striking similarities between Matt 1:21 (about Jesus) and Luke 1:77 (about John).

αὐτὸς γὰρ σώσει   τὸν λαὸν αὐτοῦ   ἀπὸ τῶν ἁμαρτιῶν αὐτῶν (Matt 1:21)

τοῦ δοῦναι γνῶσιν σωτηρίας   τῷ λαῷ αὐτοῦ   ἐν ἀφέσει ἁμαρτιῶν αὐτῶν (Luke 1:77)

Is it more likely that Matthew would have taken away John's role in bringing salvation to God's people in order to focus exclusively on Jesus as the one who will deal with sin (MCH) or that Luke would have shared Jesus' role as savior with John (FH)?[49] Although Luke 1:77 may simply be highlighting John's supporting role in Jesus' ministry which Luke later describes in more detail (Luke 3:3; John was κηρύσσων βάπτισμα μετανοίας εἰς ἄφεσιν ἁμαρτιῶν), Robert K. MacEwen argues that Luke would not likely have made that point in the infancy narrative by taking the role away from Jesus if Luke 1:77 was dependent upon Matt 1:21.[50]

Although perhaps not as convincing as the FH, proponents of the MCH have likewise demonstrated that there are plausible ways to explain Matthew's redaction of Luke's infancy narrative.

MARK'S NON-USE OF THE INFANCY NARRATIVES: THE TWO-GOSPEL HYPOTHESIS AGAIN

Moving beyond Luke's use of Matthew, proponents of the 2GH are left with one more hurdle. How does one explain Mark's omission of the infancy narratives if he had access to Matthew and Luke? B. H. Streeter famously argued, "Only a lunatic would leave out Matthew's account of the Infancy, the Sermon on the Mount, and practically all the parables, in order to get

47. Huggins, "Matthean Posteriority," 19.
48. Ibid., 18–19.
49. MacEwen, *Matthean Posteriority*, 128.
50. Ibid.

room for purely verbal expansion of what was retained."[51] This colorfully highlights the potential problem the infancy narratives pose for Markan posteriority.

William R. Farmer argued that "the omission of the birth narratives, which assume such an important role in Matthew and Luke but to which Paul never refers in his letters, fits Mark's concern to shape his gospel to conform to the Pauline kerygma."[52] Moving beyond the absence of the infancy narratives in the Pauline Kerygma, he also argued that Mark, having access to Luke-Acts, draws from Peter's recorded sermons in the book of Acts, which "make no reference to Jesus' preexistence, to his genealogy, or to any of the marvelous things that happened at or following his birth."[53] On this reading of the evidence, Mark recognized that the infancy narratives did not play a role in the preaching of Peter or Paul and omitted them.[54]

Following the testimony of the early church, which closely connects the development of Mark's Gospel to Peter's preaching in Rome, Black argues that Peter omitted the birth and resurrection narratives out of a motivation to focus on "those pericopes where Matthew and Luke have for the most part common material and are generally in parallel."[55] "Peter's intention was to refer only to those incidents in the life of Jesus of which he had been an eyewitness or could personally vouch for; therefore he would say nothing about the birth and resurrection narratives or about the collection of Jesus' sayings in Luke's central section."[56]

David Peabody argues that even though Mark omitted everything from the beginning of Matthew's genealogy to the end of Luke's genealogy

51. Streeter, *Four Gospels*, 158.
52. Farmer, *Jesus and the Gospels*, 175.
53. Ibid., 172.
54. Kloppenborg critiques Farmer's explanation because it relies "upon an identification of the author of the second gospel which derives from patristic speculations and which is rejected as groundless by most Markan specialists, and upon the supposition that the speeches in Acts are substantially Petrine" ("The Theological Stakes," 100). In a curious rhetorical move he hypothetically argues from the perspective of the 2GH in support of "the most obvious explanation" for Mark's omission of Matthew and Luke's infancy narratives: Mark did not like their positive view of Jesus' kin (100). He tries to demonstrate that if proponents of the 2GH are honest with the evidence they will be forced to admit that Mark's redactional activity demonstrates an "attack on the family of Jesus" and that Mark is "combative" and "not complementary" to his source material (108). Kloppenborg does not sufficiently demonstrate why the infancy narratives, with no mention of Jesus' brothers or sisters, would have been so uncongenial to Mark's agenda to vilify Jesus' family. Matthew in particular has little attention devoted to Mary. Cf. David Peabody's response to Kloppenborg's argument ("Reading Mark," 159–85).
55. Black, *Why Four Gospels?*, 62.
56. Ibid., 14.

except the baptism of John he signals his awareness of this material in his first verse by borrowing Ἰησοῦ Χριστοῦ from Matt 1:1 and υἱοῦ θεοῦ from Luke 3:28.[57] Mark omitted this material because its divergent content made conflation nearly impossible and he may have been influenced by the negative view of genealogies in early Christianity as reflected in 1 Tim 1:4 and Titus 3:9.[58]

A final explanation of Mark's omission of the infancy narratives is that, according to the patristic evidence, he never intended to produce a formal Gospel.[59] Papias draws attention to the fragmentary and non-chronological aspect of Mark.

> Mark, having become Peter's interpreter, wrote down accurately everything he remembered, though not in order, of the things said and done by Christ . . . [Peter] adapted his teachings as needed but had no intention of giving an ordered account of the Lord's sayings. Consequently Mark did nothing wrong in writing down some things as he remembered them, for he made it his one concern not to omit anything that he heard or to make any false statement in them.[60]

"Mark was never meant to be an independent Gospel."[61] It was not intended to be a literary masterpiece and was not produced for wide circulation. This observation is grounded in the patristic evidence and potentially explains the omission of the infancy narratives along with many of the apparent irregularities of Mark in comparison to the other Gospels.

Similar to the FH and MCH, proponents of the 2GH can provide possible explanations for why Mark would have done what he did to his sources.

RESPECT, NEUTRALITY, OR OPPOSITION: EXPLORING REDACTIONAL ATTITUDES

If we assume with the 2DH that the infancy narratives are independent then there is no need to entertain the question of what Luke would have thought about Matthew, Matthew would have thought of Luke, or Mark would have thought about both. Because of the extensive nature of the redaction,

---

57. Peabody, "Reading Mark," 174.
58. Ibid., 172–73; cf. Shuler, "Genre Criticism," 478–9.
59. Black, *Why Four Gospels?*, 30–32.
60. Eusebius, *Eccl. Hist.* 3.39.15–16 as translated in Holmes, *Apostolic Fathers*, 739–40.
61. Black, *Why Four Gospels?*, 44.

however, this question becomes acute for proponents of the 2GH, FH, and MCH.

Luke's attitude toward his predecessors is normally discussed in reference to his prologue. The first words of the Gospel are Ἐπειδήπερ πολλοὶ ἐπεχείρησαν ἀνατάξασθαι διήγησιν. Is ἐπεχείρησαν a negative comment on the results of the prior attempts or a neutral description of the difficulty inherent in the intention behind the formation of these prior accounts?[62] Luke's connection of himself to these prior attempts with κἀμοί in verse three and his connection of these attempts to the eyewitnesses suggest a positive assessment while Luke's focus on accuracy and research likely indicate that he viewed his current project as an improvement on past attempts.[63] Why compose another Gospel at all if there were nothing positive to add to the predecessors? With this in mind, McNicol, Dungan, and Peabody are correct to conclude that "[m]ore than likely there is mild implied criticism of the earlier works."[64]

Some interpreters view the redaction as antagonistic.[65] From the perspective of the MCH, Hengel argues that Matthew redacts his infancy narrative "in deliberate opposition to Luke" as "a deliberate counterpart to Luke's account, which Matthew finds offensive."[66] Kloppenborg argues that proponents of the 2GH must admit that "[a]n eirenic view of Mark is not possible. On the 2GH, Mark is combative, not complementary."[67] From the perspective of the FH, Landry argues that "Luke's Gospel represents something akin to a hostile takeover" and "Luke's birth narrative is designed to compete with Mathew's, and in effect to eclipse it."[68] Franklin describes Luke as redacting Matthew's infancy narrative in direct opposition to Matthew's theology.[69]

---

62. In support of a neutral reading of Luke's attitude in the prologue see Nolland, *Luke 1–9:20*, 6; Marshall, *Luke*, 41; Bock, *Luke 1:1—9:50*, 55–56. For a sustained argument that Luke's prologue demonstrates a negative view of his canonical predecessors see Landry, "Luke's Revision," 52–57.

63. Fitzmyer, *Luke I-IX*, 291–92.

64. McNicol et al., *Beyond the Q Impasse*, 52.

65. According to Poirier, there is a widespread assumption among proponents of the FH that Luke wrote to displace or supplant Matthew ("Introduction," 6–11). I do not think this view of Luke's attitude to his sources deserves to be linked to the FH as a whole.

66. Hengel, *Four Gospels*, 200.

67. Kloppenborg, "Synoptic Problem," 108.

68. Landry, "Luke's Revision," 51, 71.

69. Franklin, *Luke*, 360.

Others have a neutral or positive way of expressing the redactional attitude. For example, Black writes:

> Precisely because of its orientation toward the Christian Jews of Palestine, the Gospel of Matthew came to be seen by Paul and his disciple Luke as a not wholly suitable instrument for the evangelization of the Gentiles, although by virtue of its being the Gospel of the original church of Jerusalem and of its having the authority of the twelve apostles it was irrevocably the fundamental document of the Christian faith.[70]

This way of putting the issue conveys respect for the source material along with a recognition that it was "not wholly suitable" for the Gentile mission. McNicol, Dungan, and Peabody likewise argue that "[a]lthough Luke uses his own compositional agenda in Lk 1:5–2:52 to provide the setting for his narrative, he also demonstrates great respect for the general content of Mt 1:1—2:23 within this section of his narrative."[71]

The early to mid-second century circulation of the four Gospels in one manuscript collection indicates that early Christians did not read them as antagonistic toward each other or intended to replace each other.[72] This historical reality demonstrates that if the Gospel authors were trying to actively oppose each other they failed spectacularly. They either did not sufficiently make their intentions known to the earliest readers or the content of their Gospels lacked the clarity needed to make later readers aware of this intention. The early acceptance of the fourfold-Gospel collection should give modern interpreters some pause when attributing extreme combative or antagonistic attitudes to the Gospel authors.

The heavy redaction of the infancy narratives by each Evangelist certainly indicates a desire to make distinct points about the significance of Jesus and to tell the story of Jesus in a more persuasive and compelling way to a particular audience in light of particular rhetorical goals and apologetic needs. On a broader scale, without some such desire there would have been no need to even write another Gospel. Beyond this observation, guesses about Luke's attitude toward Matthew or Matthew's attitude toward Luke (appreciation, indifference, or antagonism) are speculative and likely reveal

---

70. Black, *Why Four Gospels?*, 53.
71. McNicol et al., *Beyond the Q Impasse*, 50.
72. David Trobisch makes a compelling case for the publication of the canonical edition of the New Testament by the mid-second century (*First Edition of the New Testament*). Marcion demonstrates that some Christians exclusively used one Gospel but the equally early use of the fourfold Gospel was more geographically widespread.

more about the modern interpreter's presuppositions concerning the nature of earliest Christianity.

CONCLUSION

If all we had were the infancy narratives of Matthew and Luke in isolation it would perhaps be difficult to argue for literary dependence. Shared dependence upon a prior tradition would be the most likely hypothesis. We do not, however, have the narratives in isolation but as integral parts of their respective Gospels. The infancy narratives are thus an important, but not the only, piece of the puzzle.

The explanations discussed above provide possible reasons for why Luke would have treated Matthew the way he did in the infancy narratives or vice versa but none of these explanations are strong or compelling enough to end the discussion. The most that can be achieved by proponents of the 2GH, FH, or MCH is to demonstrate that the infancy narratives do not automatically discredit or disprove their hypotheses. This goal has been achieved and proponents of the 2DH cannot simply point to the infancy narratives as evidence for their hypothesis without further argumentation. "[T]he differences in the introductory sections of these two Gospels do not necessarily preclude contact one with another."[73]

The inconclusiveness of the internal literary evidence in source criticism is likely an insurmountable problem. Francis Watson aptly notes,

> "An interpretation based on an incorrect dependence hypothesis might well produce plausible reasons why evangelist A may have modified what he finds in gospel B, even if in reality B was dependent on A or both were dependent on C . . . If one interprets a gospel on the basis of a source-critical hypothesis, one does so at one's own risk."[74]

This could lead us to abandon source criticism completely in favor of narrative criticism but the reality of Jesus as a historical figure and the growth of earliest Christianity as a historical phenomenon prevents this move.[75] The Gospels are not just fictional stories with an interesting protagonist; source criticism is required by the historical nature of the evidence.[76]

---

73. McNicol et al., *Beyond the Q Impasse*, 47.
74. Watson, *Gospel Writing*, 156.
75. Cf. Ibid., 157.
76. Watson rightly argues that "the 'real', historically- and theologically-significant Jesus cannot be detached from the process of reception that reaches its *telos* in the

Black cogently argues, "[A]ll that internal literary criticism can do is show how an existing text could have originated in more than one way. But the decision as to which is the correct way requires the help of history, if it is to be reached at all."[77] The external patristic evidence concerning the order of the Gospels is an important historical key and while many interpreters doubt that the patristic evidence is clear, unified, or reliable enough to get us through the impasse its neglect will only further weaken any proposed solution.[78]

BIBLIOGRAPHY

Bellinzoni, Arthur J., ed. *The Two-Source Hypothesis: A Critical Appraisal.* Macon, GA: Mercer University Press, 1985.

Black, David Alan. *Why Four Gospels? The Historical Origins of the Gospels.* 2nd ed. Gonzalez, FL: Energion, 2010.

Brown, Raymond E. *The Birth of the Messiah: A Commentary on the Infancy Narratives in the Gospels of Matthew and Luke.* Upd. ed. New York: Doubleday, 1993.

Carslon, Stephen C. "Clement of Alexandria on the 'Order' of the Gospels." *New Testament Studies* 47 (2001) 118–25.

Derrenbacker, Robert A., Jr. "The 'External and Psychological Conditions under Which the Synoptic Gospels Were Written': Ancient Compositional Practices and the Synoptic Problem." In *New Studies in the Synoptic Problem: Oxford Conference, April 2008. Essays in Honour of Christopher M. Tuckett*, edited by Paul Foster et al., 435–58. Leuven: Peeters, 2011.

Drury, John. *Tradition and Design in Luke's Gospel.* Atlanta: John Knox, 1977.

---

canonical gospel narratives" (*Gospel Writing*, 157).

77. Black, *Why Four Gospels?*, 37. This conclusion is indirectly supported by Garrow's recent argument in support of the MCH, which explores the conventions and constraints of contemporary scribal practice ("Streeter's 'Other' Synoptic Solution," 215–219). Cf. Derrenbacker, "'External and Psychological Conditions," 435–58. Historical considerations outside of the Gospels themselves are needed to move though the impasse.

78. This is perhaps the greatest weakness of the MCH. The clearest connection of the infancy narratives to the order of the Gospels and the earliest explicit reference to the order of the Gospels is found in Eusebius' (c. A.D. 260–c. 340) record of Clement of Alexandria's (c. A.D. 150–c. 215) account of the teaching of the "earliest elders" (cf. Peabody, "Reading Mark," 183). "Clement has set down a tradition of the earliest elders about the order of the Gospels, and it has this form. He used to say that the earliest written gospels were those containing the genealogies" (Eusebius, *Ecclesiastical History* 6.14.5 as translated in Black, *Why Four Gospels?*, 27). This quote has often been used to support the 2GH but Stephen C. Carlson has argued that "earliest written" (προγράφω) should be translated as "published openly" ("Clement of Alexandria on the 'Order' of the Gospels," 118–25). Clement would then not be making a statement about the order of composition but about the non-literary and haphazard circulation of Mark in comparison to the public publication and circulation of Matthew and Luke.

Farmer, William R. *Jesus and the Gospels: Tradition, Scripture, and Canon.* Philadelphia: Fortress, 1982.

Farrer, A. M. "On Dispensing with Q." In *Studies in the Gospels: Essays in Memory of R. H. Lightfoot*, edited by D. E. Nineham, 55–88. Oxford: Blackwell, 1955.

Fitzmyer, Joseph A. *The Gospel According to Luke I-IX: Introduction, Translation, and Notes.* Anchor Bible 28. New York: Doubleday, 1981.

Foster, Paul, et al., eds. *New Studies in the Synoptic Problem: Oxford Conference, April 2008. Essays in Honour of Christopher M. Tuckett.* BETL 239. Leuven: Peeters, 2011.

France, R. T. *The Gospel of Matthew.* NICNT. Grand Rapids: Eerdmans, 2007.

———. "Scripture, Tradition and History in the Infancy Narratives of Matthew." In *Gospel Perspectives: Studies of History and Tradition in the Four Gospels*, edited by R. T. France and David Wenham, 2:239–66. Sheffield: JSOT, 1981.

Franklin, Eric. *Luke: Interpreter of Paul, Critic of Matthew.* JSNTSup 92. Sheffield: JSOT, 1994.

Garrow, Alan. "Streeter's 'Other' Synoptic Solution: The Matthew Conflator Hypothesis." *New Testament Studies* 62/2 (2016) 207–26.

Goodacre, Mark. *The Case Against Q: Studies in Markan Priority and the Synoptic Problem.* Harrisburg, PA: Trinity, 2002.

Goulder, M. D. *Luke: A New Paradigm.* JSNTSup 20. Sheffield: Sheffield Academic Press, 1989.

Hagner, Donald A. *Matthew 1–13.* WBC 33a. Dallas: Word, 1993.

Hengel, Martin. *The Four Gospels and the One Gospel of Jesus Christ: An Investigation of the Collection and Origin of the Canonical Gospels.* Harrisburg, PA: Trinity, 2000.

Holmes, Michael W. *The Apostolic Fathers: Greek Texts and English Translations.* 3rd ed. Grand Rapids: Baker Academic, 2007.

Huggins, Ronald V. "Matthean Posteriority: A Preliminary Proposal." *Novum Testamentum* 34 (1992) 1–22.

Kloppenborg, John S. "The Theological Stakes in the Synoptic Problem." In *The Four Gospels, 1992: Festschrift Frans Neirynck*, edited by F. van Segbroeck et al., 93–120. BETL 100. Leuven: Peeters, 1992.

Landry, David T. "Luke's Revision of Matthew's Infancy Narrative." In *Reading Ideologies: Essays on the Bible and Interpretation in Honor of Mary Ann Tolbert*, edited by Tat-siong Benny Liew, 45–75. Bible in the Modern World 40. Sheffield: Sheffield Phoenix, 2011.

MacEwen, Robert K. *Matthean Posteriority: An Exploration of Matthew's Use of Mark and Luke as a Solution to the Synoptic Problem.* LNTS 501. London: Bloomsbury, 2015.

Machen, J. Gresham. *The Virgin Birth of Christ.* Grand Rapids: Baker, 1930.

Marshall, I. Howard. *The Gospel of Luke: A Commentary on the Greek Text.* NIGTC. Grand Rapids: Eerdmans, 1978.

McNicol, Allan J., et al. *Beyond the Q Impasse: Luke's Use of Matthew: A Demonstration by the Research Team of the International Institute for Gospel Studies.* Valley Forge, PA: Trinity, 1996.

Nolland, John. *Luke 1–9:20.* WBC 35a. Dallas: Word, 1989.

Peabody, David. "Reading Mark from the Perspectives of Different Synoptic Source Hypotheses: Historical, Redactional, and Theological Implications." In *New Studies in the Synoptic Problem: Oxford Conference, April 2008. Essays in Honour of Christopher M. Tuckett*, edited by Paul Foster et al., 159–85. BETL 239. Leuven: Peeters, 2011.

Poierier, John C. "Introduction: Why the Farrer Hypothesis? Why Now?" In *Marcan Priority without Q: Explorations in the Farrer Hypothesis*, edited by John C. Poirier and Jeffrey Peterson, 6–11. LNTS. London: T. & T. Clark, 2015.

Shuler, Philip. "Genre Criticism and the Synoptic Problem." In *New Synoptic Studies*, edited by William R. Farmer, 467–80. Macon, GA: Mercer University Press, 1983.

Stein, Robert H. *Studying the Synoptic Gospels: Origin and Interpretation*. 2nd ed. Grand Rapids: Baker, 2001.

Stendahl, Krister. "Quis et Unde? An Analysis of Matthew 1–2." In *The Interpretation of Matthew*, edited by Graham Stanton, 69–80. 2nd ed. Edinburgh: T. & T. Clark, 1995.

Streeter, B. H. *The Four Gospels*. New York: Macmillan, 1924.

Trobisch, David. *The First Edition of the New Testament*. Oxford: Oxford University Press, 2000.

Watson, Francis. *Gospel Writing: A Canonical Perspective*. Grand Rapids: Eerdmans, 2013.

11

The Origin of Jesus' Speeches in the Fourth Gospel[1]

ANTONIO PIÑERO
Universidad Complutense de Madrid

INTRODUCTION

THE ORIGIN AND FUNCTION of the fourth Gospel is without a doubt one of the most prominent issues in New Testament studies. And the issue surrounding the origin and function of the long speeches/discourses of Jesus in that Gospel has been (and continues to be) the subject of much debate. Raymond E. Brown provided an excellent survey of the *status quaestionis*, up to about 1980, in his commentary on the Gospel of John.[2] Two additional books, both written by Gonzalo Fontana-Elboj,[3] serve as an excellent complement to Brown's treatment of the subject. In those books Fontana-Elboj discusses the problems associated with the origins of this Gospel and its compositional process, including the origin of Jesus' speeches.[4]

1. Original in Spanish. Translated by Thomas W. Hudgins.
2. Brown, *John*.
3. Fontana-Elboj, *El Evangelio de Juan*, and Fontana-Elboj, *Los orígenes del cristianismo*.
4. In the field of Spanish philology, it is worth noting the work of Vidal, *Evangelio*

Despite all of the possible caveats regarding its strongly hypothetical nature, I think that the interpretative hypothesis of Fontana-Elboj is highly plausible. What follows is a brief summary of his position. Since I follow his argument in general and situate my own hypothesis within his, it is helpful to sketch his position before moving into those elements that are my own. Really though, my position is just an extension of the hypothesis set forth by Fontana-Elboj.

The text of the Gospel of John is the product of a particular group of people, a community that believed in Jesus, whose remote origins are traced back to the region known as Samaria. This community was formed just a few years after the death of Jesus on the cross. The tremendous upheaval brought about by the Jewish War (A.D. 66–70) prompted them to flee from their homes and move to Ephesus, where they found another group of Samaritans.[5]

The author or authors of the Gospel of John have little or nothing to do with the historical John—one of the twelve disciples/apostles, Jesus' favorite disciple, and the brother of James. A careful analysis of the Gospel and other secondary sources has led scholars to suggest two mythical founders of the Johannine community: (1) the "beloved disciple," and (2) Philip. By the second century, the "beloved disciple" and the apostle John came to be viewed as one and the same person, both mythical in nature. They sort of obscured the person of Philip, to the point that it is difficult to determine if the community referred to the apostle Philip or the deacon mentioned in Acts, since both persons appear in the sources.

THE PHASES OF COMPOSITION

A "Gospel" is nothing more than a "theological flag" about the person and mission of Jesus that was flown by diverse and important groups of Jesus' followers. The flags were woven by different reconstructions of the person of Jesus. They are a reflection of what those communities believed about the identity of the resurrected (and ascended) Messiah. These reconstructions were made up of oral and written traditions that were preserved in the memory of these communities. The Gospels were not written in a single sitting. Instead, different individuals formed them over a period of time with

---

y Cartas de Juan. It seems to me a very interesting hypothesis, though I am strongly inclined towards the general hypothesis of Fontana-Elboj.

5. Some inscriptions of the city of Ephesus testify to the existence of a Samaritan group in the city.

varying levels of involvement. With regard to the composition of the fourth Gospel, researchers have identified several phases.

The First Phase

According to Fontana-Elboj, the first phase of the Gospel of John consisted of an individual or individuals recording their memories of Jesus in writing. The pre-existing structure of the Gospel of Mark was used as a sort of template. This posed no real problem for them. The first version of the Gospel of John probably included an account of the Passion, in which the beloved disciple plays a pretty significant role, and certain Samaritan traditions, such as the call of Nathanael (John 1:43–51) and the woman at the well (John 4:1–42). To these was added the narrative structure found in the Gospel of Mark, though they left out a significant portion of its details and content. The Gospel of Mark has often been referred to as a Passion narrative with a long introduction.[6] Jesus' death and resurrection are the focal events of the Gospel. These events are interpreted in a Pauline manner, different than the Judeo-Christian communities of James and Peter. The Gospel of John is also situated within a reinterpretation of the person and mission of Jesus from a Pauline perspective.

That this first phase of the Gospel of John employs a similar structure to that of the Gospel of Mark can be deduced from the existence of Papyrus Egerton 2, which has these characteristics, just with a Johannine flavor.

What does it mean for a New Testament text to be reinterpreted from a Pauline perspective? In my opinion, by comparing the contents of a New Testament text and the ideas presented therein with other theological perspectives with other texts of the same corpus, researchers can demonstrate whether a text has a Pauline understanding of the person and mission of Jesus. Generally speaking, the Pauline tradition ascribes a much higher, almost divine, view of the person of Jesus. He is greater than just a mere prophet or earthly messiah. The Pauline tradition interprets Jesus' death and resurrection as redemptive events designed by God. They affect the history of the whole world, not just Israel. And they affect not only humanity, but the whole of creation, since even creation is set free from the burden of

---

6. Thomas W. Hudgins, in our joint blog on the study of the New Testament (aptly called "Across the Atlantic" since he is on one side of the Atlantic and I am on the other), has pointed out that the idea of a passion narrative with a long introduction is not entirely unique to the Gospel of Mark. In fact, Matthew and Luke share this emphasis on the last week of Jesus' life, though not quite as much as Mark, and the Gospel of John is focused heavily on the last twenty-four hours of Jesus' life (http://www.pineroandhudgins.com/search?q=%22last+week+of+Jesus%27+life%22).

injustice brought about by sin. Jesus' death on the cross is viewed as a sacrifice offered to God, an act predetermined by God himself from eternity past. God accepted the life-sacrifice of his messianic agent as an atonement, or ransom, for the sins of mankind. The sacrifice on the cross was vicarious in nature, the offering of a righteous person—the death of the Messiah as the son of God—who died for the life and salvation of others, even though it was them who actually deserved to die. The death of Jesus was followed by his resurrection, a sign of God's vindication and that God had indeed accepted the sacrifice.

This theological concept of a vicarious sacrifice is grounded more in Greek thought than that of the Jewish people. Those who believed in the Messiah and continued to practice the Law would be resurrected like Jesus. But each individual was responsible for accepting this event as the ultimate act of universal salvation in order to experience the redemptive value of the cross. Such acceptance is an act of faith in what God did through the death of their Messiah.

A Pauline interpretation also involves an inclusive view of redemption. Instead of only the Jews being saved, the redemption secured by Jesus' death on the cross is open to the Gentiles as well. No longer was this redemption viewed as exclusively Jewish, that is exclusively for the chosen people of God. Now the Gentiles were able to be saved on an equal footing with the Jewish people. Even though the Mosaic Law remained binding for those Jews that placed their faith in the Messiah (who, by the way, never abolished the Law or its requirements for the chosen people), the Law would not be fully valid for the Gentiles. The Law only affects those who are born Jewish. Those elements that are binding are the circumcision, dietary laws, and laws pertaining to ritual purity. The Gentiles are saved by believing that Jesus is the Messiah and by fulfilling those parts of the Mosaic Law that they can, namely the Decalogue and the law of the Messiah (i.e., the law of love).

Based on all of this, it is believed that the authors of those Gospels written after Mark, particularly the Johannine Gospels composed during phase one, accepted in some way, though perhaps not completely, this Pauline-Markan theological structure.

The Second Phase

During the second phase, certain material was added, material which could be called Lukan in nature. This process of absorption, whereby the author or authors of the fourth Gospel incorporated material from one of the other Synoptic Gospels, is impossible to explain with any certitude. That the

Gospel of Luke also had its origins in Ephesus is one plausible explanation. There was not much distance, geographically speaking, between the Lukan and the Johannine communities—they were basically neighbors—and so material could move from one community to the other, if the parties involved were interested and chose to include it in their Gospels. That appears to be what happened, at least in the case of the Lukan material that was brought into the Johannine text.

This hypothetical transfer of material could explain the appearance of the following material in the fourth Gospel: (1) part of the story of the healing of the royal official's son (John 4:46–54; Luke 7:2–9); (2) the mention of the family with whom Jesus was friends—Martha, Mary, and Lazarus of Bethlehem (John 11:1–5; Luke 10:38–41); (3) certain details surrounding the Passion and the appearances of Jesus in Jerusalem (John 20). It is possible that the pericope of the adulteress (John 8:3–11) also came from these Lukan circles; some manuscripts actually include the passage in the third Gospel. The real evidence, though, that Lukan material was carried into the Johannine Gospels lies in the fact that some material is only found in Luke and John. One explanation is they share the same geographical location, namely Ephesus.

The Third Phase

The third phase involves the inclusion of additional material that contained the sayings of Jesus. This material was included in the fourth Gospel, as it existed at that point having passed through phases one and two. But it was not added as a single discourse unit or in one particular location. The additional material is scattered all over the Johannine text. This includes the prologue-hymn (John 1:1–18) and some speeches and monologues of Jesus that had a marked theological stamp entirely their own. For example, these speeches have nothing to do with the material found in the so-called "Q source" (used by Matthew and Luke) or the topics covered in the "Little Apocalypse" (Mark 13). The Johannine Jesus does not obsessively announce the coming of the kingdom of God. Instead, his message is twofold: (1) that he himself is the true (real, physical, and ontological) son of God the Father; (2) that he is the existential Revealer of knowledge pertaining to salvation; this knowledge he imparts to his disciples, but the "world" does not understand it at all. These speeches are concentrated in the "I" statement of Jesus that he is equal to the Father (John 10:30): "*I* and the Father are one." The "I" is pre-existing, and his revelation on the earth is knowledge that leads to salvation. The substance of this revelation was the union of the Revealer with the Father and the union of a mystical community with the same Father through oneness with Jesus, generated by the faith in him as Revealer (John 17:21). The theological situation of these speeches of the Johannine Jesus and his claims, which was so different from how the person and mission of Jesus actually was, has practically no resemblance to the traits of the Jesus found in the Synoptic Gospels.

Evidence of "Diverse Hands" in Composition

An important feature of these speeches is that they were written down by different people ("diverse hands"), despite their basic theological unity. It is not neceesary to dwell on this point, since it has been demonstrated time and again in the commentaries. But Fontana-Elboj pauses to focus on two details that are more than sufficient to prove his point. The double reality (i.e., diversity of hands and theological unity) is seen, as he points out in his book *El Evangelio de Juan*,[7] in the following two ways:

1. *The apparent clumsiness in how the speeches were brought into the text.* Jesus ends one of the speeches in the Farewell Discourse with the following statement: "Get up. Let us leave" (John 14:31). The problem is another speech follows what Jesus says in 14:31, and that speech is three chapters long! Sometimes a speech is inserted in the narrative in a very awkward and problematic place, almost as if those who put it there did so unwittingly or without any knowledge of the content of the immediate context. Compare, for example, Jesus' complaint in John 16:5: "But now I am going to him who sent me; and none of you asks me, 'Where are you going?'" Compare this, however, to John 13:36, where Peter specifically asks Jesus, "Lord, where are you going?" And then there is Thomas' declaration in John 14:5: "We do not know where you are going. How can we know the way?"

2. *The haphazard repetition of themes.* The repetition of ideas or details gives the inevitable impression that very similar traditions about Jesus (with only slight variation) have just been piled one on top of the other in the fourth Gospel. One example is the first farewell discourse (John 14:1–31) and the repetition of the same themes in the second discourse (John 16:4–33). Those discourses were similar narratives, though only slightly different, that had lives of their own before being included in the Gospel of John.

---

7. Fontana-Elboj, *El Evangelio de Juan*.

Evidence of Prior Knowledge of the Synoptic Gospels

The content that was absorbed into the Gospel of John necessitates some prior knowledge of the Synoptic Jesus. In other words, the audience must have had a broader knowledge about Jesus than what is presented about his life and mission in the fourth Gospel. In modern linguistics, this is referred to as "intertextuality" (i.e., a text presupposes the existence of a previously written text that explains the new text in some way). Such speeches already existed before being introduced into the narrative framework of the fourth Gospel. This content (and the collective speeches of Jesus in John) would not make sense to a readership that was unfamiliar with the material found in the other Gospels, specifically the Synoptic Gospels. Given this, the Johannine audience must have known about the life of Jesus. Otherwise, an absolutely different image of Jesus would have emerged, one that was irreconcilable with the other Gospels (of which the authors knew, hypothetically speaking, since in the fourth Gospel we find Synoptic material [at the least material from Luke]). And the author or authors, as we have said, were familiar with these other Gospels, and they would not have wanted to present some radically different image of Jesus to the audience/community for whom the fourth Gospel was intended.

THE STRUCTURE AND CONTENT OF THE JOHANNINE SPEECHES

The structure and content of the Johannine speeches also provide material for reflection. A simple comparison of this material with the speeches of the historical Jesus (with all the caveats of the critical methodology affords) in the Synoptic Gospels demonstrates that the Johannine speeches are (1) repetitive in their content and (2) have a mystical, semi-poetic format, which some might call "semitheatrical." The Jesus of the fourth Gospel does not teach the Sermon on the Mount, nor does he teach the so-called "Lord's Prayer"; he does not speak in parables, nor do his speeches have the characteristic features of the Synoptic Jesus. The speeches of the Johannine Jesus have a mystical-symbolic tone, very different than the speeches of the Synoptic Jesus. These speeches have a spiral structure: Jesus expounds a thought, develops it from different angles, and then returns full circle before picking up another topic that is slightly connected to the one he just left. This format is repeated. In the fourth Gospel, the speeches of Jesus sometimes have a double meaning, are packed with irony, and lead to misunderstanding, which requires further explanation from the Savior. They give the impression of being profound meditations of Jesus himself about: (1) his role as the Revealer, (2) his special relationship with God the Father, (3) how people need to place their faith in him as the one from heaven, and (4) unity with him.

There are also numerous theological differences between the Jesus of the Synoptic Gospels and the fourth Gospel. Important theological themes of early Christianity that are present in the Synoptics are absent in the fourth Gospel. In place of them are new concepts, seemingly unknown to the previous Gospels—concepts such as "life," "witness," "truth," "grace," "light/darkness," "up/down," etc. Given these differences, the vast majority of Johannine scholars have wondered what inspired the diverse hands that made this Gospel and especially those latter hands that inserted the speeches of the Johannine Jesus into the previously established Markan framework.

This is a hotly debated issue, and scholars have different opinions about what is going on here. The following is a brief summary:[8]

1. Some believe that the presentation of the Johannine Jesus is patterned after Hellenistic Jewish speculations about personified Wisdom (Prov 8:22–31 and Wis 7:22—8:1), making Jesus Wisdom incarnate. This theology was shaped and complemented by Philo and his ideas about the divine Logos.

2. Others argue that the world of the fourth Gospel has many similarities with the thought and theology of the Essenes of Qumran. Certain lexical parallels between the Gospel of John and the Qumran texts are surprising, such as "spirit of truth" (John 14:17 = 1QS 4:21) and "light of life" (John 8:12 = 1QS 3:7). Another similarity is the dualism of light and darkness, truth and error, etc., shared by the Dead Sea Scrolls and the Gospel of John.

3. Others argue that the ideological world of the fourth Gospel is part of the beginnings of "gnosis." In the first century "gnosis" was still developing, not a well-established religious-philosophical system. The latter stage is designated at Gnosticism rather than "gnosis." According to this view, the figure of Jesus-Logos descends into the world, bodily, reveals salvation to men, and then ascends to the Father. This is very similar to the image found in gnosis, which has a Redeemer/Revealer/Savior. And that must have had a huge impact on the ideas found in the fourth Gospel and, to a lesser extent, those of Paul of Tarsus.

---

8. For more information, see my book *Guía para entender el Nuevo Testamento*, 393–95.

These three views are not mutually exclusive, but rather complement one another. All of them have as a common denominator the fact that they were composed in an environment of marginal Judaism, which certainly gave birth to gnosis (probably a pre-Christian movement that was born within Judaism, significantly influenced by Plato, which interprets Genesis through Timaeus), but which also encompasses the field of Jewish speculations about the divine and its projection into the world (Logos, Wisdom, Presence) that began to occur when Greek philosophy, in its essential tenets, became popular among the educated environments of the Hellenistic world from the third century B.C.

THE SPEECHES AS PROTO-GNOSIS

The Gospel of John has certain features that fit well with "proto-Gnosis" (a well known term). This refers to the infancy stage of what would, in an intellectual environment, eventually grow into full-blown Gnosticism (in less than fifty years). The two main theological characteristics found in the fourth Gospel only come together in Gnosticism: (1) the use of dualism (up/down; light/darkness; etc.); (2) the concept of the Redeemer/Revealer who descends from heaven, (suffers,) and then ascends to heaven from where he came.

The authors of these speeches are comfortable with these "protognostic" concepts to express their conception of the Messiah and his doctrine of salvation. There are two "poles," so to speak. Individuals have a choice to make—one pole or the other. Either they can accept the revelation of the Sent One or reject. In the fourth Gospel, everything is described in terms of its distance to/from these poles. Life, truth, light, and up all represent salvation; death, lie, darkness, and down are the opposites of the aforementioned descriptions and represent the opposite of salvation (i.e., lostness). The world, though, is not bad in and of itself, but only by its rejection of salvation, by not acknowledging Jesus as the incarnate Word, Revealer, and Savior of humankind. Jesus is the hero from above, from heaven, from the light, from the knowledge. His Father is God. The Jews are the paladins of down, in the world of darkness, of misunderstanding. Their father is the devil (John 8:44). In this same line of thinking, the authors of the speeches affirm that faith is to know (John 14:7), and that eternal life consists of knowing God and the One he sent (John 17:3). Jesus is the model of the true Gnostic, knowing from where he comes and to where he goes.

The Gospel of John treats only a "protognostic mental mark," since in this work certain ideas of gnosis are not accepted, though they will become present in the late second century A.D. Thus John does not reject the world as intrinsically evil; he defends at all costs the incarnation of the Sent One (something unthinkable in later in Gnosticism). He thinks that this Sent One is not embodied in successive characters, but appears only once in human history, namely in Jesus of Nazareth, a person who enters the human terrain of sufferings and death; the message of Jesus is not only for a chosen few ("spiritual" people who participate with their spirit in a special way in the divine nature), but for all who are ready to accept with faith that Jesus is the Revealer.

THE ORIGIN OF THE SPEECHES IN JOHN

Before setting forth a hypothesis concerning the source of the speeches of the Johannine Jesus, it is important to point out a small section found in Fontana-Elboj that readers might overlook. This quote, however, is important and needs to be highlighted, since it might provide the key to identifying the origin of the speeches of the Johannine Jesus. This observation serves as the real foundation of our proposal: the striking resemblance in both form and content between these speeches and the Odes of Solomon, an idea that had already been pointed out by Adolf von Harnack in 1910.[9] These Odes[10] and and the speeches in the fourth Gospel came from a very similar Judeo-Christian environment that is marked by striking theological and lexical affinities. It is as if both came from the same native soil, a mystical and protognostic branch of Judeo-Christianity, which certainly was not the majority of Christianity at that time. Fontana-Elboj rightly points out that the most remarkable comparison between these two works is the similar "tono extático, propio de una asamblea litúrgica,"[11] in which the prophets and inspired teachers played a very important role. The author of the Odes is clearly identified in his inspired and enthusiastic song as the Savior. As Peral and Alegre, who provided translation and commentary to the text in Castillian, have said:

> En este proceso de la salvación, la figura del Salvador pierde su peculiaridad y carácter único, pues el aedo, al transformarse en «Hijo», se convierte a su vez en «Salvador» de los demás, realizando (en cuanto identificado con el Hijo) la ascensión al cielo y el descenso a los infiernos (cf. OdasSl 36; 17; 42) a fin de que la salvación se realice en todas sus dimensiones ... De

9. Harnack, *Ein jüdisch-christliches Psalmbuch*.
10. Díez Macho and Piñero, *Apócrifos del Antiguo Testamento*, 3:79–130.
11. Fontana-Elboj, *El Evangelio de Juan*, 139.

ahí que las fronteras entre el «hijo propio» y el «hijo adoptivo» sean tan difusas y fluctuantes que en muchos textos resulte difícil determinar cuál es el «hijo» que está hablando en ellos. Por eso también el aedo puede recibir los títulos de Hijo de Dios (cf. OdasSl 36,3), Señor, Mesías y Cabeza de la comunidad (cf. OdasSl 17,16s).[12]

The commentary on this text by Fontana-Elboj seems absolutely relevant to our objective:

> La identificación del aedo con Cristo acabará por generar finalmente que sea Cristo mismo quien *habla por su boca sin ninguna mediación*. Exactamente, tal como lo hacen los autores de los discursos joánicos [...] (Cabe pensar que las Odas) fueron compuestas en un ambiente en el que determinadas formas litúrgicas –llamémosle parateatrales– animaban a que los miembros más dotados intelectual, estética (y espiritualmente) asumieran en primera persona la voz del Cristo preexistente que dominaba su teología. Así la comunidad joánica contó con un acervo de textos independientes, procedentes con casi total seguridad de manifestaciones litúrgicas parateatrales, que acabaron integrados en un texto evangélico que era... desde su origen como un receptáculo en el que se integraron todo tipo de innovaciones doctrinales.[13]

---

12. Díez Macho and Piñero, *Apócrifos del Antiguo Testamento*, 3:86–87. Trans. "In this process of salvation, the figure of the Savior loses his unique character and peculiarity, since the bard, once transformed into 'Son,' becomes as a result the 'Savior' of others, performing (as identified with the Son) the ascension into heaven and the descent into hell (cf. Odes of Solomon 36; 17; 42) so that salvation may be realized in all its dimensions... Hence the boundaries between the 'son' and the 'adoptive son' are so diffuse and fluctuating that in many texts it is difficult to determine which 'son' is speaking to them. That is why the bard can also receive the titles Son of God (cf. Odes of Solomon 36:3), Lord, Messiah, and Head of the community (see Odes of Solomon 17:16."

13. Fontana-Elboy, *Los orígenes del cristianismo*, 140. Trans. "The identification of the bard with Christ will eventually indicate that it is Christ himself who speaks through his mouth without any mediation. In the same way, like the authors of the Johannine discourses... [This would lead one to think that the Odes] were composed in an environment in which certain liturgical forms--let's call them parateatrics--encouraged the most gifted members (intellectually, artistically, and spiritually) to assume in the first person the voice of the pre-existing Christ who had his theology mastered. Thus the Johannine community had a collection of independent texts, deriving most likely from parateatrical liturgical manifestations, that ended up being integrated in a Gospel text, which was... from its beginning the recipient of all kinds of doctrinal innovations." Fontana-Elboj proposed the hypothetical origin to the Montanist prophetesses, Prisca and Maximilla (ibid., 355–56). The prophets claimed to be the human voice of the Holy Spirit. As I wrote in my book *Cristianismos derrotados*: "Montano, y sus dos

Now, reinforced with these ideas, a hypothesis is presented regarding the origin of these speeches, which is deduced from the points made by Fontana-Elboj. Hopefully it will add some contour to the discussion at hand. Just as Revelation does not expressly say that the whole text was to be read aloud in a liturgical context, that point can be deduced without a doubt from just looking at the text as a whole.[14] In the same way, it is highly plausible that the Gospel of John was read in liturgical services as the text was being constructed. Within this framework, *the speeches of Jesus were uttered by the prophets in that community, imbued with the spirit of the Master, and they spoke like Jesus without any distinction of persons.*[15]

---

profetisas principales, Prisca y Maximila, pensaban que en ellos habitaba el Espíritu Santo, y que la divinidad utilizaba mecánicamente sus órganos fonadores para profetizar, al igual que un músico experto pulsa las cuerdas de su lira y ésta emite los sonidos que él quiere. Como instrumentos del Espíritu desempeñaban la función de 'Paráclito', es decir, de Consolador, prometida por Jesús para después de su partida (Jn 14, 15). En efecto, el Señor no había revelado todo; quedaban muchas cosas por aprender y esas las enseñaría el Paráclito, el Espíritu enviado por el Salvador, por medio de sus bocas. Montano sostenía que se cumplía así lo afirmado por Jesús en el evangelio de Juan: 'Cuando llegue él, el Espíritu de la verdad, os irá guiando hacia toda la verdad, porque no hablará por su cuenta, sino que os comunicará todo lo que oyere y os interpretará lo que habrá de venir. El manifestará mi gloria, porque, para daros la interpretación, tomará de lo mío' (Jn 16, 12-14). De acuerdo con ello el nuevo movimiento, lo que hoy denominamos montanismo, se titulaba en verdad 'Nueva Profecía' y 'Nuevas Visiones'" (*Cristianismos derrotados*, 125). Trans. "Montano, and his two principal prophetesses, Prisca and Maximilla, thought that the Holy Spirit was dwelling in them, and that God mechanically used his prophesying organs to prophesy, just as an expert musician pulsates the strings of his lyre and it produces the sounds that he wants. As instruments of the Spirit they played the role of the 'Paraclete', that is, the Comforter, promised by Jesus after his departure (John 14, 15). In fact, the Lord had not revealed everything; Many things remained to be learned and these would be taught by the Paraclete, the Spirit sent by the Savior, through their mouths. Montano maintained that this was fulfilled in Jesus' words in the Gospel of John: 'When he comes, the Spirit of truth, will guide you to all truth, for he will not speak on his own account, but will communicate everything he hears. And he will interpret to you what is to come. He will manifest my glory, because to give you the interpretation he will take of mine' (John 16:12-14). Accordingly, the new movement, what we now call Montanism, was in truth titled 'New Prophecy' and 'New Visions.'"

14. See García-Ureña, *Apocalipsis*.

15. It is difficult to overstate the enormous importance of the early Christian prophets as interpreters and facilitators, who were responsible for updating the teaching of a Jesus, who had been dead now for some time, to the particular circumstances of the community in which they exercised the gift of prophecy. It is well known that different (and abundant) words of the prophets, spoken at the direction of the spirit of Jesus, entered the Synoptic tradition without any record of its secondary origin. That is, they did not enter the tradition with the note, "This is what Jesus said by the mouth of the prophet" (or something like that), but simply as "Jesus said." Hence the number of speeches of Jesus that are not accepted as authentic by critical scholars.

As the bard of the Odes of Solomon, the person of the prophet—or the best of the Johannine prophets—gives way and the person of Jesus begins to speak in his stead. Now, and this point is very important, it seems impossible that a community that was familiar with the Synoptic material, at least the Gospel of Mark and that of Luke, would fail to notice that those speeches had nothing to do with similar speeches of the earthly Jesus. After all, they had "transcribed" Mark and Luke and absorbed them into the Johannine narrative. Therefore, it is very plausible that attendees to the liturgical office of the Johannine community *explicitly presupposed* that the prophets who pronounced such speeches were not talking on behalf of the earthly Jesus, as in Mark and Luke, but in the name of the resurrected Jesus, the heavenly Revealer. Therefore, they would have been aware that the speeches were from a divine being, not the human person that had previously been and no longer existed as such, since he had been transmuted into an exalted-to-heaven being. With the words of Fontana-Elboj, such prophets, and of course their listeners, would be aware that in their liturgical services they were representing a "paratheatrical action," whose main and almost unique actor was the Risen One.

If someone asked listeners of that community, who were highly mystical, if the words they had heard were those of the "historical Jesus" (to use a modern-day expression; i.e., the Master from Galilee who went city to city along the dusty roads of Galilee announcing the imminent coming of the kingdom of God and the need to repent), they would no doubt say no, absolutely not. The words they heard were from the very "lips of Jesus," physically spoken by one of the prophets of the community, but actually the words of the spiritual Jesus, of the heavenly Jesus, the resurrected Jesus, the real Jesus, not the earthly Jesus. Therefore—the audiences of these liturgical offices—if they were talking about writing a "biography" of the earthly Jesus, which for them was not true because it would only refer to the physical aspect of his identity, and they were asked about the speeches of Jesus that they were about to hear, they would argue that these speeches were not valid for this alleged "biography" of an earthly Jesus. These speeches, they would argue, represented another Jesus, the authentic one, the Exalted/Resurrected One; they did not refer at all to the physical Jesus.

So, why are these speeches found in the Gospel of John today, as if they were the words of the "historical Jesus"? The answer to this question was given, centuries ago, preserved by Eusebius in his *Ecclesiastical History*:

> But, last of all [the Gospel authors], seeing that the [other] Gospels presented [only] the bodily [interpretation] of Jesus,

encouraged by some people he knew and inspired by the [Holy] Spirit, composed a spiritual gospel.[16]

This, Eusebius records, was "the account of Clement," referring to Clement of Alexandria and his *Hypotyposeis* (*Adumbrationes*).

According to this idea of a single author, mentioned by Clement, the prophets who uttered these speeches of the resurrected Jesus—and their listeners alike—would have thought they were talking about the real Jesus, that is, with the awareness that they were transmitting the true image of Jesus, which would only be fully understood *after his death and resurrection*. And they would think that prophets from other groups, in other communities of believers, such as the "Synoptic" communities—but definitely not the mystical group of the "beloved disciple"—had updated the words of the "historical Jesus." But the prophets of their mystical group, composed of "true knowers," would hold that they were not transmitting the words of the "Jesus of history," a physical Jesus, one made of flesh (as was described in the other Gospels). These mystical prophets were the means by which the heavenly Revealer spoke to their community.

The Johannine Jesus declared: "But the Advocate, the Holy Spirit, whom the Father will send in my name, will teach you all things and bring to your remembrance all that I said to you" (John 14:26). Only through the illumination of the Spirit, which the disciples would receive after the death and resurrection of the Messiah, would the Messiah be fully understood through the (Johannine) prophets, who in ecstatic trance uttered the words of Jesus in the liturgical meetings of their believing community (also Johannine). Therefore, it is very plausible that the audience of these inspired prophets of the Johannine community believed the words they heard were actually the words of the risen Jesus, not the historical Jesus. It was not the Jesus of Galilee or Jerusalem, but the heavenly Jesus. And if, hypothetically speaking, they lived among us today with that mentality, those prophets and their audience would never allow those speeches to be included with the biographies of the earthly Jesus.

Once the beauty and depth of these speeches entered subsequent hands, or the hands of the final redactor of the fourth Gospel, to embed within them material found in previously written Gospels, and—after some years had passed—once the Gospel had circulated in that form, subsequent readers would no longer be able to distinguish between the possible words of the earthly Jesus, which exist in the fourth Gospel as a result of the first two phases of composition, and the words of the heavenly Christ. And so they were admitted into the Gospel and were transmitted over many

---

16. Eusebius, *Eccl. Hist.* 6.14.7.

centuries until higher criticism was applied to biblical text at the beginning of the nineteenth century, a period in which people began to seriously doubt that the Gospel of John had the same degree of historicity as the Synoptic Gopsels. It was then decided that this material could in no way be used to reconstruct the life of the historical, or earthly, Jesus.

CONCLUSION

A hypothesis is not the same thing as fact. Moreover, it is difficult to present a strict test for this type of proposal, just as there is no perfect instrument to prove the existence of the alleged "Revelation discourse-source" of Rudolf Bultmann or his whole hypothesis of the three sources for the Gospels. However, our hypothesis—once explained and using it as a template or backdrop—can serve as an explanation of the origin of the discourses of Jesus in the Gospel of John. The "paratheatrical representation"[17] in a liturgical office explains how members of the Johannine group could accept, without any difficulty, those speeches proclaimed by their prophets, since they were not the words of the earthly Jesus, but rather those of the mystical, legitimate, and realistic Jesus, given so that people could understand the truth and deep essence of that historical Jesus, whose true identity physical eyes simply could not perceive. This also explains how in an environment where people tended to believe in events like this, and without the type of criticism we have today, Christian readers of the second century—after the death of those who had witnessed these "paratheatrical representations" by the prophets—believed that such words interpreted the true historical Jesus and served as a complement to the speeches of Jesus in the Synoptic Gospels. But today, that is simply no longer possible.

BIBLIOGRAPHY

Brown, Raymond E. *John*. 2 vols. London: Geoffrey Chapman, 1978.
Díez Macho, A., and A. Piñero. *Apócrifos del Antiguo Testamento*. Vol. 3. Madrid: Ediciones Cristiandad, 2002.

---

17. This style of liturgical or semi-liturgical paratheatrical representations is very old. They might have originated in Israel in the style of the prophets who spoke by the mouth of Yahweh, which sometimes involved significant and symbolic displays like marrying a prostitute, being yoked to something, etc. The authors of the psalms in the liturgical context of the Temple also spoke by the mouth of Yahweh and did so with such displays, so that people knew that it was not them who spoke, but actually the divinity.

Fontana-Elboj, Gonzalo. *El Evangelio de Juan: La construcción de un texto complejo. Orígenes histórico y proceso compositivo*. Monografías de Filología Clásica 24. Zaragoza: Prensas de la Universidad de Zaragoza, 2014.

———. *Los orígenes del cristianismo de Asia Menor (A. 70–135): Textos e historia*. Collecció Instrumenta 49. Barcelona: Prensas de la Universidad de Barcelona, 2015.

García-Ureña, Lourdes. *El Apocalipsis: Pautas literarias de lectura. Con prefacio de Adela Yarbro-Collins*. Colección Textos y estudios 'Cardenal Cisneros' de la Biblia Políglota Matritense 79. Madrid: Editora del CSIC, 2013.

Harnack, Adolf von, ed. *Ein jüdisch-christliches Psalmbuch aus dem ersten Jahrhundert* (the Odes . . . of Salomon, now first published from the Syriac version by J. Rendel Harris, 1909; aus dem Syrischen übersetzt von Johannes Flemming, bearbeitet und herausgegeben von Adolf Harnack, (= Texte und Untersuchungen zur Geschichte der altchristlichen Literatur, Archiv für die von der Kirchenväter-Kommission der kgl. preussischen Akademie der Wissenschaften), Hinrich'sches Buchhandlung. Leipzig 1910.

Piñero, Antonio. *Cristianismos derrotados: ¿Cuál fue el pensamiento de los primeros cristianos heréticos y heterodoxos?* Madrid: EDAF, 2007.

———. *Guía para entender el Nuevo Testamento*. 5th ed. Madrid: Trotta, 2016.

Vidal, Senén. *Evangelio y Cartas de Juan: Génesis de los textos juánicos*. Bilbao: Editorial Mensajero, 2013.

12

Wisdom and the Sojourning Saints or Christ and the Wandering Sinners?

The Wilderness Wandering Motif in Hebrews as a Reaction to Wisdom of Solomon

PAUL A. HIMES
Baptist College of Ministry

INTRODUCTION

DAVID ALAN BLACK'S CONTRIBUTIONS to the field of New Testament studies have ranged far and wide from the Gospels to the Pauline Epistles, from Greek linguistics to textual criticism, and from the highly technical to the spiritual and practical. I am delighted to contribute this essay in his honor.

One should not be surprised that among his scholarly contributions he has published at least five journal articles on Hebrews, focusing especially on discourse and literary analysis.[1] Black has especially emphasized one key fact about Hebrews: the "close liaison between the thought of the author

---

1. "The Problem of the Literary Structure of Hebrews," "Hebrews 1:1–4," "A Note on the Structure of Hebrews 12, 1–2," "Literary Artistry in the Epistle to the Hebrews," and "Who Wrote Hebrews?"

and the structure of his writing."[2] Indeed, "form and content, syntax and meaning, are inseparable."[3]

Another homily, Wisdom of Solomon, also utilizes sophisticated structure and rhetoric to make a key theological point. The similarities between Wisdom and Hebrews have long been noted.[4] This essay, however, proposes to take the standard analysis one step further. Whereas Wisdom portrays the wilderness generation as a beacon of excellence in contrast to the idolatrous Egyptians, the stepchildren of Lady Wisdom herself, the author of Hebrews focuses on their unbelief and ultimate failure. The two homilies, then, represent competing *Wirkungeschichte* on Exodus and Numbers. While Wisdom consistently paints a picture of "the ungodly *versus* the Wilderness Generation," Hebrews declares in response, "The ungodly *are* the Wilderness Generation." Considering the rhetorical and linguistic similarities between the two, as well as the extent that the wilderness generation plays a significant role in the theology of both, this essay will propose that Hebrews contains a deliberate theological counterpoint to Wisdom.[5]

The first section of this essay will provide a brief introduction to the story of the wilderness wanderers in both books, the second section will discuss positive points of contact[6] between Wisdom and Hebrews, and the final section will examine negative points of contact, or areas where Hebrews seems to be reacting specifically against Wisdom's view of the wilderness generation.[7]

---

2. Black, "Structure of Hebrews 12, 1–2," 111.

3. Black, "Literary Artistry," 50.

4. E.g., Wright, "Structure of the Book of Wisdom," 184. Lane, *Hebrews 1–8*, cxxxix. Even L. D. Hurst suggests that the author of Hebrews was familiar with Wisdom of Solomon, though he does not speculate on the degree of influence the latter might have exerted (*Epistle to the Hebrews*, 12).

5. The idea that a New Testament writer might react negatively to Wisdom of Solomon is not an unparalleled thesis elsewhere in biblical studies. In 2011 Jonathan A. Linebaugh published "Announcing the Human: Rethinking the Relationships Between Wisdom of Solomon 13–15 and Romans 1.18—2.11," arguing that the Apostle Paul was deliberately reacting against the ethnocentrism of Wisdom.

6. The term "points of contact" seems to be the best way to describe the relationship between these two texts without assuming my thesis. Linebaugh uses the term in his article "Announcing the Human" regarding Romans and Wisdom (e.g., 217), and I will borrow the term for my essay as well.

7. I am presuming here with the vast majority of scholarship that Wisdom was written decades before Hebrews, probably sometime between 100 B.C. and A.D. 40, as Peter Enns argues in "Wisdom of Solomon and Biblical Interpretation," 213; cf. a very similar date range in Helyer, *Exploring Jewish Literature*, 290. Note that Enns himself prefers a date during the reign of Caligula.

THE WILDERNESS WANDERERS IN WISDOM OF SOLOMON AND HEBREWS

The "wilderness wanderer" theme in Wisdom is first developed in chapter 11, yet 9:18 and chapter 10 provide a "hinge" between the two main sections of the book.[8] Wisdom 9:18 makes the fascinating statement that men are "saved by wisdom" (τῇ σοφίᾳ ἐσώθησαν).[9] From here, the author discusses a series of heroes whom Wisdom enabled, naturally transitioning into a discussion of the "holy people" (λαὸν ὅσιον, i.e., the Exodus-wilderness generation). From this point onward the author focuses on the wilderness wanderers in contrast to pagans, and the remainder of the book is essentially a "midrash of the Exodus event" and the subsequent wilderness adventures.[10] The intent is clearly homiletical at both the corporate and the individual level: the readers are to look to these stories as a guide for their own relationship to Wisdom.[11] Thus, in this retelling of the biblical story, the wilderness wanderers shine through as heroes, Lady Wisdom's chosen nation. From the very beginning they are identified as "the righteous people and the blameless seed" (10:15). In 11:1, the last direct reference to Lady Wisdom, she is said to have been the impetus for their "works" via the hand of Moses.[12]

Yet as scholars have long noted, Wisdom radically glosses over virtually any part of the story that might reflect negatively on the wilderness

---

8. For a discussion of the rhetorical function of a "hinge" as an "Intermediary transition . . . carried out by a unit of text which stands between two major sections of the discourse," see Guthrie, *Structure of Hebrews*, 105–6 (the term "hinge" in a rhetorical sense seems to have been coined by H. Parunack). For discussion on the outline of Wisdom of Solomon, see the following sources: Reese, "Plan and Structure," esp. 392–93, 397; Reider, *Book of Wisdom*, 2–3; Helyer, *Exploring Jewish Literature*, 288–90; Winston, *Wisdom of Solomon*, 10–12. All four of these authors see a major transition from chs. 10 to 11.

9. Septuagint text taken from Rahlf's *Septuaginta*, and New Testament Greek text taken from the Nestle-Aland, 27th ed., both via *Accordance* 8.4. Septuagint English translations are this writer's own, but New Testament quotations in English taken from the English Standard Version (Crossway, 2001). Finally, lexical searches conducted via *Accordance* 8.4 and the *Thesaurus Linguae Graecae*.

10. Wright, "Structure of Wisdom 11–19," 176–77.

11. Burkes, "Wisdom and Apocalypticism," 41; cf. also Enns, "Wisdom of Solomon," 214–15.

12. As Glicksman states in *Wisdom of Solomon 10*, 135, "Immediately following Wis 11:1, the topic shifts to the wilderness wanderings. At that point, the agent of salvation also changes from Wisdom to the Lord (cf. 11:4, where 'you' refers to the Lord). The figure of Wisdom does not appear after 11:1, but based on the opening passages in Wisdom 10 it can be assumed that she assists in the Lord's further acts of liberation, which are recounted in the rest of the book."

wanderers.[13] To begin with, Wis 10:15–21 refers to and expands on the Song of the Sea in Exodus 15.[14] The whole theme from this point forward is summarized in Wis 10:15: "She rescued the sanctified and blameless seed from the oppressing nation," where the "sanctified and blameless seed" clearly refers to the wilderness wandering generation. The subsequent retelling of the story of the Exodus generation substantially "sanitizes" the character of the wilderness wanderers themselves, always painting them in a positive light compared to the heathen.[15]

In Wis 11:4 (drawing from Exodus 17) the Israelites are depicted as simply calling out to God in their thirst (ἐδίψησαν καὶ ἐπεκαλέσαντό σε). In light of the Torah text, Joseph Reider aptly states, "This is hardly true: in Ex. 17:3 f. the people murmured against Moses and were almost ready to stone him. Apparently Pseudo-Solomon aims to prove the blamelessness of the chosen race."[16] Wisdom does tacitly admit that this "thirst" is a negative aspect of the wilderness wandering, but Wis 11:8–10 states that the cause of their thirst was not because they were ungodly, but rather "so that they would know how the pagans [rather than themselves] were judged" (v.8, δείξας διὰ τοῦ τότε δίψους πῶς τοὺς ὑπεναντίους ἐκόλασας). In other words, this "chastening" (παιδεύω, v. 9) was not punishment nor, strictly speaking, correction, but rather "education."[17] Wisdom 12 further contrasts the

---

13. For some of the more informative treatments on this topic, see Lucas, "Intra-Jewish Interpretive Debate?" 70, 83–88; Bosman, "Theological Paraphrasing," 1–7; Cheon, *Exodus Story* (much of the book, but see esp. 51, 88, 111).

14. Enns, "Retelling," 1–2.

15. The contrast between the Children of Israel and the pagan Egyptians is, perhaps, the key theme of the entire second half of Wisdom. See especially Nickelsburg, *Jewish Literature*, 210; Gilbert, "Literary Structure," 30; and Wright, "Structure of the Book of Wisdom," 176–77.

16. Reider, *Book of Wisdom*, 140.

17. Samuel Cheon states, "The water event was intended to show that God benefited the Israelites through the same element of creation by which he punished their enemies in the first plague, in which water was used as a retaliation against the Egyptians' slaying of the Israelite infants (vv. 5–7)." Also, "It was intended to teach the Israelites how God punished their antagonists in the first plague (vv. 8–10)" (*Exodus Story*, 26–27). Indeed, one suspects that "the educational reinterpretation of punishment events" would be a valid summary of much of Wisdom's theology (see especially the discussion in Cheon, *Exodus Story*, 67, 88, 111–12). On p. 112, Cheon aptly states, "[The author of Wisdom] interprets the negative settings as God's opportunities to teach his children the Israelites. So the Israelites' suffering is not God's judgment caused by their wrongdoing, but a test initiated by the Lord as their father"; similarly, on p. 88 Cheon states, "[The author] uses the Greek term πεῖρα to indicate God's testing for the education of the righteous." See also Reider, *Book of Wisdom*, 187, who emphasizes how "the writer's standpoint is that the Israelites were not chastised in punishment, but for warning and admonition" (note especially 16:6). Indeed, this incident also was included for "educational"

nature of "educational chastening" for the Israelites vs. "punishment" for the pagans, which transitions into an extended discourse on idolatry (12:24 and 27 function as a "hinge" here with their use of the plural θεούς).

After this theological treatise on idolatry (ending at 15:19), the author of Wisdom once again contrasts the children of Israel with the ungodly; while the heathen were "punished appropriately," the Israelites were shown grace (16:1–2).[18] Passaro points out that Wisdom 16 is "an elaborate fresco" that "collects Exodus themes with originality and deliberate freedom but eliminates the violent aspects of the accounts of the Exodus (omitting, for example, the element of the people's request for food)."[19] In the same chapter, instead of portraying the Israelites as murmuring and being *punished* with serpents (the incident in Num 21:5–9), the author of Wisdom prefers to focus on the radical contrast between what the Israelites experienced and what the pagans experienced (16:8–11). The latter fell dead at the mere sting of locusts and flies, while the former "conquered" (νικάω) the bite of poisonous snakes.[20] Shortly thereafter, in 16:20–29, the author also "interprets the manna event as God's pedagogy for the righteous."[21]

Thus, as far as the anonymous author is concerned, the Israelites are not sinners but saints. In 17:2, Israel is once again called the "holy nation" (ἔθνος ἅγιον) and contrasted with those persecuting them. The persecutors subsequently suffered by being exposed to a horrible fire (17:6—"a fire of its own accord, full of fear"), while God's "saints" (ὁσίοις) were given a "flaming pillar" to their benefit (18:3; note the same word ὁσίοις in 18:5).

Furthermore, the children of Israel provide God with the opportunity to demonstrate simultaneously the rescue of the righteous and the destruction of their enemies (18:7). Indeed, no higher praise of the Exodus generation can be offered than that of 18:9: "For the holy children of good men sacrificed in secret, and made a divine covenant in harmony, so that the

---

purposes (εἰς ἀνάμνησιν ἐντολῆς νόμου σου).

18. Cf. Reider, *Book of Wisdom*, 4–5, and his discussion of the contrast between Israel and Egypt.

19. Passaro, "The Serpent and the Manna," 179; note also where he speaks of a "re-presentation of the state of the people during the Exodus" (182) and where he argues that in Wis 16:6–7, Num 21:6–9 is "reinterpreted as an event in which is revealed the divine pedagogy which leads to conversion" (189).

20. Cheon aptly states, "Pseudo-Solomon indicates that the Israelites were not killed, but were only being destroyed by the attack of the serpent that God sent. He does not use the language τοὺς θανατοῦντας found in Numbers to describe the serpent. Rather, he seems to emphasize a psychological effect of the fearfulness caused by the serpent . . ." (Cheon, *Exodus Story*, 51).

21. Ibid., 67.

saints would similarly receive good things and perilous things, the fathers now initiating the singing of praises."

Even when referring to one of the darkest points of Israel's wandering, their sinful actions are deemphasized. In 18:20–21, the author admits that even the "righteous" are touched by the "taste of death," and many died, yet there is no direct statement of the wanderers' culpability. The unnamed Aaron, on behalf of the Israelites, faces down "wrath" (τῷ θυμῷ and τὸν χόλον) along with a rather vague "one who destroys" (ὁ ὀλεθεύων), yet God himself is deliberately omitted from the picture. In other words, whatever happened, it most certainly was not God's punishment for sin.

In the conclusion of chapter 19, the wilderness wanderers are described as gladly remembering all God's mighty works (19:9–10), leading to a rousing declaration of God's exaltation of his people.[22] The entire book culminates in the summary of 19:22: "For in accordance with all things, Lord, you exalted and glorified your people, and you did not ignore them, standing by them in every time and place."[23] In this way, Wisdom of Solomon ultimately portrays the wilderness wanderers as examples to be emulated, a people who possessed an intimate relationship with God their Redeemer.

In contrast to Wisdom, Hebrews consistently portrays the wilderness generation as foils to the true people of God (with some exceptions, e.g., Moses).[24] Hebrews gives extensive treatment to the wilderness wanderers in two major discourse units, 3:7—4:13 and 12:18–29.[25] In addition, the

22. In between this point and the conclusion, the author mentions the incident with the quail (Num 11:31–35 rather than Exodus 16, because of the expression ἐκ θαλάσσης ἀνέβη in Wis 19:12). Yet this once again serves as a contrast between the righteous and the wicked. The quails come up from the sea "for their comfort" (εἰς γὰρ παραμυθίαν). This last word, "comfort," is deliberately juxtaposed with τιμωρία in the next line in v. 13 (notice the parallelism of "the quails came up out of the sea for their comfort" vs. "punishments came upon the sinners"), which then segues into a discussion of Sodom as "sinners *par excellence*."

23. Reese, *The Book of Wisdom*, 198, notes, "Continuing to recapitulate as many themes as possible from the entire work, the Sage pictures the Israelites as singing about God's saving acts while they march through the Red Sea and the desert (vv. 9–12)"; Note also Enns, *Exodus Retold*, 127, who suggests that in 19:8 "Ps-Solomon is apparently concerned to show that the crossing of the sea was a unified national event."

24. As Ernst Käsemann stated in *Wandering People*, "Hebrews intends to show the Christian community the greatness of the promise given it and the seriousness of the temptation threatening it. For this reason, it sets before its eyes the picture of Israel wandering through the wilderness" (17).

25. There will be debate over the exact boundaries of these discourse units, and many would see 4:1–14 as a separate though related section. See Guthrie, *Structure of Hebrews*, 66–67, 73, 78–79; Lane, *Hebrews 1–8*, 1, 72, 83, 95–96; 445–46. Guthrie sees 12:18–24 as its own discourse unit while Lane prefers to focus on 12:14–29 as its own unit. The exact boundaries of these discourse units do not affect this essay's thesis.

wilderness wanderers are negatively alluded to in 6:4–6 and 10:26–31, as we shall see.

Hebrews' account radically departs from Wisdom's in 3:9. Whereas in Wisdom the Israelites bask in the glory of God's work and reap great benefits from his marvelous deeds, in Heb 3:9–10 the opposite is asserted: "Your fathers put me to the test and saw my works for forty years. Therefore I was provoked with that generation . . ." Both Wisdom and Hebrews stress the mighty acts of God for Moses' generation; yet in the latter, being partakers of such glory failed to save those traveling with Moses, due to their "evil, unbelieving heart" (3:12).

In Hebrews 4, the wilderness wanderers are held up to the audience as an illustration of "how people should *not* respond to God and his revelation."[26] The key word "rest" functions to develop the contrast between the wilderness wanderers and the current generation.[27] While "rest" eluded the former, the author of Hebrews indicates that the current audience still possesses "an opportunity to enjoy the Sabbath-Rest mentioned in Psalm 95."[28] The contrast is further heightened later in the passage by juxtaposing the wilderness generation's disobedient reaction towards the Good News against the audience's acceptance of it.[29]

Hebrews 12:18–24 is a "highly stylized periodic sentence" which "consists of rhythmic phrases detailing the horrors of Mt. Sinai set over against the joys of Zion."[30] In 12:25, the author of Hebrews "parenthetically continues the warning" of previous verses by contrasting the wilderness wanderers and the listeners.[31] The wilderness wanderers, despite the fearful and awesome display at Mt. Sinai, failed to hear God; the current generation is to heed the warning offered by their fate and offer God "acceptable worship, with reverence and awe" (12:28).[32]

---

26. Guthrie, "Hebrews," 995.

27. For one of the better discussions of the theology of "rest" in Hebrews, see Khiok-Khng, "Theology of 'Rest,'" 2–33.

28. Brand, "Sabbath Rest," 8; cf. Johnson, "Scriptural World of Hebrews," 246: "According to Hebrews, Psalm 95 therefore extends a rest for God's people that Joshua could not enter but Jesus already has, namely, God's own rest on the seventh day of creation . . ."

29. Thompson, "Hebrews," 232; Attridge, *Hebrews*, 125; Guthrie, "Hebrews," 955.

30. Guthrie, *Structure of Hebrews*, 133.

31. Attridge, *Hebrews*, 379.

32. For a more thorough discussion of the symbolism of Zion and Sinai in Hebrews 12, see Son, *Zion Symbolism*.

POINTS OF POSITIVE CONTACT BETWEEN WISDOM AND HEBREWS: PARALLELS IN STYLE, RHETORIC, AND MOTIF

A comparison of Hebrews and Wisdom reveals that, in spite of the mysteries surrounding their authorship and composition, they share a similar rhetorical style and goal. Both are homilies, and both utilize rhetorical devices such as *inclusio*, hook words, etc. This does not, of course, prove that Hebrews is reacting against Wisdom. It does raise the likelihood, however, that both draw from the same rhetorical well (perhaps even the same *Alexandrian* well), which then amplifies the likelihood that Hebrews was familiar with Wisdom.[33] Similarly, while the fact that Hebrews' "theology of the wilderness wanderers" is radically opposed to that found in Wisdom does not prove that the former is a deliberate reaction to the latter, the possibility is heightened the more similar Hebrews and Wisdom appear to be, especially in light of the significant role the wilderness wanderers play in both books.

The rhetorical and homiletical nature of Wisdom and Hebrews has been well established. Both Wisdom and Hebrews are sermons, specifically designed to call the readers away from debilitating action: idolatry for the former, apostasy (i.e., unbelief) for the latter.[34] Wisdom could be further classified as an *apologia*, a defense of the superiority of Judaism for the suffering Alexandrian Jews.[35] Wisdom, however, is an *internal* defense against Hellenistic culture; rather than converting the heathen *per se*, Wisdom "intends rather to fight against the attraction exercised on some members of the Jewish community by . . . the centres of Greek social life."[36] Frank

---

33. Wisdom of Solomon's provenance as Alexandria is generally not debated (see Winston, *Wisdom of Solomon*, 3; Helyer, *Exploring Jewish Literature*, 290). The possibility that Hebrews possesses points of contact with Alexandrian writing in general has been noted for a long time (see the discussion in Hurst, *Hebrews*, 7-11; Rohr, *Der Hebraerbriefe*, 5-6, as well as his citation of Heigl on p. 6). Indeed, there was even a tendency to suggest Philo provided the theological background for Hebrews, though this has been decisively refuted (thus Rohr states regarding Hebrews' concept of the Son, "Eine solche Verbindung mit der Materie wäre für Philo geradezu ein Greuel . . ." (6); see also the extensive treatment by Hurst, the entire first chapter of *The Epistle to the Hebrews*, where he lays to rest any possibility that Hebrews depended on Philo for its theology.

34. For the former, see Reider, *Book of Wisdom*, 10-11; Baslez, "The Author of Wisdom," 36; Zimmermann, "The Book of Wisdom," 12.

35. See, for example, Thyen, *Der Stil of Jüdisch-Hellenistischen Homilie*, 26-27 ("Der Zweck, den der Alexandriner mit seiner Schrift verfolgte, ist eine Apologie des in der Diaspora unter dem Zwang, der Willkür und ἀφροσύνη der βασιλείς leidenden Judentums"); Cheon, *Exodus Story*, 111-12.

36. Baslez, "The Author of Wisdom," 36 (I omitted Baslez's reference to "the court of

Zimmerman adds, "The book specifically directs its polemics against the faithless among the Jewish population, who have lost faith in their religion, betook to the ways of the Gentiles and had intermarried."[37]

Similarly, the author of Hebrews clearly intends his epistle to function as a warning against a falling away within the community of faith. The author first introduces the Wilderness Generation motif in Heb 3:7, and there extrapolates from the use of ἡμέραν in Psalm 95:7 (LXX Ps 94) that the same temptation that faced the wilderness wanderers also faces the epistle's audience (3:12–13).[38] As William Lane stresses, "today" is a "catchword" that functions to confront the listeners of the homily with the seriousness of the warning.[39]

Central to the warnings of both homilies is the story of the wilderness generation in the Torah. Both Wisdom and Hebrews rely on the Torah texts, though as noted above Wisdom radically reworks the texts to suite its ends. To transition to the Exodus story, Wisdom 10 "uses a storyline drawn from the Books of Genesis and Exodus while employing vocabulary found throughout the Septuagint."[40] Wisdom 10:19 seems to parallel the descriptions in Exodus 15:1–18.[41] Later, Wis 11:5–14 seems to draw from Exod 1:17–22 and 7:14–24 while the reinterpretation of the rebellion in Wis 18:20–25 utilizes Num 17:6–15 LXX (16:41–50 in the MT).[42] Noticeably absent is any allusion to Psalm 95/94.

In Hebrews, the warning passages of 3:7—4:13, 6:4–6 and 12:18–29 all depend on the Torah accounts of the wilderness wanderers, and even Heb 10:26–31 draws from Deut 17:6 and 32:35–36, both occurring within warnings against idolatry.[43] Psalm 95[94] is utilized as the starting point

---

the last Lagides" and "the Greek system of education" since I am not as willing to place the *apologia* in such a specific context as Baslez).

37. Zimmermann, "The Book of Wisdom," 12.

38. Attridge, "Let Us Strive," 280–81; Guthrie, "Hebrews," 955. This is summed up well by Surur Mohammed Yisak: "The author of Hebrews wanted his audience to visualize themselves as being in the wilderness with God's rest before them. He wanted them to realize the danger that faced them, but to know the way to respond to it . . . he wanted his audience to avoid the repetition of their forefather's unbelief" ("The Use of the Old Testament in Hebrews," 118).

39. Lane, *Hebrews 1–8*, 87. See also the discussion in Allen, "More Than Just Numbers," 139.

40. Glicksman, *Wisdom of Solomon 10*, 147. Glicksman also notes how Wisdom here borrows from the language of Psalms, Proverbs, and Sirach.

41. Ibid.; Enns, "Retelling," 1–2.

42. Cheon, *Exodus Story*, 34 and 87.

43. For my discussion of the Torah as the backdrop for Heb 6:4–6, I am indebted to Mathewson, "Reading Heb 6:4–6." On Heb 10:26–31, I am drawing especially from

(Heb 3:7) for the wilderness story precisely because it is a *critique* of the wilderness generation (Heb 3:7–19 actually functions as a "commentary" on Ps 95:7–11)[44], yet even here Psalm 95 depends on Deuteronomy.[45] The passage also draws heavily from Numbers 12–14: the concept of the ἀπιστία and πονηρός heart stems from these chapters.[46]

Furthermore, Dave Mathewson has made a convincing case that the warning of Heb 6:4–6 also contains an inter-textual allusion to the Kadesh-Barnea incident in Numbers and Deuteronomy 11.[47] As for 10:26–31, Jason Whitlark, among others, has pointed out that this section is drawing from Deut 17:6 and 32:35–35.[48]

As will be discussed further below, both Wisdom's and Hebrews' wilderness narratives function as a critique against idolatry. While Hebrews' critique of idolatry is somewhat more subtle, Jason Whitlark argues that "[w]hen the author [of Hebrews] chooses texts and images from the Septuagint as warnings, he consistently draws upon texts whose larger literary contexts are warnings against idolatry."[49] Wisdom, on the other hand, is much more outspoken in its critique, to the extent that Jonathan A. Linebaugh can declare, "The function of 15.1–4 within Wisdom of Solomon's critique of false-religion is therefore to establish the irreducible difference between Jew and Gentile on the basis of the non-idolatry of the former and the false-worship of the latter. More concisely, Wisdom of Solomon's anthropological dualism is built on Israel's immunity from idolatry"; indeed, "Israel is different because Israel is not idolatrous."[50]

Significantly both Hebrews and Wisdom utilize similar rhetorical devices in their homiletical development. As Addison G. Wright has noted,

---

Whitlark, "Warning," esp. 384–92.

44. Lane, *Hebrews 1–8*, 83.

45. Allen, "More Than Just Numbers," 135–39.

46. Lane, *Hebrews 1–8*, 85–86.

47. Mathewson, "Reading Heb 6:4–6," 222 (Mathewson also states, "The author's primary 'intertextual' quarry is the narrative accounts from Exodus and Numbers 13–14, overlaid with the lists from Nehemiah 9 and Psalms which recount what God did on behalf of his people"). See especially 215–21 in Mathewson's article for the specifics.

48. Whitlark, "Warning," 392; cf. O'Brian, *Letter to the Hebrews*, 376; Lane, *Hebrews 9–13*, 375–76.

49. Whitlark, "Warning," 384. In his book *Resisting Empire*, Whitlark goes so far as to say that "resisting the benefits of assimilating to the pagan imperial culture appears to be the primary concern in Hebrews" (51), though this writer is not yet willing to go that far.

50. Linebaugh, "Announcing the Human," 221–22.

The use of symmetrical arrangement, announcement of subjects, *mots crochets* and inclusions is attested in biblical and extra-biblical literature alike. Up to now *the systematic use of all of these indices of structure in a single work has apparently been observed only in the Epistle to the Hebrews.* To that work *can be now be added the Book of Wisdom,* and one may be permitted to speculate whether this structural characteristic was an occasional feature of Alexandrian rhetoric and another instance of Alexandrian contact in the Epistle to the Hebrews.[51]

Wright's observations are validated with even a cursory examination. Both homilies display significant rhetorical skill in transitioning between sections.[52] Wisdom utilizes words such as διψάω (11:4, 14) and βασανίζω (16:1–4) as *inclusio* to mark out discourse units within the discussion of the wilderness wanderers and their idolatrous foils.[53] Key words are strung together to give cohesion to discourse units; for example, in Wisdom 14 εἴδωλον provides cohesion for this discourse unity with five occurrences (out of the six total for the book).[54] In addition, words such as ἀντί function as "hinge words" in such places as 16:2, facilitating the shift from the punishment of Israel's enemies to the blessings given in the wilderness.[55]

Similar rhetorical techniques have been well documented in Hebrews. George Guthrie, for one, has developed an outline around various rhetorical elements including cohesion shifts, *inclusio*, repeated themes, etc.[56] The sections on the wilderness wanderers draw heavily from these rhetorical elements. For example, 3:7–19 contains two "high-level cohesion shifts," one at 3:7a and the other at 3:12.[57] The entire section of 3:7–4:2 is held together by various key words and expressions, namely "heart," "day," "today," "harden,"

---

51. Wright, "Structure of the Book of Wisdom," 184; emphasis added.

52. See Reese, "Plan and Structure," 391, and Guthrie, *Structure of Hebrews*, 94–111.

53. Reese, "Plan and Structure," 398. An *inclusio* can function on the macro-level as well. As Linebaugh notes, "Together with 19.1–12, the retelling of the Exodus in 10.15–21 forms an *inclusio* around *Wisdom*'s theological re-interpretation of Israel's deliverance from Egypt and subsequent wanderings in the wilderness" (*God, Grace, and Righteousness*, 61).

54. For other examples, see Passaro, "The Serpent and the Manna," 181–2; Reese, *Book of Wisdom*, 109.

55. Wright, "Structure of the Book of Wisdom," 177; cf. Bellia and Passaro, "Infinite Passion," 309.

56. See all throughout Guthrie's *Structure of Hebrews*. Naturally Guthrie and others are indebted to the seminal work of Albert Vanhoye, *La structure littéraire*.

57. Guthrie, *Structure of Hebrews*, 66.

"enter in," "belief," "rest," and "hear his voice."⁵⁸ Heb 3:12–19 is also held together, as a subunit, via an *inclusio* utilizing βλέπω and ἀπιστία.⁵⁹

In their homiletical strategy, both Wisdom and Hebrews rely on the development of contrasts. As David Winston notes, chapters 11–19 of Wisdom are built around the following contrasts between the wilderness wanderers and the Egyptians: (1) thirst-quenching water vs. blood (11:1–14); (2) hunger vs. plenty (16:1–4); (3) Egyptian suffering from insects vs. Jewish deliverance via a bronze serpent (16:5–14); (4) "thunderstorms" vs. "rain of manna" (16:15–29); (5) darkness vs. light (17:1–18:4); (6) death of the Egyptian firstborns vs. safety of Israel's firstborns (18:5–25); and (7) Egyptian drowning vs. Israel's safety in the Red Sea (19:1–9).⁶⁰ As Linebaugh notes, "The Egyptian plagues are set in antithetical pairs (diptychs) with events from Israel's wilderness sojourn, thereby constructing a symmetrical theology of history . . ."⁶¹

In the same way, Hebrews utilizes a series of comparisons that stresses the preeminence of one entity or group over another. Thus Michael W. Martin and Jason A. Whitlark see in Hebrews a "five-part epideictic syncritical project of Hebrews . . . [which] compares corresponding representatives of the old and new covenants, arguing consistently that the new covenant representative is superior to the old covenant representative."⁶²

Interestingly, both Wisdom and Hebrews follow a homiletical strategy found at least twice elsewhere in Second Temple works, namely the "Hall of Fame" motif that encourages the audience to emulate the characters being described.⁶³ Thus Wisdom has a "Hall of Wisdom" in Wisdom 10, where Lady Wisdom is the enabler (e.g., 10:1, 5b, 6, 9, etc.). Similarly, 1 Macc 2:51–61 is a "Hall of Mighty Deeds" with God himself as the enabler (v. 61, ὅτι πάντες οἱ ἐλπίζοντες ἐπ' αὐτὸν οὐκ ἀσθενήσουσιν); the point of this section is to cause the audience to imitate "the works of the fathers" and so, like them, receive "great glory and an eternal name" (2:51). Sirach 44.16—50:21

---

58. Ibid., 66–67.

59. Ibid., 78–79;

60. Winston, *Wisdom of Solomon*, 11–12. Cf. Gilbert, "Literary Structure," 30; Nickelsburg, *Jewish Literature*, 210.

61. Linebaugh, *God, Grace and Righteousness*, 62.

62. Martin and Whitlark, "Choosing What Is Advantageous," 386. For Martin and Whitlark, these comparisons are basically "Angels vs. Jesus," "Moses vs. Jesus," "Aaronic high priests vs. Jesus," "Levitical priestly ministry vs. the Melchizidekian priestly ministry," and "Sinai vs. Zion." For more discussion on contrasts in Hebrews, see Lane, *Hebrews 1–8*, 73; Koester, *Hebrews*, 262; and Guthrie, *Structure of Hebrews*, 73.

63. Some would prefer to date Hebrews post-A.D. 70. This would have no impact on the thesis of this essay, and so for the sake of convenience and personal preference I will lump Hebrews with "Second Temple literature."

consists of a "Hall of Honorable Men" (44:1: Αἰνέσωμεν δὴ ἄνδρας ἐνδόξους), though the author spends considerably more time recounting their deeds than any of the other books. Thus Hebrews 11's "Hall of Faith" represents a homiletical sub-genre already popular in second temple literature.[64]

Elsewhere, Wis 7:22–28 and Heb 1:1–4 exhibit a fascinating point of contact lexically and rhetorically. The former attributes to Lady Wisdom a number of superlative characteristics: Lady Wisdom is μονογενές, ἅγιον, etc.; she is the "most moving Mover" (πάσης γὰρ κινήσεως κινητικώτερον σοφία) and even the "smoke and power of God" (ἀτμὶς γάρ ἐστιν τῆς τοῦ θεοῦ δυνάμεως; compare with Heb 1:3, where τῷ ῥήματι τῆς δυνάμεως αὐτου is applied to Jesus himself). The use of πολυμερής (LXX *hapax legomena*) is strikingly similar to the cognate πολυμερῶς (a New Testament *hapax*) in Heb 1:1. More significantly, Lady Wisdom (in 7:26) is declared to be the ἀπαύγασμα of God. This word does not occur in published Greek literature before the LXX, and is significantly rare even in the first century, occurring only in Philo (another Alexandrian text), Heb 1:3, and possibly 1 Clem 36:2 (the date is debatable, and Clement is citing Hebrews anyways). Thus Hebrews and Wisdom share similar rare terminology in a context that deals with the superlative excellence of a particular figure.[65] Indeed, Wis 7:22–28 and Heb 1:1–4 are rhetorical siblings, though far from twins.[66]

---

64. As Linebaugh notes, "Establishing a theological principle by appealing to a series of canonical heroes was common practice in early Judaism" (*God, Grace, and Righteousness*, 57 n. 50).

65. Thus John Paul Heil declares that the language of 1:3 would cause the hearers to be "reminded of an impressive resemblance of the Son to the personified divine wisdom described in Wis 7:25–26" (*Hebrews*, 31). Nonetheless, one must be cautious in going too far with this parallel. As Amy L. B. Peeler appropriately points out, "It needs to be recognized that in the opening sentence the author of Hebrews is not drawing from Wisdom/Word descriptions alone. He brackets his *Sophia* and *Logos*-like statements about Christ with an assertion that Christ is God's heir (1.2, 4). None of the texts surveyed, however, describe God's Wisdom or his Word as God's heir of all things" (*You Are My Son*, 26). Similarly, Peter T. O'Brian states, "[The author's] carefully chosen language points to a Christology that is advanced beyond wisdom speculation" (*Letter to the Hebrews*, 53). I believe Peeler's and O'Brian's approach is more profitable than that of, e.g., Salevao, *Legitimation*, 359, who possibly goes a bit too far when he states, "In calling Christ the 'reflection' or 'radiance' of the 'glory of God' the author used ideas and terms derived from Wisdom literature. He was in fact identifying Christ with the divine Wisdom of God." We might, however, agree with J. A. F. Gregg when he states that Wisdom "belonged to the mental furniture of the N. T. writers" (*The Wisdom of Solomon*, lx).

66. As tempting as it might be to further develop an argument based *solely* on lexical similarities, much of Wisdom's and Hebrews' shared vocabulary or phrases are hardly unique in Jewish Hellenistic literature. As a further caution, one should note that in 1970 Ronald Williamson (*Philo and the Epistle to the Hebrews*) decisively refuted the idea that Hebrews was lexically indebted to Philo (pages 11–83 of Williamson's

Thematically, for both Wisdom and Hebrews, the person of Moses features prominently in transitions. Both homilies view Moses as an example *par excellence* of Wisdom on the one hand and faith and faithfulness on the other (compare Wis 10:16, 11:1 with Heb 3:3-5, 11:23-29). Significantly, Moses is the last person to be discussed in Wisdom's "Hall of Wisdom" (10:16), thus enabling a transition from individual to the children of Israel themselves.[67] Then, in Wis 11:1-3, Moses serves as the transition from the discussion of Wisdom to a discussion of the children of Israel.[68]

Surprisingly, Moses plays a more significant role in the later homily. In Heb 3:5, Moses assists in transition by completing the contrast with Christ and ushering in the first discussion of the wilderness generation.[69] Also, Moses functions as the paradigm of faithfulness (Heb 3:5; 11:23-28), an example for the audience to emulate.[70] However, as we shall see, Moses' relationship to the wilderness wanderers in Hebrews differs radically from Wisdom.

In conclusion, Wisdom and Hebrews share some fascinating similarities, especially in rhetorical structure and technique; at the surface level, they may be closer than any other two documents in Hellenistic Judaism written by separate authors (not including the Synoptic Gospels). At the very least, they both draw from the same rhetorical well.

POINTS OF NEGATIVE CONTACT: HEBREWS AS A THEOLOGICAL REACTION TO WISDOM

To declare that Hebrews attacks certain portions of theology that Wisdom supports, in of itself, proves nothing about their relationship. Yet two factors must be considered: first, Hebrews is clearly not attacking a "strawman" but rather a specific motif of Second Temple theology, and Wisdom

---

work consists of one of the most detailed lexical comparisons between two texts ever published in biblical studies). Fortunately for this writer's thesis, Williamson does argue that Hebrews owes more to the vocabulary of the LXX then it does to Philo (see esp. 14-16). Interestingly, though, Williamson suggests that the author of Hebrews "seems to have had a special interest in the four volumes which go to make up the historical account of the Maccabean rebellion" (14-15).

67. Webster, "Structural Unity," 105.

68. Ibid., 102.

69. Martin and Whitlark, "Choosing What Is Advantageous," 395. Cf. also Scott, "Jesus' Superiority," 206; and Lane, *Hebrews 1-8*, 73.

70. See Spicq, *L'Épitre Aux Hébreux*, 1:274: "fidélité de Moïse est exaltée" so that there might be "des migrateurs modeles qui peuvent encourager les derniers pélerins et leur render confidance."

of Solomon represents the most influential purveyor of that motif (i.e., "the wilderness wanderers as heroes"). Secondly, while on the one hand we must grant Samuel Sandmel's concerns about "parallelomania," nevertheless, the areas where Hebrews displays negative contact with Wisdom are specific lexical parallels with a similar motif (i.e., the wilderness wanderers) rather than generic thematic parallels with dissimilar contexts.[71] Consequently, the possibility that the later document is reacting specifically against the earlier becomes significantly more likely.

Within Wisdom's *apologia* of the wilderness wanderers, the matter of "works" (ἔργα) functions prominently. Even before Wisdom initiates the wilderness motif, the homily declares that the one who opposes Lady Wisdom will evidence "worthless works" (3:11). Yet Lady Wisdom herself is intimately associated with the works of God (8:4, αἱρετὶς τῶν ἔργων αὐτοῦ). In regards to the wilderness generation, Wisdom 11:1 declares that Lady Wisdom "favored their works (ἔργα)" through Moses; in contrast, the pagans committed "unholy" works (12:4, ἔργα . . . ἀνασίους). The pagans can evidence familiarity with God's works (13:7, ἐν γὰρ τοῖς ἔργοις αὐτοῦ ἀναστρεφόμενοι), yet still fail to acknowledge the one true God due to their idolatry (13:10, οἵτινες ἐκάλεσαν θεοὺς ἔργα χειρῶν ἀνθρώπων). In other words, the "works" of the Israelites and the "works" of the pagans are contrasted sharply based on their relationship to Wisdom.

Yet Hebrews declares that the wilderness generation is no better than the pagans. Thus in Heb 3:9 (drawing, as noted, from Ps 95[94]), the wilderness wanderers saw God's own "works" (καὶ εἶδον τὰ ἔργα μου), yet turned against him (cf. 4:10, where the implication is that the wilderness wanderers did *not* "rest" from their "works"). In other words, whereas in Wisdom the Israelites have access to God's own works via Lady Wisdom, Hebrews argues that it was precisely at this point of contact with God's "works" in the wilderness that Israel turned away from God.

The contrast may be taken a step further. Whitlark has suggested that the expression "dead works" (νεκρῶν ἔργων) in Heb 6:1 and 9:14 is possibly thematically parallel to the "dead things" in Wis 13:10 (νεκροῖς) and "working dead things" (νεκρὸν ἐργάζεται) in 15:17.[72] In Wisdom, those terms are

71. See Sandmel, "Parallelomania," 1–2, where he focuses on two key concepts: specificity and context. Neglect of either of these when comparing texts can result in "parallelomania" (the term "parallelomania" itself did not originate with Sandmel). Regarding the dangers of "parallelomania" in Hebrews, specifically, Harold Attridge's cautions are worth heeding: "Parallels to its imagery and language from apocalyptic, Jewish philosophical and Greek religious sources can often be suggestive about the significance of the text or about the presuppositions of its original audience, but they cannot be by themselves decisive for exegesis of Hebrews" ("Let Us Strive," 287–88).

72. Whitlark, "Warning," 391.

in reference to the pagans and their idolatry. Indeed, one of the key points of Wisdom is that the Israelites, unlike the pagans, were not idolaters. In John Barclay's words, "The main fact [in Wis 15:2–4] that the author wants to convey is precisely that God's people do not worship idols, because they know God and recognise his power. In the preceding critique of idolatry, criticism is leveled at those who do not know God and thus do not deduce his superior power . . ."[73] Yet in Heb 6:1, the exhortation to leave the "foundation of repentance from dead works" is a precursor to the strong warning of 6:4–6 which, as Mathewson argues, has strong lexical ties to Numbers and Deuteronomy.[74] Thus, in light of the fact that the wilderness wanderers constitute the primary foil for the audience of Hebrews, the statement that the audience should avoid "dead works" seems to implicate the wilderness wanderers as guilty of precisely that very sin, idolatry.[75] Furthermore, in Heb 9:14, the effectiveness of Jesus Christ in purging one from "dead works" is held up as superior to the methodology of the Old Covenant (quite possibly because the wilderness wanderers kept going back to "dead works").[76]

We have already mentioned Whitlark's statement about the link between Hebrews' use of warning passages from the LXX and the danger of idolatry. To reiterate, Heb 10:26–31, a text once more dealing with the wilderness wanderers, draws from Deut 17:6 and 32:35–36, both of which discuss idolatry in the context.[77] If Whitlark's basic premise here stands,

---

73. Barclay, "I Will Have Mercy," 91.

74. Mathewson, "Reading Heb 6:4–6," 211–21.

75. Regarding the topic of idolatry, Wisdom's obvious omission of the Golden Calf incident (Exod 32) is worth mentioning. Often the *absence* of a key item may declare volumes about a text's agenda. In 15:2–4, "Wisdom of Solomon alludes to Moses' confident words in the aftermath of the Golden Calf, but in the same sentence Wisdom of Solomon exonerates Israel from idolatry (Wis 15.2–4)" (Linebaugh, "Announcing the Human," 232). Bluntly stated, "There is no room for the Golden Calf in Wisdom of Solomon's anthropological dualism" (ibid.). Barclay concurs: "The author of *Wisdom of Solomon* makes no mention of the Golden Calf, and it is hard to imagine how he could have done so . . . The Golden Calf is too flagrant a sin to be mentioned here . . ." ("I Will Have Mercy," 91). On the other hand, King L. She argues that "apostasy in Hebrews should be understood in light of the golden calf episode . . . Put simply, Exod 31:18—34:35 is the controlling text to reveal his understanding of apostasy and covenant" (*Exodus in Hebrews*, 27). If correct, this would further amplify the significant divergence of Hebrews from Wisdom of Solomon when they develop the same motif.

76. Lane, *Hebrews 9–13*, 240, states, "The effectiveness of the blood of Christ derives from the qualitatively superior character of his sacrifice. His sacrifice achieved what the old cultus could not accomplish, namely, the decisive purgation of conscience and the effective removal of every impediment to the worship of God."

77. Whitlark, "Warning," 392. Whitlark also points out that the expression "living God" (e.g., Heb 3:12) was often used in contrast to idols in Jewish literature.

then Hebrews is attacking the potential of idolatry, exemplified by the wilderness wanderers.[78]

In Wis 14:12, idolatry is directly linked with πορνεία, while in Wis 14:23–27 idolatry is the cause of a whole host of evils, including ἀπίστια.[79] In fact, the pagans are given opportunity to believe (πιστεύω—12:2 in light of 12:8–10), but ultimately fail to do so.[80] In contrast, the wilderness wanderers put their trust in God (πιστεύω in 16:26, 18:6 [note also σωτηρία in 18:7] and 14:5, indirectly by analogy). Thus the wilderness wanderers believe and the immoral pagans do not.

Yet Hebrews blatantly challenges that assumption, to the extent that an entire discourse unit on the wilderness wanderers (3:12–3:19) is held together as an *inclusio* via the use of ἀπίστια and βλέπω.[81] Incredibly, ἀπίστια is linked with πορνεία in Heb 3:12 (καρδία πονηρὰ ἀπιστίας). Significantly, then, whereas in Wisdom the pagans are characterized by πορνεία and ἀπίστια, Hebrews applies both terms to the wilderness wanderers. Indeed, "faith" is consistently held up as the *opposite* of what characterizes the wilderness wanderers, those who fell away (see especially the use of πίστις in Heb 4:2, 6:12, 10:38–39). Thus the author of Hebrews pursues a polemic against unbelief, immorality, *and* idolatry, all associated with the wilderness wanderers, three particular sins that the author of Wisdom claims they were immune to.

Nestled within the *inclusio* of Heb 3:12–19 is one of eleven references to Moses by name in Hebrews. Surprisingly, Wisdom never mentions Moses by name and speaks of him sparingly. When Moses does appear, though, he is shown to be in strong solidarity with the wilderness generation. In Wis 11:1, Moses (the "holy prophet") is the means by which Lady Wisdom causes the "works" of the wilderness wanderers to be successful. Later, in 18:5, in reference to Exodus 2, that "one child" (ἑνὸς τέκνου), Moses, is linked to the rescue of the "multitude of children" (πλῆθος τέκνων) via the Exodus.

Yet Hebrews juxtaposes Moses *against* the wilderness generation. The negative description of the children of Israel (3:12–19) follows immediately on the heels of Moses' positive depiction (3:5): "This portion of Hebrews considers the distant past by contrasting the faithfulness of Moses (3:1–6) with the faithlessness of the wilderness generation (3:7–4:13)."[82] Moses, in

---

78. I am intrigued by Whitlark's thesis in *Resisting Empire*, 51 ("Often overlooked in the study of Hebrews is the extensive figured polemic against idolatry"), though I am not quite willing to agree with him on the "primary concern" of Hebrews.

79. Lucas, "Intra-Jewish Interpretive Debate?," 88.

80. Cf. also the interesting statement in Wis 18:13.

81. Regarding the *inclusio*, see Guthrie, *Structure of Hebrews*, 78–79.

82. Koester, *Hebrews*, 262.

a sense, is the mediator of the old covenant to the wilderness wanderers (9:19), yet *despite* his best efforts, the Israelites often "set aside the Law of Moses" and fell afoul of God's wrath (10:28). Whereas in Wisdom Moses is linked closely with the wilderness generation as righteous recipients of God's grace, in Hebrews Moses stands in stark contrast with the people of Israel, an Israelite of faith versus a generation of unbelief.

Moses, however, was not the only one to accompany the children of Israel through the Exodus and beyond. In Wis 10:17, the pillar of fire of Exod 13:21–22, Num 14:14, etc. is identified with Lady Wisdom herself (καὶ εἰς φλόγα ἄστρων τὴν νύκτα).[83] Thus Lady Wisdom burns for her people with the "flame of the stars"; in contrast, the pagans have no "radiant flame of stars" (17:5—ἄστρων ἔκλαμποι φλόγες) to give them light and hope. In fact, this is a significant sub-theme in Wisdom: fire acts beneficially for Lady Wisdom's people, but works against pagans (see 16:16–22, 18:1–4, 19:20–21).

In contrast, Hebrews associates the theme of fire negatively with the wilderness wanderers. If Mathewson is correct that Heb 6:4–6 is meant to be read against the backdrop of "the wilderness generation and the Kadesh-barnea incident," then the word φοτίζω is most likely an allusion to "the light that God provided for the wilderness generation in the desert."[84] Indeed, Mathewson has convincingly demonstrated via the lexical parallels of Neh 9:12, 19 and Ps 105 (LXX 104):39 that this verb can indeed refer specifically to the "pillar" that went with the Israelites.[85] In contrast to Wisdom, in Heb 6:4 the "light" is not seen as an "enabler" or "protector," but rather that which the wilderness wanderers abandon.

The "fire" motif links negatively to the wilderness wanderers in two other places. First, in Heb 10:27, those who imitate Moses' generation (see 10:28) have only "fearful expectation of judgment, and a fury of fire" to look forward to.[86] As Lane states, "The description of judgment as a fire that devours and utterly destroys recalls the actual experience of the followers of Korah who were consumed by fire because they had shown contempt

---

83. See the discussion in Enns, *Exodus Retold*, 57.
84. Mathewson, "Reading Heb 6:4–6," 211, 215.
85. Ibid., 215–16.
86. Further evidence that the wilderness wanderers are the backdrop for this warning can be seen in the expression "sinning deliberately" which "derives from Num 15:22–31, where a distinction is made between those who unintentionally transgress God's commandments (vv 22–29) and the person who sins 'defiantly,' who must be 'cut off from his people' because he has despised the Lord (vv 30–31)" (Lane, *Hebrews 9–13*, 292).

for God (Num 16:35; 26:10)."[87] Secondly, in Heb 12:29, with the wilderness wanderers once more serving as the backdrop (vv. 25–26), the audience is warned that "our God is a consuming fire," "a clear allusion to Deut 4:24 LXX."[88] In other words, just as the wilderness wanderers were in danger of fire, so also are those who turn their back on the Word. As Peter O'Brian succinctly summarizes, "None may presume upon the grace of God."[89]

CONCLUSION

Much more could be said regarding the wilderness wandering motif in both Wisdom and Hebrews. At the very least, however, this much has been established: (1) Hebrews and Wisdom share remarkably similar rhetoric, terminology, structure, and homiletical characteristics; (2) For both Hebrews and Wisdom, the wilderness wandering generation plays a key role in the development of their argument, perhaps even to an unparalleled degree among Second Temple literature; (3) Hebrews utilizes many of the same motifs as Wisdom when dealing with the wilderness wanderers, yet causes these same motifs to reflect negatively on the wilderness generation.[90] Consequently, there is a high probability that the author of Hebrews knew of Wisdom of Solomon; if so, the likelihood increases that parts of Hebrews are a deliberate reaction to Wisdom of Solomon's theology.[91]

Wisdom of Solomon declares, "Behold the wilderness generation and imitate them!" In response, Hebrews warns, "Do not be like the wilderness

---

87. Lane, *Hebrews 9–13*, 293. Lane also sees Isa 26:11 utilized in this context.

88. Ibid., 487. For an extensive discussion of all the potential intertextuality in this text, including Haggai 2:6 and Psalm 95 (94 LXX), see ibid., 475–87.

89. O'Brian, *Letter to the Hebrews*, 493.

90. I reject, however, the notion that the author of Hebrews was anti-Semitic. For further discussion, see Kim, *Polemic*; Williamson, "Anti-Judaism?"; and Fischer, "Covenant Fulfillment," 187.

91. I trust the reader will allow one side note in honor of my former doctoral advisor. As is well-known, David Alan Black is one of the few remaining scholars who holds to the Pauline authorship of Hebrews (see his book *The Authorship of Hebrews*). While I myself prefer Apollos (who was, after all, a skilled homiletical orator from Alexandria!), this essay may have the ironic function of offering support to Dr. Black's views on authorship in the following manner. First, if this essay is generally correct, and if Linebaugh is correct that the Apostle Paul was reacting specifically against Wisdom of Solomon, then Hebrews becomes the only other New Testament book other than Romans to offer a specific rejoinder to Wisdom of Solomon. Second, of all the other books of the New Testament, 1 Cor 10:1–18 especially concerns itself with the apostasy of the wilderness generation. Thus Hebrews shares significant thematic parallels with two major Pauline epistles.

generation, for their carcasses lie smoldering in the wilderness via unbelief." In contrast to the wilderness wanderers, Hebrews visualizes a living community who have placed their faith in the Ἀπαύγασμα of God himself and as a result have discovered Wisdom.[92]

BIBLIOGRAPHY

Allen, David. "More Than Just Numbers: Deuteronomic Influence in Hebrews in Hebrews 3:7–4:11." *Tyndale Bulletin* 58 (2007) 129–49.

Attridge, Harold W. *The Epistle to the Hebrews*. Hermeneia. Philadelphia: Fortress, 1989.

———. "'Let Us Strive to Enter That Rest': The Logic of Hebrews 4:1–11." *Harvard Theological Review* 73 (January–April 1980) 279–88.

Barclay, John M. G. "'I Will Have Mercy on Whom I Will Have Mercy': The Golden Calf and Divine Mercy in Romans 9–11 and Second Temple Judaism." *Early Christianity* 1 (2010) 82–106.

Baslez, Marie-Françoise. "The Author of Wisdom and the Cultured Environment of Alexandria." In *The Book of Wisdom in Modern Research*, edited by Angelo Passaro and Guiseppe Bellia, 33–52. Berlin: de Gruyter, 2005.

Bellia, Giuseppa, and Angelo Passaro. "Infinite Passion for Justice." In *The Book of Wisdom in Modern Research*, edited by Angelo Passaro and Guiseppe Bellia, 307–28. Berlin: de Gruyter, 2005.

Black, David Alan. *The Authorship of Hebrews: The Case for Paul*. Topical Line Drives 1. Gonzalez, FL: Energion, 2013.

———. "Hebrews 1:1–4: A Study in Discourse Analysis." *Westminster Theological Journal* 49 (1987) 175–94.

———. "Literary Artistry in the Epistle to the Hebrews." *Filología Neotestamentaria* 7 (1994) 43–52.

———. "A Note on the Structure of Hebrews 12, 1–2." *Biblica* 68 (1987) 543–51.

———. "The Problem of the Literary Structure of Hebrews." *Grace Theological Journal* 7 (1986) 163–77.

———. "Who Wrote Hebrews? The Internal and External Evidence Reexamined." *Faith and Mission* 18 (2001) 3–26.

Bosman, Hendrik L. "The Theological Paraphrasing of History: The Exodus Tradition in the Wisdom of Solomon." *HTS Teologiese Studies* 68/1 (2012) 1–7.

Brand, John. "Sabbath-Rest, Worship, and the Epistle to the Hebrews Celebrating the Rule of Yahweh." *Didaskalia* 1/2 (March 1990) 3–13.

Burkes, Shannon. "Wisdom and Apocalypticism in the Wisdom of Solomon." *Harvard Theological Review* 95 (January 2002) 21–44.

---

92. I am grateful to Dr. Black for his academic and spiritual mentorship, to Drs. Hudgins and Akin for inviting me to contribute, and to my seminary student Seth Folkers for reading an early draft of this paper and making suggestions (and especially for pointing me to Mathewson's article). This essay had its origins in a paper written for Dr. George Guthrie in a doctoral seminar on Hebrews, and I am grateful for comments by him and fellow student Joe Greene. Naturally any mistakes, lapses of logic, "parallelomania," or outright heresy remain the sole responsibility of this writer.

Cheon, Samuel. *The Exodus Story in the Wisdom of Solomon: A Study in Biblical Narrative*. JSPSup 23. Sheffield: Sheffield Academic, 1997.
Enns, Peter. *Exodus Retold: Ancient Exegesis of the Departure from Egypt in Wis 10:15–21 and 19:1–9*. HSM 57. Atlanta: Scholars, 1997.
———. "A Retelling of the Song of the Sea in Wis 10, 20–21." *Biblica* 76 (1995) 1–24.
———. "Wisdom of Solomon and Biblical Interpretation in the Second Temple Period." In *The Way of Wisdom: Essays in Honor of Bruce Waltke*, edited by J. I. Packer and Sven K. Soderlund, 212–25. Grand Rapids: Zondervan, 2000.
Fischer, John. "Covenant, Fulfillment and Judaism in Hebrews." *Evangelical Review of Theology* 13 (April 1989) 175–87.
Gilbert, Maurice. "The Literary Structure of the Book of Wisdom: A Study of Various Views." In *The Book of Wisdom in Modern Research*, edited by Angelo Passaro and Guiseppe Bellia, 19–32. Berlin: de Gruyter, 2005.
Glicksman, Andrew T. *Wisdom of Solomon 10: A Jewish Hellenistic Reinterpretation of Early Israelite History through Sapiential Lenses*. Deuterocanonical and Cognate Literature Studies 9. Berlin: de Gruyter, 2011.
Gregg, J. A. F. *The Wisdom of Solomon*. CBSC. Cambridge: Cambridge University Press, 1909.
Guthrie, George H. "Hebrews." In *Commentary on the New Testament Use of the Old Testament*, edited by G. K. Beale and D. A. Carson, 919–95. Grand Rapids: Baker Academic, 2007.
———. *The Structure of Hebrews: A Text-Linguistic Approach*. Supplements to Novum Testamentum 73. Leiden: Brill, 1994.
Heil, John Paul. *Hebrews: Chiastic Structures and Audience Response*. CBQMS 46. Washington, D.C.: The Catholic Biblical Association of America, 2010.
Helyer, Larry R. *Exploring Jewish Literature of the Second Temple Period*. Downers Grove, IL: InterVarsity, 2002.
Hurst, L. D. *The Epistle to the Hebrews: Its Background of Thought*. SNTSMS 65. Cambridge: Cambridge University Press, 1990.
Johnson, Luke Timothy. "The Scriptural World of Hebrews." *Interpretation* 57 (July 2003) 237–50.
Käsemann, Ernst. *The Wandering People of God: An Investigation of the Letter to the Hebrews*. Translated by Roy A. Harrisville and Irving L. Sandberg. Minneapolis: Augsburg, 1984.
Khiok-Khng, Yeo. "The Meaning and Usage of the Theology of 'Rest' (Κατάπαυσις and σαββατισμός) in Hebrews 3:7—4:13." *Asia Journal of Theology* 5 (April 1991) 2–33.
Kim, Lloyd. *Polemic in the Book of Hebrews: Anti-Judaism, Anti-Semitism, Supersessionism?* Eugene, OR: Wipf & Stock, 2006.
Koester, Craig R. *Hebrews*. AB 36. New York: Doubleday, 2001.
Lane, William L. *Hebrews 1–8*. WBC 47a. Nashville: Thomas Nelson, 1991.
———. *Hebrews 9–13*. WBC 47b. Nashville: Thomas Nelson, 1991.
Linebaugh, Jonathan A. "Announcing the Human: Rethinking the Relationship Between Wisdom of Solomon 13–15 and Romans 1.18–2.11." *New Testament Studies* 57 (2011) 214–37.
———. *God, Grace, and Righteousness in Wisdom of Solomon and Paul's Letter to the Romans: Texts in Conversations*. NovTSup 152. Leiden: Brill, 2013.

Lucas, Alec J. "Unearthing an Intra-Jewish Interpretive Debate? *Romans* 1, 18–2,4; *Wisdom of Solomon* 11–19; and *Psalms* 105(104) –107(106)." *Annali di Storia dell'Esegesi* 27/2 (2010) 69–90.
Mathewson, Dave. "Reading Heb 6:4–6 in Light of the Old Testament." *Westminster Theological Journal* 61/2 (Fall 1999) 209–25.
Martin, Michael W., and Jason A. Whitlark. "Choosing What Is Advantageous: The Relationship between Epideictic and Deliberative Syncrisis in Hebrews." *New Testament Studies* 58 (2012) 379–400.
Nickelsburg, George W. *Jewish Literature between the Bible and the Mishnah*. 2nd ed. Minneapolis: Fortress, 2005.
O'Brian, Peter T. *The Letter to the Hebrews*. Pillar New Testament Commentary. Grand Rapids: Eerdmans, 2010.
Passaro, Angelo. "The Serpent and the Manna or the Saving Word. Exegesis of Wis 16." In *The Book of Wisdom in Modern Research*, edited by Angelo Passaro and Guiseppe Bellia, 179–93. Berlin: de Gruyter, 2005.
Peeler, Amy L. B. *You Are My Son: The Family of God in the Epistle to the Hebrews*. Library of New Testament Studies. London: T. & T. Clark, 2014.
Reese, James M. *The Book of Wisdom, Song of Songs*. OTM. Wilmington, DE: Michael Glazier, 1983.
———. "Plan and Structure in the Book of Wisdom." *Catholic Biblical Quarterly* 27 (October 1965) 391–99.
Reider, Joseph. *The Book of Wisdom*. JAL. New York: Harper, 1957.
Rohr, Ignaz. *Der Hebraerbriefe und die Geheime Offenbarung des Heiligen Johannes*. Bonn: Peter Hanstein, 1932.
Salevao, Iutisone. *Legitimation in the Letter to the Hebrews: The Construction and Maintenance of a Symbolic Universe*. JSNTSup 219. London: Sheffield Academic, 2002.
Sandmel, Samuel. "Parallelomania." *Journal of Biblical Literature* 81/1 (March 1962) 1–13.
Scott, Brett R. "Jesus' Superiority Over Moses in Hebrews 3:1–6." *Bibliotheca Sacra* 155 (April–June 1998) 201–10.
She, King L. *The Use of Exodus in Hebrews*. Studies in Biblical Literature 142. New York: Peter Lang, 2011.
Son, Kiwoong. *Zion Symbolism in Hebrews: Hebrews 12:18–24 as a Hermeneutical Key to the Epistle*. Paternoster Biblical Monographs. Colorado Springs: Paternoster, 2005.
Spicq, Ceslas. *L'Épitre aux Hébreux*. Vol. 1. Paris: Gabalda, 1952.
Thesaurus Linguae Graecae. University of California, 2009. http://tlg.uci.edu.
Thompson, James W. "The Hermeneutics of the Epistle to the Hebrews." *Restoration Quarterly* 38 (1996) 229–37.
Thyen, Hartwig. *Der Stil of Jüdisch-Hellenistischen Homilie*. Göttingen: Vandenhoeck & Ruprecht, 1955.
Vanhoye, Albert. *La structure littéraire de l'épitre aux Hébreux*. Lyon: Desclée de Brouwer, 1962.
Webster, Edwin C. "Structural Unity in the Book of Wisdom." *East Asia Journal of Theology* 4 (April 1986) 98–112.
Whitlark, Jason A. *Resisting Empire: Rethinking the Purpose of the Letter to "the Hebrews."* Library of New Testament Studies. London: T. & T. Clark, 2014.

———. "The Warning against Idolatry: An Intertextual Examination of Septuagintal Warnings in Hebrews." *Journal for the Study of the New Testament* 34/4 (2012) 382–401.

Williamson, Clark M. "Anti-Judaism in Hebrews?" *Interpretation* 57/3 (July 2003) 266–79.

Williamson, Ronald. *Philo and the Epistle to the Hebrews*. ALGHJ. Leiden: Brill, 1970.

Winston, David. *The Wisdom of Solomon*. AB 43. Garden City, NY: Doubleday, 1979.

Wright, Addison G. "The Structure of the Book of Wisdom." *Biblica* 48 (1967) 164–84.

———. "The Structure of Wisdom 11–19." *Catholic Biblical Quarterly* 27 (January 1965) 28–34.

Yisak, Surur Mohammed. "The Use of the Old Testament in Hebrews: Understanding the Interpretive Method of the Writer of Hebrews." ThM diss., Southeastern Baptist Theological Seminary, 2007.

Zimmermann, Frank. "The Book of Wisdom: Its Language and Character." *Jewish Quarterly Review* 57 (July 1966) 1–27.

13

Contextualizando y actualizando la traducción al español de la gramática griega de David Alan Black

Stephen H. Levinsohn
SIL International

INTRODUCCIÓN

"Para el estudiante de lengua española, el griego se asemeja más a su lengua materna que a otros idiomas"[1] y no faltan lecciones en las que los traductores ya adaptaron el texto de David Alan Black[2] para explotar las similitudes entre los dos idiomas. Este artículo considera unas áreas en las que el proceso de contextualización podría llevarse todavía más allá. Ya que ambos idiomas son de la clase "pro-drop" (no tienen que utilizar un pronombre para indicar el sujeto), hay gran correspondencia en el uso y no-uso de los *pronombres*, lo cual debería impactar la presentación tanto de las conjugaciones verbales como de la traducción de los verbos indicativos (§1). Otros rasgos en común incluyen el uso de los *demostrativos* (§3), la voz *media* (véase la "media reflexiva" del español—(§4), el modo *subjuntivo*

---

1. Black, *Aprenda a leer el griego del Nuevo Testamento*, 7.
2. Black, *Learn to Read New Testament Greek*.

(§5), y ciertas variaciones en el *orden* relativo de las oraciones dentro de la frase (§6). Un resultado de estas semejanzas es que las comparaciones con inglés, francés, y alemán no serán beneficiales para el lector hispano.

Este artículo presenta también varios avances en cuanto a nuestro entendimiento de las variaciones en el *orden* de los elementos de los sintagmas y oraciones (§6), de las diferencias entre los *participios* pre-nucleares y pos-nucleares (§7), de las construcciones *perifrásticas* (§8), de la función del *artículo* (§9), de la identificación y funciones de los *aspectos marcados* (§10), y de la *segmentación* de los textos en secciones y párrafos (§11).

EL USO DE LOS PRONOMBRES

Tanto el griego como el español son idiomas "pro-drop," lo que quiere decir que no tienen que utilizar un pronombre para indicar el sujeto, ya que el verbo incluye una desinencia (terminación) de persona y número.[3] Por ejemplo, la primera persona singular de la voz activa de "desatar" en español consiste en la desinencia -*o* agregada a la raíz *desata-* (*desat-o*),[4] y la forma correspondiente en griego se forma de la misma manera, al añadir -ω a la raíz λύ- (λύ-ω). El siguiente cuadro compara las desinencias de la voz activa en ambos idiomas.

	Singular		Plural	
1.	-ω	-o	-μεν	-mos
2.	-εις	-s	-τε	-´is
3.	-ει		-ουσι(ν)	-n

Este cuadro facilita el aprendizaje de la morfología del griego, ya que ciertas pares de desinencias manifiestan semejanzas fonológicas con el español. Se nota también que en ambos idiomas, la diferencia entre la segunda persona singular y la tercera es solamente una *s*.

El hecho de que los dos idiomas son "pro-drop" tiene varias implicaciones para la gramática en cuanto al uso y no uso de los pronombres. En primer lugar, lo normal será no utilizar un pronombre al traducir un verbo

---

3. Black (*Aprenda a leer el griego del Nuevo Testamento*, §18) utiliza el término "sufijos primarios" para referirse a estas desinencias.

4. Cuando -*o* se agrega a *desata-*, se suprime la última vocal de la raíz.

griego al español. Por ejemplo, ἔχει no quiere decir "él tiene," sino "tiene"[5] y "el sufijo de persona y número ω" significa "-o" y no "yo."[6]

En segundo lugar, la sugerencia de que las desinencias de persona y número del griego tienen "su origen probablemente en la unión de pronombres personales independientes a la raíz del verbo"[7] no le aclarará nada al estudiante hispano. Aún si la hipótesis fuese cierta (y es poco probable, ya que tanto el griego clásico como el idioma indo-europeo clásico sanscrito colocan el sujeto antes del verbo y tienen desinencias verbales para persona y número), el punto clave en la comparación entre el verbo griego y el español es la semejanza entre los dos juegos de desinencias.

En tercer lugar, el uso de los pronombres personales que se refieren a los sujetos cambia poco entre el griego y el español. En ambos idiomas, se emplean para destacar un *contraste* con otro sujeto, como en Mateo 5:22 (ἐγὼ δὲ λέγω ὑμῖν "Pero *yo* os digo"),[8] donde "'yo' contrasta con 'a los antiguos' (v 21)."[9] Se utilizan también para establecer el *tema* del que trata un discurso, como en Juan 8:12 (Ἐγώ εἰμι τὸ φῶς τοῦ κόσμου "*Yo* soy la luz del mundo").

En resumen, los pronombres que se refieren a los sujetos en griego típicamente se traducen al español con pronombres. En cambio, cuando el griego no emplea un pronombre para referirse abiertamente al sujeto, el español tampoco lo hará, salvo en las traducciones que emplean "usted(es)," debido a la ambigüedad resultante. Así que la RV95 no necesita un pronombre al traducir Lucas 6:46 (Τί δέ με καλεῖτε, Κύριε κύριε. . .;) "¿Por qué me llamáis 'Señor, Señor'. . .?" En cambio, la ambigüedad entre "ustedes" y "ellos" o "ellas" obliga a la NVI a emplear un pronombre: "¿Por qué me llaman *ustedes* 'Señor, Señor'. . .?"

EL CASO ACUSATIVO

En inglés, la diferencia entre el caso nominativo y acusativo del griego se expresa principalmente "por el orden de las palabras: el sujeto precede al verbo, y el objeto lo sigue sin cambio alguno de la forma."[10] Existe otro rasgo en español que facilita la diferencia entre los dos casos: la preposición "a" que

5. Ibid., §3.
6. Ibid., §12.
7. Ibid., §21.
8. Si no se indica la versión española que corresponde al griego, se ha tomado de la Biblia Reina Valera de 1995 (Sociedades Bíblicas en América Latina).
9. Ibid., §65.
10. Ibid., §28.

"[p]recede al complemento directo cuando este es de persona determinada o está de algún modo personificado,"[11] como en "Los hombres ven *a* los apóstoles." Además, cuando el complemento se antepone al verbo, lo sigue un pronombre acusativo, como en "Estos hombres *los* ven los apóstoles."

De modo que, cuando se considera el caso acusativo del griego, sería beneficial para el estudiante hispano hacer referencia a las ocasiones en las que una señal que corresponde al acusativo se manifiesta también en español.

LOS DEMOSTRATIVOS

Tanto en griego como en español, "[e]l demostrativo de cercanía... indica algo cerca, mientras que el demostrativo de lejanía... indica algo más lejos."[12] Muchas veces, cuando la referencia del demostrativo es *anafórica* (se refiere a un concepto mencionado en el contexto), "cerca" quiere decir que el concepto es el centro de atención o "temático," mientras que "lejos" indica lo contrario (no es temático). Por ejemplo, en Hechos 10:36 (οὗτός ἐστιν πάντων κύριος "este es Señor de todos"), el "uso de un demostrativo de proximidad hace que Jesucristo vuelva el centro de atención interino (temático), en vez de Dios (si se suprime la partícula relativa en 36a) o del mensaje (si la conserva)."[13] En Hechos 10:9 (Τῇ δὲ ἐπαύριον, ὁδοιπορούντων ἐκείνων "mientras [aqu]ellos iban por el camino"), en cambio, el "uso del demostrativo distal ἐκείνων 'aquellos' indica que, ahora, el centro de atención no será ellos."[14]

LA VOZ MEDIA

En griego, "[l]a voz media... representa al sujeto actuando en su propio interés o participando intensamente en los resultados de la acción del verbo."[15] Sucede lo mismo en español: "voz que vincula el sujeto de un verbo... con el participante que experimenta el proceso denotado por el predicado"[16] y

---

11. *Diccionario*, I.3.

12. Black, *Aprenda a leer el griego del Nuevo Testamento*, Lección 11.

13. Levinsohn, *Hechos*, 55.

14. Ibid., 44. Para una discusión más extensa de las funciones de los demostrativos griegos, inclusive la diferencia entre ἐν ταῖς ἡμέραις ἐκείναις ("en aquellos días") y ἐν ταῖς ἡμέραις ταύταις ("en estos días"), véase Levinsohn, "Unified Linguistic Description of οὗτος and ἐκεῖνος," 206–19.

15. Black, *Aprenda a leer el griego del Nuevo Testamento*, §81.

16. *Diccionario*, II.2262.

que se expresa normalmente por medio de los verbos reflexivos. Así que lo más claro para el estudiante hispano sería enseñarle que la voz media del griego corresponde a la voz media del español. De modo que no es necesario escribir acerca de Mateo 27:5 (ἀπήγξατο "se ahorcó"), "El pronombre reflexivo "se" no aparece expresamente en el griego,"[17] ya que el verbo reflexivo es una parte integral de la voz media en español.

Black considera que "[l]a proporción de ocurrencias de la voz media reflexiva en el Nuevo Testamento es en realidad muy escasa. Es más usual encontrar el sentido reflexivo expresado por un verbo en la voz activa acompañado por un pronombre reflexivo griego."[18] En realidad, parece que el uso de la voz media o del pronombre reflexivo depende del verbo. Por ejemplo, el pronombre reflexivo se emplea cinco veces en Juan con ποιέω "hacer" (5:18, 8:53, 10:33, 19:7, 19:12), pero la voz media se utiliza cuatro veces con νίπτω "lavar" (9:7 [bis], 9:11, 9:15). Un verbo en Juan que se manifiesta en ambas formas es διαζώννυμι "atarse a la cintura." El pronombre reflexivo se usa en 13:4, pero la voz media en 13:5 y 21:7.

EL MODO SUBJUNTIVO

Aunque el modo subjuntivo del griego presenta muchos desafíos para los hablantes del inglés, es menos problemático para el hispanohablante, ya que el subjuntivo se emplea con frecuencia en español y muchos de sus usos (aunque no todos) son los mismos en ambos idiomas. Vale la pena, pues, destacar no sólo las diferencias,[19] sino también las similitudes.

En las oraciones principales, el subjuntivo se emplea en griego y en español en las *exhortaciones* de primera persona plural (γρηγορῶμεν καὶ νήφωμεν "vigilemos y seamos sobrios"—1 Tesalonicenses 5:6) y las *prohibiciones* (Μὴ κρίνετε "No juzguen a nadie"—Mateo 7:1). En cambio, el subjuntivo no entra en español en las *declaraciones enfáticas* (ἀμὴν λέγω ὑμῖν, οὐ μὴ ἀπολέσῃ τὸν μισθὸν αὐτοῦ "de cierto os digo que no perderá su recompensa"—Mateo 10:42) o las *preguntas* (Τί ποιῶμεν ἵνα ἐργαζώμεθα τὰ ἔργα τοῦ θεοῦ; "¿Qué debemos hacer para poner en práctica las obras de Dios?"—Juan 6:28).

En las oraciones subordinadas, el subjuntivo se emplea en ambos idiomas en las oraciones *finales*, siempre, en el caso del español, que los sujetos de las dos oraciones sean diferentes (Μὴ κρίνετε, ἵνα μὴ κριθῆτε "No juzguen

---

17. Black, *Aprenda a leer el griego del Nuevo Testamento*, §82.
18. Ibid.
19. No faltan ocasiones en las que Black nota que "el futuro en español se utiliza generalmente para expresar la idea de la construcción griega" (Ibid., §152).

a nadie, para que nadie los juzgue a ustedes"—Mateo 7:1 [NVI]).[20] En cambio, el subjuntivo nunca entra en español en las oraciones *condicionales*.

EL ORDEN DE LAS PALABRAS, SINTAGMAS, Y ORACIONES

Esta sección trata de unas variaciones en el orden de los componentes de las frases, oraciones, y sintagmas. Ya que Black comienza con el orden de las palabras y sintagmas en la oración, haré lo mismo.[21]

Black et al. escriben que "[l]os elementos de la oración colocados en primer lugar reciben a menudo un énfasis especial."[22] Las palabras "a menudo" son importantes porque no siempre es así. Por ejemplo, "es frecuente que el sujeto vaya antes del verbo, especialmente cuando . . . introduce un nuevo asunto o se desea que haya un contraste con" algún elemento correspondiente del contexto.[23]

Estas observaciones implican que la anteposición de un elemento puede ser el resultado de una de dos motivaciones distintas, las que capta un patrón propuesto por el lingüista Simon Dik para los idiomas cuyo verbo con frecuencia precede al sujeto y al complemento, especialmente en los textos narrativos. El patrón es: P1 P2 V X:[24] (1) la posición P1 la pueden ocupar uno o más componentes TEMÁTICOS[25]; (2) la posición P2 la puede ocupar un componente FOCAL[26]; y (3) "X" se refiere a cualquier otro componente de la oración que esté presente. 1 Juan 1:5 ilustra las dos posiciones ante-verbales P1 y P2:

P1	P2	V
ὁ θεός	φῶς	ἐστιν
Dios	luz	es

---

20. Si el sujeto no cambia, se utiliza "para" y un infinitivo para introducir las oraciones finales (véase Juan 6:28, citado arriba).

21. Black, *Aprenda a leer el griego del Nuevo Testamento*, §35.

22. Ibid.

23. Ibid., §170.

24. Dik, *The Theory of Functional Grammar*, 363.

25. El *tema* "es la entidad de la que trata principalmente el enunciado" (Dik, *The Theory of Functional Grammar*, 130).

26. El *foco* "es la parte que indica lo que el hablante pretende que sea el cambio más importante y destacado que debe hacerse en la representación mental del oyente" (Dooley y Levinsohn, *Análisis de discurso*, §11.1).

La oración comienza con el sujeto temático ὁ θεός, para indicar un cambio del tema de las oraciones anteriores, que era ἡ ἀγγελία "el mensaje." Le sigue el elemento focal φῶς. Su ubicación antes del verbo le da énfasis: "Dios es luz."[27]

1 Juan 1:4 tiene dos oraciones, una principal y una final, cada una con un componente temático en P1:

	P1	V	S		P1	V
καὶ	ταῦτα	γράφομεν	ἡμεῖς,	ἵνα	ἡ χαρὰ	ᾖ πεπληρωμένη
y	estas cosas	escribimos	nosotros	para que	ἡμῶν vuestro gozo	sea completo

En la primera oración, ταῦτα se refiere a lo que Juan acaba de escribir en los versículos anteriores e indica un cambio de tema de ἡ κοινωνία ἡ ἡμετέρα ("nuestra comunión"). La anteposición del sujeto de la oración final indica otro cambio de tema, a ἡ χαρὰ ἡμῶν "vuestro gozo" y lo sigue un comentario acerca de "vuestro gozo" que es el foco de la oración: el sintagma verbal ᾖ πεπληρωμένη "sea completo."

En cambio, el componente antepuesto en la primera oración de 1 Juan 1:7 está en posición P2:

	P2	V
ἐὰν δὲ	ἐν τῷ φωτὶ	περιπατῶμεν
si pero	en la luz	andamos

La anteposición de ἐν τῷ φωτί da énfasis al contraste con "en las tinieblas" (v. 6): "Pero si andamos *en (la) luz*."

Ahora, consideremos Mateo 27:54:

	P2	V	S
Ἀληθῶς	θεοῦ υἱὸς	ἦν	οὗτος
verdaderamente	de Dios hijo	era	éste

Una vez más, la anteposición del complemento (θεοῦ υἱός) le da énfasis. Además, "la posición del posesivo genitivo θεοῦ antes de su sustantivo hace que sea enfático":[28] "Verdaderamente éste era Hijo de Dios."

Sin embargo, el orden genitivo—sustantivo no siempre da énfasis al genitivo. Véase Mateo 5:30: καὶ εἰ ἡ δεξιά σου χεὶρ σκανδαλίζει σε. Aunque

27. Black, *Aprenda a leer el griego del Nuevo Testamento*, §170.
28. Ibid.

el adjetivo δεξιά "derecha" se ubica antes del sustantivo χείρ "mano," el contexto indica que el énfasis contrastivo cae en "mano," ya que el v 29 habla de "tu ojo derecho": "Y si tu mano derecha te es ocasión de caer."

De la misma manera, el orden complemento—verbo no siempre da énfasis al complemento. Esto se ve en Mateo 8:2: Κύριε, ἐὰν θέλῃς δύνασαί με καθαρίσαι. La última oración de la frase no da énfasis a "me," sino a "limpiar": "Señor, si quieres, puedes limpiarme." O sea, el verbo καθαρίσαι se ha *pospuesto* para énfasis (véase abajo).

Para reconocer cuando un orden indica que un componente ha sido antepuesto para énfasis y cuando no, nos toca tener en cuenta otro factor; a saber, el "Principio del Flujo Natural de la Información."[29] En los sintagmas y oraciones que obedecen este principio, los componentes que comunican la información establecida se colocan antes de los que comunican información nueva o *no*-establecida.[30] En Mateo 5:30, por ejemplo, el orden genitivo—sustantivo del sujeto conforme con este principio:

establecida	no-establecida
ἡ δεξιά σου	χεὶρ
la derecha tu	mano

El orden complemento—verbo en la última oración de Mateo 8:2 también conforme con el principio:

establecida	no-establecida
με	καθαρίσαι
me	limpiar

En la primera oración de 1 Juan 1:7, en cambio, el orden complemento—verbo *quebranta* el principio y da énfasis a la información no-establecida, o sea, la antepuesta:

	P2: no-establecida	V: establecida
ἐὰν δὲ	ἐν τῷ φωτὶ	περιπατῶμεν
si pero	en la luz	andamos

En resumen, cuando el orden de los constituyentes de un sintagma nominal es modificador—sustantivo, se determina primero si el orden es conforme con el Principio del Flujo Natural de la Información. Si es conforme,

---

29. Comrie, *Language Universals and Linguistic Typology*, 127–28.
30. Véase Firbas, "Comparative Word-Order Studies," 115.

entonces el modificador *no* se ha enfatizado. En los otros casos, *sí* se ha enfatizado.[31]

De la misma manera, cuando una oración comienza no con el verbo sino con otro constituyente, hay dos factores que considerar:

1. si el constituyente ante-verbal es temático (en posición P1) o no;
2. si el orden es conforme con el Principio del Flujo Natural de la Información.

Si el constituyente es temático y/o el orden conforma con el principio, entonces *no* se ha enfatizado. En los otros casos, *sí* se ha enfatizado.[32]

A veces, un orden que conforma con el Principio del Flujo Natural de la Información resulta en la ubicación de "una palabra fuera de su orden natural" para enfatizarla.[33] Así que en Mateo 8:2 (citado arriba), el verbo καθαρίσαι "limpiar" se ha pospuesto al complemento μέ "me." Algo semejante se ve en Hechos 10:3: εἶδεν ἐν ὁράματι φανερῶς ὡσεὶ περὶ ὥραν ἐνάτην τῆς ἡμέρας ἄγγελον τοῦ θεοῦ εἰσελθόντα πρὸς αὐτὸν καὶ εἰπόντα αὐτῷ, Κορνήλιε "vio en una visión claramente, como a la hora novena del día, a un ángel de Dios que se le acercó y le dijo: —¡Cornelio!" (RV adaptada). En este versículo, es el *complemento* el que se ha pospuesto. "La introducción del ángel y lo que hacía hacia el final de la oración indica que es el enfoque principal."[34]

La diferencia entre los constituyentes temáticos y focales se aplica también a las *oraciones subordinadas*. Afortunadamente, lo que se escribe aquí acerca del griego se aplica igualmente al español.

En ambos idiomas, las oraciones subordinadas que se colocan antes de la oración principal típicamente sirven de fondo para la principal y, en la mayoría de los casos, también indican un cambio de escena. Esto se ve en Hechos 9:23: Ὡς δὲ ἐπληροῦντο ἡμέραι ἱκαναί, συνεβουλεύσαντο οἱ Ἰουδαῖοι ἀνελεῖν αὐτόν "Pasados muchos días, los judíos decidieron en consejo matarlo." La oración subordinada de tiempo Ὡς δὲ ἐπληροῦντο ἡμέραι ἱκαναί "llena la posición P1 para indicar un cambio del tiempo de los acontecimientos de 20–22."[35]

---

31. Para una presentación más detallada sobre este tema, véase Levinsohn, *Adjective-Noun Ordering*.

32. Para una discusión más detallada del Principio del Flujo Natural de la Información en griego, véase Levinsohn, *La aplicación del estudio de los rasgos discursivos*, §3.1.

33. Black, *Aprenda a leer el griego del Nuevo Testamento*, §170.

34. Levinsohn, *Hechos*, 42.

35. Ibid., 49.

En Hechos 10:41, en cambio, la oración subordinada se ubica después de la principal: ἡμῖν, οἵτινες συνεφάγομεν καὶ συνεπίομεν αὐτῷ μετὰ τὸ ἀναστῆναι αὐτὸν ἐκ νεκρῶν "a nosotros que comimos y bebimos con él después que resucitó de los muertos." En este versículo, la expresión temporal es una parte integral del enfoque de la frase.[36]

La misma diferencia se observa con las oraciones condicionales. En 1 Juan 1:8, por ejemplo, la oración condicional que comienza la frase indica un cambio de situación que sirve de fondo para la oración principal: ἐὰν εἴπωμεν ὅτι ἁμαρτίαν οὐκ ἔχομεν, ἑαυτοὺς πλανῶμεν "Si decimos que no tenemos pecado, nos engañamos a nosotros mismos." En 1 Tesalonicenses 3:8, en cambio, la oración condicional se ubica después de la oración principal y es una parte integral del enfoque de la frase: νῦν ζῶμεν ἐὰν ὑμεῖς στήκετε ἐν κυρίῳ "ahora vivimos si vosotros estáis firmes en el Señor."[37]

LAS ORACIONES PARTICIPIALES

Black reconoce tres usos básicos de los participios griegos: como adjetivo, como sustantivo y como adverbio. En el último caso no lleva artículo.[38] Esta sección se fija en el uso adverbial y destaca una diferencia importante entre los participios que se colocan antes de la oración principal y los que la siguen.

Cuando una oración participial se coloca *antes* de la principal, casi siempre indica "alguna circunstancia en la cual sucede la acción del verbo principal."[39] El efecto de expresar estas circunstancias y acciones en forma participial es ponerlas en fondo en comparación con la acción principal. Esto se ve en Marcos 5:25–27:

| καὶ γυνὴ οὖσα ἐν ῥύσει αἵματος δώδεκα ἔτη | "Y una mujer que desde hacía doce años padecía de flujo de sangre |

---

36. Véase también Hebreos 10:26 (Ἑκουσίως γὰρ ἁμαρτανόντων ἡμῶν μετὰ τὸ λαβεῖν τὴν ἐπίγνωσιν τῆς ἀληθείας, "Si pecamos voluntariamente después de haber recibido el conocimiento de la verdad").

37. Black, *Aprenda a leer el griego del Nuevo Testamento*, §170.

38. Ibid., §131.

39. Ibid. Para una discusión más detallada de las oraciones participiales, véase Levinsohn, *Adverbial Participial Clauses* (presentado a la conferencia internacional sobre discurso y gramática "Illocutionary force, information structure and subordination between discourse and grammar," Universeit Ghent, Belgia). La presentación nota que, en raras circunstancias, una oración participial pre-nuclear es el enfoque de la frase (está en posición P2). Véase, por ejemplo, 2 Cor 11:23: παραφρονῶν λαλῶ , "Hablo como si estuviera loco."

καὶ πολλὰ παθοῦσα ὑπὸ πολλῶν ἰατρῶν	y habiendo sufrido mucho a manos de muchos médicos
καὶ δαπανήσασα τὰ παρ' αὐτῆς πάντα	y habiendo gastado todo lo que tenía
καὶ μηδὲν ὠφεληθεῖσα	y de nada habiéndole servido,
ἀλλὰ μᾶλλον εἰς τὸ χεῖρον ἐλθοῦσα,	antes habiéndole ido peor,
ἀκούσασα περὶ τοῦ Ἰησοῦ,	habiendo oído hablar de Jesús
ἐλθοῦσα ἐν τῷ ὄχλῳ ὄπισθεν	habiéndose acercado por detrás entre la multitud
ἥψατο τοῦ ἱματίου αὐτοῦ	tocó su manto"

El efecto de utilizar siete oraciones participiales antes de la principal es ponerlas en fondo en comparación con la acción más transcendental: "tocó su manto."

En cambio, las oraciones participiales que *siguen* a la principal muchas veces agregan datos importantes acerca de la acción principal, especialmente cuando están en el tiempo presente (es decir, cuando tienen aspecto imperfectivo). Esto se ve en Marcos 1:7: καὶ ἐκήρυσσεν λέγων, "Ἔρχεται ὁ ἰσχυρότερός μου ὀπίσω μου. . . "Y predicaba, diciendo: 'Viene tras mí el que es más poderoso que yo. . .'" Lo transcendental en este versículo no es el hecho de que Juan predicaba, sino el contenido de lo que predicaba, lo cual se presenta en la oración participial pos-nuclear.

Aun cuando una oración participial pos-nuclear tiene aspecto aorístico, puede comunicar una información más importante que la de la oración principal. Esto se ve en Hechos 28:25:

ἀσύμφωνοι δὲ ὄντες πρὸς ἀλλήλους ἀπελύοντο	"Al no estar de acuerdo entre sí, comenzaron a irse
εἰπόντος τοῦ Παύλου ῥῆμα ἕν, ὅτι Καλῶς τὸ πνεῦμα τὸ ἅγιον ἐλάλησεν διὰ Ἠσαΐου τοῦ προφήτου πρὸς τοὺς πατέρας ὑμῶν . . .	después de esta última declaración de Pablo: 'El Espíritu Santo les habló acertadamente por medio del profeta Isaías a los antepasados de ustedes . . .'" (NVI)

Este orden causa que los lectores se fijen no tanto en el suceso de que los judíos salían de la casa sin ponerse de acuerdo, sino en lo que Pablo les dijo antes de su salida.

Ahora consideremos Hebreos 12:1-2:[40]

---

40. Black (*Aprenda a leer el griego del Nuevo Testamento*, §171) no hace una diferencia entre las funciones de las oraciones participiales pre-nucleares y pos-nucleares.

Τοιγαροῦν καὶ ἡμεῖς τοσοῦτον ἔχοντες περικείμενον ἡμῖν νέφος μαρτύρων,	"Por tanto, nosotros también, teniendo en derredor nuestro tan grande nube de testigos,
ὄγκον ἀποθέμενοι πάντα καὶ τὴν εὐπερίστατον ἁμαρτίαν,	habiéndonos despojado de todo peso y del pecado que nos asedia,
δι' ὑπομονῆς τρέχωμεν τὸν προκείμενον ἡμῖν ἀγῶνα	corramos con paciencia la carrera que tenemos por delante,
ἀφορῶντες εἰς τὸν τῆς πίστεως ἀρχηγὸν καὶ τελειωτὴν Ἰησοῦν,	puestos los ojos en Jesús, el autor y consumador de la fe"

La primera oración participial describe la situación en la que hemos de realizar las acciones principales. Le sigue una segunda oración participial pre-nuclear que describe una acción que nos toca haber hecho antes de la principal. Luego vienen las oraciones nuclear y pos-nuclear que expresan la intención primordial del autor: no sólo de "correr la carrera con perseverancia,"[41] sino de correrla con los ojos puestos en Jesús.

LAS CONSTRUCCIONES PERIFRÁSTICAS

Como Black indica, a veces los participios aparecen con el verbo copulativo εἰμί para formar lo que se denomina una construcción perifrástica.[42] Nos limitamos en esta sección a las ocasiones cuando el participio está en el presente (con aspecto imperfectivo).[43]

Típicamente, cuando un idioma tiene dos formas imperfectivas—una sencilla y otra perifrástica—, la perifrástica es más *estática*.[44] Así que la forma sencilla utilizada en el griego de Juan 8:2 (καὶ καθίσας ἐδίδασκεν αὐτούς "y sentándose, les enseñaba") quiere decir que Jesús estaba enseñando[45] (activo) cuando las autoridades "le trajeron una mujer sorprendida en adulterio." En cambio, la forma perifrástica empleada en Lucas 21:37 (Καὶ ἦν διδάσκων τὸ καθ' ἡμέραν ἐν τῷ ἱερῷ "De día enseñaba en el Templo") refleja el hecho de que Jesús *solía* enseñar en el templo, sin sugerir que lo hacía continuamente, sin pausa.

---

41. Ibid.

42. Ibid., §131 (7).

43. Para una presentación detallada del contraste entre las formas perifrásticas y sencillas, véase Levinsohn, "Copula-Participle Combinations," §§2–3. La sección 3 describe la diferencia entre las dos formas cuando el participio es perfecto.

44. Ibid., §2. Véase BDAG εἰμί §11.f.

45. El uso del imperfecto perifrástico del español no corresponde a su uso en griego.

La diferencia entre las dos formas se ilustra en las oraciones infinitivas de Lucas 9:29 (ἐν τῷ προσεύχεσθαι αὐτόν—sencilla) y 9:18 (ἐν τῷ εἶναι αὐτὸν προσευχόμενον—perifrástica).[46] Aunque la RV traduce ambas expresiones "Mientras oraban," la forma sencilla de 9:29 comunica que Jesús estaba orando (activo) cuando "la apariencia de su rostro cambió." En cambio, se entiende del 9:18 que, aunque Jesús oraba aparte, hubo por lo menos una ocasión en la que interrumpió sus oraciones para interrogar a sus discípulos. Así que la forma perifrástica nos deja entender que Jesús oraba, sin sugerir que lo hacía continuamente, sin pausa.

La forma perifrástica se usa en la presentación de eventos *iterativos*,[47] ya que se permite entender de su naturaleza estática que la acción se realizaba repetidas veces sin sugerir que se hacía continuamente. De modo que en Lucas 4:44 (καὶ ἦν κηρύσσων εἰς τὰς συναγωγὰς τῆς Ἰουδαίας "Y predicaba en las sinagogas de Galilea"), la forma con la cópula es más apropiada para comunicar que Jesús solía predicar en las sinagogas sin sugerir que era la única cosa que hacía durante ese tiempo (véase Mateo 4:23).

En Lucas 2:51 (καὶ ἦν ὑποτασσόμενος αὐτοῖς), la naturaleza estática de la forma perifrástica la capta la RV al traducirla: "y les estaba sujeto."[48]

Ambas formas se encuentran en Hechos 12:5 (ὁ μὲν οὖν Πέτρος ἐτηρεῖτο ἐν τῇ φυλακῇ· προσευχὴ δὲ ἦν ἐκτενῶς γινομένη ὑπὸ τῆς ἐκκλησίας πρὸς τὸν θεὸν περὶ αὐτοῦ [NA28] "Así pues, Pedro era custodiado en la cárcel, pero la iglesia hacía oración ferviente a Dios por él" (LBLA). La forma sencilla (ἐτηρεῖτο) refleja el hecho de que Pedro estaba custodiado continuamente en la cárcel. La naturaleza estática de la forma con la cópula (ἦν . . . γινομένη), en cambio, sugiere "más bien que su oración era ferviente y en serio, y no que era constante."[49]

Finalmente, en Hechos 8:28, la forma perifrástica (ἦν τε ὑποστρέφων καὶ καθήμενος ἐπὶ τοῦ ἅρματος αὐτοῦ [NA28] "volvía sentado en su carro" sirve de *fondo* para la acción más importante que se expresa de forma sencilla: καὶ ἀνεγίνωσκεν τὸν προφήτην Ἠσαΐαν "y leía al profeta Isaías" (LBLA).

---

46. La posición no marcada del sujeto en las construcciones perifrásticas es entre el verbo copulativo y el participio (Levinsohn, "Copula-Participle Combinations," §1).

47. Véase Fanning, *Verbal Aspect*, 315.

48. La construcción "acentúa la continua obediencia de Jesús a sus padres" (Black, *Aprenda a leer el griego del Nuevo Testamento*, §131).

49. "The word [ἐκτενῶς] has rather the idea that their prayer was *earnest* and *fervent*, than that it was constant" (Barnes, *Acts of the Apostles*, 217).

EL ARTÍCULO

Aunque Black utiliza el término "artículo definido" para referirse al artículo griego, es mejor suprimir la palabra "definido," y esto no es meramente porque "[e]l griego no tiene ningún artículo *indefinido*."[50] El término "definido" no encaja bien con el significado del artículo en griego, ya que el artículo indica, no que la entidad es definida, sino que es congnitivamente identificable. "Se puede considerar que su presencia con un nominal sirve de instrucción del autor a los lectores, indicando que procesen la información comunicada de tal manera que la identidad del referente no sea ambigua."[51] En Lucas 8:8, por ejemplo, el referente de Ὁ ἔχων ὦτα ἀκούειν "El que tiene oídos para oír" es indefinido (Jesús no se refiere a ninguna persona específica), pero sí se puede *identificar* del contexto como cualquier persona que acaba de oír lo que Jesús dijo.

Ya que hay solamente un artículo en griego, el artículo es el miembro marcado de un par de términos, en contraste con su ausencia. Se representa su naturaleza marcada así: +Identificable.

Toca recordar que, cuando se emplea la forma marcada de un par de términos, la característica asociada con la forma marcada está presente. Cuando no se utiliza, en cambio, no se comunica nada acerca de la presencia o ausencia de la característica—no se ha indicado nada acerca de esa característica. De modo que no es cierto que la función de la forma que carece de la marca sea la opuesta de la forma marcada.[52] En el caso del griego, esto quiere decir que, aunque las expresiones con el artículo como ὁ Ἰησοῦς (literalmente, "el Jesús") son +Identificable, no es necesariamente el caso de que la ausencia del artículo (Ἰησοῦς) indique que la expresión sea no-identificable.

Observando cómo las cartas del Nuevo Testamento comienzan, notamos que, a veces, la primera frase no contiene ningún artículo. Así que en 1 Pedro 1:1–2 (Πέτρος ἀπόστολος Ἰησοῦ Χριστοῦ ἐκλεκτοῖς παρεπιδήμοις διασπορᾶς Πόντου, Γαλατίας, Καππαδοκίας, Ἀσίας καὶ Βιθυνίας, κατὰ πρόγνωσιν θεοῦ πατρός ἐν ἁγιασμῷ πνεύματος εἰς ὑπακοὴν καὶ ῥαντισμὸν αἵματος Ἰησοῦ Χριστοῦ "Pedro, apóstol de Jesucristo, a los expatriados de la dispersión en el Ponto, Galacia, Capadocia, Asia y Bitinia, elegidos según el previo conocimiento de Dios Padre en santificación del Espíritu, para obedecer y ser rociados con la sangre de Jesucristo"), las referencias a Dios y al

---

50. Black, *Aprenda a leer el griego del Nuevo Testamento*, §33.

51. Levinsohn y Dubis, "Use of the Greek Article." La material de esta sección se basa en este artículo, que cita a varios autores recientes que concluyen que la función asociada con la presencia del artículo griego es la identificación.

52. Levinsohn, *Discourse Features*, ix.

Espíritu Santo carecen del artículo aunque tanto Pedro como los lectores de la carta las podrán identificar. Esto sugiere que el autor de una carta griega da por sentado que, cuando los destinatarios la reciban, su "representación mental" no contenga ningún concepto activo; o sea, que sea una pizarra en blanco.[53]

Sin embargo, no es siempre el caso que todas las referencias al comienzo de una carta carecen del artículo. Por ejemplo, en 1 Tesalonicenses 1:1 (Παῦλος καὶ Σιλουανὸς καὶ Τιμόθεος τῇ ἐκκλησίᾳ Θεσσαλονικέων ἐν θεῷ πατρὶ καὶ κυρίῳ Ἰησοῦ Χριστῷ "Pablo, Silvano y Timoteo, a la iglesia de los tesalonicenses en Dios Padre y en el Señor Jesucristo"), la referencia a la reunión de los tesalonicenses (τῇ ἐκκλησίᾳ Θεσσαλονικέων) lo tiene. Esto sugiere que Pablo, Silvano y Timoteo conciben la reunión como algo que se está realizando cuando la carta se los lea, y así identificable desde su punto de vista.[54]

De acuerdo con las observaciones anteriores, Heimerdinger y Levinsohn propusieron el patrón siguiente:

1. La activación con nombre de un participante es *sin* el artículo.

2. Las referencias subsiguientes son *con* el artículo.[55]

El mismo patrón sirve de regla por defecto para cualquier entidad, inclusive los sustantivos abstractos.[56]

Si observamos el comienzo de los libros del Nuevo Testamento que no sean cartas escritas a destinatarios nombrados, se nota que el artículo está presente con algunas expresiones. Por ejemplo, la epístola a los Hebreos comienza con las palabras Πολυμερῶς καὶ πολυτρόπως πάλαι ὁ θεὸς λαλήσας τοῖς πατράσιν ἐν τοῖς προφήταις "Dios, habiendo hablado muchas veces y de muchas maneras en otro tiempo a los padres por los profetas." En este caso, el autor da por sentado que los lectores puedan identificar a quiénes se refieren las expresiones para Dios (ὁ θεός) y los profetas (τοῖς προφήταις).

---

53. Cuando se utilizan nombres para identificar a los escritores o destinatarios de una carta en el Nuevo Testamento, las referencias siempre carecen del artículo.

54. La referencia a los Tesalonicenses carece del artículo porque los escritores se imaginan la presencia de sólo *algunos* de sus ciudadanos. Cuando un sustantivo común se utiliza al comienzo de una carta del Nuevo Testamento para identificar a los escritores o destinatarios, lo normal es utilizar el artículo. En 2 Juan 1 y 3 Juan 1, por ejemplo, Ὁ πρεσβύτερος tiene el artículo porque el autor cuenta con que los lectores sean capaces de identificar "el anciano" de su conocimiento previo de quién les estaría escribiendo una carta de tal naturaleza (véase Jackman, *John's Letters*, 175).

55. Heimerdinger y Levinsohn, "Definite Article," 18.

56. Véase Black, *Aprenda a leer el griego del Nuevo Testamento*, §33.

Ahora, consideremos Juan 1:1: Ἐν ἀρχῇ[57] ἦν ὁ λόγος "En el principio era el Verbo." La presencia del artículo con λόγος exige que los lectores identifiquen el referente con algo en su conocimiento enciclopédico (o sea, el conjunto de conocimientos que han adquirido a lo largo de los años). Walvoord y Zuck escriben que la expresión "se usaba ampliamente tanto en la enseñanza filosófica griega, como en la literatura sapiencial y filosófica judía. Juan escogió este término porque era conocido [por] sus lectores."[58] Al mismo tiempo, los comentaristas notan que las palabras introductorias Ἐν ἀρχῇ reproducen el comienzo del libro de Génesis (véase la versión de la Septuaginta) y ὁ λόγος también hace presente la misma narración, al aludir a la expresión "y Dios dijo," repetida siete veces.[59] De modo que la presencia del artículo con λόγος probablemente dirige a los lectores a identificar "el Verbo" con la Persona Divina a la que Dios Padre hablaba en el principio.

Pasamos ahora a la tercera frase de Juan 1:1: καὶ θεὸς ἦν ὁ λόγος "y el Verbo era Dios." Black nota que "La regla de Colwell (publicada en 1933) declara que los nominativos predicativos sin artículo que preceden a la cópula... son por lo general definidos en su significado" y "El resultado es que θεός tiene un significado casi seguramente definido."[60] No obstante, Turner y Mantey, entre otros, concluyen que la omisión del artículo antes de θεός indica que ὁ λόγος y ὁ θεός no se refieren a la misma Persona Divina.[61] Al contrario, la presencia del artículo con θεός habría *identificado* al referente de ὁ λόγος con ὁ θεός.[62]

Ya notamos que no es necesariamente el caso que la ausencia del artículo indique que la expresión sea no-identificable. Más bien, "Si el referente de un substantivo sin artículo es único y activo, entonces se le da prominencia.... Es decir, si un substantivo griego tiene un referente único y activo, pero carece de artículo, entonces está 'enfatizado' o destacado."[63] Así que en Hechos 10:34, "La referencia explícita a Pedro (Πέτρος), que no es necesaria para identificarlo, destaca lo que dice. La ausencia del artículo con su nombre aumenta la prominencia ... e implica que el discurso es el punto

---

57. Aunque Black (Ibid.) sugiere que ἐν ἀρχῇ "carece del artículo por [la] influencia del hebreo," ya hemos notado que lo normal en el griego del Nuevo Testamento es introducir los conceptos sin artículo.

58. Walvoord y Zuck, *El conocimiento bíblico*, 19.

59. Véase, por ejemplo, Milne, *John*, 31.

60. Black, *Aprenda a leer el griego del Nuevo Testamento*, §169.

61. Turner y Mantey, *John*, 54.

62. "Al expresar la relación así, Juan evita el error de una identificación total de las dos personas" (traducción de Milne, *John*, 34).

63. Levinsohn, *La aplicación del estudio de los rasgos discursivos*, §3.2.

culminante de la conversación."⁶⁴ De la misma manera, en 1 Corintios 2:16 (ἡμεῖς δὲ νοῦν Χριστοῦ ἔχομεν "Pues bien, nosotros tenemos la mente de Cristo"), νοῦν Χριστοῦ "es un componente focal antepuesto a la posición P2 para darle prominencia (contrastiva). La supresión del artículo aumenta esta prominencia."⁶⁵

Esta sección termina con una breve discusión del artículo con los adjetivos y demás modificadores que siguen al sustantivo, como en ὁ ποιμὴν ὁ καλός (palabra por palabra, "el pastor el bueno"—Juan 10:11) y στολὴν τὴν πρώτην ("vestido el mejor"—Lucas 15:24).⁶⁶ Básicamente, la presencia del artículo con un modificador es como una instrucción a "anclarlo"⁶⁷ a un sustantivo identificable (o, en términos tradicionales, a interpretar el modificador como atributivo.⁶⁸ Así que, en el sintagma ὁ ποιμὴν ὁ καλός, el segundo artículo ancla καλός ("bueno") al sustantivo identificable ὁ ποιμὴν ("el pastor").

En Mateo 4:12 (κατῴκησεν εἰς Καφαρναοὺμ τὴν παραθαλασσίαν "habitó en Capernaúm, ciudad marítima"), el artículo ancla παραθαλασσίαν al sustantivo Καφαρναούμ. En este ejemplo, el sustantivo carece del artículo, ya que no se ha introducido anteriormente en el Evangelio pero, ya mencionado, entra en la representación mental de los lectores y pasa a ser identificable. A menudo, cuando el sustantivo no tiene artículo pero el adjetivo sí lo tiene, la expresión adjetival se traduce en español con una oración subordinada de relativo. Así que la traducción de Mateo 4:12 en la NVI es "a Capernaúm, que está junto al lago."

En Lucas 18:13 (ἱλάσθητί μοι τῷ ἁμαρτωλῷ "ten compasión de mí, que soy pecador"), el artículo ancla el sustantivo modificante ἁμαρτωλῷ al pronombre μοί y, una vez más, la expresión adjetival se traduce con una oración subordinada de relativo.⁶⁹

---

64. Levinsohn, *Hechos*, 31.

65. Levinsohn, *La aplicación del estudio de los rasgos discursivos*, §3.2.

66. Tradicionalmente, los adjetivos con artículo que siguen a los sustantivos con o sin artículo se ubican en las posiciones atributivas segunda y tercera, respectivamente (Wallace, *Greek Grammar*, 306–7). Para una discusión más extensa de la presencia y la ausencia del artículo con los adjetivos y las oraciones infinitivas, véanse las secciones correspondientes de Levinsohn y Dubis, "Use of the Greek Article."

67. "Una entidad textual está Anclada si el SN [sintagma nominal] que la representa está enlazado, por medio de otro SN o 'Ancla' adecuadamente contenido en [el primer SN], a otra entidad textual" (traducción de Prince y Cole, "Given-New Information," 236).

68. Véase Black, *Aprenda a leer el griego del Nuevo Testamento*, §44 (1).

69. Contraste Black (Ibid., §33), que considera que las traducciones españoles no captan la presencia del artículo en esta oración.

Cuando a un sustantivo con artículo le sigue un adjetivo sin artículo (p. ej., Ἡ ἀγάπη ἀνυπόκριτος "El amor... sin fingimiento"—Romanos 12:9), el adjetivo no está anclado al sustantivo,[70] y se entiende como "*adjetivo predicativo*":[71] "El amor sea sin fingimiento."

En resumen, el artículo no señala que el sustantivo que modifica sea "bien definido,"[72] sino que es identificable; es decir, que el lector debe procesar la información comunicada de tal manera que la identidad del referente no sea ambigua. En cambio, la ausencia del artículo no comunica nada de manera positiva (p. ej., "Énfasis indefinido" o "Énfasis cualitativo").[73] Al contrario, no indica si el referente es identificable o no.

ASPECTOS MARCADOS Y NO-MARCADOS

Como Black observa, "el aspecto se refiere al punto de vista de la acción que el hablante decide presentar al oyente" y "Las tres categorías del aspecto en el griego son el aorístico, el imperfectivo y el perfectivo."[74]

Ciertos lingüistas han asociado el aspecto escogido con un grado específico de intensidad. Por ejemplo, Black (reproduciendo el esquema de Stanley Porter)[75] considera que "el aspecto aorístico es el término no marcado, y los aspectos imperfectivo y perfectivo los marcados con mayor intensidad. El aspecto aorístico es también el típico, usado como un telón contra cuyo fondo se puede ver el resto de las acciones. El aspecto imperfectivo es el del 'primer plano,' que contrasta con el aorístico, mientras que el perfectivo es el aspecto de 'marcado al máximo,' e importante en cualquier lugar en el que se utilice."[76] Para Robert Longacre, en cambio, el aorístico se emplea en las narraciones para los eventos del primer plano, el imperfectivo para los del fondo, y el perfecto para los que no son muy dinámicos.[77] El cuadro que sigue contrasta sus posiciones.[78]

70. "Una unidad que no está 'anclada' se puede denominar flotante" (traducción de Crystal, *Dictionary of Linguistics and Phonetics*, 20).

71. Black, *Aprenda a leer el griego del Nuevo Testamento*, §44.

72. Ibid., §169.

73. Ibid.

74. Ibid., §167. En vez del término "perfectivo" (Ibid.) que "expresa acción terminada" (*Diccionario*, II.1684), prefiero hablar del aspecto perfecto, ya que incluye "el estado o condición resultante... de una acción ya completada" (Black, *Aprenda a leer el griego del Nuevo Testamento*, §15).

75. Porter, "Prominence: An Overview," 57.

76. Black, *Aprenda a leer el griego del Nuevo Testamento*, §167.

77. Longacre, "Mark 5.1–43," 177.

78. Para este cuadro en inglés, véase Levinsohn, "Aspect and Prominence," 162.

Aspecto	Aorístico	Imperfectivo	Perfecto
Porter	no marcado ("fondo")	primer plano	marcado al máximo
Longacre	primer plano	fondo	no muy dinámico

Una solución a este desacuerdo la ofrece le Teoría de la Relevancia.[79] Según esta teoría, toca distinguir entre el uso no-marcado cuando es el aspecto más relevante o apropiado para presentar un evento y los usos marcados cuando otro aspecto hubiera sido lo esperado.[80]

Por ejemplo, habrá muchas ocasiones en las que el imperfectivo es el aspecto más apropiado para presentar un evento. Como ejemplo concreto, consideremos la última frase de Marcos 10:52: καὶ ἠκολούθει αὐτῷ ἐν τῇ ὁδῷ "y seguía a Jesús por el camino." En este contexto, el autor quiere comunicar no sólo que Bartimeo comenzó a seguir a Jesús, sino que lo continuaba (un evento del primer plano). De la misma manera, el imperfectivo en Lucas 2:41 (Καὶ ἐπορεύοντο οἱ γονεῖς αὐτοῦ κατ' ἔτος εἰς Ἰερουσαλὴμ τῇ ἑορτῇ τοῦ πάσχα "Iban sus padres todos los años a Jerusalén en la fiesta de la Pascua") es el aspecto más apropiado para presentar esta costumbre de los padres de Jesús (un evento que sirve de fondo para los descritos en los siguientes versículos).

Ahora, consideremos Marcos 15:14: ὁ δὲ Πιλᾶτος ἔλεγεν αὐτοῖς, Τί γὰρ ἐποίησεν κακόν; "Pilato dijo: —¿Pues qué mal ha hecho?" En este versículo, el imperfectivo (ἔλεγεν "decía") no parece el aspecto más apropiado para presentar lo que Pilato preguntó (nótese el uso del pretérito simple en la RV). Más bien, es un uso marcado que comunica al lector que debe buscar "implicaciones adicionales que compensarán el esfuerzo adicional en el procesamiento [la interpretación] de la frase."[81] En este caso, la implicación más probable es que la pregunta se ha metido al fondo en relación con los eventos siguientes, para destacarlos.[82]

Juan 8:31 (Ἔλεγεν οὖν ὁ Ἰησοῦς πρὸς τοὺς πεπιστευκότας αὐτῷ Ἰουδαίους, Ἐὰν ὑμεῖς μείνητε ἐν τῷ λόγῳ τῷ ἐμῷ, ἀληθῶς μαθηταί μού ἐστε "Dijo entonces Jesús a los judíos que habían creído en él: —Si vosotros permanecéis en mi palabra, seréis verdaderamente mis discípulos") parece otra ocasión en la que el aspecto imperfectivo (Ἔλεγεν "decía") se ha utilizado de

79. Véase Wilson y Sperber, *Meaning and Relevance*.
80. Véase Zegarač, "Relevance Theory and the Meaning of the English Progressive," 29.
81. Gutt, *Translation and Relevance*, 41.
82. Lo mismo sucede en Marcos 15:12. Para una discusión detallada de la alternación entre los verbos aoristos y imperfectos en Marcos 15:11–15, véase Levinsohn, "Aspect and Prominence," 172–73.

manera marcada. Dada la importancia de lo que Jesús dijo y los resultados descritos en los próximos versículos, el propósito de emplear una forma marcada probablemente es el de destacar sus palabras.

En resumen, en vez de decir que los eventos descritos con el aspecto imperfectivo son inherentemente de fondo (Longacre) o de primer plano (Porter), debemos distinguir entre las ocasiones cuando su uso es no-marcado (lo que comunica sólo que el evento se ha presentado como no terminado) de aquellas cuando su uso es marcado (con implicaciones que varían según el contexto).

Para reforzar este punto, consideremos otro versículo tratado por Black: Romanos 6:13:[83]

(a) μηδὲ παριστάνετε τὰ μέλη ὑμῶν ὅπλα ἀδικίας τῇ ἁμαρτίᾳ,   "ni tampoco presentéis vuestros miembros al pecado como instrumentos de iniquidad,

(b) ἀλλὰ παραστήσατε ἑαυτοὺς τῷ θεῷ ὡσεὶ ἐκ νεκρῶν ζῶντας   sino presentaos vosotros mismos a Dios como vivos de entre los muertos,"

El mandato (a) es una prohibición y Black nota que "Se usa generalmente μή con el imperativo de presente para prohibir la continuación de una acción en curso."[84] En cambio, el aspecto del mandato (b) es aorístico, que "no se preocupa por las veces que una acción debe ocurrir, sino por el hecho de que debe ocurrir."[85] El uso de ambos aspectos en este versículo parece no marcado, de modo que no debemos insistir ni que el primero se haya metido al fondo en comparación con el segundo (Longacre) ni *vice versa* (Porter).[86]

Un uso del verbo en el presente que siempre es marcado es el *presente histórico*, ya que lo normal es describir los eventos pasados con el aoristo. Se encuentra con frecuencia en los Evangelios de Mateo, Marcos y Juan, por ejemplo, "cuando el escritor introduce nuevos sucesos o personajes," como en Marcos 1:40: Καὶ ἔρχεται πρὸς αὐτὸν λεπρός "Viene a él un leproso."[87]

Comúnmente, no es el evento presentado en el presente histórico el que se destaca, sino los sucesos siguientes. Así, en Marcos 1:21 (Καὶ εἰσπορεύονται εἰς Καφαρναούμ "Entran en Capernaúm"), lo importante no

---

83. Black, *Aprenda a leer el griego del Nuevo Testamento*, §167.
84. Ibid., §158.
85. Ibid., §167.
86. Aunque Black (Ibid.) destaca el aspecto presente (imperfectivo) del participio ζῶντας "vivos," tampoco es un uso marcado.
87. Ibid., §22.

es el acto de entrar en el pueblo, sino lo que sucede después de la entrada. De la misma manera, cuando una pregunta se introduce con el presente histórico, como en Juan 1:48 (λέγει αὐτῷ Ναθαναήλ, Πόθεν με γινώσκεις; "Le dijo Natanael: —¿De dónde me conoces?"), lo importante no es la pregunta, sino la respuesta (en este caso, ἀπεκρίθη Ἰησοῦς καὶ εἶπεν αὐτῷ, Πρὸ τοῦ σε Φίλιππον φωνῆσαι ὄντα ὑπὸ τὴν συκῆν εἶδόν σε "Jesús le respondió: —Antes que Felipe te llamara, cuando estabas debajo de la higuera, te vi")[88] Así que el uso del presente histórico para introducir la pregunta destaca la respuesta.

A veces, el suceso destacado por el presente histórico no se presenta en seguida, sino después de la descripción de otros eventos. Esto se ve en Mateo 28:10: τότε λέγει αὐταῖς ὁ Ἰησοῦς, Μὴ φοβεῖσθε· ὑπάγετε ἀπαγγείλατε τοῖς ἀδελφοῖς μου ἵνα ἀπέλθωσιν εἰς τὴν Γαλιλαίαν, κἀκεῖ με ὄψονται "Entonces Jesús les dijo: —No temáis; id, dad las nuevas a mis hermanos, para que vayan a Galilea, y allí me verán." Antes de describir este encuentro anticipado de Jesús con sus discípulos, interviene el informe de la guardia a los sumos sacerdotes (vv. 11–15). Sin embargo, el uso del presente histórico en el v. 10 crea la expectativa del cumplimiento de las palabras de Jesús.

LA SEGMENTACIÓN DE UN TEXTO

"El análisis del discurso de cualquier texto comienza por lo general tratando de dividirlo en secciones principales, secciones menores, y párrafos"[89] y el criterio básico que se utiliza para su segmentación es que cada unidad propuesta "trate de un solo tema. Si el tema cambia, entonces comienza una nueva unidad."[90]

Se pueden citar varios rasgos textuales que apoyan las divisiones propuestas en base de un cambio de tema.[91] Éstos incluyen los siguientes:[92]

1. Un *sintagma u oración inicial o antepuesto* (es decir, en posición P1— véase §6) que comunica el cambio de tema o un cambio de situación. Black se refiere a los sintagmas que comienzan con Περὶ δέ ("Acerca de"): "en cada caso Pablo introduce un nuevo tema."[93] Cita también

---

88. Para una discusión detallada del presente histórico en Marcos 11:1–7, véase Levinsohn, "Aspect and Prominence," 170–71.

89. Black, *Aprenda a leer el griego del Nuevo Testamento*, §172.

90. Traducción de Beekman y Callow, *Translating the Word of God*, 279.

91. Véase Levinsohn, *Gálatas*, §4.1.

92. Para una lista más completa de los rasgos que apoyan las divisiones, véase Levinsohn, *Discourse Features*, capítulo 8.

93. Black, *Aprenda a leer el griego del Nuevo Testamento*, §172.

el sintagma μετὰ ταῦτα ("después de estas cosas") que "comienza normalmente una nueva sección en el Evangelio de Juan."[94]

2. Ciertas *conjunciones* o la *ausencia de una conjunción*. Black observa que "en el Evangelio de Mateo... τότε indica a menudo que comienza una nueva sección"[95] o, más específicamente, "una sub-sección de una unidad más grande."[96] En una carta como Gálatas, por ejemplo, no se encuentra ninguna conjunción entre el saludo inicial y el cuerpo de la carta (1:6), ni entre el cuerpo de la carta y el saludo final (6:18).

3. Una *clausura* como ἐν τοῖς λόγοις τούτοις "con estas palabras" (1 Tesalonicenses 4:18, refiriéndose a la totalidad del pasaje anterior) o ἀμήν "Amén" (Gálatas 1:5).

4. Una estructura *quiástica*, con "un paralelismo inverso" en la segunda parte de la estructura.[97] 1 Corintios 10:6–11 sirve de ejemplo, ya que el v. 11 corresponde al 6, el 10 al 7, y el 9 al 8.[98]

6	ταῦτα δὲ τύποι ἡμῶν ἐγενήθησαν, εἰς τὸ μὴ εἶναι ἡμᾶς ἐπιθυμητὰς κακῶν, καθὼς κἀκεῖνοι ἐπεθύμησαν.	"Estas cosas sucedieron como ejemplos para nosotros, para que no codiciemos cosas malas, como ellos codiciaron.
7	μηδὲ εἰδωλολάτραι γίνεσθε καθώς τινες αὐτῶν, ὥσπερ γέγραπται, Ἐκάθισεν ὁ λαὸς φαγεῖν καὶ πεῖν καὶ ἀνέστησαν παίζειν.	Ni seáis idólatras, como algunos de ellos, según está escrito: «Se sentó el pueblo a comer y a beber, y se levantó a jugar.»
8	μηδὲ πορνεύωμεν, καθώς τινες αὐτῶν ἐπόρνευσαν καὶ ἔπεσαν μιᾷ ἡμέρᾳ εἴκοσι τρεῖς χιλιάδες.	Ni forniquemos, como algunos de ellos fornicaron, y cayeron en un día veintitrés mil.
9	μηδὲ ἐκπειράζωμεν τὸν Χριστόν, καθώς τινες αὐτῶν ἐπείρασαν καὶ ὑπὸ τῶν ὄφεων ἀπώλλυντο.	Ni tentemos al Señor, como también algunos de ellos lo tentaron, y perecieron por las serpientes.

---

94. Ibid.
95. Ibid.
96. Levinsohn, *Hechos*, 15.
97. Black, *Aprenda a leer el griego del Nuevo Testamento*, §171.
98. Aunque es cierto que, en muchas estructuras quiásticas, "la línea del centro es la recibe el mayor hincapié" (Ibid.), este pasaje demuestra que no siempre es así. Ya que el pasaje "se dirige a nosotros (*ejemplos para nosotros... para amonestarnos a nosotros*)," "se esperaría que las exhortaciones también se presentarían en primera persona. Como consecuencia, cuando Pablo cambia de primera a segunda persona en 7 (y una vez más en 10), el efecto es dar más potencia a la exhortación" (traducción de Levinsohn, *Non-Narrative Discourse Analysis*, 75).

10	μηδὲ γογγύζετε, καθάπερ τινὲς αὐτῶν ἐγόγγυσαν καὶ ἀπώλοντο ὑπὸ τοῦ ὀλοθρευτοῦ.	Ni murmuréis, como algunos de ellos murmuraron, y perecieron por mano del destructor.
11	ταῦτα δὲ τυπικῶς συνέβαινεν ἐκείνοις, ἐγράφη δὲ πρὸς νουθεσίαν ἡμῶν. . .	Todas estas cosas les acontecieron como ejemplo, y están escritas para amonestarnos a nosotros. . ."

5. Una estructura *inclusiva*, cuando un pasaje comienza y termina con más o menos la misma expresión. Una vez más, 1 Cor 10:6–11 (arriba) sirve de ejemplo, ya que comienza con ταῦτα δὲ τύποι ἡμῶν ἐγενήθησαν "Estas cosas sucedieron como ejemplos para nosotros" y termina con ταῦτα δὲ τυπικῶς συνέβαινεν ἐκείνοις "Todas estas cosas les acontecieron como ejemplo."

6. Una *pregunta retórica* que introduce un tema. Por ejemplo, la pregunta retórica τίς ὑμᾶς ἐβάσκανεν. . . "¿quién os fascinó. . .?" (Gálatas 3:1) introduce un nuevo tema.

7. Una *referencia aparentemente redundante* a una entidad. En Gálatas 5:2, por ejemplo, la referencia aparentemente redundante "yo, Pablo" (ἐγὼ Παῦλος) apoya una subdivisión.

8. Un *vocativo*. "En las cartas de Pablo, los vocativos como 'hermanos' aparecen a menudo al principio de un nuevo párrafo."[99]

9. Un verbo de *orientación* que introduce un nuevo tema, como Γνωρίζω "os hago saber" (Gálatas 1:11).

10. Una oración que *reintroduce un concepto* que no apareció en el contexto inmediato sino en una sección más temprana. Por ejemplo, Ἔχοντες . . . ἀρχιερέα μέγαν "teniendo un gran sumo sacerdote" (Hebreos 4:14) no se refiere a nadie en el contexto inmediato, sino al ἀρχιερέα τῆς ὁμολογίας ἡμῶν "sumo sacerdote de nuestra profesión" que se mencionó en 3:1.

Aunque los rasgos textuales descritos arriba se pueden citar para apoyar las divisiones propuestas en base de un cambio de tema, puede haber otras motivaciones por su presencia. Por ejemplo, los vocativos se emplean no sólo al inicio de una nueva sección, sino también para destacar una proposición importante. Véase el vocativo largo de Gálatas 4.19: τέκνα μου, οὓς πάλιν ὠδίνω μέχρις οὗ μορφωθῇ Χριστὸς ἐν ὑμῖν "Hijitos míos, por quienes vuelvo a sufrir dolores de parto, hasta que Cristo sea formado en vosotros," "cuyo efecto es dar prominencia al resto de la oración; o sea, el

---

99. Black, *Aprenda a leer el griego del Nuevo Testamento*, §172.

20."[100] Las preguntas retóricas, las referencias aparentemente redundantes y los verbos de orientación también se emplean para destacar alguna información que está por presentarse.[101]

Es de recordar, pues, que las divisiones del texto se proponen primordialmente en base de un cambio de tema. Luego el texto se examina para verificar si se presenta un juego de rasgos que apoya la división propuesta.

Gálatas 5:13 sirve de ilustración, ya que la RV95 y la VP proponen una división principal entre los vv 12 y 13, pero la RV60 no la reconoce. Los rasgos textuales que apoyan esta división incluyen el sujeto inicial Ὑμεῖς "vosotros" que indica un cambio de atención de "los que se perturban" (12), el vocativo ἀδελφοί "hermanos" (13) y el retorno al tema de la libertad cristiana, que se mencionó por última vez en 5:1. Además, Pablo comienza sus exhortaciones directas a los gálatas en 5:13.

El único rasgo contradictorio es que la conjunción de apoyo γάρ "porque" (13) indica que lo que sigue refuerza lo anterior. Es por esto, tal vez, que otros eruditos y versiones proponen una división entre los vv 15 y 16. Sin embargo, los rasgos textuales que apoyan una división allí son pocos: el verbo de orientación Λέγω "digo" y la conjunción de "progresión (desarrollo)" δέ.[102]

Se concluye que a la división principal entre los vv. 12 y 13, cuya base es un cambio de tema, le apoya un juego amplio de rasgos textuales.

CONCLUSIÓN

Este artículo destaca varias semejanzas entre el griego del Nuevo Testamento y el español que puedan aumentar el beneficio para los hispanohablantes de la traducción de la gramática de David Alan Black; las que tienen que ver con los pronombres, la morfología verbal, el caso acusativo, los demostrativos, la voz media, el modo subjuntivo, y el orden especialmente de las oraciones dentro de una frase. También describe unos avances en nuestro entendimiento de las diferencias entre los participios pre-nucleares y posnucleares, de la naturaleza de las construcciones perifrásticas, del significado de las variaciones en el orden de los elementos de los sintagmas y oraciones, de la función del artículo, de cuándo y por qué un aspecto se ha utilizado de manera marcada, y de la segmentación de los textos en secciones y párrafos. Muchos de este segundo grupo de temas los trata el doctor Black en

---

100. Levinsohn, *Gálatas*, 58.
101. Levinsohn, *Non-Narrative Discourse Analysis*, §§.8.7, 8.8, 8.10.
102. Levinsohn, *La aplicación del estudio de los rasgos discursivos*, §3.3.

la última lección de su gramática (la 26), pero ciertas secciones anteriores anticipan una discusión posterior; por ejemplo, la §33 sobre el artículo.

No se han mencionado hasta ahora los términos utilizados para referirse a los diferentes niveles de la jerarquía sintáctica del griego. Este artículo ha tratado de emplear los términos encontrados en las gramáticas escolares, que también son las preferidas en el diccionario de la Real Academia; a saber, palabra—sintagma—oración—frase. Sin embargo, la influencia del inglés a lo largo de las Américas causa problemas especialmente en el entendimiento de este último, debido a ser un "amigo falso" con "phrase" (sintagma) en inglés. Por eso, creo que sería aconsejable destacar esta área, la primera vez que surge en la gramática y, además, incluir un glosario de los términos técnicos utilizados en la gramática.

Finalmente, vale la pena observar que, si los autores de la traducción de la gramática de Black deciden actualizarla conforme a observaciones como las contenidas en este artículo, estarán continuando una tradición honorable que se ha manifestado en inglés, por ejemplo, cuando la gramática de Friedrich Blass[103] fue revisada por Albert Debrunner[104] y, luego, por Robert W. Funk.[105]

BIBLIOGRAPHY

Barnes, Albert. *Notes on the New Testament, III: The Acts of the Apostles*. Glasgow: Blackie, 1846.

Bauer, Walter, et al. *A Greek-English Lexicon of the New Testament and Other Early Christian Literature*. 4ª ed. Chicago: University of Chicago Press, 1957.

Beekman, John, y John C. Callow. *Translating the Word of God*. Grand Rapids: Zondervan, 1974.

Black, David Alan. *Learn to Read New Testament Greek*. 3ª ed. Nashville, TN: B&H Publishing Group, 2009.

———. *Aprenda a leer el griego del Nuevo Testamento*. Traducido por Thomas W. Hudgins, Lesly J. Hudgins, y Fiorella Polo. González FL: Energion Publications, 2015.

Blass, Friedrich. *Grammatik des Neutestamentlichen Griechisch*. Göttingen: Vandenhoeck und Ruprecht, 1896.

———, y Albert Debrunner. *Grammatik des Neutestamentlichen Griechisch*. 4ª ed. Göttingen: Vandenhoeck und Ruprecht, 1913.

———, y Albert Debrunner. *A Greek Grammar of the New Testament*. Traducido y revisado por Robert W. Funk. Chicago: Chicago University Press, 1961.

Comrie, Bernard. *Language Universals and Linguistic Typology*. 2ª ed. Chicago: University of Chicago Press, 1989.

103. Blass, *Grammatik des Neutestamentlichen Griechisch*.
104. Blass y Debrunner, *Grammatik des Neutestamentlichen Griechisch*.
105. Blass y Debrunner, *Greek Grammar*.

Crystal, David. *Dictionary of Linguistics and Phonetics*. 4ª ed. Oxford: Blackwell, 1997.
Diccionario de la Lengua Española. 23ª ed. México: Real Academia Española, 2014.
Dik, Simon. *Functional Grammar*. Amsterdam: North-Holland, 1978.
———. *The Theory of Functional Grammar. Part I: The Structure of the Clause*. Dordrecht: Foris, 1989.
Dooley, Robert A., y Stephen H. Levinsohn. *Análisis de discurso: Manual de conceptos básicos*. Versión castellana de Marlene Ballena Dávila; Lima: Instituto Lingüístico de Verano, 2007.
Fanning, Buist M. *Verbal Aspect in New Testament Greek*. Oxford: Clarendon Press, 1990.
Firbas, Jan. "From Comparative Word-Order Studies." *BRNO Studies in English* 4 (1964) 111–26.
Gutt, Ernst-August. *Translation and Relevance: Cognition and Context*. Oxford: Basil Blackwell, 1991.
Heimerdinger, Jennifer y Stephen H. Levinsohn. "The Use of the Definite Article before Names of People in the Greek Text of Acts, with Particular Reference to Codex Bezae." *Filología Neotestamentaria* 5 (1992) 15–44.
Jackman, David. *The Message of John's Letters*. Leicester: Inter-Varsity Press, 1988.
Levinsohn, Stephen H. *Adverbial Participial Clauses in Koiné Greek: Grounding and Information Structure* (presentado a la conferencia internacional sobre discurso y gramática "Illocutionary force, information structure and subordination between discourse and grammar," Universeit Ghent, Belgia; https://www.sil.org/resources/archives/68396, 2008).
———. *La aplicación del estudio de los rasgos discursivos a la exégesis del Nuevo Testamento* (http://www.recursosteologicos.org/Documents/Exegesis_Discursivo.pdf, 2009).
———. "Aspect and Prominence in the Synoptic Accounts of Jesus' Entry into Jerusalem," *Filología Neotestamentaria* 23 (2010) 161–74.
———. *Discourse Features of New Testament Greek: A Coursebook on Its Information Structure and Other Devices*. 2ª ed. Dallas: SIL International, 2000.
———. *A Fresh Look at Adjective-Noun Ordering in Articular Noun Phrases* (presentado a la conferencia internacional de la Society of Biblical Literature, Londres; https://www.sil.org/resources/archives/68397, 2011).
———. "Functions of Copula-Participle Combinations ('Periphrastics')." En *The Greek Verb Revisited: A Fresh Approach for Biblical Exegesis*, editado por Steven E. Runge y Christopher J. Fresch, 307–326. Lexham Press, 2016.
———. *Los rasgos discursivos comparativos aplicados a la traducción de Gálatas* (http://www.recursosteologicos.org/Documents/Galatas_traduccion_discursivo.pdf, 2009).
———. *Los rasgos discursivos comparativos aplicados a la traducción de los Hechos de los Apóstoles* (http://www.recursosteologicos.org/Documents/Hechos_traduccion_discursivo.pdf, 2009).
———. "The Relevance of Greek Discourse Studies to Exegesis." *Journal of Translation* 2:2 (2006) 11–21. Online at http://www.sil.org/siljot/2006/2/48004/siljot2006-2-02.pdf.
———. *Self-Instruction Materials on Non-Narrative Discourse Analysis* (https://www.sil.org/resources/archives/68640, 2015).

———. "Towards a Unified Linguistic Description of οὗτος and ἐκεῖνος." En *The Linguist as Pedagogue: Trends in the Teaching and Linguistic Analysis of the Greek New Testament*, editado por Stanley E. Porter y Matthew Brook O'Donnell, 204-16. Sheffield: Sheffield Phoenix Press, 2009.

———. y Mark Dubis. "The Use of the Greek Article in 1 Peter: A Case Study." En *The Article in Post-Classical Greek*, editado por Daniel H. King. Dallas TX: SIL International (en prensa).

Longacre, Robert E. "Mark 5.1–43: Generating the Complexity of a Narrative from Its Most Basic Elements." En *Discourse Analysis and the New Testament: Approaches and Results*, editado por Stanley E. Porter y Jeffrey T. Reed, 169-96. Sheffield: Sheffield Academic Press, 1999.

Milne, Bruce. *The Message of John*. Leicester: InterVarsity Press, 1993.

Porter, Stanley E. "Prominence: An Overview." En *The Linguist as Pedagogue: Trends in the Teaching and Linguistic Analysis of the Greek New Testament*, editado por Stanley E. Porter y Matthew Brook O'Donnell, 45-74. Sheffield: Sheffield Phoenix Press, 2009.

Prince, Ellen F., y Peter Cole. "Toward a Taxonomy of Given-New Information." *Radical Pragmatics*. Editado por Peter Cole. New York: Acadamic Press, 1981.

Turner, George Allen, y Julius R. Mantey. *The Gospel According to John: The Evangelical Commentary*. Grand Rapids: Eerdmans, 1964.

Wallace, Daniel B. *Greek Grammar Beyond the Basics: An Exegetical Syntax of the New Testament*. Grand Rapids: Zondervan, 1995.

Walvoord, John F., y Roy B. Zuck. *El conocimiento bíblico: Un comentario expositivo, Nuevo Testamento*, Tomo 2. Traducido por Julián Lloret y Jack Matlick. Puebla, México: Ediciones Las Américas, 2001.

Wilson, Deirdre, y Dan Sperber. *Meaning and Relevance*. Cambridge: Cambridge University Press, 2012.

Zegarač, Vladimir. "Relevance Theory and the Meaning of the English Progressive." *University College London Working Papers in Linguistics* 1 (1989) 19-31.

www.ingramcontent.com/pod-product-compliance
Lightning Source LLC
Chambersburg PA
CBHW071238230426
43668CB00011B/1489